APPLIED ART·

DRAWING
PAINTING
DESIGN and
HANDICRAFT

ARRANGED FOR SELF·INSTRUCTION
OF TEACHERS, PARENTS, AND
··STUDENTS··

by

PEDRO·J·LEMOS
Director, Museum of Fine Arts
Leland Stanford Junior University
Editor "The School Arts Magazine"

1920

PACIFIC PRESS PUBLISHING ASSOCIATION
··MOUNTAIN VIEW, CALIFORNIA··
PORTLAND, ORE.· KANSAS CITY, MO. · BROOKFIELD, ILL.· ST. PAUL, MINN· CRISTOBAL, C. Z.

Dedicated to
Henry Turner Bailey
Pathfinder of
American Art
Education

FOREWORD

Art, when combined with life's environment, becomes a growing human benefit. Utility may become attached to art without subtracting from the beauty of art. Every handicraft or manufactured object may become an article of beauty, when art is added, and still retain its utility.

Drawing, painting, design, color, modeling, and handicraft are each an important element in art. To know something or much of each will help that much toward better understanding of the whole. Each is an important link in the study of art, and the true artist acknowledges its importance.

Something of these elements, therefore, has been presented in the following pages. Each element is presented separate and interwoven, that the reader may recognize art as a unifying cord which weaves all the products of mankind into a pattern of beauty.

The majority of the pages are illustrations. Pictures tell more than can be explained in many pages. Only enough reading matter has been included to unify the illustrations. For the beginner, though he be of mature years, the first chapters contain important foundations. Each succeeding chapter presents progressive suggestions for the teacher and the student, and guidance for the parent desiring an interesting form of vocational art study for the young artist.

The purpose of the book is not that the pupil copy and repeat or adhere to its pages rigidly. It is hoped that they will stimulate interest and create a desire to do original work. Each reader and student should adopt that part and begin at that point which his personal training requires. Originality and personal inventiveness are important factors in the progress of art study, and should be encouraged.

The book includes the fruit of many years' experience in both teaching and professional practice. In it are given those problems found to yield the greatest practical response in the briefest period.

Many of the illustrations are by students and fellow artists who have liberally given of their work. To these I express my appreciation. May the readers, young and old, learn the beauty of nature, learn to picture her messages, and to add harmonies from her storehouse of line, form, pattern, and color, that will beautify their everyday living. To these will come the richness of enthusiasm.

PEDRO J. LEMOS.

(6)

CONTENTS

GRAMMAR GRADES

ACADEMIC GRADES

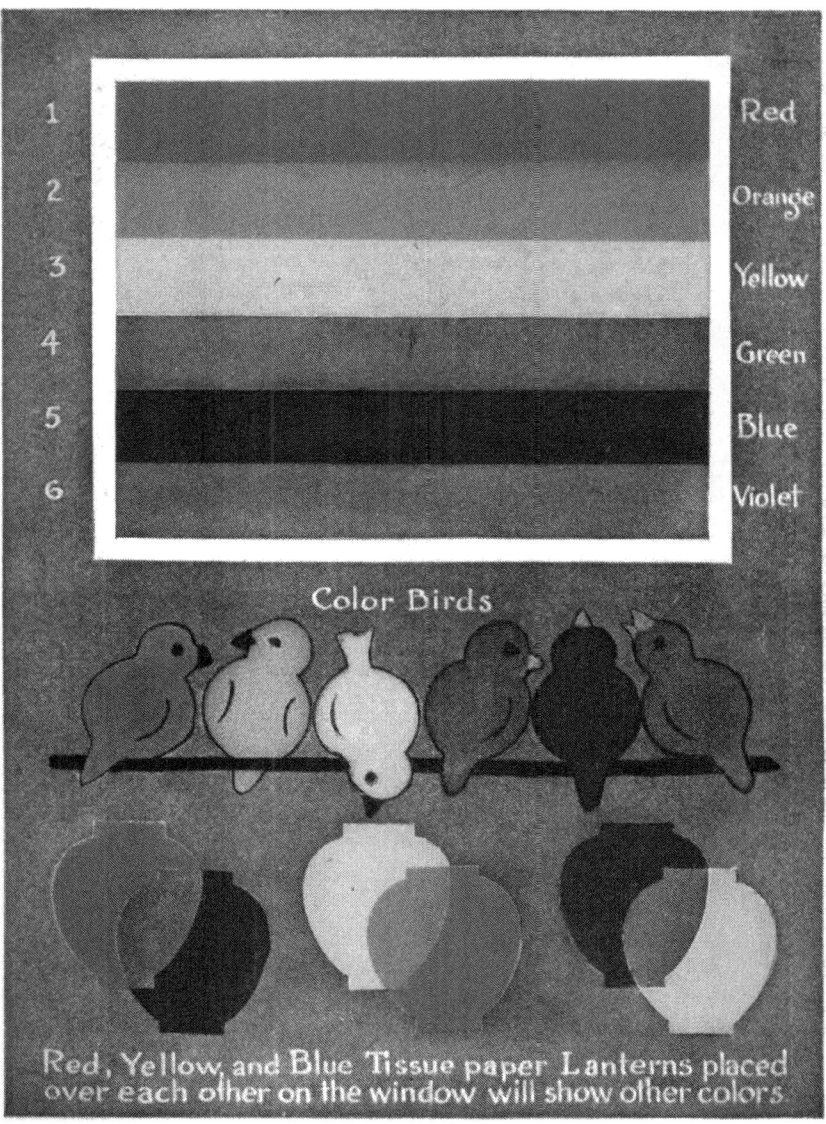

A RAINBOW HARMONY

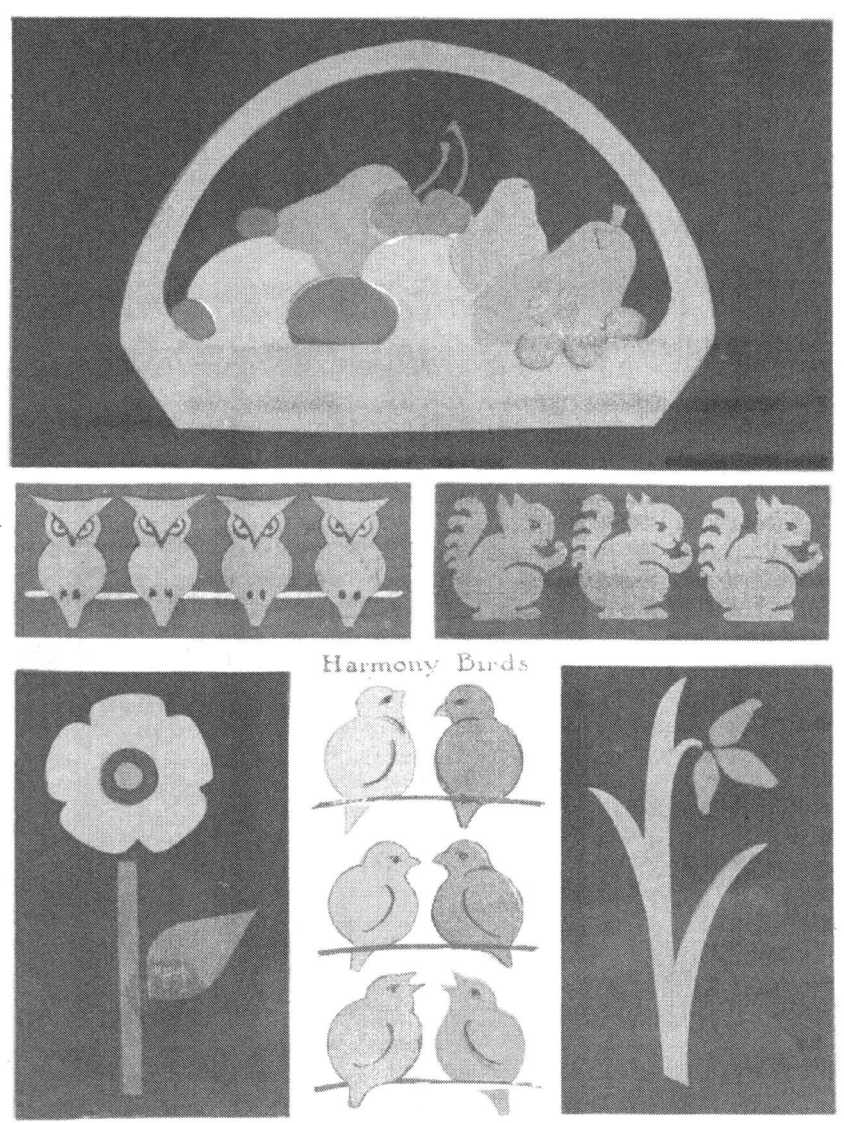

Harmony Birds

CUT PAPER COLOR HARMONIES

THE FIRST YEAR

DRAWING AND COLORING

THE FIRST LESSONS IN DRAWING should be on simple subjects, for a subject that is too difficult discourages. And progress is best made with lessons that give foundation instruction in the beginning.

EVERY SUBJECT IN NATURE HAS A SHAPE; and if this shape is observed, and then planned on the paper beforehand, the subject itself can be drawn over the shape with comparative ease. The lines of the subject may not always be just the shape of a circle or a square, but these forms may be the general shape of the object. If we use such shapes as guide lines, we have a controlling shape to guide our drawing.

BY OBSERVING AND COMPARING, we can learn much in drawing. If we observe the shapes of flowers and fruits and the forms of trees and houses, we shall be better able to draw them, as we shall remember these shapes, and make our drawings similar to them.

THE MOST GENERAL AND MOST FAMILIAR SHAPE is the circle. The circle is the shape of the earth, of the moon, and of the sun, as well as of many fruits and flowers. The circle has been used as a form in drawing by every nation of the world, and it has been found in the earliest records of mankind.

TO MAKE A CIRCLE FIRST, use a button, a piece of money, or other round object, as a guide. Holding it with the finger tips of one hand, draw around it on a piece of paper. If this is done on a stiff piece of paper, the circle cut from the paper can be used as a guide for other circles. Draw a number of circles on a piece of paper, making the outlines lightly. Then with a soft pencil go over these outlines one after another, seeing how firm and smooth the circles can be made. Also see if you can make the ending of the line meet the beginning perfectly, so that there will not be a joint where the two points meet.

CONFIDENCE IN DRAWING will be learned by making lines firmly and with a free stroke. Slow, hesitating lines are as bad as fast, careless ones. By drawing lines over and over around a guide line, first going slowly and then faster, you will get good practice for gaining control of your pencils or crayons.

A PENCIL SHOULD NOT BE SHARPENED with a long, slender point, nor with a blunt, squatty point. It should not be held so close to the point that the point cannot be easily seen, nor so far from the end that the pencil cannot be easily controlled.

THE BEST PENCILS TO DRAW WITH at the beginning are those which have a large, soft lead and a fairly large wood portion. Hard pencils are good for several purposes, such as preliminary outlines and mechanical drawing, but they should not be used for free-hand drawing and sketching. Hard pencils make indentations in the paper wherever used; and where erasing is necessary, the eraser will not remove these indentations.

THE BEST PENCILS FOR CHILDREN are those which have very large wooden portions, or even large crayons, as they can be more easily held, and little fingers are better able to draw with something that is "holdable."

PAPER FOR DRAWING should be of a soft and slightly rough surface. Smooth or glazed paper should not be used. Drawing Manila paper is widely used, because it is not as expensive as other paper, and has a cream color, which is pleasanter for the eyes than white, as the latter reflects light too strongly.

FOR ERASING, a soft eraser is best, as it will not roughen the paper or destroy the surface for further drawing. Erasing is necessary to make corrections. We should endeavor to see how little erasing is necessary. If we are constantly thinking that we can erase and correct, we may become careless, and find that we are using the eraser as much as our pencil. At the same time, we should erase wherever we recognize an imperfection, and correct our drawing. When erasing, do so with care. Do not carelessly remove any of the part not intended to be erased. Erasing is an important part of drawing, and we should take out parts of drawing with as much thought and care as we add them.

A SLANTING POSITION is best for drawing. A stiff cardboard can be used for such purpose, since the usual slant of school desks is not enough to place the paper with all parts at nearly equal distance from the eye. It is proper to turn the sheet of paper, when drawing, to any position that will permit the lines to be drawn most easily. Generally lines drawn toward one are most easily produced; and if lines are in different directions on the subject, turn the paper so that the line can be drawn as nearly perfect as possible.

INDIVIDUAL METHODS SHOULD BE ENCOURAGED in all phases of art, even when we are doing or teaching the beginning of art. The fact that some one else did good work with a certain tool or in a certain manner is no real proof that we must do likewise. Art work is best when it is individual. For a whole class or group of students to do work just alike would be a disadvantage, even though their work were perfect. It is better that each student have perfect or good results but expressed in his own way. Therefore we should study the good results of others' work, but aim to do our work equally well in our own way.

A GOOD BEGINNING PROBLEM toward recognizing form is to draw a number of circle guide lines and see how many objects we can find that will come within or be most easily made with the circle. We may also produce many objects with the use of a large and a small circle. We shall find that the circles may be placed partly over one another to make some of the shapes, or portions of circles combined with complete circles.

ANIMAL AND BIRD FORMS can be made by the use of such guide forms, and many interesting groups made by children in this way. By the addition of a few marks for ears and eyes, for feet and tail, considerable action can be obtained. This will show us that certain shapes control many objects, and that it is of first importance that the mass, or larger parts, be expressed first. The smaller details added next are more easily made correct if the larger parts are first placed properly.

LINE DIRECTIONS are sometimes difficult to determine. In many objects, we find that the forms are made by one line meeting another. If the direction of these lines as they approach each other is varied a little, our drawing becomes faulty. If one line is incorrect, it may ruin our whole drawing, in that we have added other lines in relation to the incorrect one.

TO RECOGNIZE LINE DIRECTIONS more easily, a good problem for practice is the drawing of grasses or weeds or simple branches, which show parts going in different directions. If there is a main line, this main line should be drawn first, and the next in importance drawn branching from it or drawn toward it — whichever is the easier way to secure the proper connection. This should be done in pencil or black crayon until a fairly good drawing can be made. It is not necessary to put in all the shading and small parts. At present, we shall be content to have merely the main directions, expressed in strong, black lines.

LEAF AND FLOWER FORMS are good studies at the beginning. They may be placed on the paper, and a light pencil line drawn around them, and the pencil or crayon used to fill them in, making a silhouette of each shape. If the pencil strokes or crayon lines are made in one direction only, they will look better. The next step is to outline them without tracing around the object, and then fill in with solid lines. The third step is to use the crayon or pencil and make the silhouette shape without a preliminary outline.

WHEN DRAWING FROM NATURE FORMS, we should recognize the beautiful lines and shapes that occur in leaves and flowers. We shall find that some are circular, and others are bell-shaped, trumpet-shaped, triangular, or long and narrow. Whatever the shape may be, we should study it carefully before drawing it. If we decide that it is triangular, we should ascertain whether it is a narrow triangle or a wide triangle, because otherwise we may have our object within the right general form but the exact shape may be wrong.

THE DRAWING OF TREES may be made very similar to that of leaves. In fact, leaves very often are found to resemble the shape of the tree from which we took them. Dry trees, or trees without foliage, can be drawn very much as we have drawn the twigs or the grasses with our crayon. In this way, the drawing of simple things with certain portions will help us in drawing larger things with similar parts.

BLACK AND WHITE DRAWINGS of plants and trees can be made with black and white crayon on gray paper. We must decide what parts of the subject are best expressed with white and which will look best in black. We can then draw them the same as we did when we used only black, but we will use white for certain parts. This will make the subjects more interesting; because, while no color is used, color is suggested in that some parts are darker than others.

THE USE OF COLOR is important to know; and the order of colors, as well as the colors that are best to use together, can be taken up from the very beginning. Nature would be uninteresting compared with its present wonderful coloring if every part of it were of one color. We find lovely colors in flowers and trees, fishes and other sea forms; and birds and animals are often covered with beautiful color harmonies and fascinating patterns. Nature gives good harmonies in color arrangements; and in later chapters, we shall copy some of these and use them.

THE RAINBOW IS A PERFECT HARMONY OF COLOR. In it we find colors arranged next to others in harmonies. Yellow, red, and blue are called primary colors, because they cannot be made by mixing other colors together, but they do make other colors if mixed together.

Yellow and red make orange, yellow and blue make green, and blue and red make violet. In the rainbow, these colors are in this order: yellow, green, blue, violet, red, and orange. Any two of these neighboring colors used together make a good color combination. Good combinations are red and green, blue and orange, and yellow and violet. These combinations are made by using any one of the primary colors (yellow, red, and blue), and mixing the remaining two together to make the companion color.

HARMONY BIRDS can be made by cutting a paper bird out of each of the six harmony colors and arranging them in proper order. Also arrange the harmony birds in harmonious pairs. Also cut tulips and bells from colored paper and group them in pleasing color combinations until you are very familiar with good color combinations.

WHEN COMBINING ANY COLORS or colored objects, remember the combinations used with the harmony birds and keep the same colors together. If we wish to make a cover design or doll clothes, or color a border, we shall use two colors, and the colors will be one of the combinations used with the harmony birds.

COLORED CRAYONS, when used for coloring, should be held toward the point, and not pressed too hard, as they will break. When a color is to be made by rubbing two colors together in the same space, the first crayon should be rubbed lightly, so that parts of the paper will be left for the second color. If the paper is covered solid with the first crayon, the second color will not mix with it at all. Light rubbing will make tints of the colors, and more rubbing will increase the strength of the color.

COLORED FLOWERS AND GRASSES can be made on gray paper by making black and white crayon drawings as we did before on gray paper, then rubbing a color lightly over the white and adding the proper color over the black. We can also color the objects that we made with the circle, as well as the birds and the animals.

DESIGN

DESIGN MEANS GOOD ARRANGEMENT or good order. No design is good without thoughtful arrangement. To be orderly means to design or arrange our belongings with method. If we take several rings of paper and put them together without arrangement, they appear confused and are not good design. If we arrange them so that they balance and make a good shape, they then become designed.

CIRCLE DESIGNS may be made by pasting down colored circles of paper in interesting shapes. The circles may be folded on the edges so as to change the shape, or parts may be cut away. In this way, see how many borders and forms you can make with the circle. With two colors, make borders that will harmonize. We should use the same colors that we found to be the best when using the harmony birds. The best designs should be kept by pasting the parts down well and mounting the paper on a larger card.

WHEN PASTING OR MOUNTING examples of work, we must be careful to leave a wider margin always at the bottom of the sheet. When trimming the edges of our papers, we shall make them as straight and square as we can. If necessary, this may be done by using the edges of a book cover, as a book cover is usually straight-edged.

BIRD AND ANIMAL BORDERS may be made by pasting a row of birds or animals across a book cover or around the edge of a card. Borders of other objects, such as fruit and leaves, or books, or trees, make interesting borders also, and they can be arranged in colors.

SIMPLE BORDERS AND PATTERNS can be made with dots and dashes of different lengths made with crayons. If we will take a ruler and mark off inches and half inches on an envelope, and use it as shown, we can mark off on papers regular divisions within which we can place our design marks. Or we can cut squares or circles out of colored paper, and arrange them as borders or all-over patterns. Such borders and patterns can be used on paper boxes or paper folders, on book covers, and in many other useful ways.

HANDICRAFT

ACCURACY AND APPLICATION can be learned by handicraft. To be able to use our hands properly and to do the things that are necessary to our needs and comfort without depending always on others, is a valuable accomplishment. There are certain requirements, such as neatness and correct measuring, that are important through all workmanship. Neatness, accuracy, and good design may be first learned by paper folding.

PAPER FOLDING WILL TEACH MANY THINGS. It will show that certain shapes are the foundations of useful forms. If we take a square of paper and fold it by placing the opposite edges together, we divide it into many squares. If we fold it by placing the corners together and creasing it, we divide it into squares or triangles. A circle may be folded and divided into spaces also. Page 28 shows two squares and a circle divided by folds. The scissors are then used, and parts of the folds are cut, and little boxes and baskets made by pasting parts of the folds.

PAPER CUT-OUT BORDERS AND PATTERNS can be made by folding a strip of paper or a square or a circle. If a bird or a flower is cut out of a folded circle or square, when the paper is opened the repeated bird or flower shape will make a pretty design. We should see how many different borders we can make by cutting simple shapes out of folded paper. We should be careful not to cut too many different openings out of the same piece of paper border.

PAPER WEAVING can be used to make pretty mats. If a folded square of paper is cut as shown on page 29, other strips can be woven into it, and different patterns can be made by weaving the strips differently.

DECORATIONS may be made by using the crayons or cutting out little colored spots of paper and adding them to the paper baskets and boxes.

PAPER OBJECTS AND LITTLE PAPER MAY BASKETS may be cut out of various colored papers and pasted on other paper backgrounds. If a paper is folded and one half of a basket is cut out, we shall find that when the paper is opened, both sides of the basket will be alike. We can then use cut-out colored flowers and birds to add to the basket. Good harmonies of color will be necessary to make our cut paper baskets look well, and we should use colors that go well together.

LETTERING will look well on our paper objects and booklet covers if it is well done. Simple lettering can be made on squared paper by going from line to line and from one corner to another of the squares.

CAPITAL LETTERS are easier than the small letters, and we should practice for some time in lettering our names or the names of our town and state and school.

LETTERING WITH A PENCIL is the easiest way to begin lettering, and the use of a soft pencil on a squared paper is the best method.

TO BEGIN, make the letters I, T, C, E, F, S, G, H, L, O, U, and P as shown on the lettering page for this chapter. These letters have lines that are in the same direction as the lines on the squared paper.

THE LETTERS WITH SLANT LINES, such as B, D, K, M, N, Q, R, V, W, X, Y, and Z, should next be drawn until the slant lines can be made straight and meet at the right points.

NUMBERS should next be tried, and words and numbers combined, until they are drawn equally well.

LETTERING WITHOUT SQUARED PAPER should be practiced, and we should see how well we can do the lines of the letter without the squared paper as a guide. We can apply our lettering to little gift cards, to box covers, bookmarks, and other objects where we wish lettering to appear. We ought to be careful not to make the lettering too large or too small for the space that it is placed within.

TO LEARN FORM, make shapes with clay or other soft materials that will hold their form when pressed into shape.

TO MAKE A ROUND BALL, a small piece of clay is rolled lightly between the palms of the hand. When the clay has been rolled until it is round, it is placed on the desk, and then other parts are made and added to the round part to make objects.

FRUIT AND FLOWERS can be made by adding stems and leaves. The clay can also be flattened out, and objects made in low relief. These may be pressed out on a piece of paper.

ROUND OBJECTS made in clay or plasticine are good beginning problems for any one, and it is interesting to see how many objects can be made from a round clay ball. Other shapes can be made easily from the ball form, and then objects made that come nearest such forms.

BIRDS AND ANIMALS can be made from clay balls. Small balls can be added to the larger balls to make the heads. These birds and animals may be placed on a small tree twig set in a jar of sand, or they may be perched upon the branches of cut flower stems that are on our tables. See how many things that have been drawn can be modeled in the clay.

CIRCLE DRAWINGS

2 Applied Art

CIRCLE BIRDS AND ANIMALS

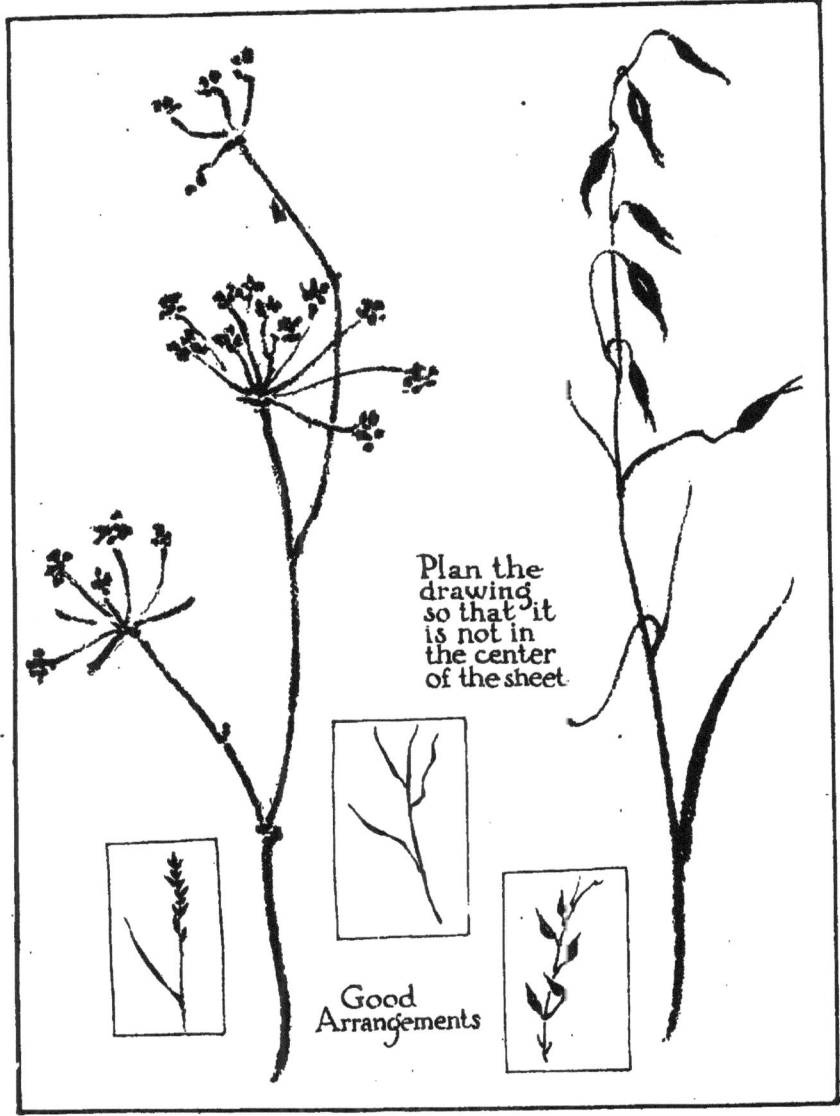

Plan the
drawing
so that it
is not in
the center
of the sheet

Good
Arrangements

LINE NATURE DRAWINGS

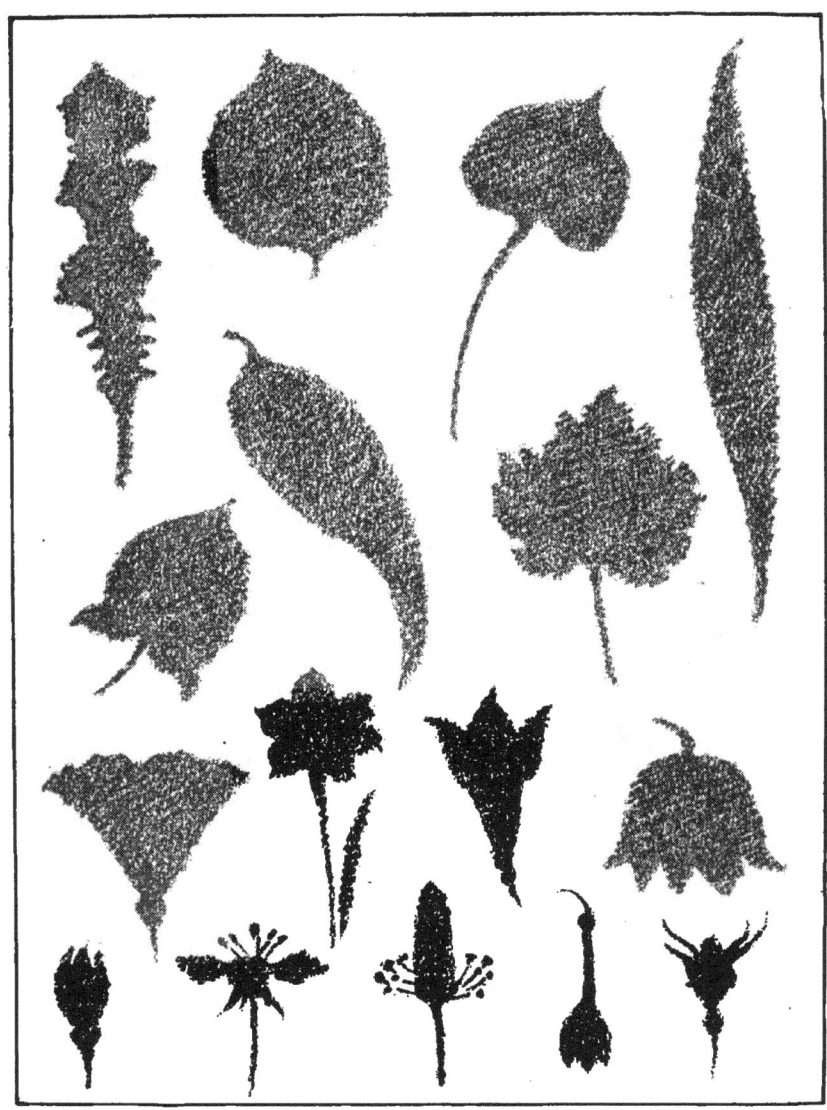

FORM NATURE DRAWINGS

LIGHT AND DARK NATURE DRAWINGS

LIGHT AND DARK CRAYON DRAWINGS

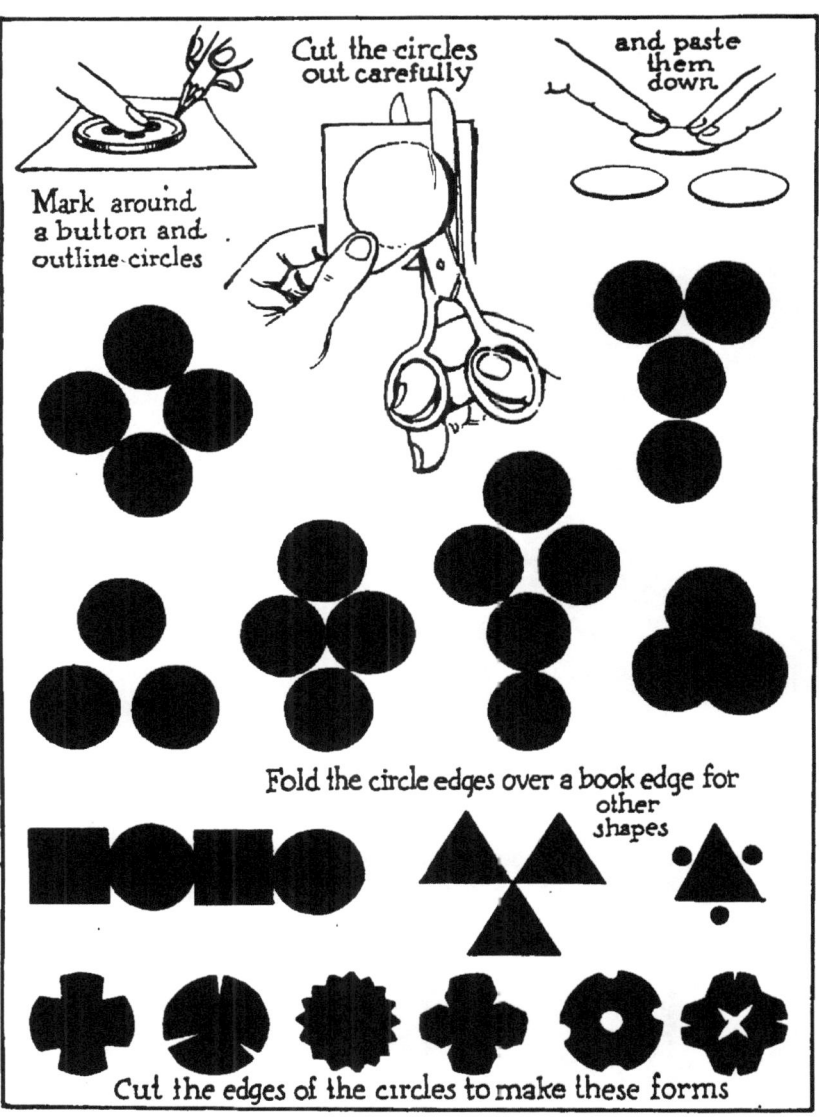

Mark around a button and outline circles

Cut the circles out carefully

and paste them down

Fold the circle edges over a book edge for other shapes

Cut the edges of the circles to make these forms

CIRCLE DESIGNS

Paste a small circle and a large circle together

Add chalk strokes making birds and animals

CIRCLE PAPER CUT-OUTS

PAPER CUT-OUT OBJECTS

Scissor
Cut-Outs

SCISSOR DESIGNING

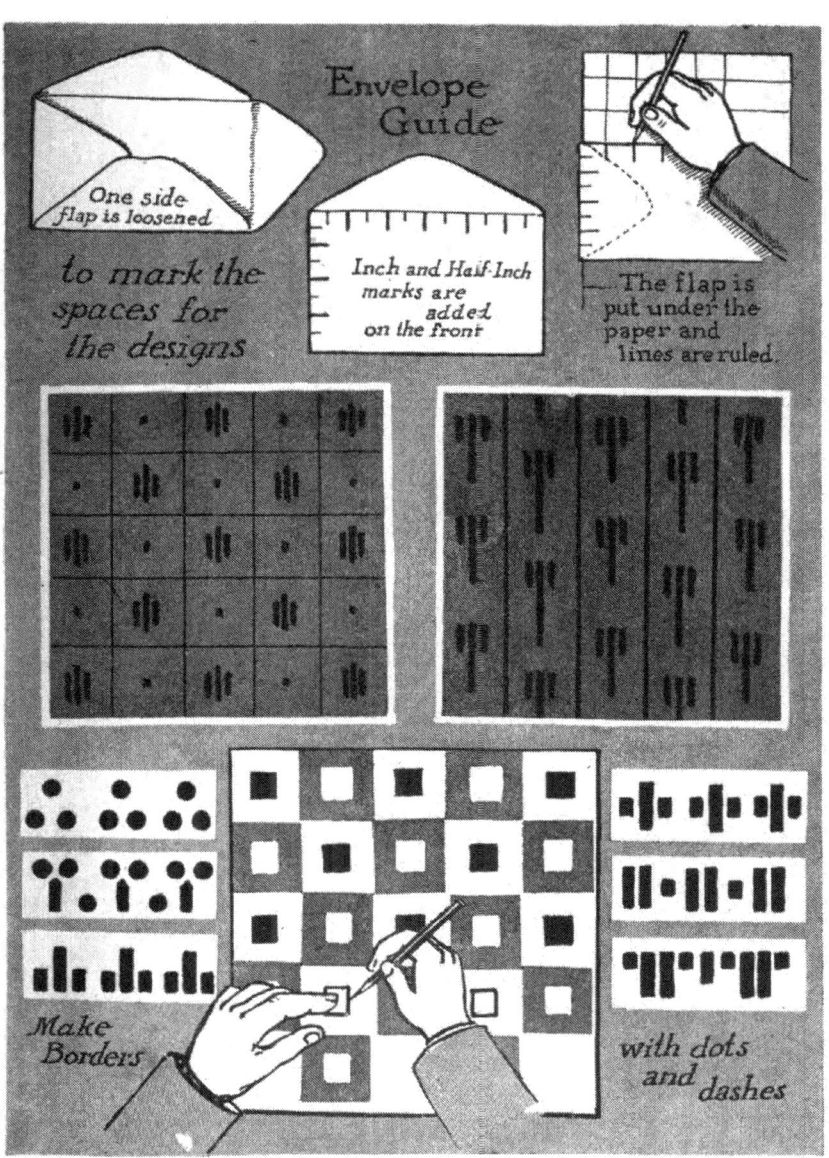

ALL-OVER PATTERNS

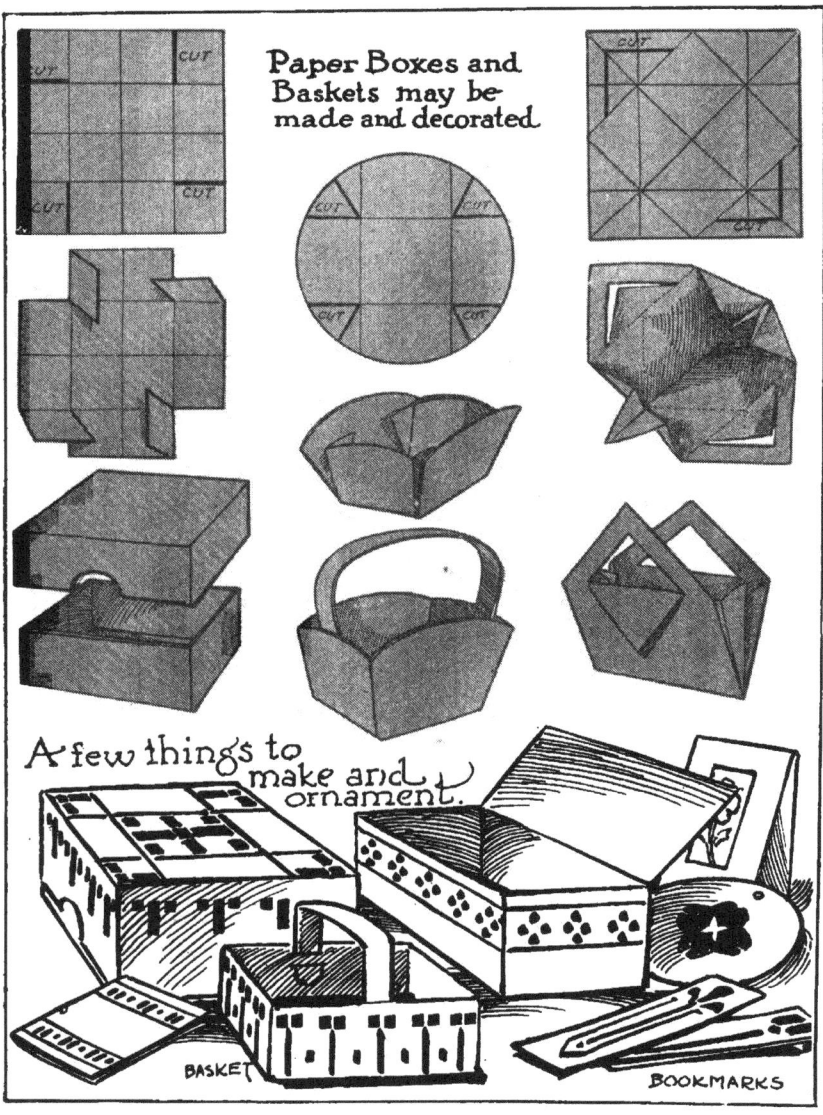

Paper Boxes and Baskets may be made and decorated

A few things to make and ornament.

BASKET

BOOKMARKS

PAPER BOXES AND BASKETS

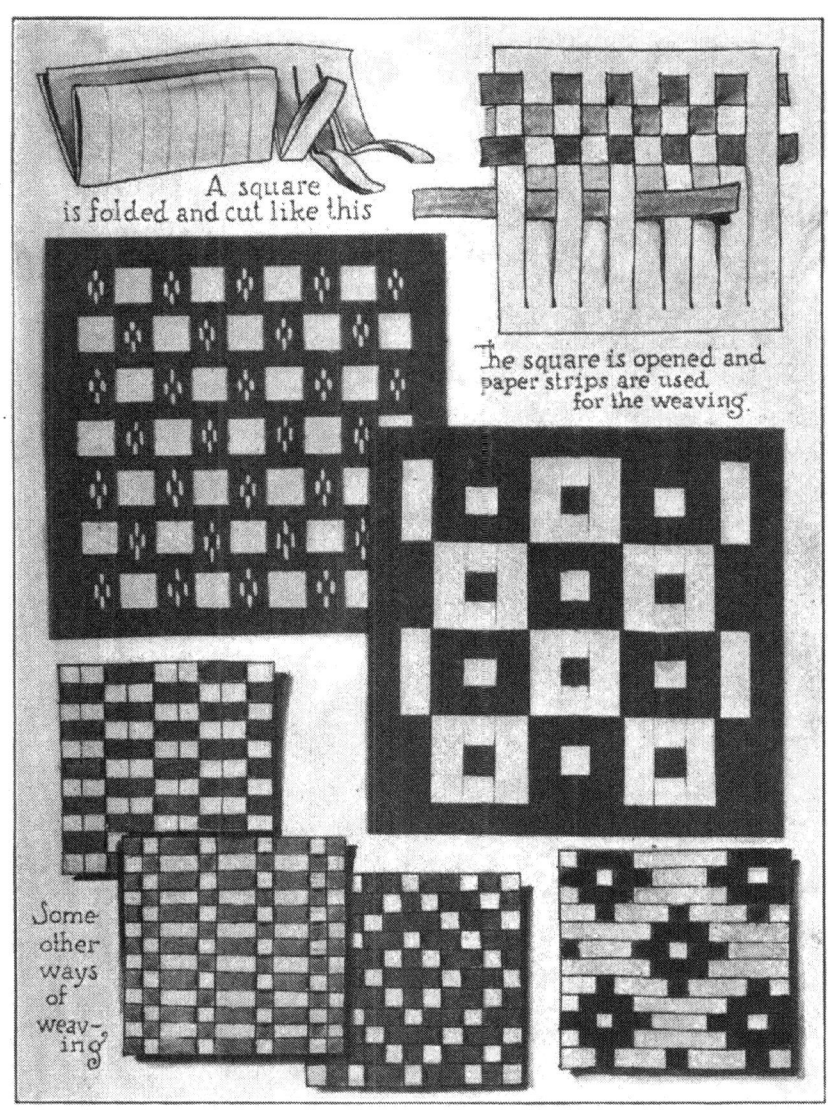

A square
is folded and cut like this

The square is opened and
paper strips are used
for the weaving.

Some
other
ways
of
weav-
ing

PAPER MAT WEAVING

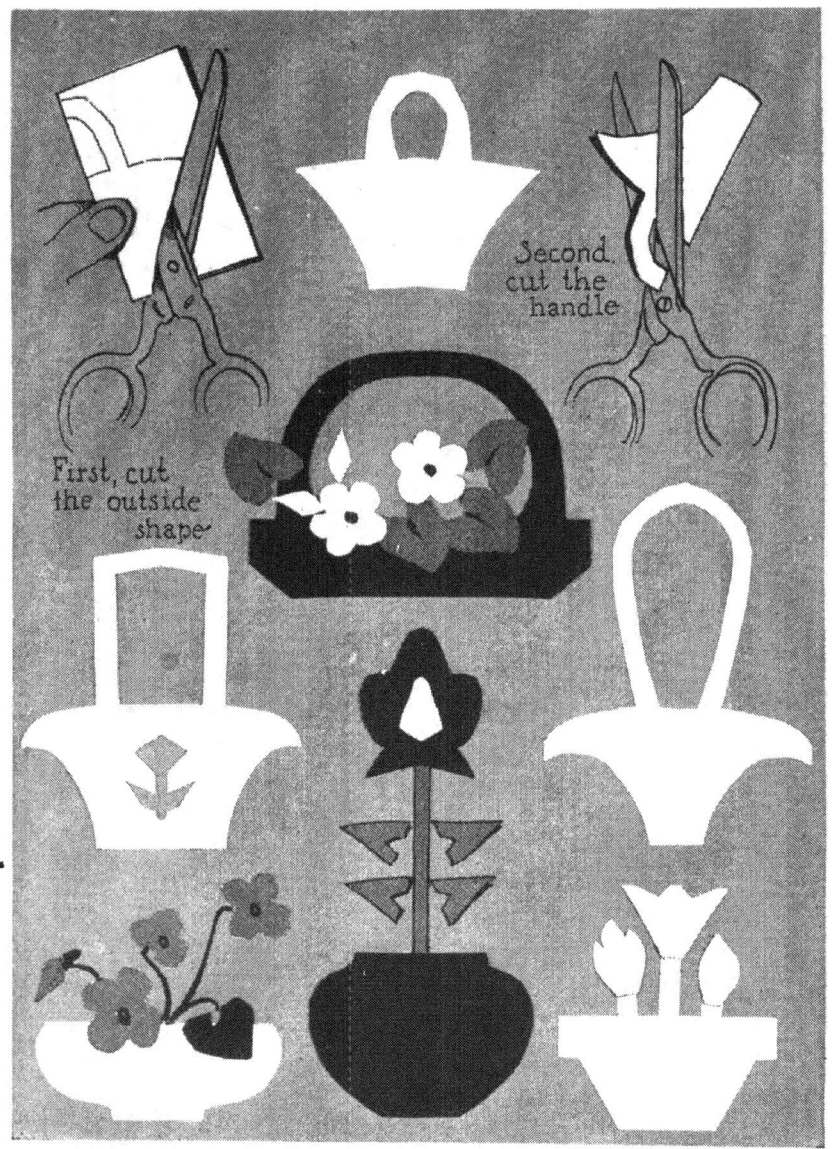

PAPER FLOWER BASKETS

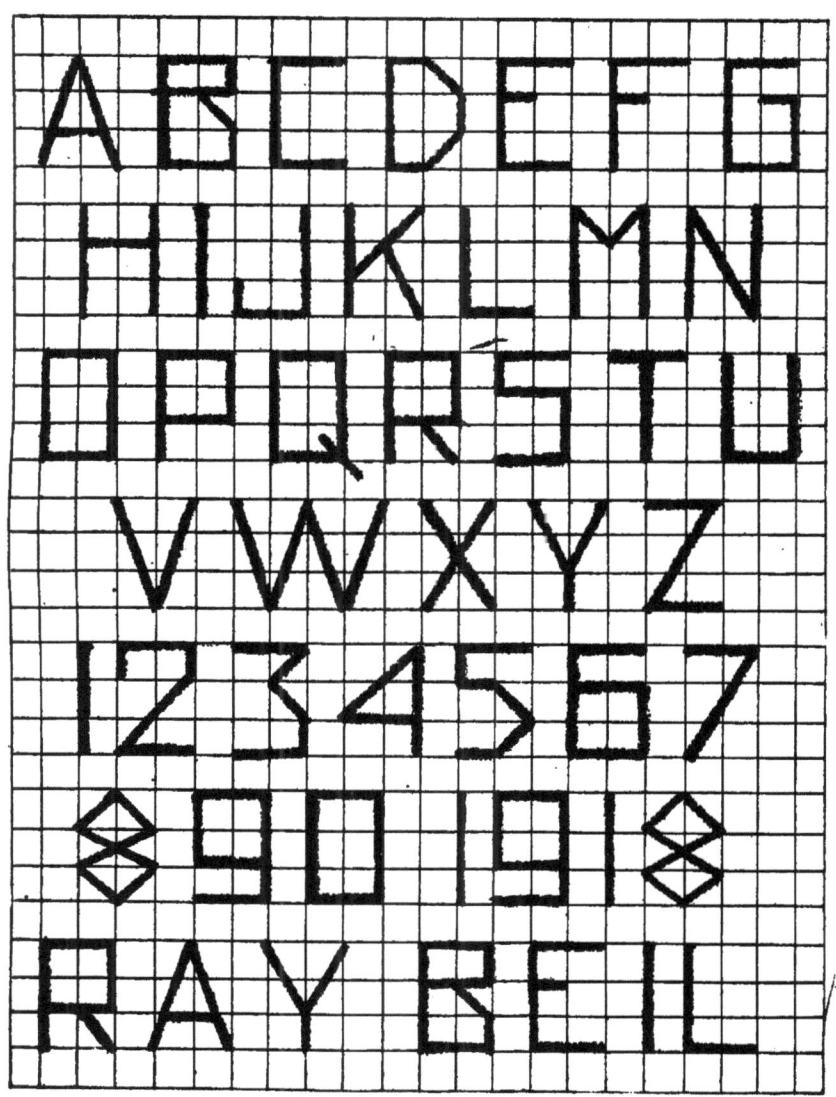

SIMPLE LINE ALPHABET

Roll a clay
ball between
the hands

Pinch
the ball
to
flatten it

Press the clay
between the thumbs
and
fingers

for
making
leaves
and
flat
objects

SIMPLE MODELED OBJECTS

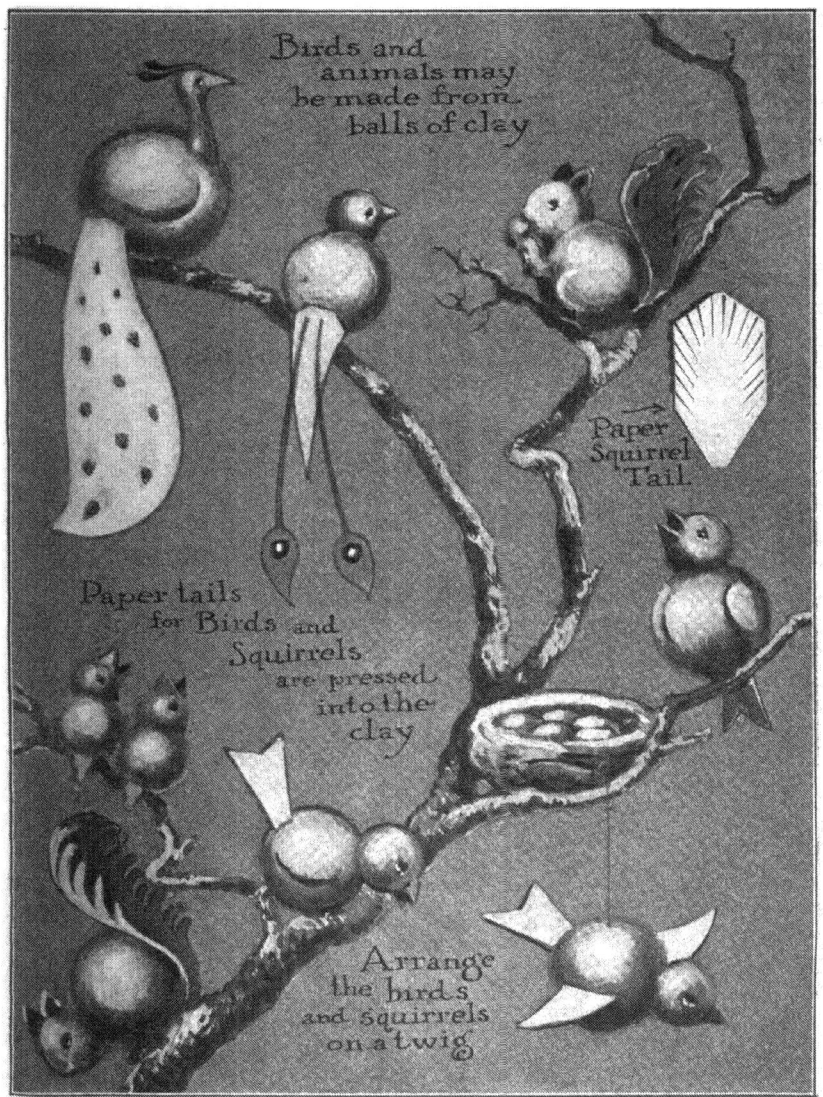

Birds and animals may be made from balls of clay

Paper Squirrel Tail

Paper tails for Birds and Squirrels are pressed into the clay

Arrange the birds and squirrels on a twig

MODELED BIRDS AND ANIMALS

3 Applied Art

TEACHER'S NOTES FOR THE FIRST YEAR

PLANT HOLDERS. When the pupils are drawing from weeds or plants, there are several devices for holding the material in position. One is a card easel with an elastic band or a string around the top. Or a piece of modeling wax is shaped so that a stem put into it will be held in upright position.

For flowers, a little bottle (a cream bottle is good) is filled with damp sand and the stem of the flower is put into it.

To hold flowers in certain positions, a wire can be bent as shown to fasten to the edge of the cup or vase.

Objects can be put on a board that is placed across the aisle toward the front of the desk rows. A second board can be placed halfway back in the aisle for those in the rear seats. A board is necessary in every other row only.

TO SHARPEN PENCILS. A pencil sharpener in a schoolroom is a good thing to have, but a hand-sharpened pencil renders a better drawn line. The teacher should illustrate the best way to sharpen a pencil, and give the reasons why. The pupil who can sharpen a pencil well and who gives proper care to the preparation of his drawing material will have an advantage over the careless pupil. As he grows older, he will be more inclined to take care of and keep in good condition every tool he uses.

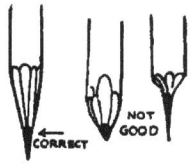

MOUNTING DRAWINGS. The best work accomplished in the class should be mounted on a dark paper mount and hung in the honor corner or exhibition space. Such work will be a stimulus to other students, and at the same time will keep before the eyes of all, the kind of work that the teacher wishes the pupils to equal.

The best drawing made of an object each week can be displayed in a special space, and then all such weekly exhibits assembled in the honor corner afterward. At the end of the term, the teacher then has the best of the work for exhibition with the average work of the pupils.

TEACHER'S LIBRARY. Every teacher should have a file of reference subjects for drawing, painting, and design and handicrafts, so that any subject needed may be easily located. An index system or alphabetical arrangement will do much toward making easier the work of the teacher. Birds and animals, flowers and trees, and other subjects should be filed so as to be easily found. A series of subjects that come within circle shapes is one collection, and subjects showing good color harmonies form another part of the first year's reference material. A number of the animal and bird pictures and good colored prints showing rich color harmonies should be kept posted in the classroom. They will cheer up the room as well as guide the pupils in their drawings and handicraft.

COLORED PAPER WINDOW AND BLACKBOARD DECORATION

CUT PAPER APPLICATIONS

THE SECOND YEAR

DRAWING AND COLORING

EVERY OBJECT IS MADE UP OF SHAPES; and when drawing from any objects, we should first try to see these different shapes, and make the general shapes of our objects before trying to put in the small parts.

"BLOCKING" is the name given to the drawing of these general shapes, because block shapes are made up of straight lines and simple shapes.

In the last chapter, we studied how to make circle shapes, and we then drew objects, birds, and animals, within these shapes. We shall now take simple objects and draw them in outline.

TO COMMENCE DRAWING OBJECTS, place them so that the simplest side is seen. The more difficult sides can be drawn later.

THE FIRST ILLUSTRATION in this chapter shows objects that have been drawn in simple outlines and from simple views. It will be seen that the flatiron comes within a general shape of a half circle, while the candlestick comes within a triangle. That the candlestick is again made up of different smaller shapes, can also be seen.

WE SHOULD COMPARE PARTS and think when we are drawing. After the general shape is made, we should then see what the most important or largest portion of the object is, and make that next. We may think in this way: The next part is less than one half of the whole shape, and it is a *little* less than one half. So we will draw it that way. Next we notice that the handle on the object joins the side a little more than one half way up. So we commence it at that point on our drawing. Then we note, by comparing, that the top part is half the size of the first part drawn, and draw it in that proportion. After we have drawn all these parts in this manner, we can look them over and compare them with the original, and correct the parts that are faulty.

THE DRAWING OF SEVERAL OBJECTS together should be the next step. The objects should be arranged either so that one does not come in front of another, like the teddy bear and the bowl and flower on page 44, or so that some of them will come in front of others, like the basket and the apples.

CRAYON DRAWINGS of these objects can be made by outlining the shapes and then filling in the outline with solid, even crayon lines.

(35)

The crayon lines should be rubbed in one direction as far as possible, and all parts should be made as even in blackness as possible. Such drawings are called silhouette drawings.

FIGURE DRAWING can be started at this time by the use of single lines and a circle. The circle will be for the head, and the lines will be for the arms, the legs, the body, the hands, and the feet. By drawing a long line first for the body, and then two for the arms and two for the legs, with a circle for the head added, it will be found that a human figure's action lines are indicated. Short lines for hands and feet are added to finish the figure.

ACTION DRAWING gives more interest than drawing objects, though to draw objects well is very necessary. Often we need to concentrate on parts of a study that are not so interesting as other parts, in order that we may know the whole subject well.

In art study, many people work at only the parts they find interesting, and later they are prevented from doing things satisfactorily, because they neglected studying certain important things earlier.

BE THOROUGH IN YOUR ART STUDY, and avoid skipping from one thing to another, or picking out only those parts that interest you. You will find that all parts are necessary to the whole subject. Learn to do them all well.

WHEN MAKING ACTION FIGURES, try to make the different lines in proportion to the parts they represent on the human figure. Avoid having one leg longer than the other, and do not make the arms so long they would reach the ground. By comparing the lengths of the arms and legs of those around you, or by looking at your own, you can tell the correct lengths.

AN ACTION MODEL made of black strips of paper as shown on page 45 can be used as a guide for action drawing. The arms and the legs can be turned to give different poses, and then single line drawings can be made from this model. We can call the model Bobby, and make a dog model to play with him. Other animals can be made and used as action models. Artists and illustrators use action models that look like human figure dolls, and that are called manikins. These manikins are used to guide artists in securing human figure attitudes in their paintings. We can use Bobby and Fido in the same way.

OBJECT DRAWING IN BLACK AND WHITE on a gray paper is an excellent way of drawing from objects. Do not try to show light and shade, or to draw the object in any position but a front view or a side view, whichever way shows the object the flattest.

COLORS IN OBJECTS are either dark or light. With white chalk or crayon, we can make all the light parts white; and with dark crayon, we can make all the dark parts. The parts that are neither dark nor light may be left for the gray paper to represent, and simply outlined with black crayon.

TOYS ARE GOOD OBJECTS TO DRAW, because they are generally simple in outline, and therefore not hard to draw. Can you draw your toys the way they have been drawn on page 46?

COLOR DRAWINGS can be made of the subjects that have been drawn in outline. Crayons can be used to fill in the spaces between the black lines. The crayons should be used lightly, so that the coloring is a tint and not a solid color.

COLORED SILHOUETTE DRAWINGS can be made. Draw a brown basket. Next, by the side of it, draw a yellow pear, an orange, some red cherries, purple grapes, a blue plum, and a green apple. These should all be drawn in silhouette.

COLORED FLOWERPOTS can be drawn with colored crayon or cut out of colored paper. A flower can be drawn growing from a flowerpot, and it should be of a color harmonious to the flowerpot.

GOOD COLOR HARMONIES are as follows: yellow and orange, orange and red, red and violet, violet and blue, blue and green, green and yellow; also, red and green, yellow and violet, and blue and orange. If we have a flowerpot in one of the colors, then the flower should be of the other color.

COLORED CHINESE LANTERNS can be made by cutting out a good shape from stiff paper and outlining two forms. Fill these two forms with yellow crayon. Then rub red crayon very strongly on the top part of one lantern, grading it gradually until it blends to a faint tint near the bottom. Do the same with the other yellow lantern, but use blue crayon. Make two more lanterns in red, and use yellow over one and blue over another. Then make two more lanterns in blue, and rub yellow on one and red on another. This will show us how such colors go together, and that a green or a red or a blue can have some of another color in it.

COLORED ACTION FIGURES can be drawn with crayons. A coat can be added to the figures to make a boy, and a skirt can be put on a figure to make a girl. When two figures are used together in different colors, the colors should be harmonious. Trousers may be added to the boy and a blouse to the girl. The blouse and the skirt can be different colors. What colors will be harmonious? The boy's coat will be dark blue and the trousers light blue. How can you make the blue lighter?

SQUARE COLOR PANELS can be made with a card two inches square. In the center of this square, place an inch square card and make a pencil line around it. It should be as near the center as possible; and you can tell when it is in the center, because the distance between the small square and the edge of the big square will be the same on all four sides. Color the small square one color, and the other space another color that will be a good harmony. If the outside color is made fainter than the color in the center square, it will be a better harmony; because when there is more of one color than another, it is best that the greater amount of color be fainter than the other.

BREEZE BIRDS AND FLUTTERING BUTTERFLIES can be cut out of folded paper and hung by strings at the window, where the breeze will cause them to move. Squirrels, birds, and fruit can be cut out of colored papers, too, and added to colored-chalk tree limbs drawn on the blackboard. The teacher may draw the main part of the picture, the children each adding part of the subject.

GOOD MARGINS WHEN MOUNTING are important. It is best to leave more space always at the bottom than on the top or the sides. Too much margin or too little margin on the mount is not good. Try to place every drawing on the mount paper so that it will be improved in appearance.

WHEN PASTING DRAWINGS, it is not necessary to paste them down solid. A little paste on the tips of the cut-out parts will hold them on the background mount firmly. Care should be taken not to use so much paste that it will show on the mount. Neatness and accuracy can be learned by pasting our drawings on mounts; and we should do it repeatedly, until we can do it rapidly and correctly the first time.

DESIGN

BLOCK TREES can be drawn by using squared paper and drawing trees as shown on page 47. Such trees can be used in many ways to decorate covers and for making borders. We should never use natural tree drawings for decorations. Natural drawings of trees are good as pictures of trees; but whenever we use any part of nature in art work to ornament anything, it should first be designed. By design we mean the arrangement or fixing over of a subject to fit its purpose. If we are to decorate a flat surface, our design should then be flat in effect to go with the flat surface.

WHEN DRAWING BLOCK TREES, we can have the lines so that they follow the square lines of our squared paper, or we can make the lines run from corner to corner. Simple shapes are the best to make, and the outlines should be made of as long lines as possible.

After we have designed several good block trees, we can use them as guides for cutting out a number of colored paper trees, which can be pasted on cards or covers, as borders and decorations.

TREE STENCILS can be made by cutting out the tree that we like best of those designed on the squared paper, and tracing around one half of it on a folded paper. By cutting out this shape and opening the paper, we shall then have a stencil. If the stencil is placed on another paper and held firmly in one place, and a crayon rubbed over the stencil, the result will be a tree design on the paper underneath the stencil. This is illustrated on page 49. If we are careful in placing our stencil when making such stencil designs, we shall find that a great deal of space can be covered in a short time by this method.

INCH BORDERS can be made by laying a ruler down and drawing a light straight line with a dot at each inch. With our crayon, we can then draw over the pencil line; or we can rule the line with the crayon. We shall also make upright lines at each inch mark. These lines should be short lines, but all of the same height. A paper held with the edge placed where we wish the lines to end will prevent our crayon from marking past the place. We can then make squares or circles or some other very simple spot shape over each inch mark. Cut-out paper squares or other shapes may be pasted on the inch lines or between the inch lines.

HALF-INCH MARKS can be added to our designs, and they may be shorter, and the ornaments that we make over them may be smaller. When we make paper baskets or boxes, these borders may be used to decorate them.

FLOWER CUT-OUTS are good designs to make, and the use of scissors will train us to make simple outlines, which is a valuable knowledge in art, and at the same time we shall learn how to cut accurately with scissors.

To make the flower, draw a simple circle or round shape and make a center shape in it. Or the edge of the flower may be drawn with an interesting shape. Next draw a thick stem to it, and a flowerpot or dish at the bottom. Leaves may be added to the flower.

TO MAKE BOTH SIDES ALIKE, fold the paper in half and outline one half of the flower and vase or bowl against the folded edge as shown on page 50. Cut this folded design out with scissors, and when it is opened out, both sides will be alike. To mount these, paste should be carefully tipped on the points of the flowers and leaves and the design pressed on a dark-colored paper. A book or other heavy weight should be placed over the design until it is pressed well.

BOOKMARKS, GIFT CARDS, PLACE CARDS, and other little useful articles can be made by cutting out small flower cut-outs and pasting them on these objects.

THE BEST POSITION for these cut-outs on the objects to which they are to be pasted, should be carefully decided, so that the cut-out will not be spoiled by being badly placed. If lettering is to be added, the cut-out should be placed so as to leave good room for the lettering. Light flowers look best on dark backgrounds, or dark flowers on light backgrounds.

TRAVEL PICTURES may be found in many magazines. These may be cut out or traced, and other cut-outs made by using them as guides. Black, gray, and white paper may be used for the different parts of the pictures. These can be used for illustrating written compositions on travel in different countries. The cut-outs may be used for tracing around to give an outline, and then crayons may be used to fill in the outline with various colors.

SILHOUETTES IN BLACK OR WHITE PAPER CUT-OUTS, showing the different methods of travel in different parts of the world, will make an interesting border for a study room. White paper will look well against the blackboard, while black or dark paper will look best if placed against a lighter background. As you study the geography of each country, suppose that you also find out what animals or kinds of wagons are used in that country, and make picture cut-outs that will best show the method of traveling.

HANDICRAFT

INSTEAD OF FLAT OBJECTS, we shall now start to make objects with several sides. While we have been doing cutting with scissors, we have been in a way drawing with them, because we cut outlines to make pictures and designs. We have made these designs and pictures on flat surfaces or to paste on flat surfaces. Now we shall cut and construct paper objects with scissors; and instead of being flat, they will have several sides. We shall also make booklets with our paper cut-outs, and cut and fold paper to represent birds and animals.

PAPER BASKETS can be made in several ways. The simplest way is to take a square of paper and fold it several times by laying the edges together and creasing it, until sixteen squares are made. Two strips are cut off, leaving nine squares, as shown on page 53, section number 4. Parts are cut as shown by the dark lines, and these are then pasted together and a handle is added. A border or design can be pasted or painted on the basket.

OTHER BASKETS can be made by cutting a circle and a strip from paper. The strip is pasted across the paper circle and creased as shown in section 1 of page 53. This permits the paper basket to come together so that it can hold things. The strip that projects beyond the circle can be cut to make a handle.

BIRD AND BUNNY BASKETS can be made by folding a paper square from corner to corner and drawing a bird or animal that will fit in the part that folds up. A handle is then added, which completes it, as shown in section 2 on page 53.

A CIRCULAR BASKET is shown on the same page in section 3. By folding a paper square from corner to corner and folding again and cutting as shown, and then opening it up and pasting the tips together, a paper basket that will stand firmly is easily made.

PAPER FURNITURE AND TOYS can be made by folding paper into squares and cutting away parts. Other parts are then pasted together, and these may be decorated to make them more interesting. If firm paper is used, the furniture or toys will be more durable. We should see, after we cut the toys and furniture shown on page 52, how many other things we can make of our own.

AN ALPHABET BOOK, or A B C book, should be made. This can be done by drawing a simple object, bird, or animal on each of the twenty-six pages of the book. The object, bird, or animal on each page should have a name commencing with the proper letter of the alphabet for that page. The letter of the alphabet should be lettered both in capital and in small letter, and the name of the object also should be lettered on the page. The subjects should be drawn in simple outline, or with simple flat colors, or they may be cut out and pasted down on the pages. A book made of silhouette subjects cut out of black paper and pasted on the pages will make an interesting alphabet book.

PAPER ANIMALS THAT WILL STAND may be made similar to those shown on pages 56 and 57. By tracing these and cutting them out and putting them together, we can learn how to make other animals and birds that will stand up likewise. It will be fun, when we are studying about birds and animals, to make some of them in paper in this way. In time, we shall have enough for a menagerie or a Noah's ark. Such a collection will delight some little sick boy or girl or some shut-in who cannot run around out of doors.

SMALL LETTERING will be studied in this chapter, as we have already made capital letters. In the history of lettering, we find that capital letters were used before small letters, and that small letters were used because they could be written more rapidly than the large ones. While capital letters are made all the same height, we find that some small letters extend above and below their main parts. The lettering page in this chapter shows an alphabet that is made up entirely of straight lines and drawn on squared paper. We should learn to letter our name and the name of our town or city and school with small lettering on squared paper. We should learn to letter well afterward without the squared paper.

ROUND BALL MODELING. With a ball of clay that has been made by rolling a piece of modeling clay between the palms of the hands, many interesting forms can be made. If we hold a strong thread between our fingers and press it into the clay, we can cut it in half. Each of these halves can be used to model little cups or vases. Some of the vases may be widest at the top, while others may be widest at the bottom. Small sticks, some flat and some pointed, may be used to shape the clay with, and our fingers may be used too. The stick points or a pencil can be used to press little spots or marks into the vases or the bowls for borders and decorations. If we make little bowls out of plasticine, we can put water into them with a few pansies or other small flowers. Thus the bowl will be useful as well as pretty. Colored beads may also be pressed into the clay vases to decorate them. Small, colored pieces of cardboard may be used in the same way.

MODELED ANIMALS can be made from halves of clay balls. A small ball should be used for a head, and a half of a ball for the body. The ball is pressed onto the half ball, and then the legs and the tail and the ears are added, or made from parts of the head and body. Let us see how many things we can make from clay balls or parts of clay balls.

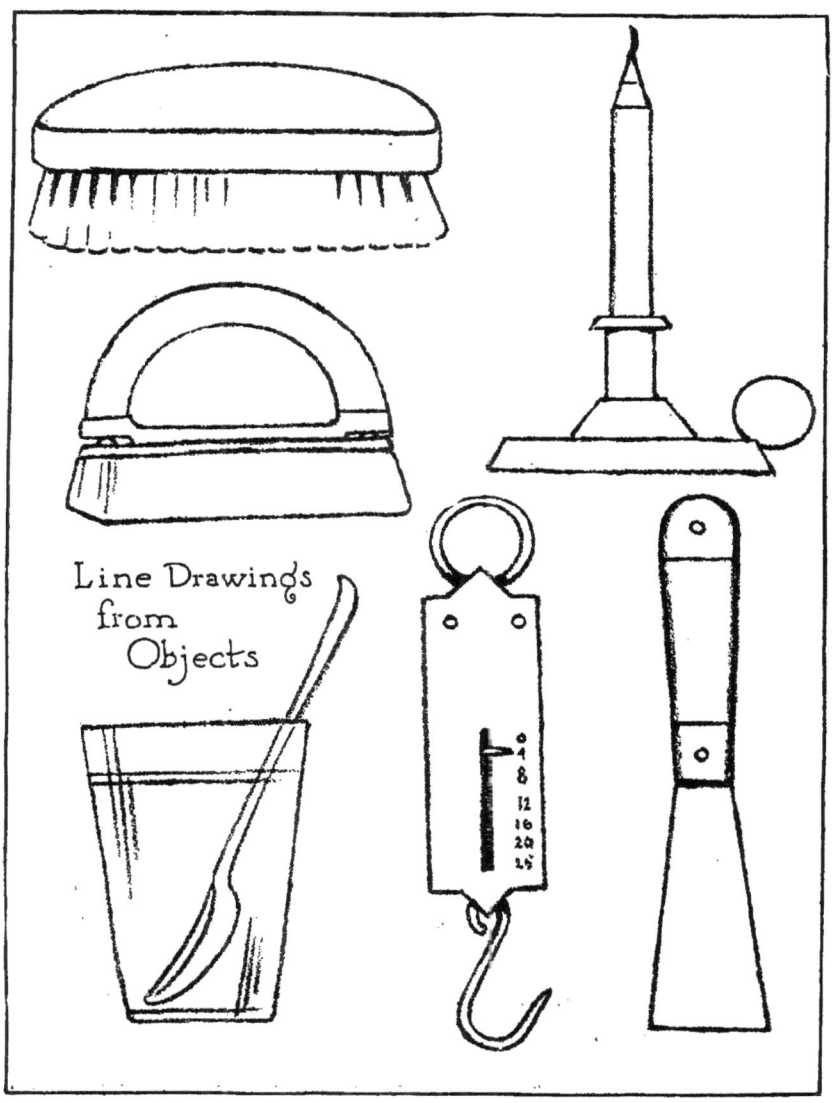

Line Drawings from Objects

LINE OBJECT DRAWING

Draw simple
groups in black
crayon

FLAT OBJECT DRAWING

ACTION DRAWING

LIGHT AND DARK OBJECT DRAWING

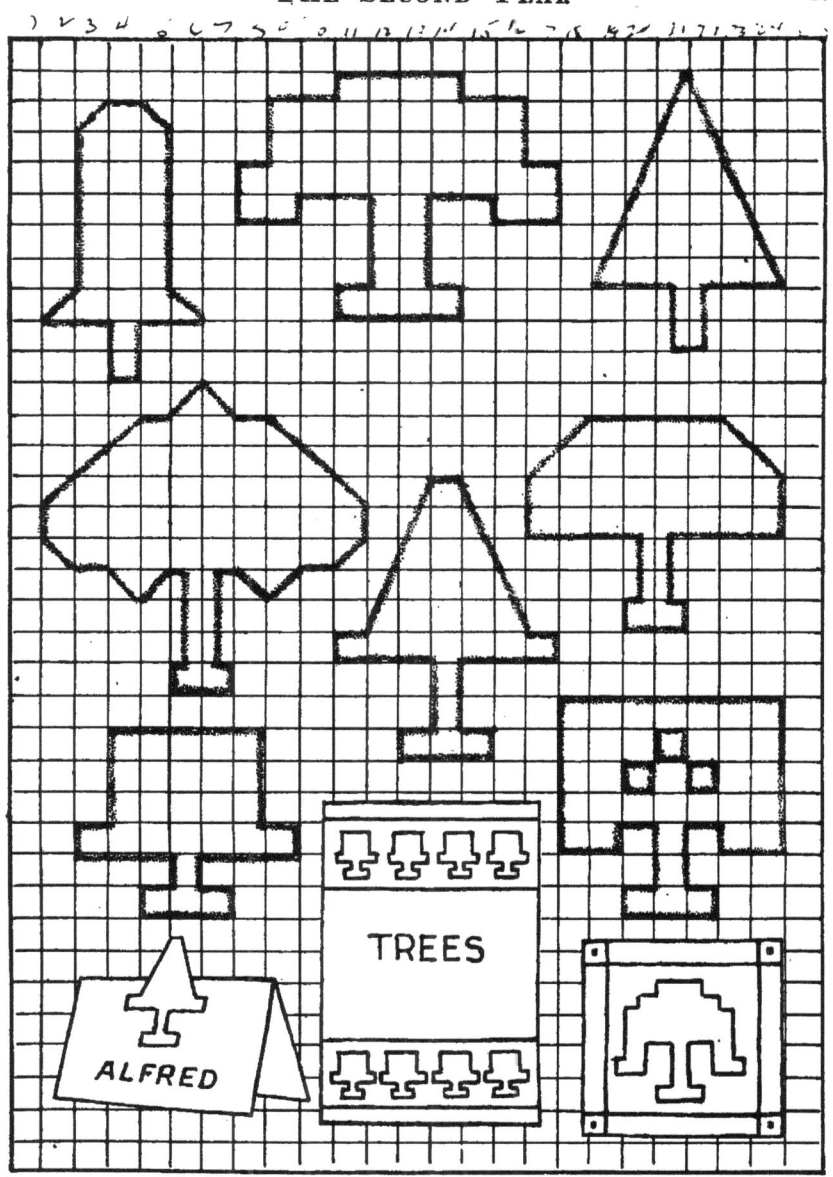

BLOCK TREE DRAWING

LIGHT AND DARK OBJECT DRAWING

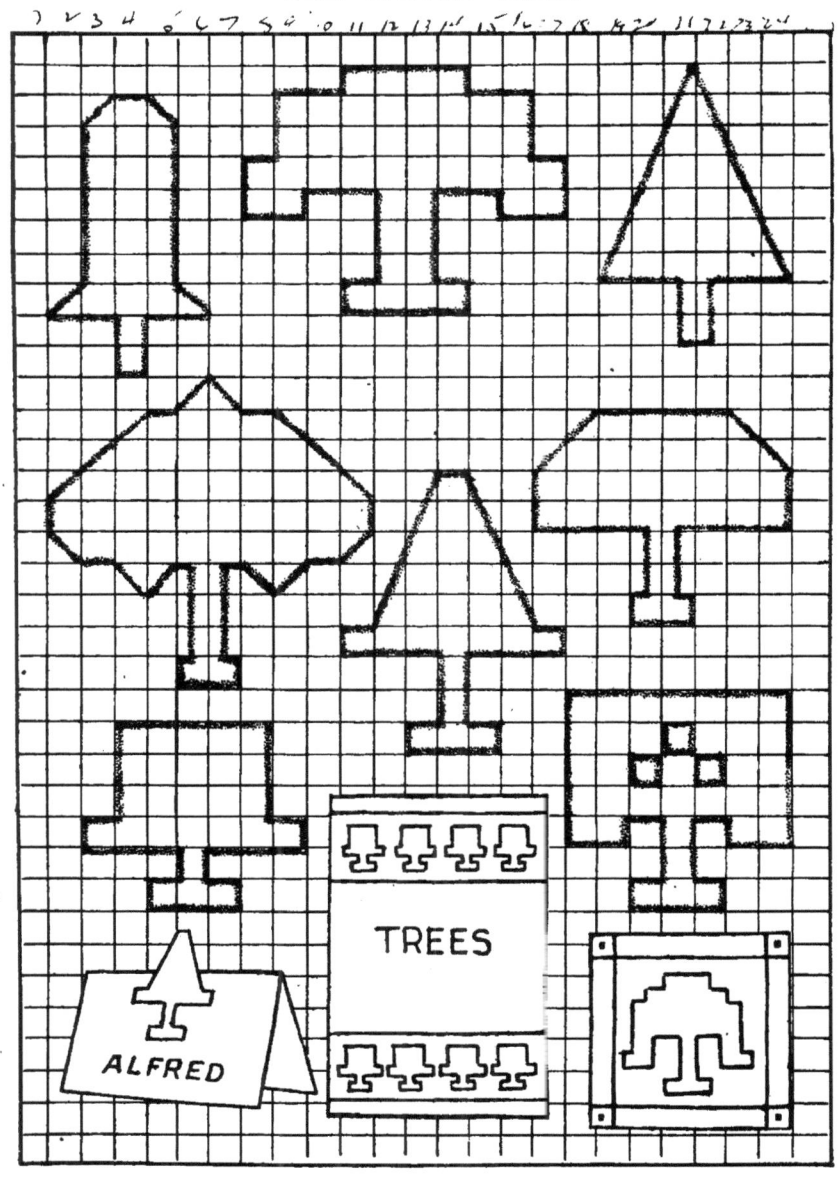

BLOCK TREE DRAWING

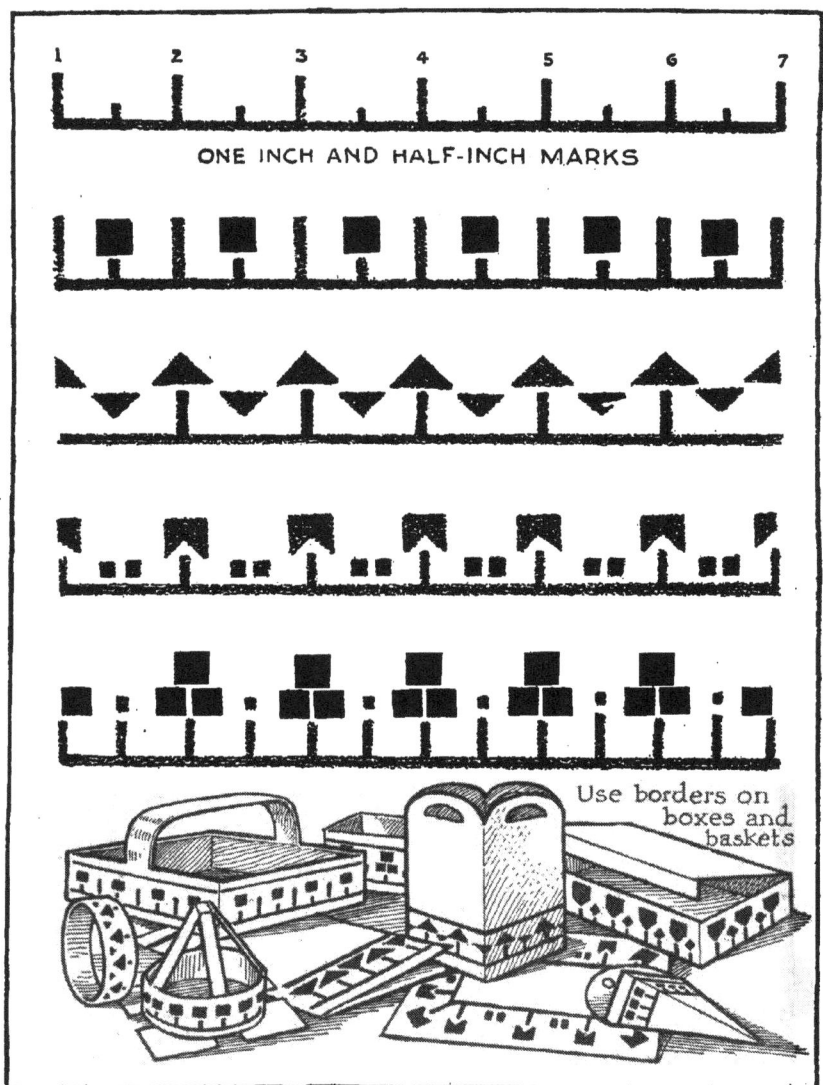

ONE INCH AND HALF-INCH MARKS

Use borders on boxes and baskets

SPOT BORDER DESIGNS

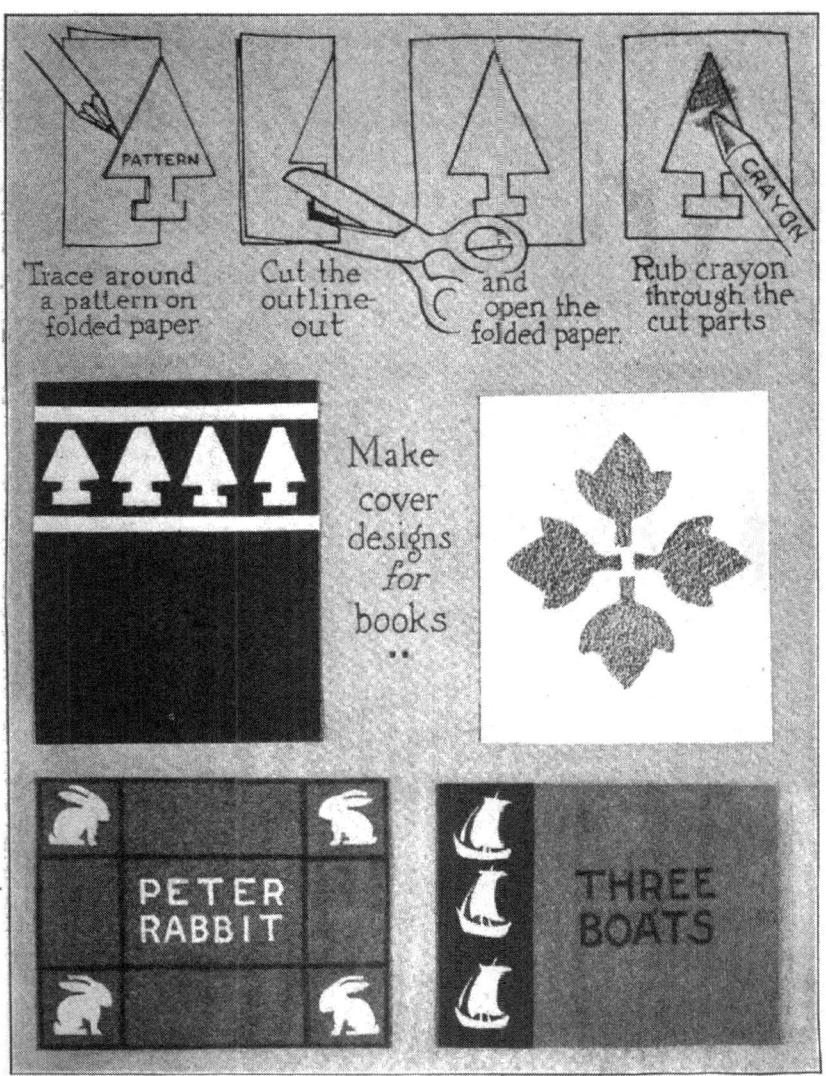

Trace around a pattern on folded paper

Cut the outline out

and open the folded paper

Rub crayon through the cut parts

Make cover designs for books ..

SIMPLE BOOKLET COVER DESIGNS

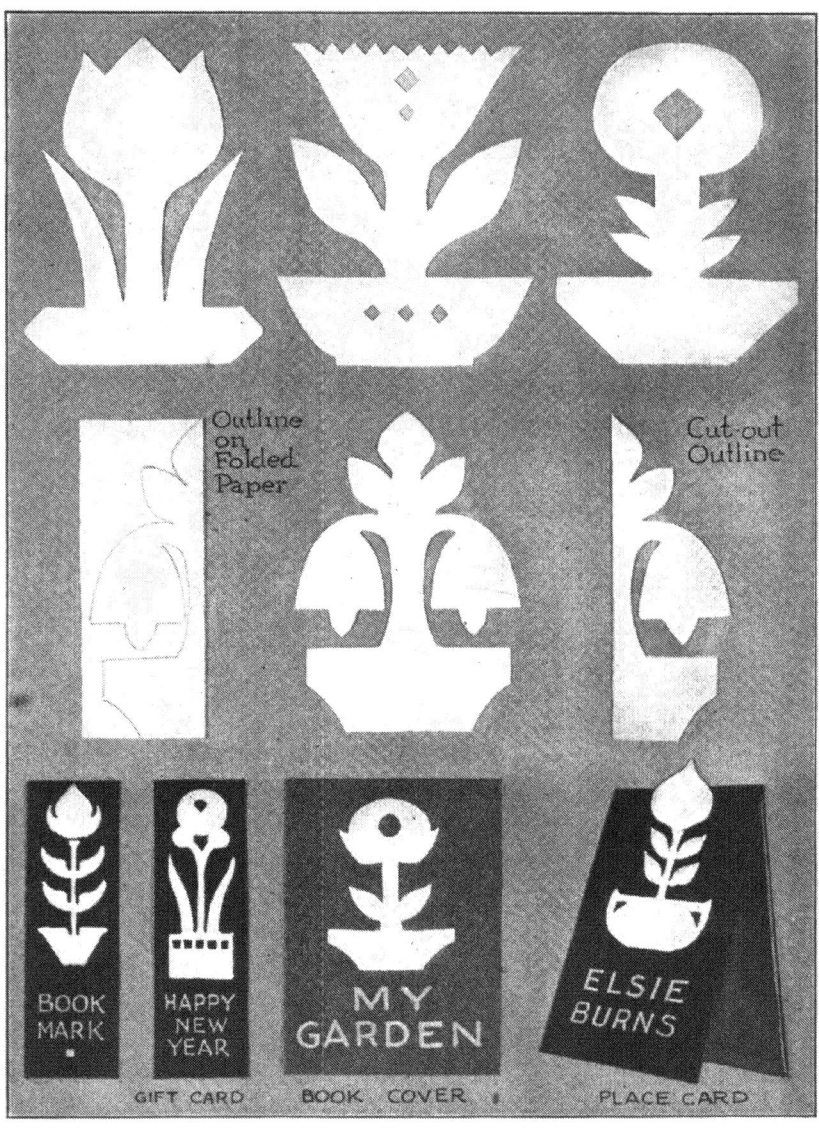

FLOWER CUT-OUTS

Trace pictures from magazines on "Land-Travel" and make cut-outs or crayon drawings

Make simple drawings

TRAVEL PICTURES

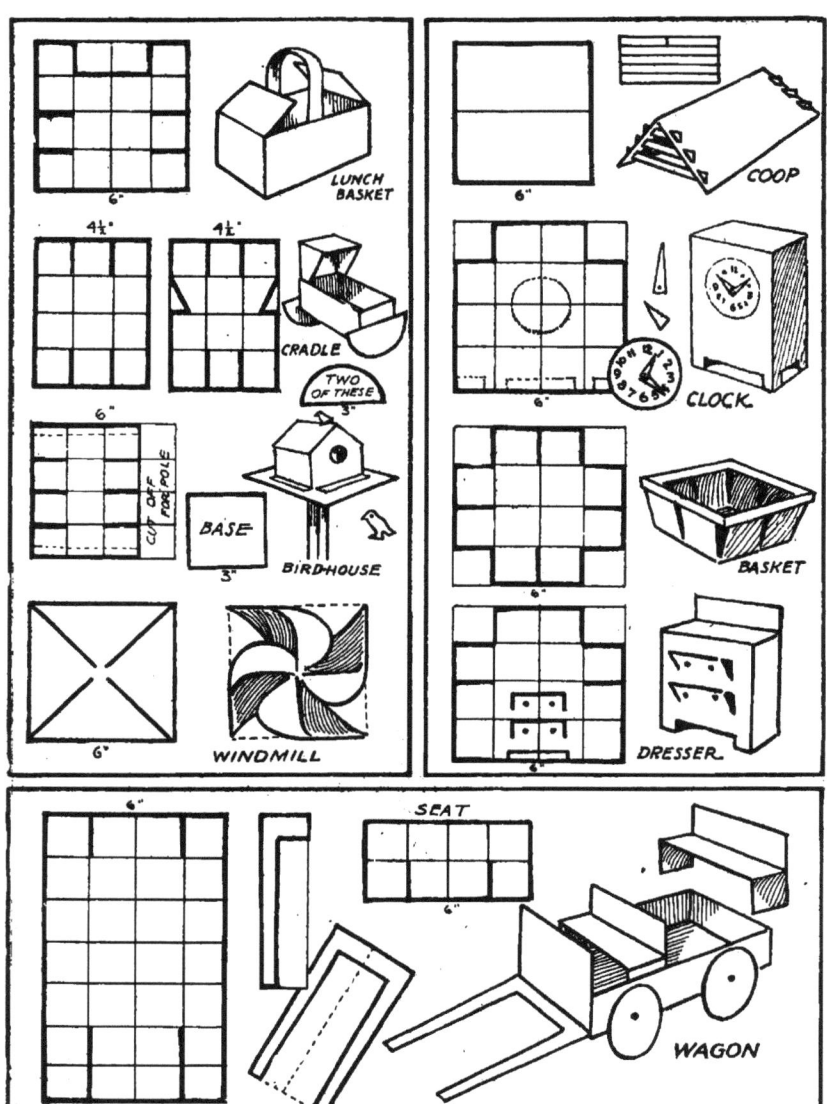

PAPER CONSTRUCTED OBJECTS

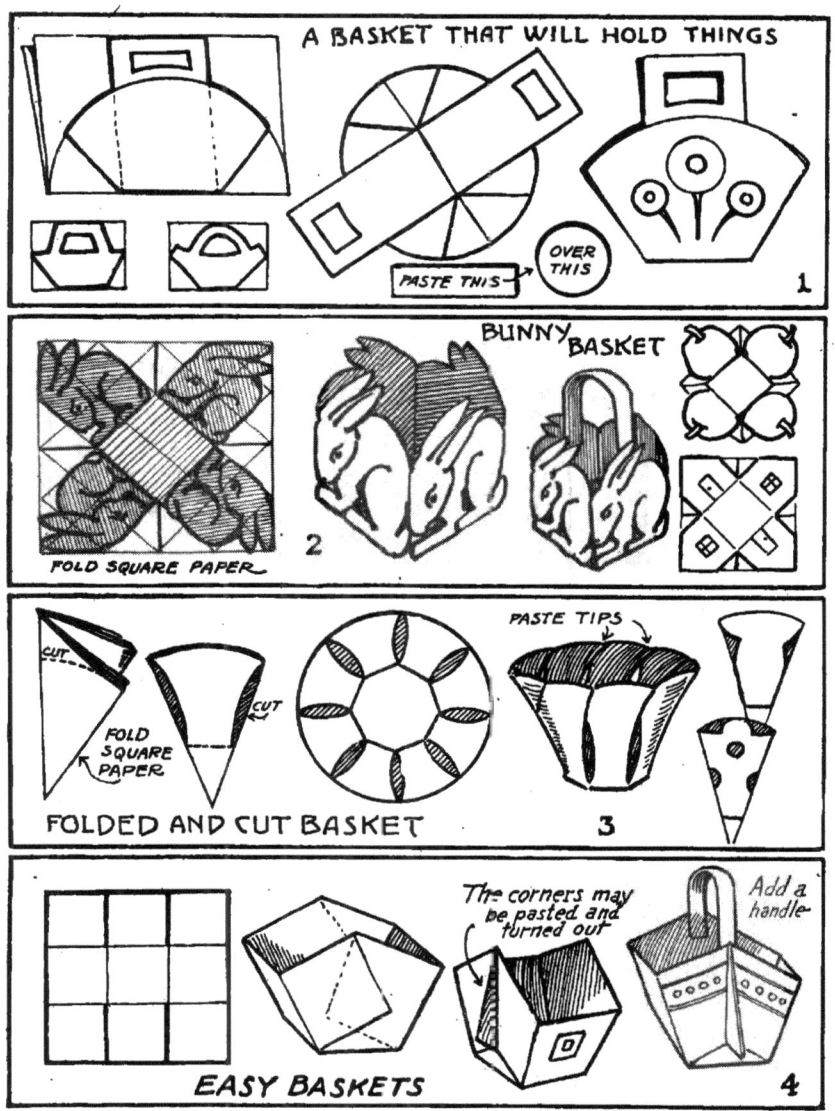

A BASKET THAT WILL HOLD THINGS

PASTE THIS

OVER THIS

1

BUNNY BASKET

FOLD SQUARE PAPER

2

FOLDED AND CUT BASKET

CUT

FOLD SQUARE PAPER

CUT

PASTE TIPS

3

EASY BASKETS

The corners may be pasted and turned out

Add a handle

4

PAPER CONSTRUCTED BASKETS

ILLUSTRATED PAPER FOLDERS

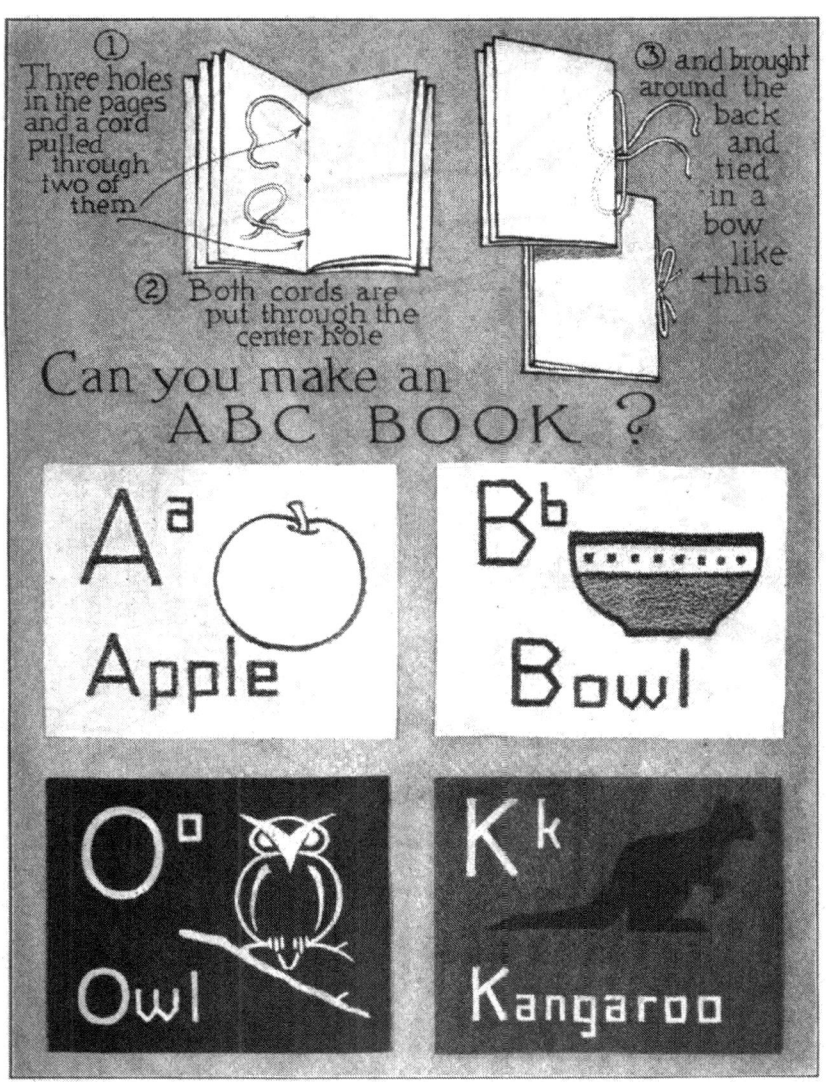

ALPHABET BOOK

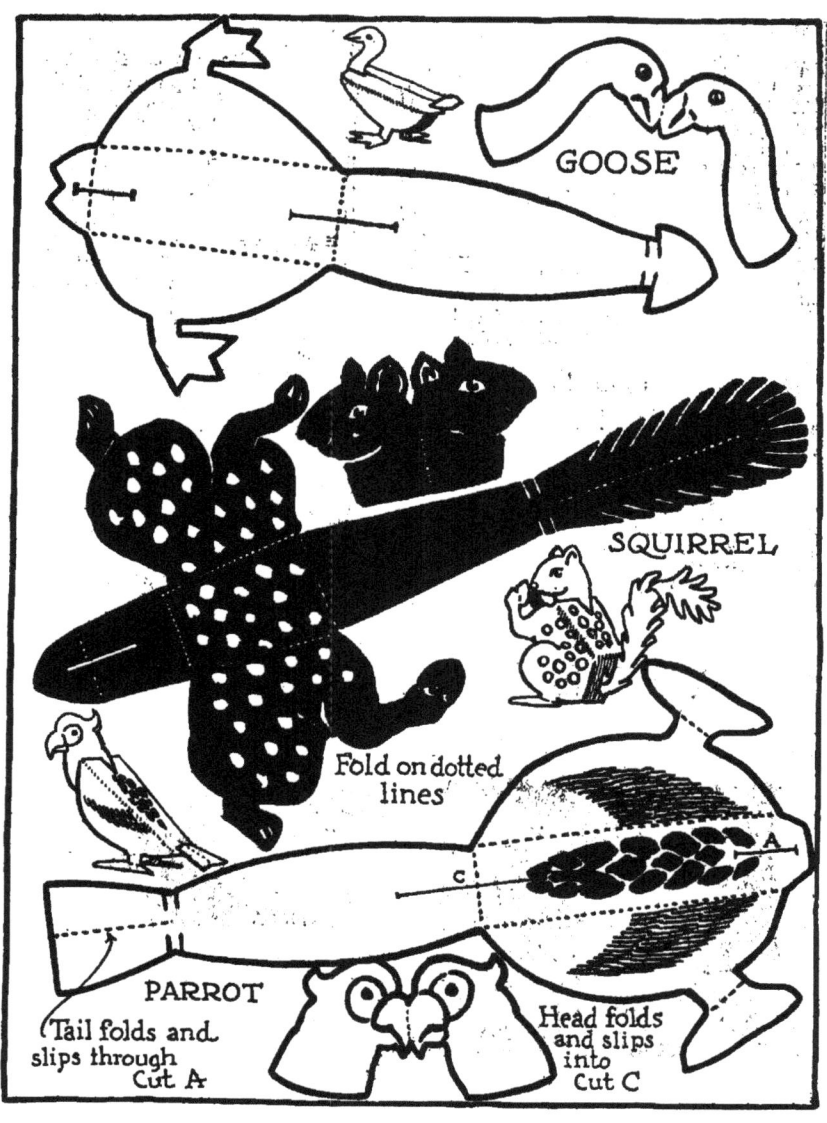

HOW TO MAKE PAPER BIRDS AND ANIMALS

PAPER ANIMALS THAT WILL STAND

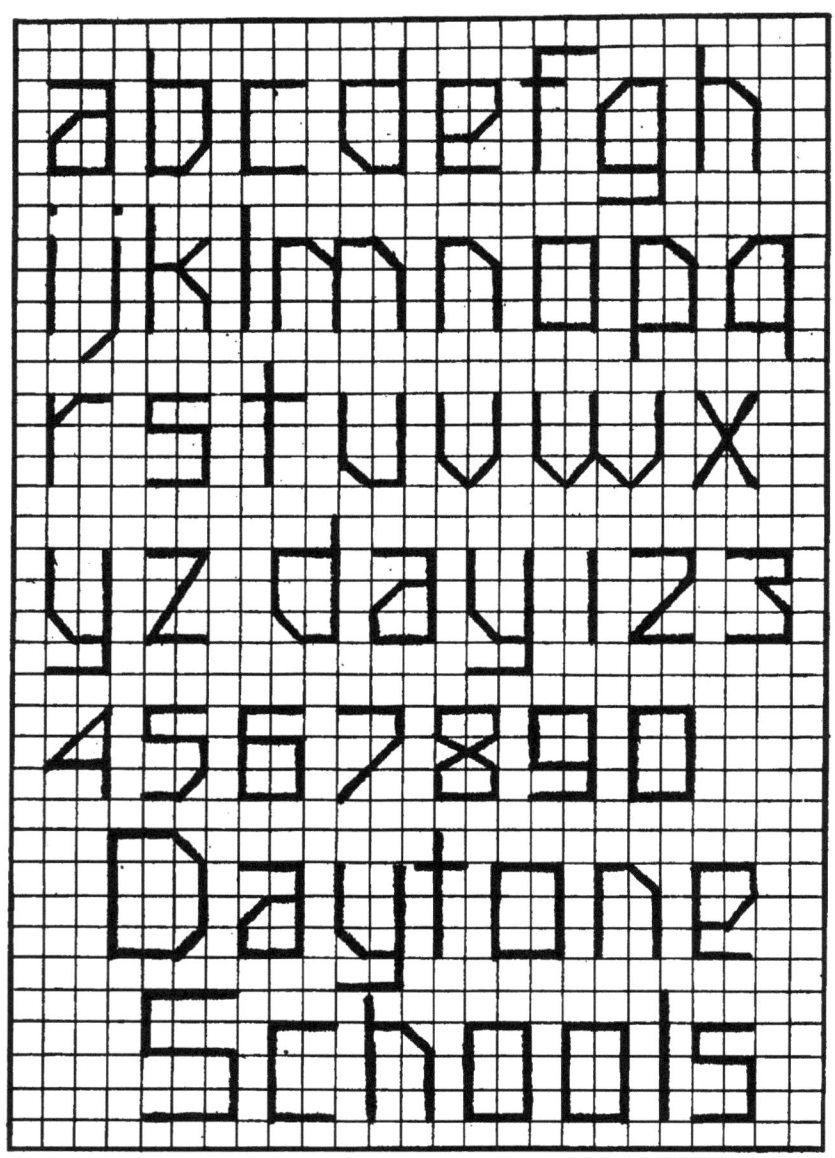

SIMPLE SMALL LETTER ALPHABET

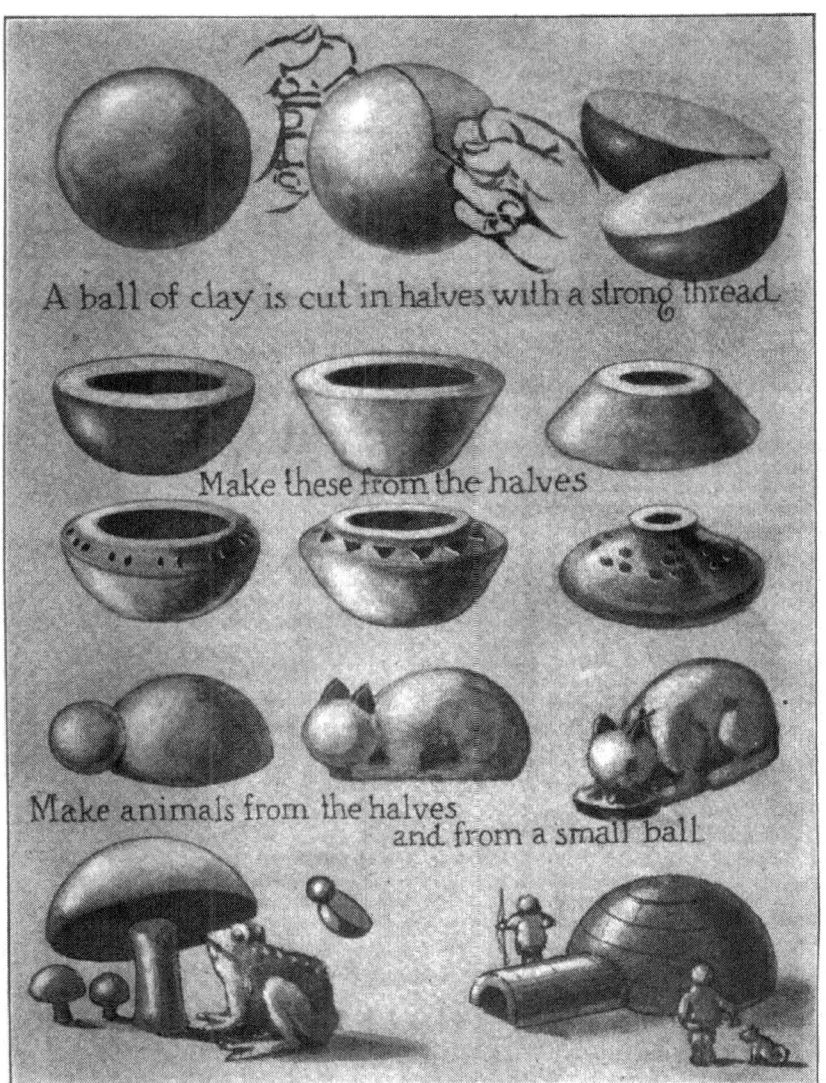

MODELING FROM A BALL FORM

TEACHER'S NOTES FOR THE SECOND YEAR

STILL LIFE COLLECTION. Considerable work and worry can be saved by the teacher who will retain simple objects that have been found good for children to draw. Bowls, old candlesticks, discarded tools and toys that have simple outlines—these should be kept so that they can be used as subjects from which to draw. If these are kept in different drawers or boxes, they can be easily found as needed, and small numbers cut from a calendar can be pasted on them, and the objects listed. This will enable a monitor or teacher to keep the collection in order. Different shades of paper or cardboard should also comprise part of this collection. These can be used to place back of the objects, to give their different parts and outline contrast. The objects should be so contrasted that their outline is clearly seen by the pupils.

SILHOUETTE BOX. When drawing silhouettes from objects, the pupils are often confused by the details and colors of the object. To give a silhouette to the objects, they may be placed between the window and a window shade, if the sun is shining. A silhouette box can be made as shown opposite, to simplify the subjects. A candle or an electric globe on an extension wire may be used to give the light needed. Such an arrangement will make silhouette drawing easier for the beginner. After some practice drawing with the use of the silhouette box, the teacher should have the pupils draw silhouettes from objects without the use of the box. Such a box can be used throughout the grades, more difficult subjects being used, or groups of objects being arranged, as the pupils advance.

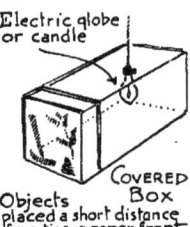

Electric globe or candle

Objects placed a short distance from tissue paper front.

COVERED BOX

PICTURE HELPS. The teacher should collect, and encourage the children to bring, everything that can be assembled in the way of pictures on the different problems in the art studies. A group of pictures of all kinds of trees and tree landscapes will prove helpful. A collection of pictures taken from magazines or posters, showing the different methods of land travel, either in this country or in foreign parts, will help the pupils in the land travel cut-out subjects.

The teacher should file away these subjects carefully, so that they can be used from term to term. Large pieces of folded paper will hold the subjects well, and these can then be placed in a drawer or portfolio where they can be easily secured as needed.

BIRDS

COSTUMED ACTION FIGURES. The teacher can make a large action figure from cardboard, and this figure can be costumed as a boy or girl of a foreign country. If the study is to be the Netherlands or the arctic regions, the costume can be chosen accordingly. As the teacher tells the story, the figures can be posed by moving the arms and the legs, and the children can then more easily make their action figure drawings.

THE CARE OF MODELING MATERIALS. Modeling wax, if kept in the pupil's desk during warm weather, is inclined to stain the books and the paper. A butter box or any box lined with paraffin paper will prevent the modeling wax from injuring the books, and will also prevent the partly finished modeling problems from being injured. The pupil's name may be added to the box. This enables the teacher to put all the boxes away in a cabinet for use on modeling day.

JOHN RAY

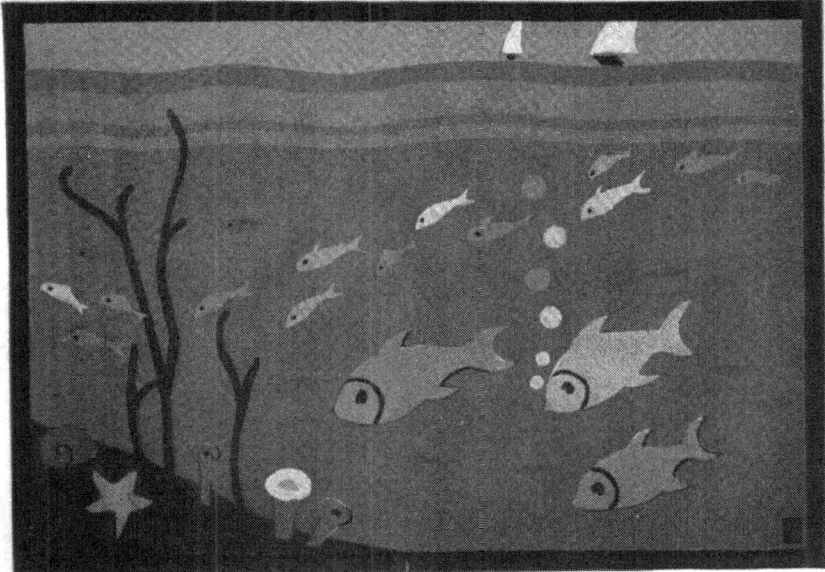

CUT PAPER PICTURES

CRAYON DRAWING — CUT PAPER PICTURES

THE THIRD YEAR
DRAWING AND COLORING

ALL THE OBJECTS AROUND US can be drawn within some simple form. If we look at a table or a chair, we find that it can be drawn within an ·oblong. If we start to draw a bell or a pear, we find that it fits well within a triangle shape. This same idea applies to everything around us. It may be furniture or fruit, or even the live things about us, such as animals and birds.

WHEN STARTING TO DRAW AN OBJECT, look for this general shape, or "form," as it is called by artists. By imagining a line from one point to the other of the object, we can quickly obtain a good idea of the shape into which the subject will fit.

LOOK ON THE WORKING CHART, page 69, and you will notice how much easier the drawing of a subject becomes if we first block. out its general form. Observe how well the little rabbit fits within the oval shape, and the basket into the square shape. The light lines you see on the working chart are known as guide lines and are sketched in very lightly. When your drawing is finished, these can be erased.

A SPLENDID PRACTICE IN DRAWING is to cut out in heavy paper some of the geometric forms shown at the top of the working page. Next trace their outline upon your sheet of drawing paper, and see how many objects you can think of that will fill the space correctly. What can you think of, for instance, that will fit well within a circle? The working page shows a peach and an umbrella. What other things can you think of that will fit in the circle? How about a pumpkin, a balloon, and an alarm clock? See if they can be drawn with circles. What shape would we need to fit an inkwell, a lily, and a fan? What shape would fit a table and a toy wagon? Let us see how many of these you can draw.

THE BEST ARTISTS IN THE WORLD always draw the general forms of their subjects first. Sometimes we meet people who think it is not important to do this, and they start in by drawing one end of their object and finishing their drawing as they go along. When they are finished, there is nearly always something the matter with their work. Maybe the head in their drawing is too large for its body, or

(61)

maybe the table is too long for its height. At any rate, people who do not stop to study the general form, or shape, of their objects first, are losing time.

WHEN YOU GO OUT WALKING, look around you and see what you can find that will fit into these simple shapes. Perhaps it will be a little, round bird sitting on a limb, or the round wheels of an automobile. Maybe it will be the oblong shape of a street car or the triangular shape of the roof of your house. This is an interesting thing to do, and it sharpens our eyes so that we notice things more carefully.

ALL THE TREES around us will really fit within these shapes. We may be walking along and see in a hedge a little tree that would fit exactly inside a triangle. Or we may be picking flowers on some hillside, and find that we are right by an oak that has a square shape. Some of the weeping willow trees look like a triangle upside down; and some of our most beautiful, tall trees, like the poplar, can be drawn inside of an oval.

THE DRAWING OF A TREE is very hard for some people, because they try to put too much in. They look at it so hard that they see too many details. They try to draw every leaf on the branches, and soon give up in despair.

A VERY GOOD PLAN in trying to draw a tree is to half close your eyes. Look at the tree that way, and you will see only its general form, or shape. This is what we should put down on our paper. It is this shape which gives our tree its character, and makes one kind of tree differ from another. Notice the trunk of the tree too. Is it long and slim, or is it short and wide? The trunk helps to give the tree character.

PEOPLE AROUND US fit into shapes too. Some people are much rounder and shorter than others. Sometimes we see a man who would almost fit into a circle; or, again, a man who is so tall he would have to be drawn inside a very slim oblong. Artists who draw figures a great deal, always draw their general forms first. They often have wooden models that they use to help them in this work. You can make a little model to help you in your work by cutting a picture like the one shown on the page of action figures. It should be jointed so you can make it do different things.

ACTION FIGURES, as these are called, are a big help in drawing people. By doing these first, we soon learn to show the character of the people and what they are doing. A man who is running looks quite different from a man who is sitting down. When a man is carrying a pail of water, he always bends to one side to balance himself. Drawing these action figures helps us to show this.

ONCE BEFORE, we made a figure that had just a straight line for a body. This time, we shall make one that looks a little more like a real person, because it has a wider body. Look at the page of action figures and see how many you can copy. Then try to make up some for yourself. When you have done this for a while, see if you can make up a picture with several people in it. Look at the pictures at the bottom of the page. See the one with the Indians in it. What shape are the tents in this picture? Look at the one with the Eskimos. What shape are their houses? Do you think you could draw them?

COLOR is something nearly every one enjoys. There is hardly a person who sees a beautiful rainbow or a delicately colored flower who is not made happy by looking at it. Some of the most beautiful rugs and paintings we have are judged beautiful mainly because of their wonderful color.

LITTLE POSTERS that are really better than many painted ones, can be made by cutting out objects in colored paper and pasting them against a good background. Then you could cut out the letters that you learned in your lettering lesson and make a poster for your school.

IN USING COLOR, be careful not to get too many bright colors together. It is better to put some bright colors and some deep, rich colors together rather than too many brilliant ones. Black backgrounds always help colors to look rich. A red flower, with a green stem, pasted on a black or dark brown background, always looks well. Colors like red and orange and yellow are called "warm" colors, because they make you feel warm. Colors like blue and green are called "cool" colors, because they make you feel cool and restful.

IN USING COLOR, it is better to try two or three kinds of color schemes before pasting down the one you intend to use. In this way, you train your eye to see color harmonies correctly.

DESIGN

SO FAR, you have made your pictures with a pencil or crayon on paper. This time, we are going to try something different. We have noticed that everything may be drawn inside of certain simple shapes. Now we are going to try to tear some of those shapes out of paper. To do this, we must work carefully, so as to be sure we are tearing in the right direction.

FIRST LET US DECIDE what we will tear out. Suppose it is to be a church. We know that most churches have tall steeples, so we must be sure to count on that. Then they have windows. We can figure to show these, too, if we think best. Take the paper in your hand and start at one corner. By using, our thumb nails to tear with, we can rip the paper without much trouble. First we go down one side, then across the bottom. Then we can start at the top and go down the other side.

KEEP YOUR EYE on the general shape of your church. Be sure its steeple is tall enough. See if you can make the rest of the church so that the steeple is not too big or too small for it. When you have finished, you can fold your paper again and tear out some doors and windows. Try tearing out a flower and a bird like those on page 72. Then try tearing out a little tree or plant in green paper, and a flower-pot in red or brown, and pasting them together.

PAPER CUT-OUTS also are very interesting. While they are easier to cut than the ones we tear, we shall find that we must not go too fast, or our scissors will cut off parts we had planned to leave. We might cut objects out of black paper and paste them on white, like the little boys in the parade on page 73, or we might cut them out of white and paste them on gray, like the picture of the goat eating grass. Sometimes the object may all be cut out of one piece of paper, or at other times it may be made up of several separate pieces of paper pasted together. We should be careful not to cut out too many long, slim pieces, because they are not only harder to cut out, but harder to paste down, too.

OUR NEXT PROBLEM is going to be more interesting still. We are going to see if we can make something with our crayons and scissors that will be useful and beautiful too. First we will take some colored papers and cut out some circles, triangles, and squares. Then we can cut some of these circles and squares in half and make other shapes, like the bowls on page 74. After we have cut these out, the next thing is to take some black paper and see if we can paste down a pretty flower or tree with our colored paper. Try several arrangements first, before you paste. Move your colored paper spots around in different ways until you have found the prettiest arrangement.

THE NEXT STEP will be to paste the flowers down. Before you have done this, take your pencil and draw a pencil line around your paper spots on the black paper, so that you will know just where to paste your flowers. When you paste, be careful not to use too much paste or to get any on the front of your flower, as that would spoil your whole picture. When the flowers and the flowerpot have been pasted down, then you can connect them with a green stem drawn with your crayons. If you do this neatly, you will have a nice little picture.

PLACE CARDS, INVITATIONS, GIFTS, AND LITTLE BOXES may all be decorated in this way. Look at the picture, and you will see how some of these flowers can be used. If they are done well, they are always good to look at. The next time you send a letter to a friend, try making one of these pretty flowers to send with it.

PEOPLE WHO DESIGN wall paper and the designs that go on curtains, rugs, and other materials, make a great deal of use of interesting spots or forms. Sometimes they arrange them in borders, sometimes they use single spots, and sometimes they make patterns of them that cover the whole surface. Big factories in America are always looking for artists who can make up interesting designs of this kind. By training your eye, when you are young, to pick out the kinds of spots that are good and really artistic, you can learn to draw or to buy the kind of things that will always look well.

DESIGNS MADE OUT OF CUT PAPER are shown on page 75. Notice that you can make a pretty border of simply a row of triangles, with a little crayon line next to them. Or you can cut out a border and beautify it by putting merely one or two spots of color on the cut-out paper. If you will use white and black paper pasted on gray paper first, you will get the best results. Then later you may try some in colored papers.

VASES have been used for thousands of years. The ancient Egyptians had some very beautiful vases in their homes. The vases designed by the Greeks are used to this day as models. Nearly everybody likes vases and has use for them at home. Oftentimes we see vases that are not very pleasing to look at. The person who designed them made something that is not attractive to the eye. Maybe the outline of the vase has too many wiggles in it, or the bottom does not look as though it would hold up the top. In vases like this, we say the "design" is bad.

SOME GOOD VASE DESIGNS are shown on page 76. A rule is printed there, too. It says, "The widest part of the form should be above or below the middle." This is because our eyes dislike monotony, and vases that are divided right in the middle like a barrel are uninteresting. Try folding some paper and see how many good vase forms you can make.

5 Applied Art

HANDICRAFT

THE STAR SHAPE has been used for many hundreds of years. We all know the story of the star of Bethlehem, and how the wise men followed it. Every time we go out on a starlight night, we can see thousands of these twinkling "flowers of the sky," as some one has called them. The star is a sort of symbol of hope and light, and is used that way by most designers.

MANY NATIONS have the star shape on their flags. The first American flag had thirteen stars to represent the thirteen states. The states of Tennessee, California, and others have stars on their flags. Most of these stars have five points. How many of us can cut out a star with that many points?

A FIVE-POINTED STAR and how it is made are shown on page 77. If you will fold a square of paper as is shown in the drawing, and cut across it with your scissors, you will unfold a perfect five-pointed star. Below are shown some flags of other nations. Notice how the English flag is made up of crosses, and the Italian of a crown and a shield.

FIVE WAYS TO MAKE STARS are shown on the next page. A six-pointed star is easier to make than a five-pointed one. Below you can see how you can use stars in your work. With your crayons and cut paper, you could make a picture of the wise men for your mother; or, if your teacher asks you for a composition, you could write one about your flag and make a pretty cover for it. A fine thing to do would be to start a star book. Get some blank sheets of paper and draw or cut out everything you can find about stars. See if you can get some pictures of snowflakes, or snow stars, as they are often called. And in some magazines, you may be able to find pictures of starfishes, or sea stars. It would not be long before your book would be full.

WE SHOULD KNOW HOW TO MAKE AN ENVELOPE. Years ago people used to make their own envelopes by simply folding over the paper on which they had written their letters. To-day envelopes are very common, and there are all kinds of shapes and sizes. Sometimes, though, when we need a certain size, we wish that we could make some of our own. On page 79, you have pictures of some envelopes and how they are made. They are not hard to do, and are interesting to try. There are three kinds here, and each one is easy to cut out. Below are some little cards for you to draw and color. You could surprise your friends by sending them a birthday or New Year card that you have made all yourself. Then you could make an envelope to fit it and mail the whole thing. See if you can make some good ones.

AFTER MAKING THE TREES, we can set them in our sand table and fix up the water. This can be made by putting a little piece of glass over some green paper and pulling the sand down over it a little. The sky could be blue paper with a rainbow cut out of colored papers, and there could be a white mountain. We could make the little log cabin, too, of a brown paper box, with a slanting red roof. A number of interesting pictures could be made in this way. I wonder if you could make one showing the old oaken bucket well and a farm-house near it.

WATER SCENES are as interesting as land pictures. It is a good plan to keep a scrapbook in which to paste your land pictures, and one for your water pictures. The Indians used their long canoes, the Chinese use their odd fishing boats, and the Venetians their gondolas. Years ago all the sea travel was done in sailboats, and it took months to cross the ocean. Now we have grand steamships that cross the ocean in only a few days. See how many pictures of boats and ships you can find and cut out. Don't forget to try to keep their character by their general shape.

IN ANCIENT TIMES, there lived an old man who built an odd boat. He was warned by God that a great flood would come over the earth, and was told to build a boat called the ark. For years, he worked on this boat, and called upon people to get ready for the time when the flood would come. People laughed at his ideas; but when the time came, the birds and the animals came into his ark. Before long, the flood came, and every one but Noah and his family was destroyed.

NOAH AND HIS ARK would make a splendid picture for you to work out. A diagram is shown on page 82, telling you how to do it. The ark is the hardest part, but it is easy if you will follow directions. Mark off, or fold off, the right number of squares, then cut it out as shown. Next you can cut out all the animals and birds and make your sand table. By cutting two pieces of paper at one time, you can cut out a pair of animals at once. The birds can be hung up by pieces of thread fastened to the biggest trees. You can color the animals with crayons or chalk.

WE CANNOT LEARN TO LETTER TOO SOON. If we can learn to letter well, we shall find that it will help to make our handwriting better. In early days, the scribes spent many months producing beautiful hand-lettered pages. To-day all our papers are printed from metal type that was first lettered by some good artist.

LETTERING is useful in many ways, such as making place cards, signs, mottoes, invitations, and other such things. Our first alphabet came from the Egyptians, who called their letters "story symbols." The most beautiful alphabet we have is called the Roman, because the Romans first designed it.

MOST LETTERS are too hard for little artists to make, but we have a kind that is very easy. It is made from cut paper, and the picture on page 84 shows you how it is done. In this way, you can make any number of letters, and paste them on your pictures or posters. Some numbers are shown, too, for you to use. See if you can make this "window alphabet," as it is called.

LAST YEAR we modeled little objects out of round shapes. This year we are going to try square ones, which are a little harder. First we will make a round ball of our clay, as we did before. Next we tap one side of our ball on a flat surface to flatten it out. Then we do this with the other sides. When we are through, we have a cube, from which we may make various objects.

TO CUT THE CUBE, we can take a thread and press it through our clay wherever we wish to separate it. In this way, we can make pillars and pyramids and prisms. You will notice that there are many interesting forms shown on page 85. Try a simple one first, like the clock. The dial of the clock may be scratched in with a toothpick or a hairpin. Next try the little house with its two windows and door. Then see if you can make the flower basket and the little armchair.

MODELING is fine practice for artists, because it helps them to think of objects from every side, instead of just one side, as is done in drawing on paper. Some of our best artists have been men who liked to model things in clay, as well as to paint. Auguste Rodin, a French sculptor, became very famous through his wonderful figures cut from marble. The French government has given copies of some of his wonderful statues to the United States. Next time you are in a park or a museum, look and see if you can find any of Rodin's statues.

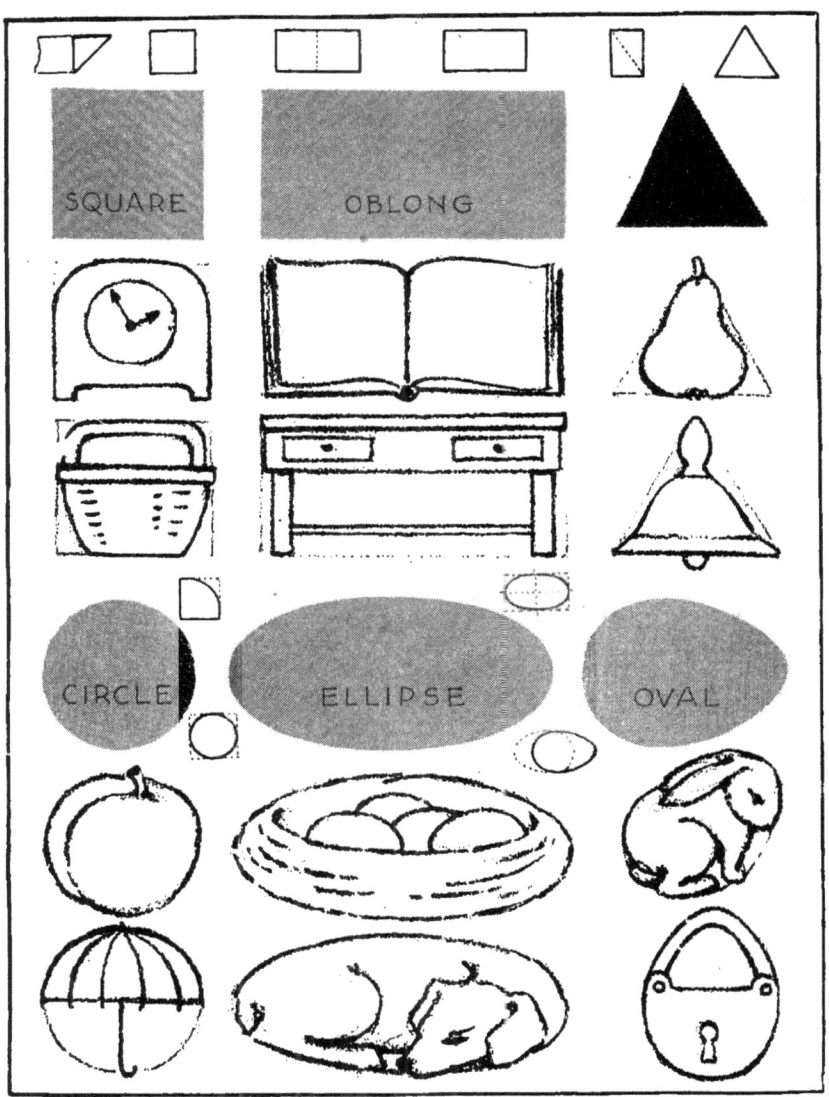

GEOMETRIC FORM DRAWING

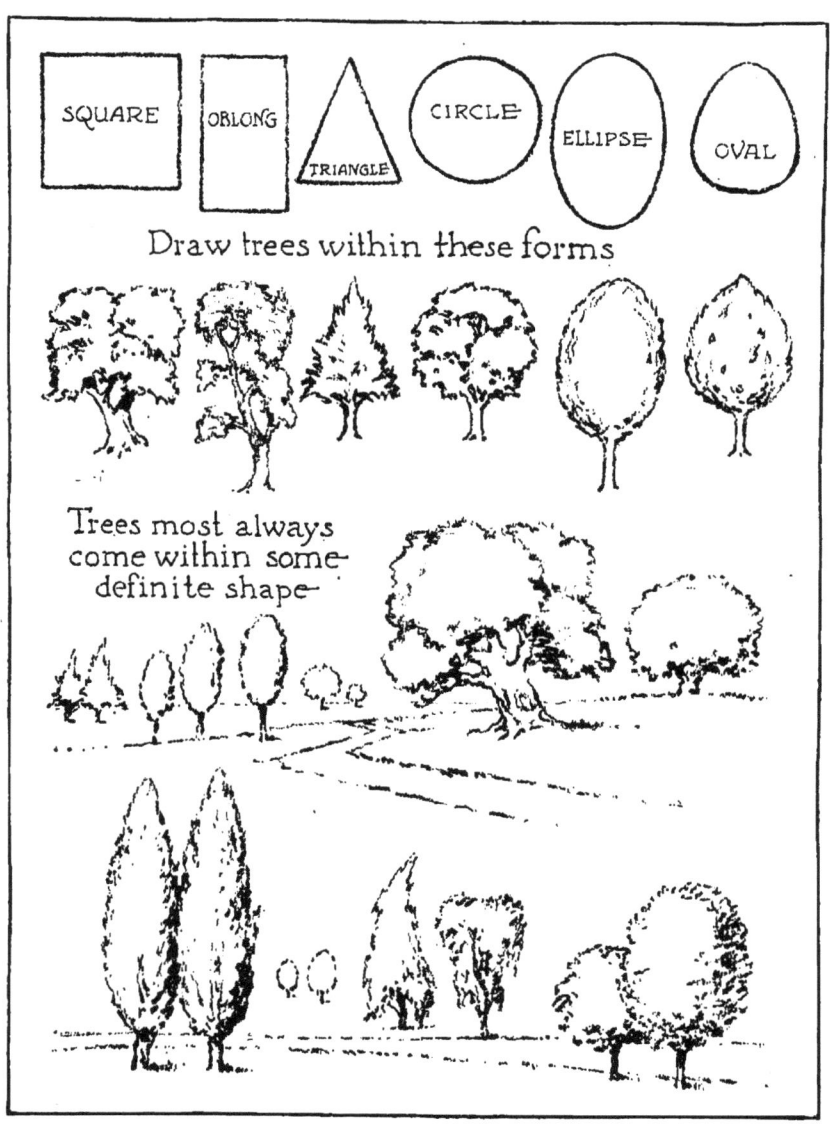

DRAWING TREES WITHIN FORMS

Make this paper model
from which to draw action figures

MAKING PICTURES WITH ACTION FIGURES

PAPER TEAR-OUTS

PAPER CUT-OUTS

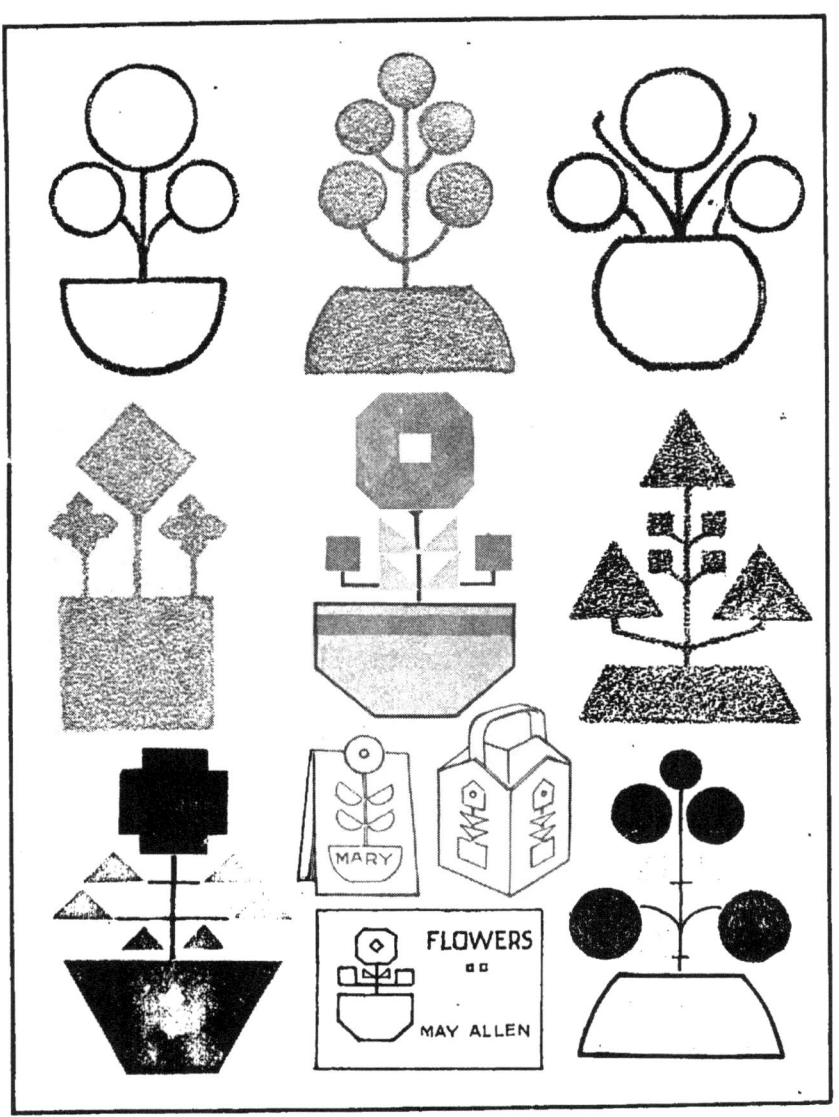

PAPER-FORM FLOWERS

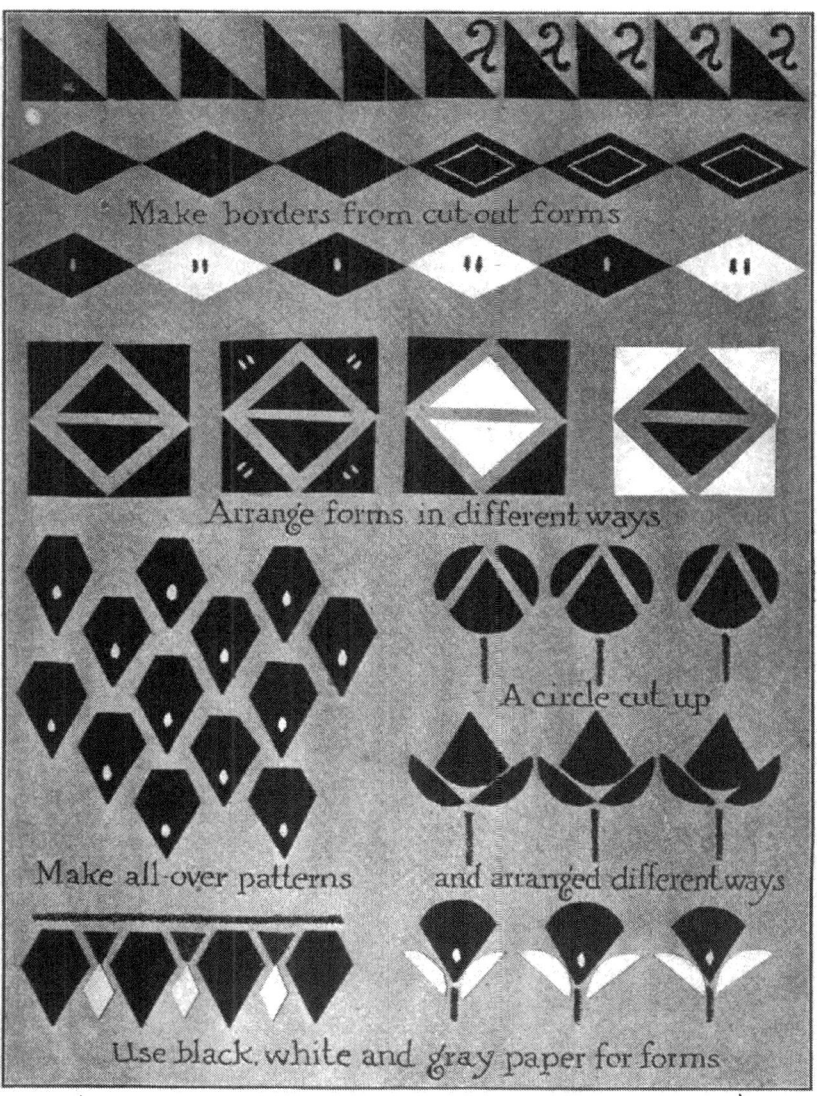

Make borders from cut-out forms

Arrange forms in different ways

A circle cut up

Make all-over patterns

and arranged different ways

Use black, white and gray paper for forms

CUT-OUT PAPER-FORM DESIGNS

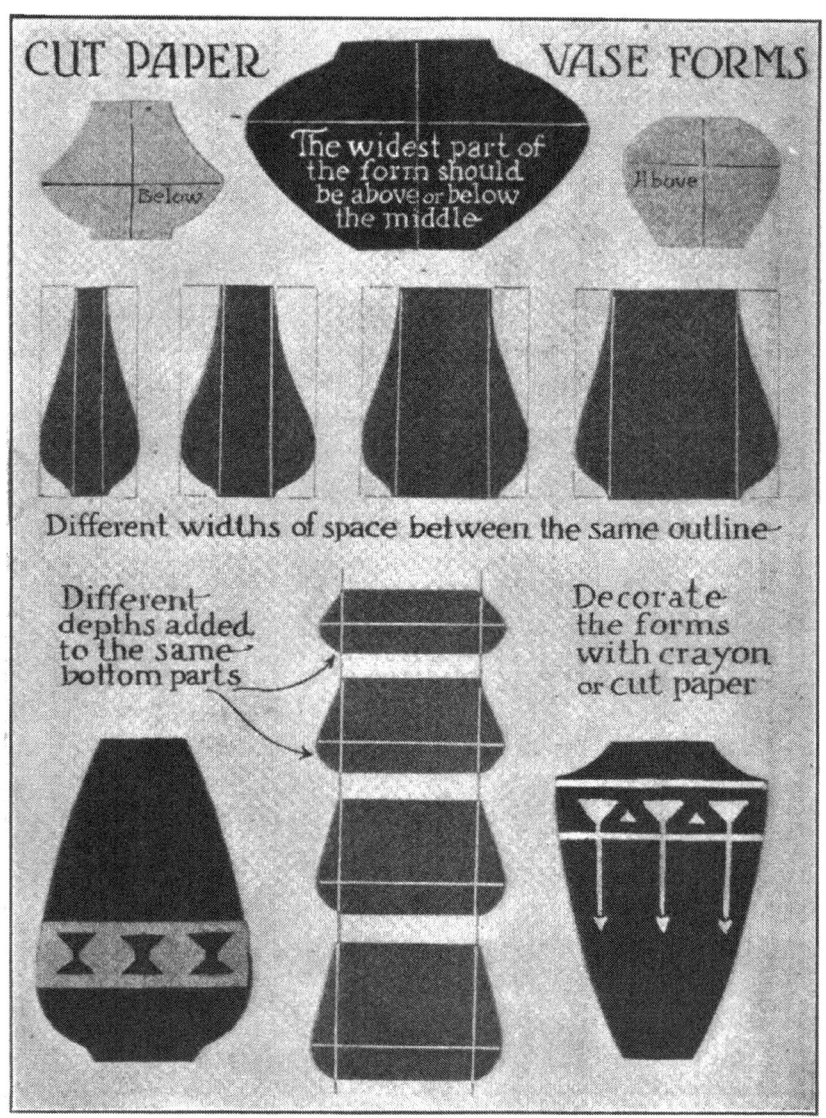

CUT PAPER VASE FORMS

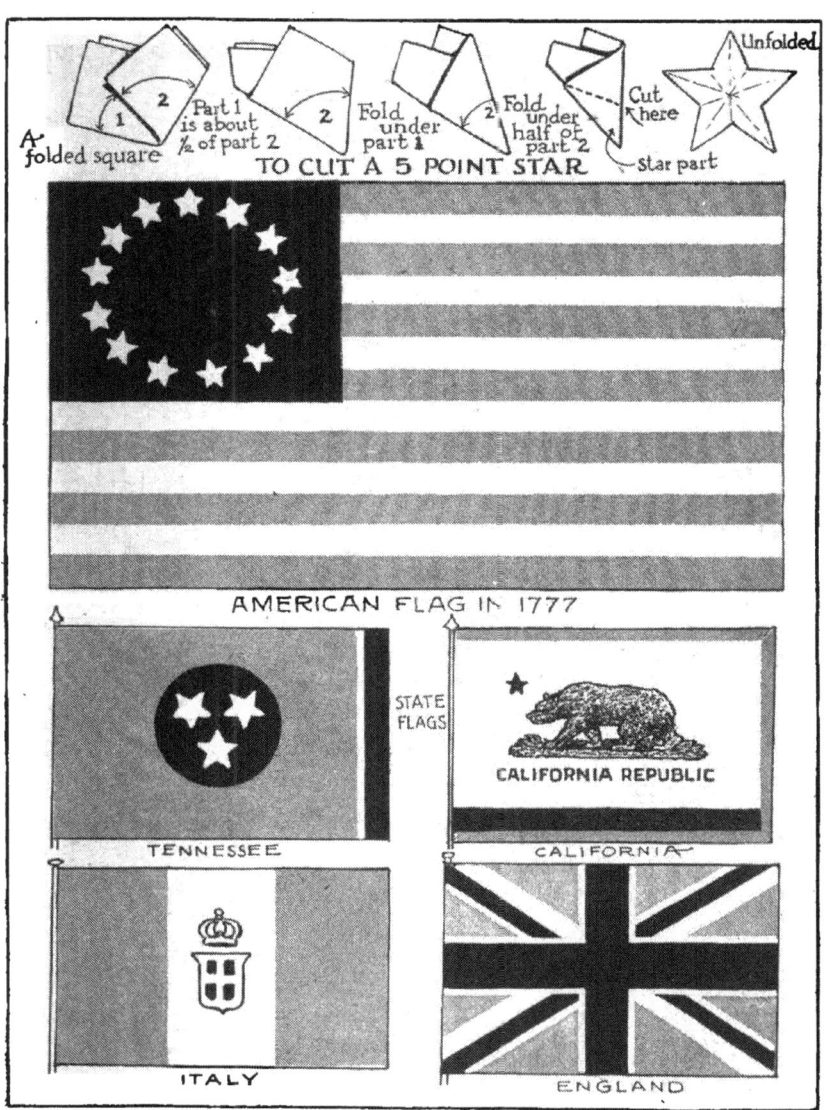

FLAG DESIGNS

STAR PAGE

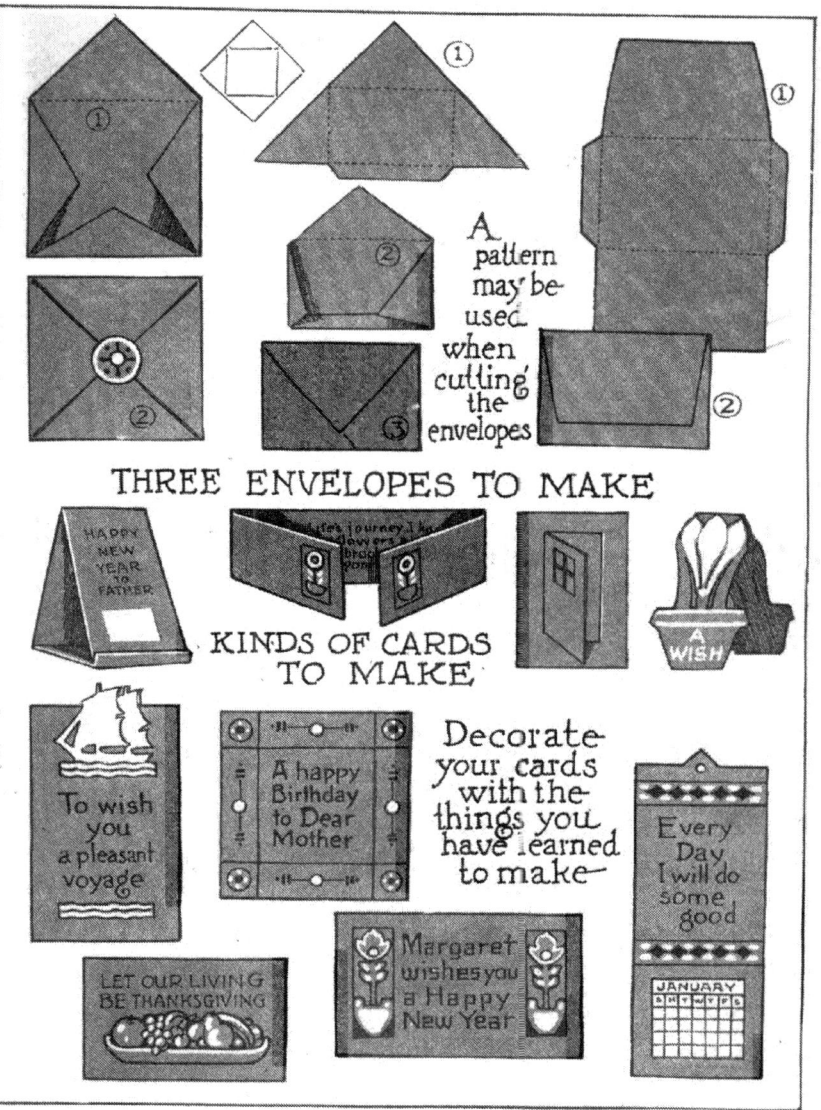

THREE ENVELOPES TO MAKE

A pattern may be used when cutting the envelopes

KINDS OF CARDS TO MAKE

Decorate your cards with the things you have learned to make

PAPER CARDS AND ENVELOPES

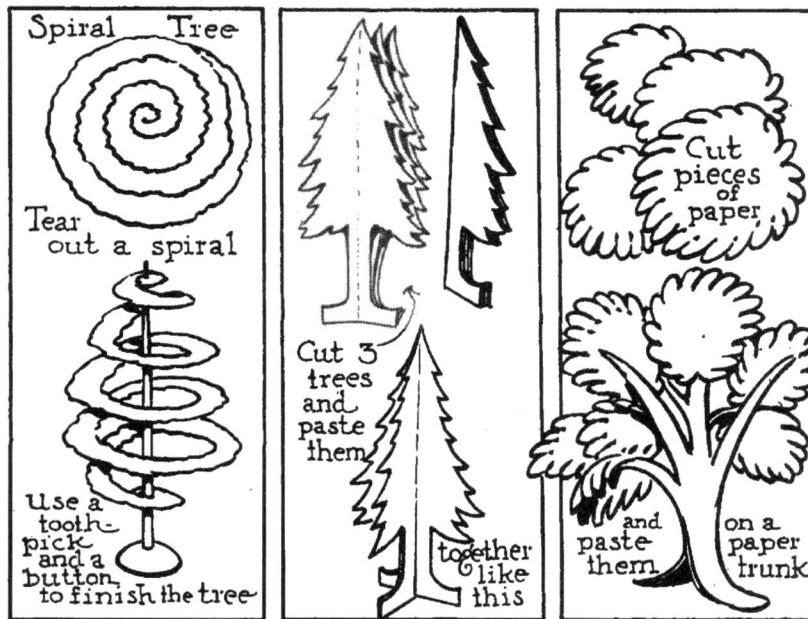

Make a landscape with paper trees and paper flowers and houses
Water will be glass over green paper and sand will be used for the ground.

PAPER TREE LANDSCAPE

Cut-out ships and boats for Water Travel

Cut large ones for the blackboard

Paste into booklets

WATER TRAVEL PICTURES

6   Applied Art

The Boat

The House

The Roof

The Deck

HOW TO MAKE A NOAH'S ARK

A PAPER NOAH'S ARK

PAPER CIRCLE CUT-OUTS

A square of paper is folded ▮ and cut→ Ǝ ◼ and opened like this

The alphabet has been made from this form

A B C D E
F G H I J K
L M N O P
Q R S T U
U W X Y Z
1 2 3 4 5
6 7 8 9 0

FOLDED PAPER ALPHABET

A ball of clay is tapped on a flat surface to flatten one side

Flatten the other sides the same way

Until a cube is made from which objects may be formed

Cut cubes into other forms

How many other things can you make?

MODELING FROM A SQUARE FORM

TEACHER'S NOTES FOR THE THIRD YEAR

CUTTING FORMS. The teacher should have a good supply of patterns as guides for the children to use to cut squares and circles from. To these should be added the other geometric forms, such as the ellipse, the oval, the rectangle, and the triangle. These forms can then be used by the pupils for the tracing outlines within which they can draw objects. If each pupil has a set of the six forms, he can learn more readily the names of each and the uses to which the various ones can be adapted. Different colors may be used for the different shapes, and the teacher can speak of them as the "red form" or the "blue form" when drilling the children in the names and description and problems of their work.

CUT PAPER BORDERS. The best way to secure good work from pupils when giving applied art problems is to have a number of the problems that have been already worked out. In showing the uses to which cut paper borders can be applied, the teacher should have boxes, cards, and booklets that have been decorated with cut paper designs. These should be brought out and displayed by the teacher, to show the pupils just how successful other pupils have been with the material. For this purpose, the teacher should retain from time to time some examples of the best work done by the pupils. These can be placed on an honor shelf.

VASE FORMS. Pictures of beautiful vases, and inexpensive vases good in form, should be used by the teacher to illustrate shapes for paper cutting. Large crayon outlines on paper, showing pleasing contours, and how vase shapes are varied by different widths and heights, should be made by the teacher for posting on the wall. The children should be asked to cut tall shapes and wide shapes, and then to decorate them with cut paper ornaments. Just where these ornaments can be most artistically placed presents a problem for the pupils and the teacher.

FLAG COLLECTION. When the study of flags becomes the problem, the teacher can display flag examples that have been secured from magazines, calendars, and other sources. It will be an easy matter for the children of a class, during a year's period, to make flags of uniform size of all the nations. Such a general problem will acquaint the class with many countries, as the next interest on their part will be to know about the people and the land to which each flag belongs. Art problems should be related to the other school subjects at every opportunity.

STAR AND SHIP COLLECTION. To help the pupils to make progress in the star and ship problems, a collection of star forms throughout the kingdoms of nature should be illustrated. While many of these are obtainable only through pictures, there are many seed pods, leaves, and shell or marine forms to illustrate this form in beautiful arrangements. Prints of ships, or silhouettes of all the types of ships, from the earliest and crudest forms to those of the present day, will make an interesting array as well as an instructive one for the class.

WATER COLOR FLOWER PAINTING

BRUSH WORK POSTERS

THE FOURTH YEAR

DRAWING AND PAINTING

BRUSH DRAWING is the subject we are going to study in our fourth year. Up to this time, we have been making our objects with paper and scissors or our crayons; but this year we are going to use our colors and our brushes. To do this work right, we ought to study some of the brush work done by people who have perfected this kind of work.

THE JAPANESE are masters of art work with a brush. In fact, they do practically all of their writing with a brush, as well as their drawing. In our first two pages of this chapter, we have some examples of work done by the Japanese. Notice, in the tree page, the strong, simple strokes that are used. The Japanese artist here has carefully studied his trees for some time before he has put a single stroke down. Then he has gone to work, and with simple, direct lines, has put down only those parts which are necessary to tell the story of the tree. Such drawings are good to study and copy. They help you to produce drawings that are simple and effective. Notice the tree in the middle of the top line. What picture could be more simple and yet so beautiful?

JAPANESE BIRD AND ANIMAL DRAWINGS are known all over the world for their beauty. People buy Japanese prints to look at and study because of the masterful way in which they are drawn. One reason why the Japanese are able to draw so well is because they learn much by drawing from memory. The Japanese teachers take their classes to museums and art galleries, and ask them to draw something from memory when they get home. This is a splendid test, as it cultivates their ability to see and remember things. After they have drawn what they can remember, then they are taken once more to see the subject they tried to draw, and to find their mistakes. In this way, the Japanese art student soon learns to be very observing, and to put down only the strokes necessary to tell the character of the object he is drawing.

WE ARE GOING TO STUDY some lessons in brush drawing, and see if we can learn to make good drawings that way. On page 97, we have some drawings of objects we see every day, such as an ink bottle, a candlestick, and a hammer. You will notice they are drawn with but one black tone, and have no shading. This kind of work is called "sil-

(87)

houette," after a famous Frenchman who used to cut out pictures, of his friends in black paper and paste them against a white background.

SILHOUETTES are good drawings to make, because they keep your work simple and strong, and help you to think only of the general character of your objects instead of unimportant details. The best way to make these drawings is to sketch in very lightly the general shape of your object, then draw it in with a brush and ink or your black water colors. Later, when you are more familiar with your brush and ink, it is a good plan to try drawing your object directly on the paper with the brush without using any pencil outlines.

DIRECT DRAWING, as this method is called, is excellent practice to give you confidence in your work. It will also teach you to leave out unnecessary lines and details. Sometimes you can leave a little white line between the black parts in your drawing, to help make the drawing plainer, like the picture of the flowerpot at the bottom of the page.

FLOWERS AND PLANTS drawn with a brush are beautiful if they are drawn right. Notice in the working drawing on page 98 how perfectly the graceful lines of the oat stalks have been shown, and the delicate edgings on the rose leaves at the bottom of the page. If we put our plants or flowers up against a window and look at them through half closed eyes, we find it easier to draw their silhouettes. In drawing plants, try to keep the stems light and graceful as most of them are.

AN IMPORTANT KNOWLEDGE TO GAIN is how to hold your brush. You will notice, on page 99, that the brush is held straight up and down. This may seem hard at first, but it is the way the Japanese do it, and it is the best way that has ever been found for this kind of work. Holding it this way helps you to make your light or heavy strokes just when you want them. After you have practiced drawing plants and flowers indoors, try sketching some growing grass and weeds out of doors.

THE HANDLING OF BRUSHES AND COLOR is an important thing to study if we expect to do successful work. It is much better to practice simple washes of color with our brushes until we become accustomed to the way they work. Most beginners have trouble in making their washes smooth and flat on the paper.

SMOOTH WASHES can be made by first dampening your paper all over with a cloth or brush wet with clear water. When this water is nearly dried off, put your wash of color wherever it is to go. Flow the color from the brush the way it is shown on page 101, with each stroke just touching the next. Work from the top of your drawing down toward the bottom. If you can work with your drawing on a board that slants a little, the wash will flow together easily.

TO MAKE TREES, foliage, and grass, we can use various methods. One way, as shown, is to put in a flat wash first. When this is still slightly wet, we drip in the darker parts, and the two tones run together, making a nice foliage effect. Another way is to paint the background first, and when it is still wet, paint the tree on it. This method, called "wet wash," is shown at the bottom of the working sheet, and is fine for keeping a drawing from looking too stiff. Still another way is to paint the tree on after the background is dry. This method is very useful in flat-toned drawings known as "decorative work."

IN DRAWING TREES, it is always best to put in the trunk and the branches first, then the foliage. We do this because this is just the way the tree grows, and it helps us to get the character of our tree right. If we put a flat wash on our paper, let it dry, then put another over the bottom half of our first wash, we find that the bottom half is darker. We can make darker shades by putting washes over one another in this way.

WHEN PAINTING A LANDSCAPE, we first put down flat washes of color for the sky or the foreground. Next we add our trees or other objects. We can do this in two ways. If we put them in when the wash is still damp, they will blend into it. If we wait until the first wash is dry, we will have a flat "decorative" drawing.

FOR LARGE SPACES, such as clouds and sky, we must always use a full brush of color and put it on fairly rapidly. Do not go over your washes when they are wet and try to retouch places you would like to change. This would make your drawing spotty and irregular. A little practice will soon help you to put on these big washes without much trouble. Practice making clouds and sky. They are important in wash work.

YELLOW, RED, AND BLUE are the colors from which all the other colors are made. We can make orange by mixing yellow and red. We can make green by mixing yellow and blue. We get violet by mixing red and blue. So if we have a box with yellow, red, and blue and a black in it, we have a set with which we can do a great deal. If we mix water with our colors, we find that they become lighter and more delicate. If we mix black with them, they become darker. In this way, we can make light and dark portions in our drawings, as well as make them in different colors.

TO MAKE A LANDSCAPE in colors, we would first put on a light wash of blue for our sky. Next we would make our foreground of a medium green. Then we would put on our trees with a darker green. And last, we might put little touches of black or brown in the tree trunks. See if you can draw in colors the picture at the bottom of the page of landscapes. Make your sky light blue and your cloud a very light yellow.

KEEP THE COLORS IN YOUR BOX CLEAN. Do not mix black into your pan of yellow, or you will spoil the clearness of the yellow. The way to mix your colors is to take a little yellow and put it on the inside of the cover of your color box. Then wash out your brush in water, and dip it into your black. Then you can take this brush full of black and mix it in with the yellow you have put on the cover. In this way, we keep our pans of color clean, and our drawings will look much brighter and clearer as a result.

DESIGN

TO BECOME ACQUAINTED WITH OUR BRUSHES AND COLORS, we shall see what we can do with them in our design work. In our work this year, we want to see what artistic drawings we can make by the good arrangement of our objects on the page. On page 103, we have a picture of a water jar and a teapot in silhouette. Do you think you could copy this with your brush and black water color? Try it.

AFTER YOUR SILHOUETTE, see if you can make the drawing on the right of this page. This time, you will notice that the drawing is made in three different washes, or "tones," as they are called. First put on your lightest tone, which is the one in the water jug. Then put in your middle tone, or the one in the teapot. Last put in your black in the inside of the teapot and the neck of the water jug. See if you can make your tones so that they look well together. Do not have your lightest tone too dark, or you will not be able to get your other tones dark enough.

THE PICTURE OF THE BOY is made the same way as the jug and the teapot are. First he is shown in silhouette, and then in tones. Before trying the one of the boy, see if you can make the one of the thistles to the right of it. Notice how well these thistles are arranged in the panel. This is one of the things in design that we want to learn. Notice that the line of the thistle's stem does not cut the picture right in half, but is over to one side. This keeps the picture from being too ugly and monotonous. Notice how gracefully the flowers grow from the main stem. All the lines in this little picture give you the impression of a plant growing upward toward the sunlight. Put in your main stem first and your flowers last.

IN DESIGN WORK, we always try to put our drawings on paper so that they will divide the space artistically. To do this, we should always avoid lines that cut our picture right in half up and down or across the middle. On page 104, you will see a picture of what is called a "finder." These finders are used by designers to help them get artistic arrangements in their drawings. They are made by folding a strip of paper at right angles, as shown in the picture. Make two of these.

IN LOOKING FOR ARTISTIC DESIGNS, an artist takes a picture or photograph he has made, and moves finders about over it until he discovers a new arrangement of its parts that looks artistic to him. Notice that on page 104, three pictures are made of different parts of the same drawing. Take some drawing you have made, and see if you can do this.

THE NEXT THING we want to do is the dividing of squares into interesting parts. We do this so that we can learn to make good designs for tiles, cushions, rugs, and stained glass windows. Later on, we can make some of these cushions and tiles. Look at the top row of squares on page 105. They are all the same size, but they look different because of the way in which they have been divided. In one square, we have a little square in the middle with lines running to the edge. In the second, we have a square turned within a square; and in the third, we have four little squares in the corners of the large square.

BY USING TONES AND COLORS, we can work up some beautiful designs from these squares. Draw two or three of these squares, and try making them first in different washes of black. After you have made some you like, then try making them in color. Suppose you use two colors, like orange and black. Use your bright colors in the smallest spots, and your black in the rest. Take the first square in the top row, for instance. You could make the little square in the center in orange, and the rest of the square in a medium wash of black. Then you could outline the whole design with a black line.

LOOK AT THE RUG DESIGNS on the lower part of page 105. You will notice they are made up of squares divided and arranged in pleasing lines. Could you make a rug design like one of these? Draw an oblong, and try one in black and white. Then try one in colors. Keep your squares simple and your work will be prettier.

HANDICRAFT

DESIGNS APPLIED to things we use, help us to make those things more beautiful if we work out the design as we should. On page 106, we have a drawing showing how to do stick printing. This work is called stick printing because the designs are put on paper or cloth by means of the ends of sticks. These sticks are cut with different designs, so that almost any number of patterns may be made.

WITH A SHARP KNIFE, notch the ends of the sticks into designs such as those shown in the picture. Do not try to make them too elaborate, as the simple designs are easier to cut, and look quite complete when repeated in patterns. The way to print these designs is as follows: Take a piece of felt or an ordinary blotter and soak it with water color paint. Then take a ruler and mark out your paper into the divisions you want to make. Put a pencil dot every place you wish to print a design. Next thumb-tack your paper over five or six layers of newspaper. Press your stick firmly on your felt pad, then transfer your design to your paper.

DESIGNS may be transferred to cloth or paper this way with but little trouble. In doing stick printing, we should be careful not to get too much paint on the end of the stick, as this makes a blurred design. Hand bags, belts, neckties, and many other things may be made attractive by this method.

STENCIL WORK is another handicraft idea, something like stick printing. In stick printing, we cut designs out of wood. In stencil work, we cut them out of oiled paper. We use oiled paper because it is easier to cut out, and because it does not catch and hold the colors we use, as an ordinary paper would. To cut these stencils properly, we must design them so as to have separate parts, like the flower shown on page 107. This is necessary; because if we do not, when the paper is cut out, the design will fall apart.

WHEN YOUR DESIGN IS CUT OUT, the next thing to do is to mark off the places where your stencil is to go, just as you did in stick printing. If you are using cloth, a little piece of hard crayon can be used to mark off these places. Next take some wax crayons and rub them evenly over the parts of the stencil you wish to color. If you thumb-tack your stencil paper down before rubbing your crayon through, there will be less chance of its being blurred. After your design has been stenciled, press a hot iron over the back of it, to set the design. Table runners, book covers, and many other useful things for your home can be made with stencil work. The next time you want to make a gift, try a stenciled table mat or table runner.

OUR HOMES would all be more beautiful if we would take more interest in the colors and designs with which we surround ourselves. We live in our homes such a good part of the time, it is important that these surroundings be harmonious. People who have not studied to find out what is good and what is not good in colors, furniture, and drapings, often surround themselves with ugly things, like haircloth sofas, marble-top tables, and bright red walls. Who could ever hope to rest and relax in such surroundings!

WE STUDIED how to divide squares and rectangles into pleasing divisions. Let us use what we have learned in making some designs. "Interior decoration" is the name given to the study of the furnishing of our homes. First we shall take an oblong that runs up and down, and plan it into a window. After we have divided it into what we think is a good arrangement, we can make some curtains and drapes for it of colored tissue paper. We can make the side curtains of heavier paper than the center one, if we like. The outlines of the windows we can make with crayon or water colors.

LETTERING

EVERY YEAR, we should keep up our study of lettering. This is a useful subject to study. On page 109, we have an alphabet to study and copy. You will notice that this alphabet is designed so that there are no hard curves in it. Yet it is agreeable to look at and easy to read, which are qualities necessary in a good alphabet. The trouble with many alphabets is that they have too many hard curves in them, and beginners find it very difficult to make them.

THIS ALPHABET is made up of letters that are nearly all based on a sort of "quarter of a circle" shape. This shape is plainly seen in the letters C and D. If you will keep this in mind, you will find the letters quite easy to copy. Observe that the tops of the letters are flat, and that the letter S looks somewhat like a Z backwards. The small letters are very much like the large ones, except that they have lines which run above and below the line. These are called "ascending" and "descending" strokes. Some numbers also are shown for you to copy. Few people can make good numbers.

A PAGE OF POEMS is shown in this chapter. Little poems like this are always appreciated. Read the one about the cradles. Did you ever before think of trees as cradles for flowers? Then read the one below it about Jack Frost and the snowflake designs he weaves. These are two lovely poems for you to read and copy. You could put little touches of cream and light gray crayons on the pussy willows, and cut the Jack Frost designs out of light blue paper and paste them on black.

LOOK UP LITTLE VERSES in magazines and books, and see if you can make up some original pictures. If your lettering is not good enough yet, you can write the verses neatly. Sometimes, if you will letter your verses on little slips of paper and then paste them down on a colored paper, you can get some beautiful effects, like the daisy poem at the bottom of the page. The moon and the stars are put in afterward with your water colors, to which white has been added.

OUR MODELING LESSON this year will show us how to make tiles. These are used for fireplaces, floors, sinks, bathrooms, and for many other purposes. A fine problem for us to work out is to make a table tile. Table tiles are useful to have on our dining tables to put hot dishes on. For this reason, we shall make them of cement, so that they will stand heat.

WE FIRST TAKE SOME PLASTICINE, or modeling wax, and model our design on it, as shown on page 111. We will use simple subjects, because then our tiles will be easier to make. Before modeling the design in the wax, it would be well to work the design out on paper until we have it just right. We can then trace this on a square of the wax and model it. Next we should put our wax design face up on a flat surface. Around it we put four strips of wood that have been oiled with linseed oil. These are to keep our plaster of Paris in place when we pour it over our model.

PLASTER OF PARIS mixed with water until it is fairly thick, can then be poured over our model, as shown in the picture, and left to set. When the plaster has set thoroughly, we can remove the wood strips and pull off our mold. We put this plaster of Paris mold face up on the table, the way we did the wax model. By oiling the face of the plaster, we keep the cement from sticking to it. We then take a mixture of about three parts of cement mixed with one part of fine sand, and mix it with water until it pours well. We pour this over our plaster mold, and let it set about three days.

WHEN THE CEMENT HAS SET, we can take it out, and we have made ourselves a little tile that is both useful and beautiful. If care is taken in following out these steps, you will be more than pleased with the results.

Japanese
Brush
Drawings

JAPANESE TREE STUDIES

JAPANESE BIRD DRAWINGS

SILHOUETTE BRUSH DRAWINGS

7 Applied Art

PLANT BRUSH DRAWINGS

Make outdoor studies from growing grass and weeds

Hold the brush in upright position

Pressing down when a heavy line is wanted

and using just the tip of the brush when making a light line

At the beginning a careful outline should be drawn.

Brush drawings of different kinds of leaves and in different positions should be made.

Commence with brush tip

then press the brush down

and end with the tip again.

Make the leaves with one stroke

BRUSH WORK DRILLS

From forms alone we may know character and age.

Ships in silhouette can be made with the brush. The rigging can be pen lines.

Brush drawing in silhouette is excellent practice.

Buildings and city outlines are good subjects for silhouettes.

Many things can be expressed in silhouettes.

A PAGE OF SILHOUETTES

Brush strokes
should just meet,
to make an
even tone

After the
first tone
drip in the
dark parts

Washes put over each other make darker shades. Hills
and trees can be made in the same way

Painted on
a wet back-
ground

Painted on
a dry back-
ground

First, the tree
branches

Then the
foliage

HOW TO DO BRUSH WORK

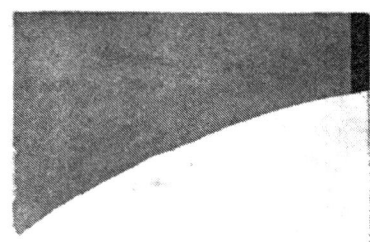

First, flat washes of color for sky or foreground

Second, the trees or objects are added. If added while the first wash is damp they will blend into it

A full brush must be used for large spaces and the color must not be retouched after it is placed

LANDSCAPE BRUSH PAINTING

BRUSH PAINTING

With finders select good parts from a brush drawing and make other drawings

ARRANGING FLOWER PICTURES

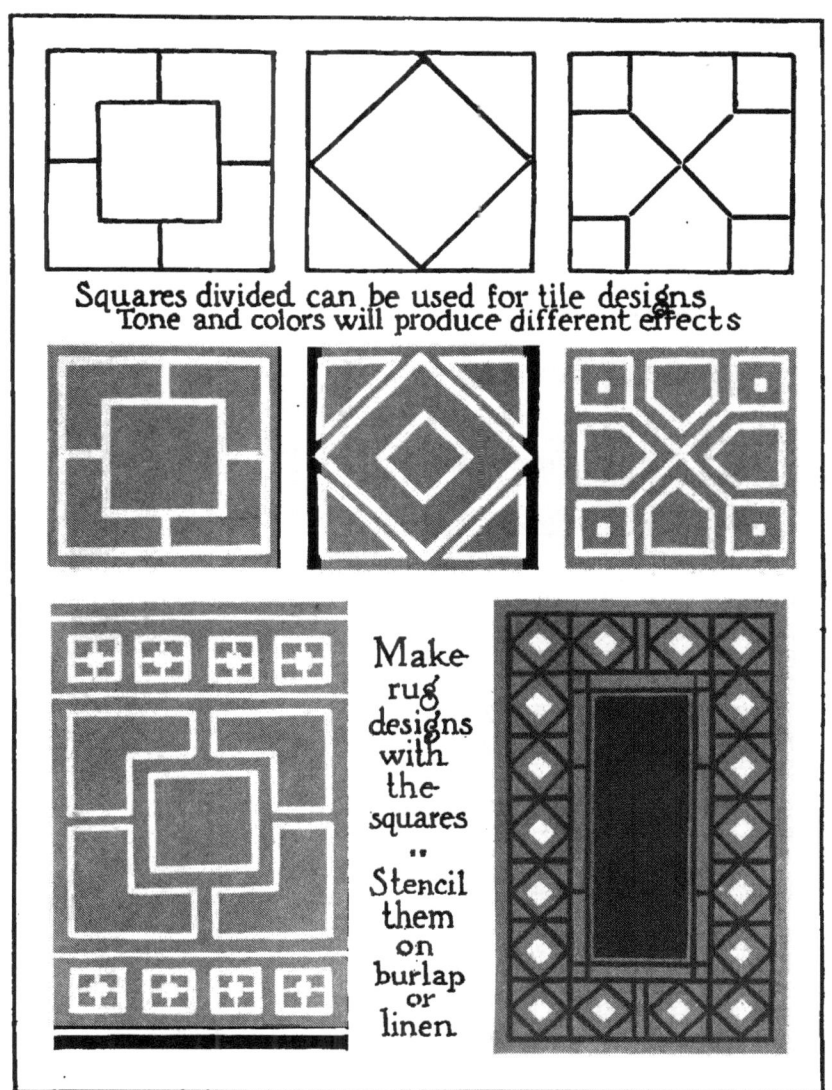

Squares divided can be used for tile designs. Tone and colors will produce different effects

Make rug designs with the squares .. Stencil them on burlap or linen

DESIGNS WITHIN SQUARES

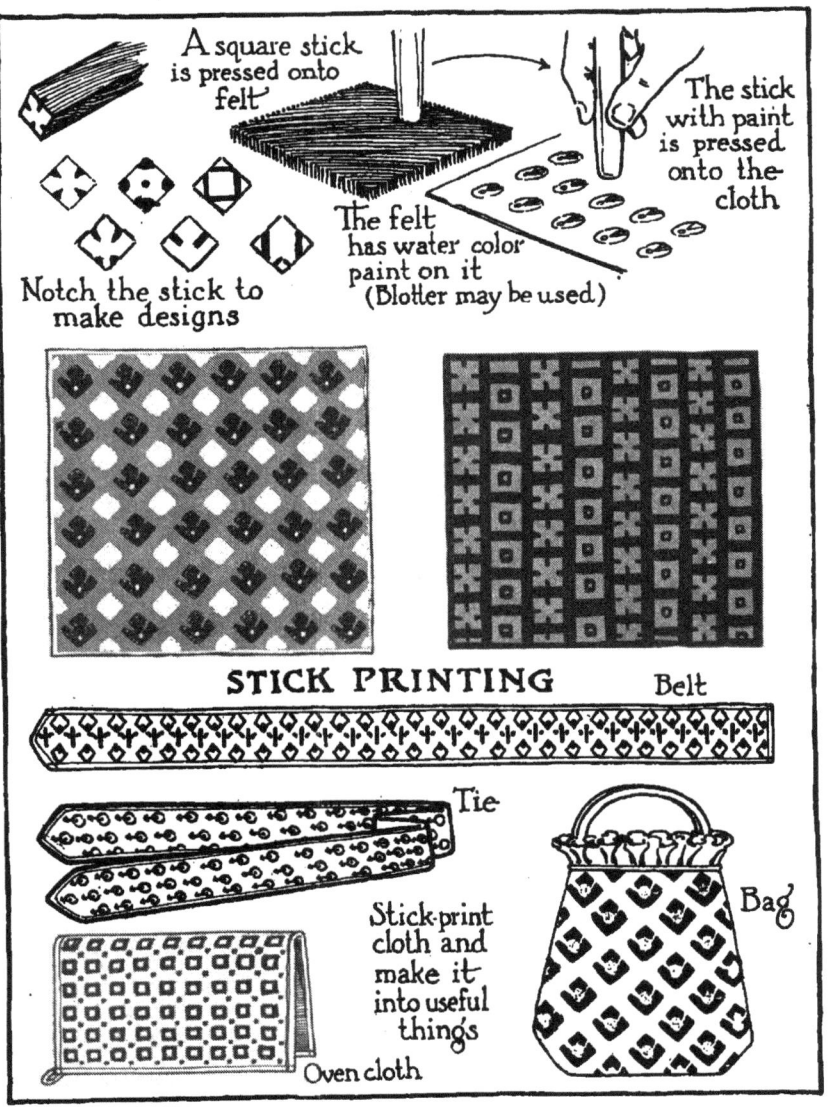

A square stick is pressed onto felt

The stick with paint is pressed onto the cloth

The felt has water color paint on it (Blotter may be used.)

Notch the stick to make designs

STICK PRINTING

Belt

Tie

Bag

Stick-print cloth and make it into useful things

Oven cloth

HOW TO STICK-PRINT

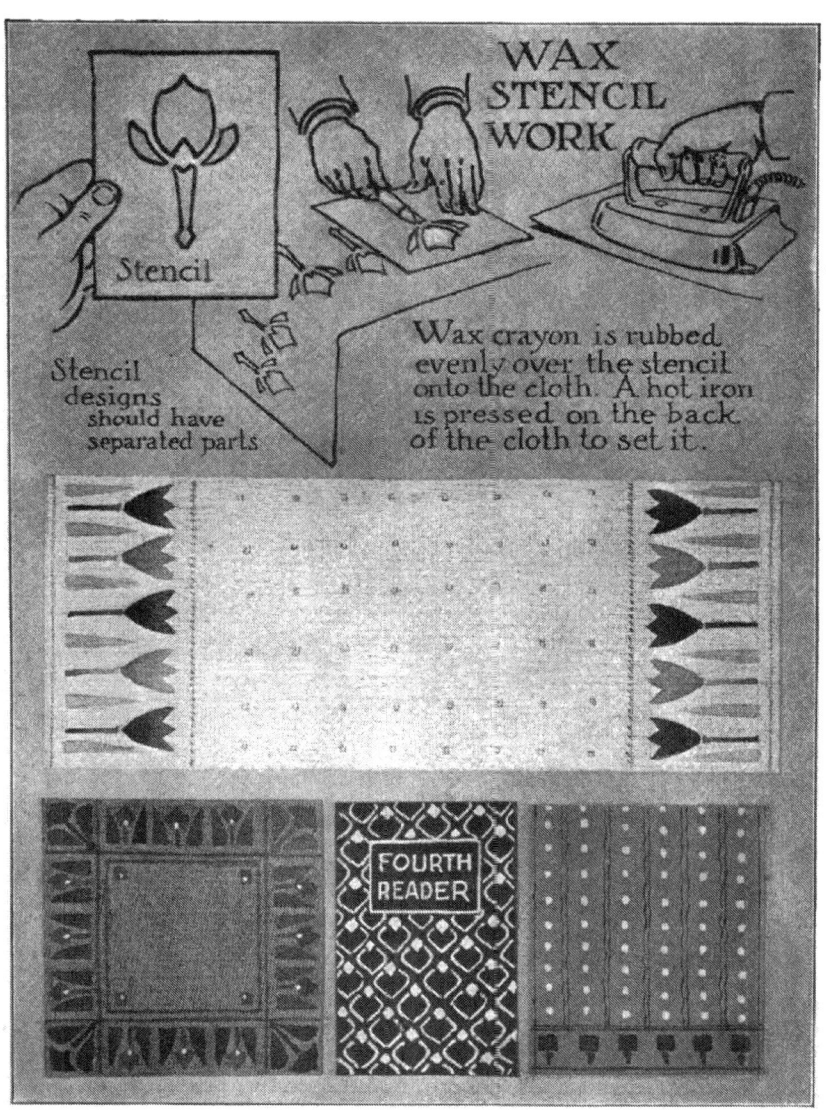

A SIMPLE STENCIL METHOD

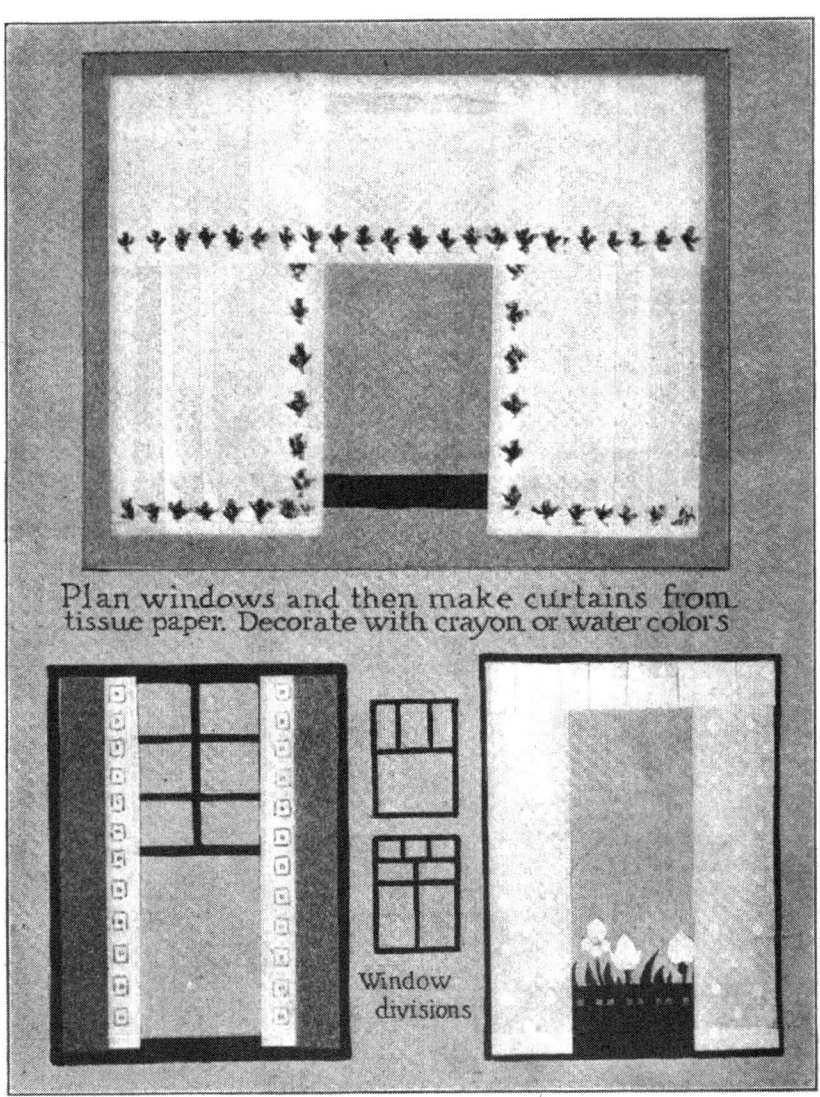

Plan windows and then make curtains from tissue paper. Decorate with crayon or water colors

Window divisions

WINDOW DESIGNS

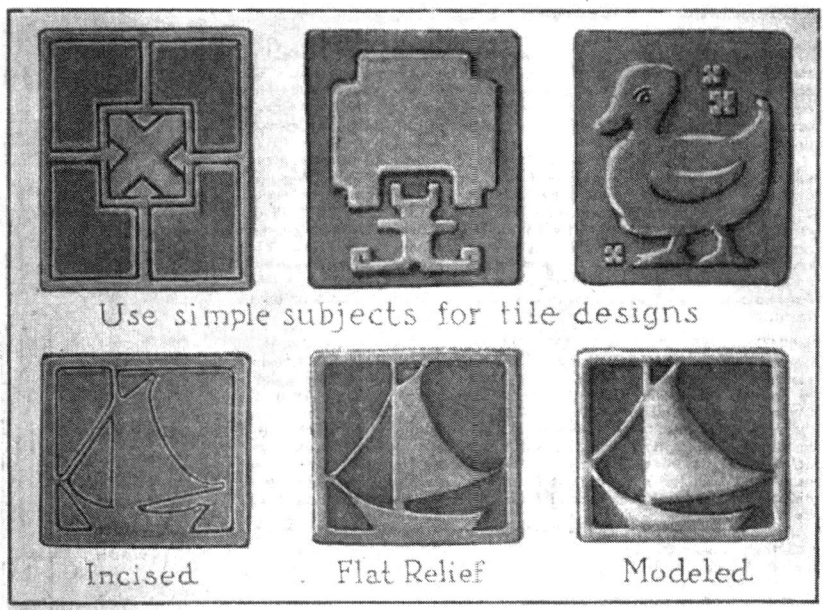

Use simple subjects for tile designs

Incised   Flat Relief   Modeled

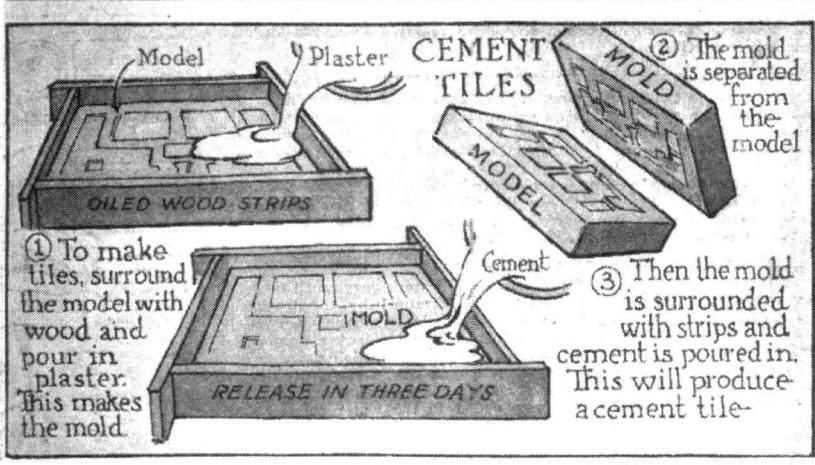

Model   Plaster   CEMENT TILES   ② The mold is separated from the model

OILED WOOD STRIPS

① To make tiles, surround the model with wood and pour in plaster. This makes the mold.

Cement

③ Then the mold is surrounded with strips and cement is poured in. This will produce a cement tile.

RELEASE IN THREE DAYS

CEMENT TILE DESIGNS

TEACHER'S NOTES FOR THE FOURTH YEAR

BRUSH DRAWINGS. A large chart of brush drills should be made by the teacher, to post up at the front of the room. The children should then be encouraged to copy these at every possible opportunity. A group of good drawings, or of reproductions of brush drawings, should be shown the children or posted on the wall, to demonstrate brush work.

If the teacher will arrange a large card or blackboard space over which a board or a large card is placed, and use this for posting good examples of work, the students can learn much from such a display. Things that they bring can be added to the collection. This will encourage the students to be on the lookout for such examples, and their observation and appreciation will be markedly sharpened. Fine examples of brush drawings are constantly appearing in magazines, and many of them are of subjects that interest children. Good Japanese prints of flowers, birds, and animals also illustrate brush work.

THE CARE OF BRUSH AND PAINTS. The children should be impressed with the importance of care of their materials. A brush abused will not give good strokes. If the children are taught early to care for their art tools, they will have a respect throughout life for other tools and equipments. The brush should be placed carefully in the box after being cleaned. If it is placed on a card and held with an elastic band, the point will be protected. If a brush dries bent, it cannot easily be used properly on the next occasion. Teach the children not to put more water into the pans of paint than is absolutely needed to moisten the color for that brush load.

Avoid having them get the habit of dipping a brush full of color and then cleaning the brush in water. This causes a waste of color and a thoughtless habit. Teach them to think carefully before they use the next color, deciding first if it is the color needed and just how much of it should be taken. Paper should not be wasted. If a small section is to be used, do not have the pupils work on a large sheet. The small section should be removed from the larger piece before it is used.

WORKING ORDER OF PAINTING MATERIAL. The pupil should arrange the painting material in an orderly way in front of him, in such a position that no waste movements will be necessary. If the paints are in one place and the cloth and the water in different places, the pupil is sure to become confused, and accidents will occur. The diagram opposite shows a good arrangement. By this arrangement, the paints, the blotting cloth, and the water are in their order as used; and once the pupil becomes accustomed to this placing, he can work very rapidly, moving from one to the other as needed, almost unconsciously.

STENCIL MATERIALS. When working with water color in stencil work, it will be found that some cloths work very much better than others. These cloths should be determined by the teacher previously, and the determination will depend largely upon the available assortment in the teacher's locality. The children can secure many remnants of cloth for small bags, doll clothes, doll house curtains, etc., from their mothers. Where wax crayons are used for stencil work, a different and coarser cloth will be found to give the best results. A little library paste added to the water colors will give more body for use on cloth. When wax crayons are used for stencil work, avoid using too much. The heat of the iron used for pressing causes the color to spread; and if the crayon is too thick, the design will look smudged.

First-
The pencil
outline and
the dark parts.

Second -
The cold
colors
are placed
in flat.

Third-
The warm
colors
are
added
flat.

Finished-
By shading
all of the
flat colors.

Wood
Duck

STEPS IN WATER COLOR PAINTING

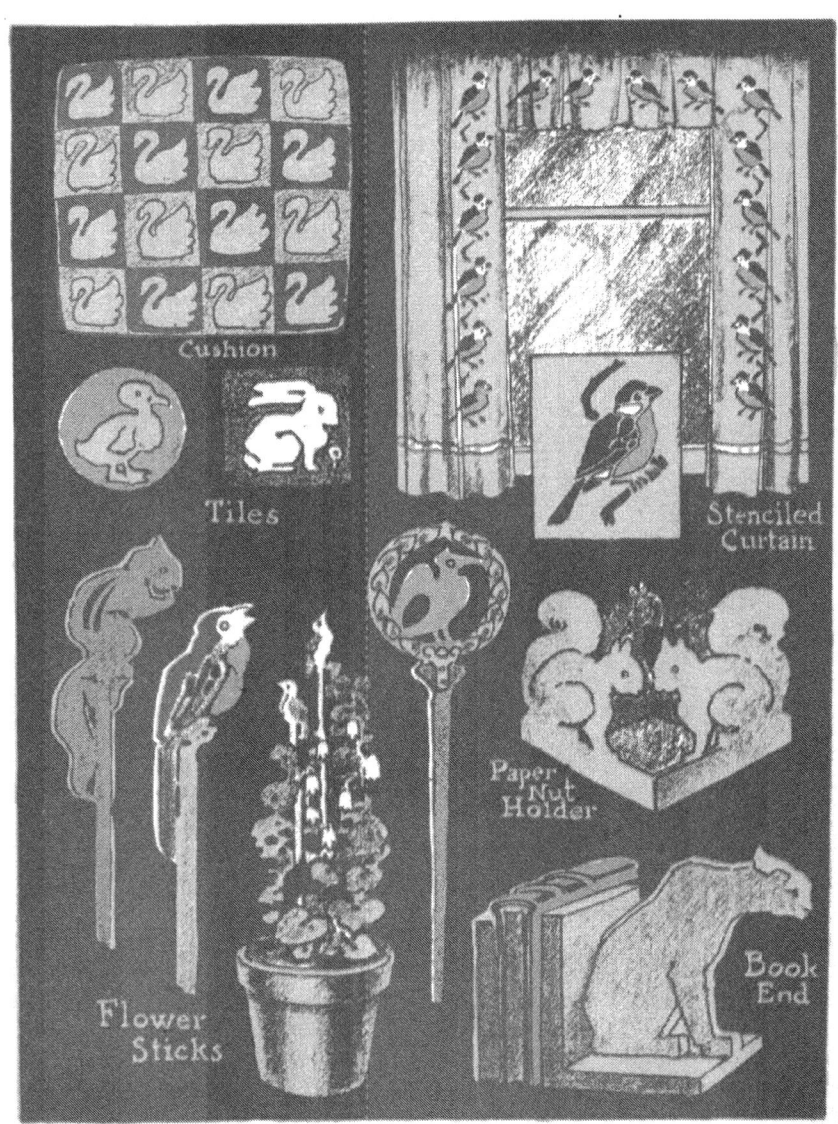

APPLIED BIRD AND ANIMAL DESIGNS

THE FIFTH YEAR
DRAWING AND PAINTING

WE STUDIED TREES very fully last year. This year, we are going to study some things that are closely related to trees. These are birds and animals. What a queer world this would be if all the birds and animals were taken out of it! It would not be nearly so interesting or happy.

MOST ARTISTS are great lovers of birds and animals, which form the foundation for many beautiful paintings and designs made in the past. James Whistler, a famous painter, was very fond of using the peacock in his designs. Rosa Bonheur, the wonderful animal painter, never tired of studying and painting horses, dogs, deer, and other animals.

BIRDS AND ANIMALS are so lively, as a rule, that it would be pretty hard for a boy or a girl to sketch them from life. Fortunately, at most libraries, there are many fine drawings, paintings, and photographs that we can see to help us out. On page 121, we have some good drawings of canary birds. In the upper right-hand corner, you are shown how to block one out in copying it. Notice that the body is made of an oval, and the head of another. After you have put these in, you can start to draw the details.

AN IMPORTANT THING to watch and study is a bird's leg. Observe how it connects with the body. Notice that the leg bends back a way just where it connects with the body, and that the bird has three toes in front, but only one behind. More people make mistakes in drawing a bird's leg than in drawing any other part of the bird.

THE JAPANESE ARTISTS are very fond of drawing birds. On page 122, you will see a picture of a woodpecker as he is printed in the dictionary, and two ways a Japanese artist would make him. How much more pleasing and interesting these last two drawings are! One of them is made with only five brush strokes, yet it tells the whole story. Below we have two drawings of a little tree squirrel, done in only a few strokes. See how fine they are. Drawings that tell the most with the fewest lines are the kind that we should try to make.

A WHOLE PAGE of drawings done by Japanese with a brush is shown in this chapter. Every one of them is a good study. It is because the artists have always been trained to observe and to handle their

(113)

brushes so well, that they are able to make drawings like this. Notice the little rabbit in the second row. He is done with just a few simple brush strokes, yet you can almost see him wiggle his nose. Look at the picture of the fox running. Every line is drawn with the idea of showing his fleetness and his sly character. The horse, the little Japanese dog at the bottom, and every other animal on the page, has been drawn in the same way. Take your brush and ink and see if you can copy the rabbit and the fox.

SOME BIRDS AND ANIMALS worked out in tones are shown on page 125. At the top, we have three good pictures of a mouse. Notice how a light background has been put in to make him stand out against it. Notice, too, how the artist has tried to show that the mouse is getting ready to jump, by accenting the muscles of the hind legs and drawing the long tail lifted from the box. While this page shows the mouse and the duck and the rooster in tones, you will observe that these tones are simple and not worked up too much. That would have spoiled the strong effect of the drawing.

WE SHOULD TRY drawing some birds with black water color. A fine page to help us is given in this chapter. First we shall make two ovals, one large and one small, with our water color. Next we add the other parts, such as the beak, the legs, and the tail. When this is done, we have a sort of silhouette of a bird. With this to work over, we can finish our bird up like the one shown in the picture. Little details like the eyes and light spots on the wings can be put in with white paint, or left white on the paper when we put on our flat washes.

ACTION DRAWINGS of birds, like those shown in the upper right-hand corner, are fine to help you get the character of birds. If you will make a whole page of these before trying a large picture of a bird, your large picture will be much better drawn. Notice the little sketch showing how to draw a bird's foot. See if you can copy it. Look at the two little birds on a limb. Observe how thin their necks are and how big their mouths. They are always hungry. We would hardly think they could grow into the beautiful birds we see flying from tree to tree.

IN DRAWING BIRDS with water colors, try to keep your strokes clean and sharp. Do not carry too much color on your brush, nor work colors into surfaces that are too wet. If you do, your drawing will not have the crisp, decided look that these in the picture possess.

NOW THAT WE ARE USING BRUSHES, we can think of color in various ways. We may make our color drawings with crayons, in cut-out papers, or with our water colors. "In trying to make birds or animals in color, the best plan would be to try them with our crayons or in cut-out paper first, until we are more acquainted with the way they look. If we wanted to draw a colored picture of the page of canary birds, for instance, we could use a sheet of brown or tan paper, and put the canary birds in with yellow crayons. The very lightest parts of the canary's breast and wings could have a touch of white; and the dark parts, like the legs, could be made with a little black or brown. It is best not to use too many colors.

ANOTHER WAY TO WORK the birds in color would be to draw and cut them out of colored paper, and mount them on some other paper. Some of the prettiest designs you will make may be done in this way. To finish them up, you can put a little of the details in with water color and a brush. The little mouse and the duck shown on page 125 would look good this way.

LATER, after we have made some drawings with crayons and in paper, we should try working them out with our brushes and water colors. Remember, half the secret of good water color work is to keep our brushes and colors clean and in good condition. Never let colors dry hard on your brush. This is bound to spoil it. Suppose we wanted to make a copy of the duck shown on page 124. First we would sketch it out carefully in pencil, so as to be sure that we have a good picture. We should be sure to make our pencil lines light, because heavy pencil lines or too much erasing spoils our paper for water color work. Do not forget to "block in" the subject lightly before making the final lines. This really saves time.

AFTER OUR SKETCH is made, we should start to lay in our flat tones of color. First we should put a light wash of yellow all over the breast and the neck. Next we could put in the red legs and beak. Then we could mix a deep blue and put that on where the dark feathers run along the back. Last we could put a light brown color just below the neck, in the tail, and on the top of the head. After these are dry, we could put in a few little dark strokes with black paint for the eye and to bring out any necessary parts. After you have made the duck, see if you can draw and color the quail. It is better not to use too many colors, as they would cut your drawing up so that it would look like a crazy quilt.

THE COLOR PAGE in this chapter shows how to paint a duck in color. After we have made one like it, let us try to paint one from a stuffed bird or a good colored picture.

DESIGN

DESIGNERS, as we said before, make a great deal of use of birds and animals in their work. Many designs are worked into rugs and beautiful tapestries. In order that these designs may be woven on the looms in the big mills, the artists find it necessary to plan their designs into what are called "geometric patterns." The lines of these geometric patterns correspond to the threads in the looms.

A SQUIRREL'S PICTURE is shown on page 127, and also the geometric design that has been made from it. You will notice that these designs are made on paper that has been divided up into little squares. The lines you make must follow the lines in these little squares, or the pattern cannot be woven on the loom. When your design has been outlined, then it can be filled in with a brush and ink. After you have made some in black and white, you could try some in flat colors, like brown and gray and red.

THE CHARACTER of most of these birds and animals is easy to make out, in spite of the fact that the lines in the designs are all straight. If you will look at the page, I am sure you can find a duck, a squirrel, a dog, a rooster, and a cat. See if you cannot.

SOME BEAUTIFUL DESIGNS are given on page 129. In this page, you will notice that the subjects have been planned so as to fit the space in which they are put. Notice how perfectly the rooster fits into his square, and how the black parts of the picture cut it up into pleasing parts. Look at the picture of the little squirrel eating a nut. See how his head and body on one side just balance the bushy tail on the other side.

CUTTING UP OUR SPACES like this is the way to make our drawings attractive and really artistic. Besides this idea, we should think of how the light and the dark parts look also. A fine example of a good arrangement of lights and darks is shown in the design of the rabbit running. Notice how the white and the black balance each other against the gray background. Notice the border of storks on page 129. It looks well whether you look at the white part or at the dark part. This is because the white and the black spots have been planned out so as to hold together well.

FLAT DRAWINGS like these are the kind you should aim to make. Do not try to take your bird or animal drawing and shade it all up with realistic shading. If you do, you will make it look smudgy and uninteresting. Besides that, you will be doing more work with less results.

On page 130 are shown a bird and some animals that would look well on posters. Notice how flat they have been made. This is the kind of work that makes the best posters our artists are turning out. Nothing is put down that does not mean something.

ATTRACTIVE POSTERS can be made by cutting out birds or animals from colored paper and pasting them against a background of another color. For instance, let us take the polar bear on the top row. He could be cut from white paper. The moon could be cut from yellow paper, and the iceberg from light blue. Then the whole thing could be pasted down on black or dark green paper. We would paste the moon down first, then the iceberg, and last, Mr. Bear.

HANDICRAFT

THIS YEAR we are going to learn how to make some interesting toys, with birds and animals as our subjects. We have in this chapter a whole page showing birds and animals that would make good toys. Every one of the subjects shown could be made into dozens of different toys and novelties that people would like to have.

SINCE THE WAR, manufacturers in the United States have tried to educate the people to buy toys made in this country. Designers have been encouraged to design toys that would be typically American. Every year, especially about holiday time, we see thousands of toys that have been produced in this country. Toys are always appreciated by children, and are a good means of both instructing and amusing them.

THE FUNNY LITTLE OWL on page 131 would make a pleasing toy. With his big, wise eyes and fuzzy face, he looks quite learned. He would make a nice garden stick to train plants up to. The blue jay would make a good garden stick, too. The little Teddy bear could be made of stuffed cloth, and so could the rabbit. Or they could be cut from wood and put on wheels for little children to play with.

ON THE NEXT PAGE, we have two ways to make jointed birds of cardboard. In the one called the eyelet bird, the different parts are fastened together with metal eyelets like those found on our laced shoes. A shoemaker could put these in for you, or a little punch can be secured that will do the work. The spear point bird is easier to make, if you do it carefully. The body of the bird has little slits in it. The legs and neck of the bird are finished off with points shaped like a spear-head. To put these points into the slits, you must first fold back the sides of the spearhead so it will slip in. When it is through, then you open out these sides again, and they hold the neck and the legs and the tail in place.

AFTER YOUR BIRDS have been finished, they can be moved so as to stand in many different ways. Look at the working page and you will see how the birds will look. They can be made of colored cardboard, or of white cardboard, or of heavy paper, and colored any way you like best.

BOYS ESPECIALLY like to work in wood. On page 133 are shown working drawings of seven toys that are easy to make from little pieces of wood like those found in apple boxes. One of the easiest is the little bird windmill. The birds may be made from wood or heavy paper, and held in place with a half spool and a little nail. The balancing horse in the upper left-hand corner is cut out of three pieces. If the wire and the stone are fastened on right, the horse will balance himself like a circus horse on the edge of the table. The donkey cart next to the horse is a toy any little girl or boy would like to have. The way to make it is shown at the top of the page. If you wanted, you could make one with two donkeys fastened to it.

THE SWINGING PARROT is made somewhat like the balancing horse, only it is simpler to construct. By means of an iron washer glued on each side of his tail, he is made to keep his balance properly. This parrot could be painted in brilliant colors, like red and green and black. The swinging peacock next to it is a most interesting toy when once made. While it may look a little difficult, it is really easy, and will give its owner much pleasure after it is done. When you swing the stone back and forth, the peacock nods first his head and then his tail, as though going out for a morning walk.

TWO OTHER BIRD TOYS are shown. When you move the two sticks back and forth, the pecking hen appears to be eating a hasty breakfast. Mr. Rooster is made with his neck fastened to pieces of broom handles used as wheels. When he is pulled along the floor, his head bobs up and down, as if he said, "I told you so!"

A PAGE OF DRAWINGS showing how to make toys from our sketches is shown next. At the top, we have a picture of a horse, and two drawings showing how it should be simplified to make a toy. Notice that in the original sketch, the horse has his legs spread apart. In the toy, only the legs on one side are shown. This is done in order to make the toy easier to cut out and construct. The last drawing of the three is the best, because its straight lines make it easy to cut out. At the same time, these straight lines give the toy character.

FOUR WAYS TO MAKE HORSES that will stand up are shown on the same page. You will notice that the one on the left is cut from only one piece of paper. The bottom is then folded so that it will stand up. The horse on the right is made of three pieces, one for the front legs, one for the hind legs, and one for the body. The body is then slipped into the grooves made at the top of the front and the hind legs. Two horses that have thickness as well as length are shown at the bottom of the page. One is made from a single piece of paper, and the other from two pieces. They do not have to be glued, but will hold together if they are folded up properly. Many other animals and birds can be made in the same way. See if you can make a rabbit or a duck in this way.

MOVABLE TOYS made of wood are an interesting problem, especially if you have a little sloyd saw with which to cut them out. These sloyd saws can be bought at hardware stores, and are very useful. If you cannot get one, you can make your movable toys of thick cardboard cut out with a knife. The way to do this is shown on page 135. On that page, we have a picture of the elephant as he generally looks, and then one simplified so that it will cut out easily. Notice how the tusk has been connected with the trunk so that it will not break off when it is cut out.

COLORING TOYS may be done in different ways. A very easy way is to color them with your wax crayons. Unless this is carefully done, they will look more or less streaky. Another way is to color the toys with opaque water colors. Opaque colors are good because they dry flatter than transparent colors. The transparent colors will do if you have no other colors. If water colors are used, you can make them permanent and more brilliant by giving them a coat of what is known as white shellac or clear varnish. This should be put on with a wide brush and also fairly rapidly, so as not to stir up the water color beneath it. Toys cut from heavy cardboard can be made quite lasting in this way.

LETTERING

WE HAVE TRIED different kinds of alphabets. On page 136 is a new one, and one that is quite professional looking. It is all made by cutting with scissors. The inside openings are made by folding the letters and cutting them out. We first cut out a piece of cardboard for the pattern of our oblong. On the edge of this pattern, we should divide it into five squares the long way and three squares the short way. The easiest way would be to use geometric paper, which is paper that is divided into little squares already. With this paper to work on, all we have to do is to measure five squares up and down and three across. When we have cut out this oblong, then we can fold it and cut out our letters. Notice how the center part is cut out of the letter O. This is shown in the upper left-hand corner of the working page. The Q is something like the O with a little tail sticking out to one side.

LETTERS like J and H are easy to cut. The letter S is one of the hardest, so a diagram of it is shown at the bottom of the page. If we follow the lines on the geometric paper closely, we shall be certain of good results. Some of the letters do not need to be folded in order to be cut. These letters are shown at the bottom of the page. An alphabet like this can be cut out of paper of any color, and is very useful in making up posters.

MODELING

MODELING ANIMALS is one of the most fascinating things that children can do. Birds and animals modeled in clay or in plasticine are a fine study for little artists. We should never get discouraged, but keep at it, and we shall soon begin to notice an improvement in our work. Some of our best sculptors have made over the same animal thirty or forty times before they made one they liked. In modeling birds or animals, we should be careful to follow the method shown on page 137. First we make the very rough shape to get the main character. Then we scrape away parts and add parts to make such portions as the head and the neck. Last we put in the details, like the rabbit's ears and his legs and eyes.

BIRDS are always built up best over an oval form, as all their bodies have this shape. Be careful, in joining the head to the body, to make the joint strong, so that the head will not fall off. Do not try to put in small details. They would spoil your masterpiece.

TEACHERS with classes in modeling can get excellent results by having a little cage or pen in which they can put a duck or a rabbit to be modeled. If this is put on a large table, the children can work around it. This keeps the model from straying too far, yet gives him plenty of freedom. A photograph of such a class is shown on page 124. Children could change places, and in this way get different poses.

•

Action Sketches from Canary Birds.

SKETCHING FROM BIRDS

Draw
Birds
and
Animals
using
Brush
Strokes.

5 Brush
Strokes

Simplified
Brush
Drawing

6 Brush
Strokes

4 Brush
Strokes

Abbreviated
Birds *and*
Animals
Tell the most with
the fewest lines.

DRAWING BIRDS AND ANIMALS WITH FEW LINES

JAPANESE BRUSH DRAWINGS

MODELING FROM LIVE CREATURES

LIGHT AND DARK CRAYONS USED ON GRAY PAPER

A small and a large oval

with other parts added

Young Birds show clearly the head and body parts.

make the foundation of a bird drawing.

HOW TO PAINT BIRDS

BLOCK BIRD AND ANIMAL PATTERNS

Block Drawings may be used as Borders for Cross-Stitch Patterns.

Several Cross-Stitch Squares may be sewed together.

Checked Cloth may be used.

Another Stitch to try.

THE USE OF BLOCK DRAWINGS

BIRDS AND ANIMALS IN DESIGN

9 Applied Art

BIRDS AND ANIMALS IN POSTERS

How many of these animals can you make into toys?

BIRD AND ANIMAL OUTLINES FOR TOY USE

APPLIED ART

PAPER BIRD TOYS

SIMPLE MECHANICAL TOYS

The Sketch Simplified for Toys

FOUR WAYS TO MAKE A HORSE THAT WILL STAND UP

Body

Front Legs

Hind Legs

The Pattern

Fold

The Body

Fold

The Head

OTHER ANIMALS AND BIRDS CAN BE MADE IN THE SAME WAY.

PAPER ANIMAL TOYS

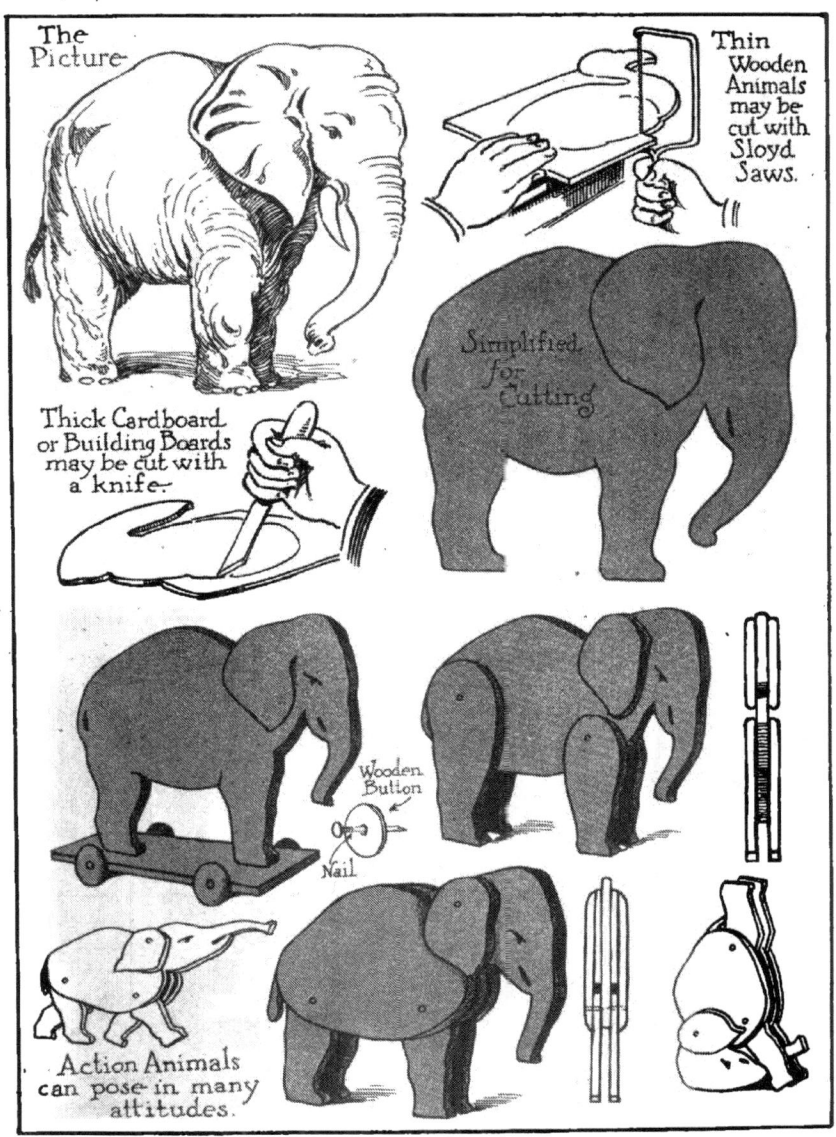

The Picture

Thin Wooden Animals may be cut with Sloyd Saws.

Simplified for Cutting

Thick Cardboard or Building Boards may be cut with a knife.

Wooden Button

Nail

Action Animals can pose in many attitudes.

FOUR WAYS TO MAKE TOYS

SCISSOR LETTERS. *INSIDE OPENINGS FOLDED AND CUT*

ANGLE CUT LETTERS *FOLDED AND CUT*

LETTERS CUT WITHOUT FOLDING

A PAPER LETTER ALPHABET

First--
the rough shape.

Second--
a closer
form.

Third--
The finished
subject.

Birds may
be started from
an oval
form.

Avoid small
details.

Put in only the
important parts.

HOW TO MODEL BIRDS AND ANIMALS

TEACHER'S NOTES FOR THE FIFTH YEAR

SKETCHING FROM ANIMALS. An additional interest in art problems can be created by the problem of sketching from live birds and animals. This sounds like a difficult problem, but if handled properly by the teacher, it need not be a failure at all. Pet canaries or kittens, pet rabbits or dogs, can be placed in a good location, so that the pupils can group around the subject and sketch it. The pupils should not endeavor to secure completed drawings, but should be content with action sketches or outline drawings. The pupils should change places from time to time, to secure new viewpoints and to follow up some particular part they wish to complete.

A simple cage to retain the bird or animal can be made from ordinary wire mesh around a light wooden frame. If this is placed on a table, it permits a clearer view to all workers. A drill of this kind occasionally will show that some of the pupils secure better results from such subjects than from still life, and it will create variation in all the work.

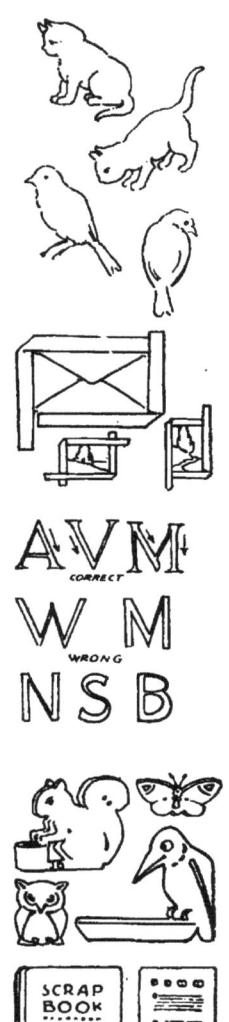

HOW TO MAKE FINDERS. To make finders for finding the best parts of pictures, a strip of cardboard should be bent at right angles. As a right angle guide, use an envelope or a book cover, as such material is usually manufactured with a true angle. Two finders should be made and preserved for locating good portions of pictures where such problems occur. If a more durable finder is desired, two pieces can be cut out of a stiff cardboard, which will give a more solid finder.

LETTERING MATERIAL. A collection of different kinds of letters, as found in advertisements and cover designs, should be mounted on cards and posted on the bulletin board for the pupils to see. Ornate or fanciful lettering should not be encouraged. Children tend to elaborate lettering and to choose intricate forms. They should be shown that plain lettering is preferable, that it is more practical and more beautiful.

A good chart to keep before the pupils is one showing the incorrect shading of the letters A, V, W, N, and M, and the incorrect spacing of the same along with the letters I, T, L, and P. Such a lesson is a never forgotten one. The pupils should also be encouraged to notice where there are good examples of lettering in their home town, as well as to note where there are incorrect uses of lettering.

ANIMAL TOYS. When toy making is to be the problem, a number of simple but good toys should be collected and displayed on a shelf, to stimulate ideas. A toy made in paper, cardboard, or thin wood by a child will be a very greatly appreciated plaything. He sees what effort and thought are needed, when he works out his toys, and he will take better care of those he possesses and of those others possess. The most successful toys should be placed on the honor shelf for a few days.

VERSES FOR ILLUSTRATION. There are many verses that lend themselves easily to illustrations. Such poems as those written by Stevenson, Seegimuller, Riley, and others are filled with word pictures. The teacher should have a number of these always ready for use. A scrapbook with verses adaptable to different months, and with child verses on different subjects, will prove an excellent help.

CRAYON DRAWING ON DARK PAPER.

DIRECT WATER COLOR ON WHITE PAPER.

STILL LIFE PAINTING

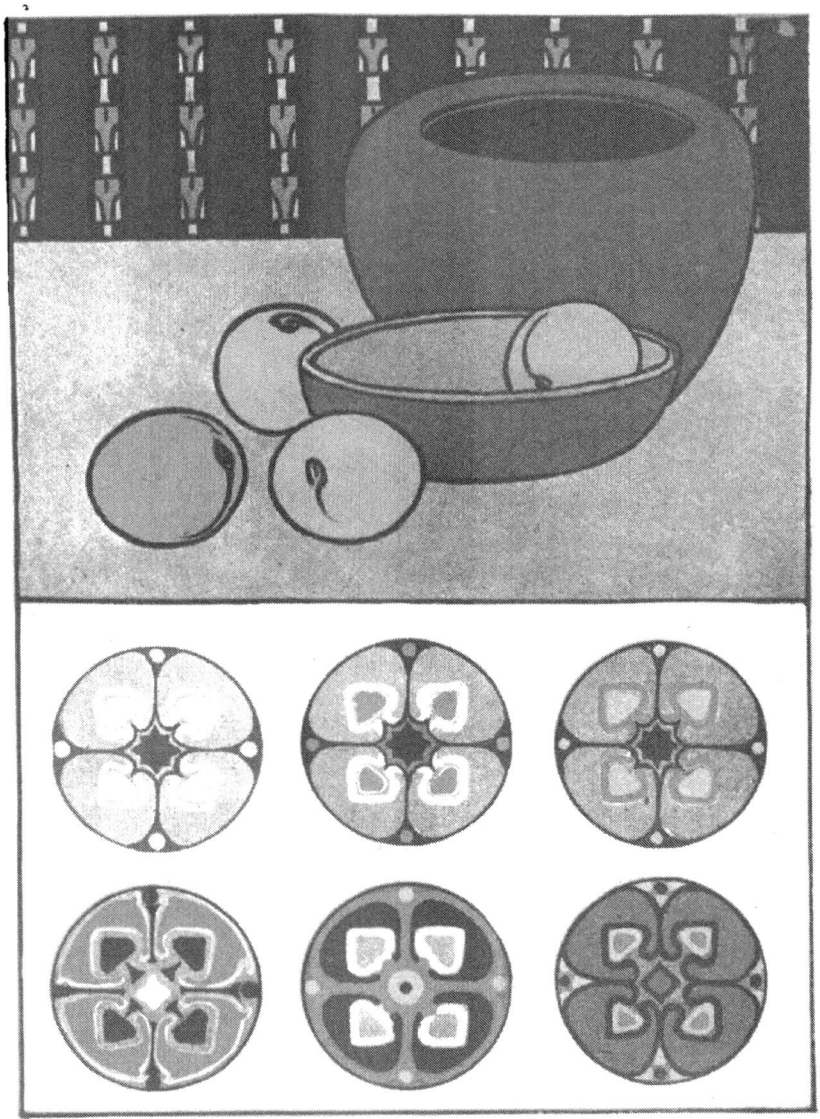

FLAT TONE STILL LIFE — ROSETTE DESIGNS

THE SIXTH YEAR

DRAWING AND PAINTING

DETAIL DRAWINGS of things in nature, such as flowers and plants, help us to get acquainted with the character of these objects, so that when we come to do the more elaborate work, we shall draw with understanding. Instead of trying to do too much, we should make careful studies of just how the leaves branch off from the main stem, or how the wheat stalk differs from an ordinary blade of grass.

A PAGE OF PLANT GROWTHS is shown in this chapter. Notice the graceful way the leaves of grass branch out from the main stalk. See the difference between the character of this drawing and that of the branch in the upper right-hand corner. Notice that the toadstools at the bottom of the page do not stick right out of the ground like toothpicks, but grow out with a graceful curve, as shown in the picture. It is by observing and studying little details like this that we become better artists.

STUDIES OF FLOWERS AND LEAVES are shown on page 148. These drawings were done with a soft pencil. The shadow parts were made with a heavier line, so as to bring out the character of the subject. By leaving out all unnecessary shading, it is easier to show the true character of the plants. The growth of the acorn and of the eucalyptus buds is much more rugged than that of the apple blossom and of the poppy. Try to copy the picture of the apple blossom, then get some real flowers and leaves and draw them with your pencil in this style. Make a whole page of these drawings, and see if your friends can tell the names of them.

STILL LIFE DRAWINGS, as those on page 149 are called, are so called from the fact that the subjects are not alive. Such subjects would be dishes, fruit, and books. Drawing from things like these is fine training and is taught in nearly every grammar and high school. In arranging these groups, we must be careful to place them in such a way that they will make pleasing pictures and not scattered or piled-up ones.

DRAW IN OUTLINES at first, so that you can give all your attention to drawing these curves and straight lines right. Some bowls are much taller than others; and sometimes, in a group, we may have a large pitcher. We should work to keep these various sizes in the right proportion to one another. In order to help the objects look round, a good plan is to accent some of our lines, as is done in the picture.

IN DRAWING OBJECTS, we find they must be made entirely different according to the position from which we are looking at them. If we have a silver dollar and look at its edge, it is simply a flat strip. If we lay it down on the table, it is a perfect circle. When we pick it up and start to lift it into the air, it begins to look less and less like a circle, until just opposite our eyes it appears to be a broad, straight line. This brings out something that we must watch for in drawing still life objects.

DRAWING OBJECTS in different positions, like those shown on the top of page 150, will help us to know how these things should be made. To get good results, we should always block our objects in light lines first. In drawing curved shapes, a good plan is to draw a straight line each way through the center of our circle, to help us get the general direction. This is shown plainly in the drawings on the top line of page 150. Notice how much narrower the bottom of the pail is in the last drawing of that row than in the second one. This is because the pail is turned more in the last drawing.

DRAWING OBJECTS WITH CURVES needs more practice than the straight object drawing. In drawing these curves, it is always best to put in the whole curve, even though part of it comes back of something else, as in the saucer in the picture. If this is done in light lines, the part you do not need can be erased easily. A candlestick is a good subject for you to try. One of them is shown here.

MEMORY DRAWING of still life objects is fine for strengthening both our memory and our observation. If we look at two or three simple objects, then go away and try to draw them from memory, we shall find that they will nearly always lack correct proportions and shapes. A second and a third trial will help us to correct these; and when we once learn to draw them right, they are there to stay. Artists in European countries make much more use of memory work than we do here, and this is responsible for the skill with which many of them draw.

USING GUIDE LINES can never be emphasized too much in drawing. It is because so many beginners fail to make good use of these that they do not get along as well as they ought. A guide line drawn through the middle of an object will help us to get its height right and also to keep it from looking as if it would tip over. Look at the page next to the one with the pails on it. You will see that the first guide lines in the top row look like a row of matches sticking up in the air.

But if we look right below this drawing, we can see how useful these lines really are. They make the right placing of our objects much easier. A group like the one shown here would be very confusing to draw without the use of guide lines.

REARRANGING OUR OBJECTS is a good way for us to train the eye as to what is an artistic arrangement and what is not. Some grown-up artists have never learned to do this right, because they have never practiced it enough. "Finders" like those shown in the picture are also a big help in making artistic groupings.

FINDERS are a help in making drawings like those of the basket and the candle on page 152. A good thing to do is first to draw the group just as it is. Do this in outline with a brush. When your drawing is finished, take your finders and pick out several sections that you think will make good pictures. Then make drawings of these. This is one of the best drills you can try. Every good artist and illustrator has done this sort of work in his early training.

WASH WORK in still life drawing may be done in several different ways. The first one we shall try will be like those shown on page 153, marked "Flat Tone Still Life." As you can see, every one of these drawings has been made with only two or three simple flat washes. One has a black background, and the rest have gray backgrounds. Our finders come in handy here to help us get a well arranged picture. After we have penciled out our drawing carefully, we can put in our wash tones. It is best to put in the lightest ones first and the darkest last.

FLAT TONE WORK may be done in crayons and charcoal too. A whole page of work done in this style is shown here. See how simply the still life drawing of the cherries and the basket on page 161 has been made. Yet it satisfies us. Our modern illustrators and poster artists are doing their work more and more this way. Soon practically all of our art work will be done like this. In using our crayons for flat tone work, we should try to keep the shades smooth, and not full of little smudge spots caused by careless work. Crayon or charcoal drawings that show a little of the paper underneath the lines are always the best kind to do.

STILL LIFE GROUPS done in cut-out paper can never be excelled for the results we get and the training given us. Look at the cut-out objects on page 162. Are they not strong and pleasing? Yet they have been done in the simplest way. Cut paper work is always a benefit because it gives us an opportunity to center all our attention on the idea of pleasing arrangements and tones without worrying over other things, like whether our color is going to dry smoothly or not. All the pictures on page 162 have been made with white and black paper pasted on a gray or a black background. The work has been done carefully, and so the results are very satisfactory. Many illustrations in magazines are not as artistic as the still life picture here of the candlestick and the open book, yet they are much more elaborate.

TWO OTHER METHODS of still life drawing are shown on page 154. The top half shows how we can make good drawings by using a half-tone wash on white paper. Little openings are left to show the "high lights," or bright spots, of our objects. While this is still holding to the simple style, it has the result of making our objects appear rounder. Below this drawing, we have one showing how to draw objects by using white crayon or water colors on gray paper. In this case, we try to draw only the light spots in our objects. This kind of drawing is a little harder than the others. For that reason, a good plan is to sketch from such things as glass bottles or tumblers, or things made of shiny metal like aluminum or brass.

OUR NEXT STEP in still life work is to try showing our objects with their high lights and shadows done in flat tones. First we should get some gray or light brown paper. After we have penciled our group lightly on it, we should decide what tone will best represent the main part of our subject. Next we paint this tone in. After it is dry, we add our important high lights with white opaque paint or a white crayon. This leaves only our shadows to do. By looking at our objects through half closed eyes, we can find where the shadows come. We paint these shadows in with a darker tone than the one we used first, and our drawing is done. A fine page showing each step in this kind of work is given in this chapter. See if you can make a drawing in this way.

COLOR can be used in many of the drawings we have already made in black and white. We can never expect to do things well in color until we have first learned to do them well in black and white. If colors are used right, they will have all the nice "spotting" of black and white drawings, and have beautiful coloring as well. Any of the drawings we have made of flower studies, can be worked out in color in an interesting way. A fine way to make colored flower studies is to get some dark shade of paper and put in our flower tints with our crayons. Then if we use a dark crayon, we can put in our outlines and accents with it. This is a quick way of making color sketches from flowers that are likely to wilt easily.

A BOOK OF FLOWERS worked out in this way would be something you would always be proud of. It could be made up like a portfolio, with loose leaves, so that you could take any flower out and work from it, if you wished. Next spring, ask the teacher if you can make a portfolio like this. The cover could be of heavy cardboard, with a cloth back to make it last well.

COLOR DRAWINGS of still life subjects are made in many schools. Still life groups give us a good chance to study color, because the colors in them do not change from day to day as do those in a flower or a plant. Then, too, some of our vases and fabrics have wonderfully rich color in them; and by trying to match these colors, we learn to see color correctly. The drawing of the apples in the pan would be a good one to try in colors. The pan could be made in a blue-gray tint, and the apples with rosy cheeks of red and orange. This subject can be done in two ways. In one, we could make all of our colors flat, as though they were cut out of paper. The other, we could shade up more with high lights and shadows, like those we did in black and white.

DESIGN

DESIGNS made with drawing instruments were practically the only kind thought of for many years. Men used things like compasses and triangles in all their design work. Many beautiful things were designed in this way. The Arabians and other Far East peoples decorate their public buildings and churches with many wonderful and exquisite designs worked out from interlacing of circles, squares, and other mechanical forms. The beautiful designs we see in the snowflakes are of this kind.

DESIGN in later years has relied a great deal upon what is known as free-hand work, or that done without the help of drawing instruments. But all good designers know how to use these instruments, and depend upon their help for certain kinds of work. Where designs are to be put in metal or carved out of stone or some similar substance, the designer generally makes his designs more mechanical. It is good for us to learn how to use a compass, a T square, and a triangle, because they will come in handy many times.

DRAWING INSTRUMENTS used in our work will teach us to be more accurate. We soon find, if we are not careful, that the designs do not come out right. Look at the compass designs on page 155, and you will see why. In the top row are three squares. The first square has a large circle inside. If we do not get one point of our compass in the exact center of the square, the other point will not draw the circle so that it touches every side of the square alike.

The way to get the center of the square is to draw a diagonal line from corner to corner of the square. When you have done this, you will find that your lines cross each other. Where they cross is the center of your square. A little design inside of the big circle has been made by putting one end of the compass on the corner of the square and swinging a curve with the other from the middle of each side.

THE SECOND SQUARE has a design in it that is made by putting one end of the compass on one corner of the square and swinging in a curve from one of the nearest corners to the one opposite it. The design in the third square is made by first finding the middle of one side of the square, and putting one end of the compass on it while you swing in a curve from one end of that side to the other end. These designs are all easily made if you are careful.

. BEAUTIFUL DESIGNS can be made by filling in the different parts of our patterns with tones of black, white, and gray. Some designs made in this way are shown on the working page. These same designs worked in black and white, or in color, make fine motifs to use on little boxes, or book ends, or any handicraft work. Such designs as these, being mechanical, are suitable for almost any piece of craft work. Where a man might not like a box with a butterfly on it, he is nearly always pleased with designs like these.

ROSETTES are designs built upon a rose shape. Every one of them is built inside a circle. Rosettes have been used by designers from the time of the earliest of their work that is known. On page 156, we have two rows of rosettes that were used by different nations. The Greek rosette and the early Italian are used a great deal at the present. In almost every big city, you can see public buildings in which a Greek rosette has been used somewhere in the architectural ornaments.

VARIOUS WAYS TO DRAW ROSETTES are shown in the third line. The first shows a design in a brush outline, the second shows it in black and white, and the third shows it in three tones. Notice how much more interesting the rosette becomes when it is worked in the three tones. This third design would make a good one to use on the top of a round box. The last two lines of the page show rosette forms that have been taken from nature. Here we have rosettes from snow crystals, shells, flowers, fruits, and many other sources. They are all different, yet they are all interesting.

THE LAST TWO DESIGNS show a rosette taken from an apple blossom, and how this same shape is seen in an apple's center if we cut it in half.

NATURE is overflowing with suggestions for designs that we may work out. Every flower, plant, rock, and tree has dozens of design ideas in it, if we will only look for them. On page 157 are some drawings showing us how to work out a design from a flower. First we have a picture of the flower in its natural form. Then we have a drawing showing the same flower worked out in curved lines, and one showing it worked out in straight lines. In the second row we have the flower worked out in three different ways. The first fits a square, the second fits an oblong, and the third a triangle. Yet, in looking at them, there is no doubt about their all being designed from the flower in the top row.

THE SAME FLOWER worked into a circle, an ellipse, and an oval, is given in the third line. So, on this page, the artist has shown us that with a little study, we can make eight or more different designs from one flower. One secret of doing these easily is to draw first the shape you want to fit your flower into, then make your flower fit inside of that form. By drawing guide lines through the center, you will make it easier to get both sides alike.

BORDERS AND PATTERNS worked from these designs are shown at the bottom of the page. Notice how interesting the designs look when repeated in borders, or in all-over patterns, like wall paper. They become more interesting still if they are worked out in colors. For a good practice in this work, take some interesting flower, and see if you can make some good designs from it. Designs like these work well in stenciled cushions and table runners. They also look well in things made of wood or metal.

HANDICRAFT

BUILDINGS constructed of paper are one of the things we shall study this year. First we shall learn to make cubes and pyramids, and other things that go toward making up building shapes. We can also use them in our still life drawing work. A page of buildings and the way to make them is shown on page 158. All these constructed objects must be first planned out in flat paper, as is shown in the diagram. Then they are folded up and pasted into place.

THE PYRAMID in the flat plan does not look much as it does when finished. See if you can make one. A good way to make the paper fold with sharp edges is to take a hard pencil and rule a strong line along the parts you wish to fold. This makes the paper fold smoothly. By looking at the drawing, you can see how to make the house and the church. What other buildings can you design? After they are done, or before, if you want, the windows and other details can be painted on.

ALPHABETS made with a medium pencil are good things to practice. It is well to start with a pencil, because when we do not have to worry about pens or brushes or ink, we can think more about the shapes of our letters. The alphabet in this chapter is artistic, and a suitable one for lettering mottoes or verses. You will see that they all have a short line to finish them off. Remember to put this on, as it makes the letters look better.

LETTERING with a pen can be done after you have made a good alphabet with your pencil. A satisfactory pen to use is one called the round writing pen. We can draw in any direction with it, without any fear of its being caught in the paper. With pens like these, we can soon learn to make the alphabet. After you have made it in ink, then try lettering two or three short mottoes with it. You could letter these on tinted paper and mount them on cardboard. A cream paper mounted on dark brown would look well. Be sure to draw some guide lines for your letters to go on, or they will run uphill and downhill.

MODELING BOWLS and curved objects seems difficult to most of us, but here is a way to do them that is really easy. First we take our clay and roll it out into long cylinder shapes. Next we take these and wind them around to make a long spiral like the one shown in the second picture of the modeling page. After this is done, we build up the sides like the third drawing. When our spiral has run out, then we can take a knife or a flat stick and flatten out or smooth down the sides. This will give us part of our vase. By making some more spirals, we can add to our vase until it is any height we want.

THIS PLAN can be used to make many interesting cylindrical things in clay. The shapes may be like a bowl or a vase, or one that is the same diameter all the way up and down. In doing this kind of work, we should be careful to roll out our cylinders so that they are the same thickness all the way along, or we shall find that our vases will look lopsided and crude. When the vases are finished, little border designs may be scratched into them with a sharp stick, a toothpick, or a hairpin. A good plan is to sketch out three or four vase and bowl designs on paper, and make sure they are artistic before making them in the clay.

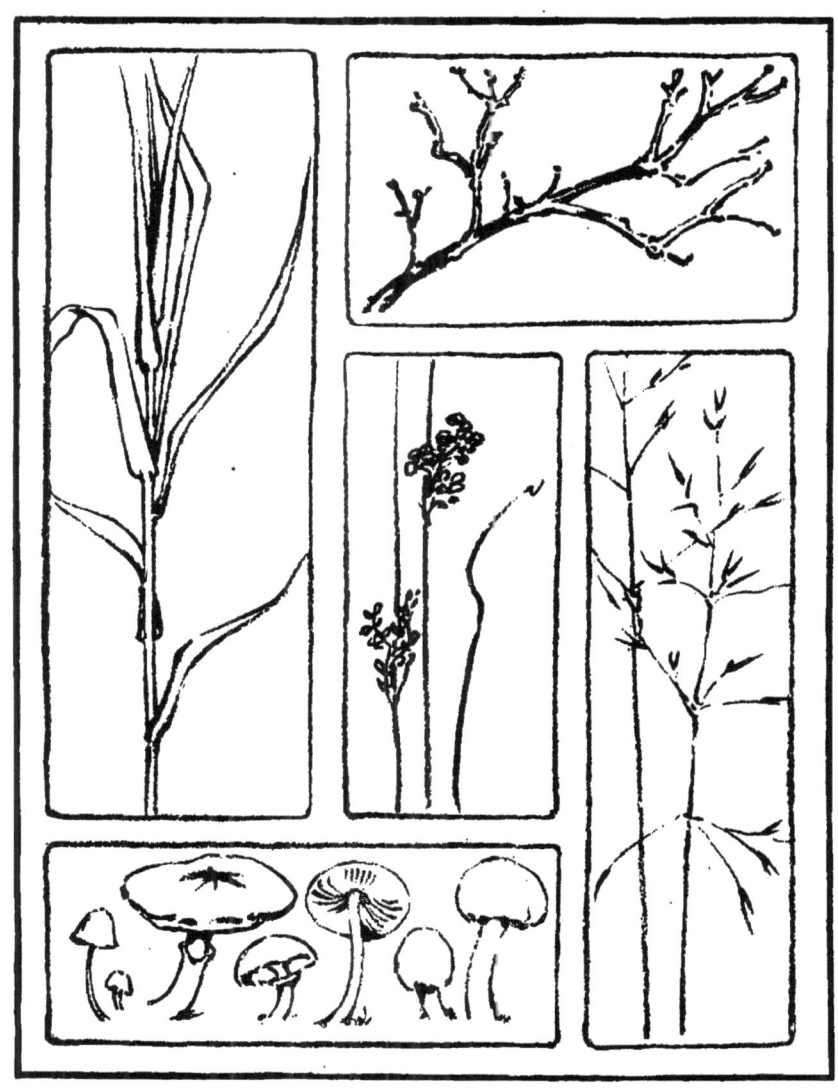

ACCENTED OUTLINE NATURE DRAWINGS

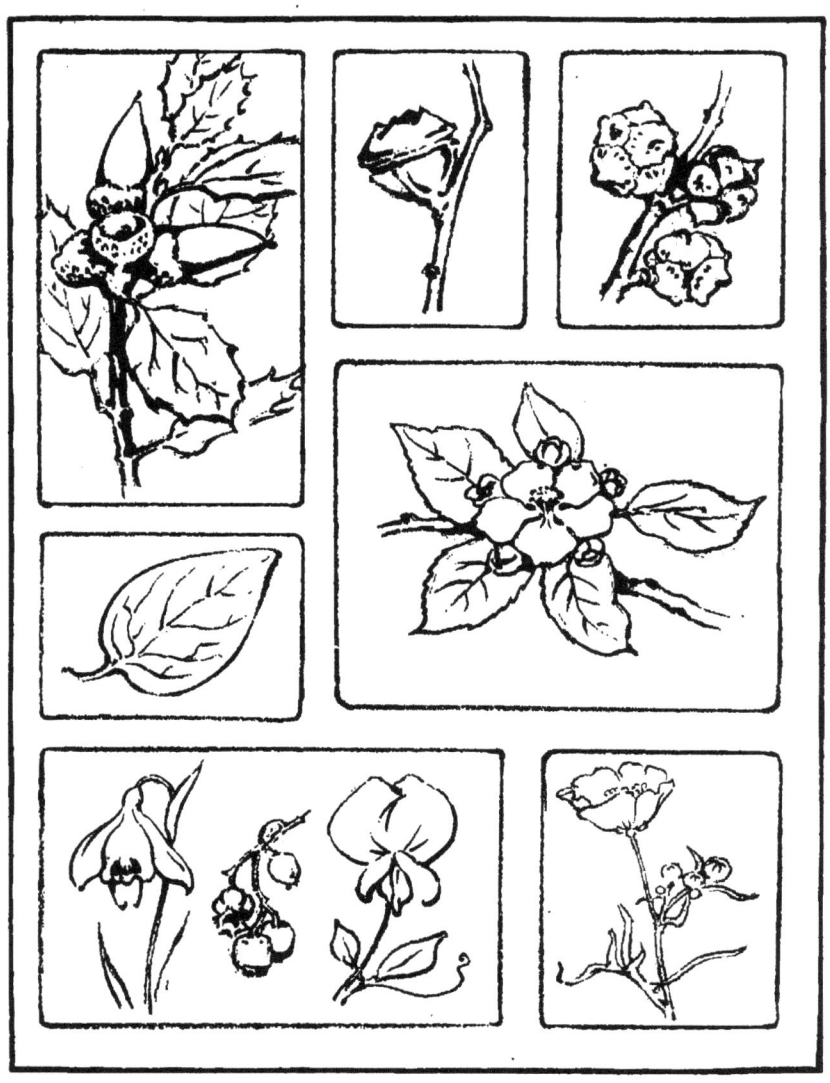

ACCENTED PENCIL DRAWINGS

ACCENTED STILL LIFE DRAWINGS

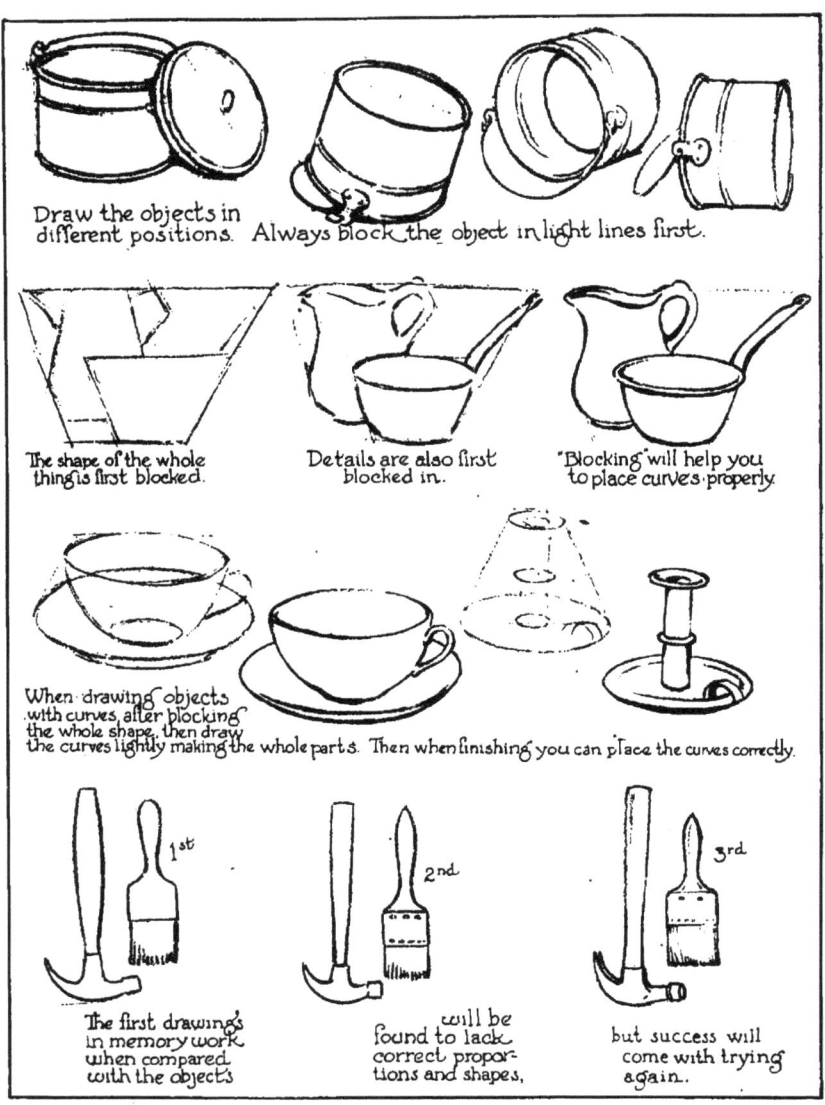

Draw the objects in different positions. Always block the object in light lines first.

The shape of the whole thing is first blocked.

Details are also first blocked in.

"Blocking" will help you to place curves properly.

When drawing objects with curves, after blocking the whole shape, then draw the curves lightly making the whole parts. Then when finishing you can place the curves correctly.

1st

2nd

3rd

The first drawings in memory work when compared with the objects

will be found to lack correct proportions and shapes,

but success will come with trying again.

THE DRAWING OF OBJECTS

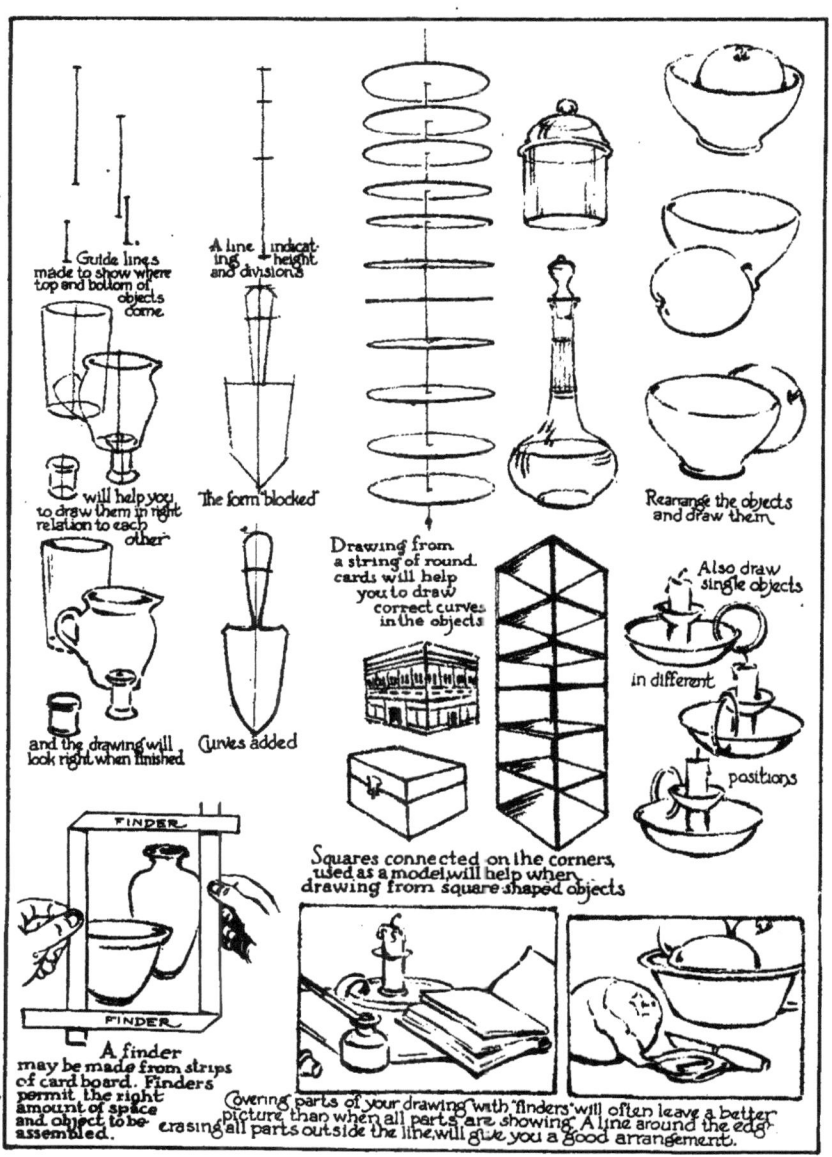

DRAWING OBJECTS IN DIFFERENT POSITIONS

Make a pleasing arrangement of objects and draw it

Use a brush

Then find several sections that will make good pictures

PICTURE ARRANGEMENTS

FLAT TONE   BRUSH
STILL LIFE   WORK

STILL LIFE BRUSH DRAWING

Half-tone Wash on White Paper

White Water color

White Paint or Crayon on Gray Paper

Crayon

HIGH LIGHT OBJECT DRAWINGS

Compass
Designs
within
Squares
and
Circles

COMPASS DESIGNS

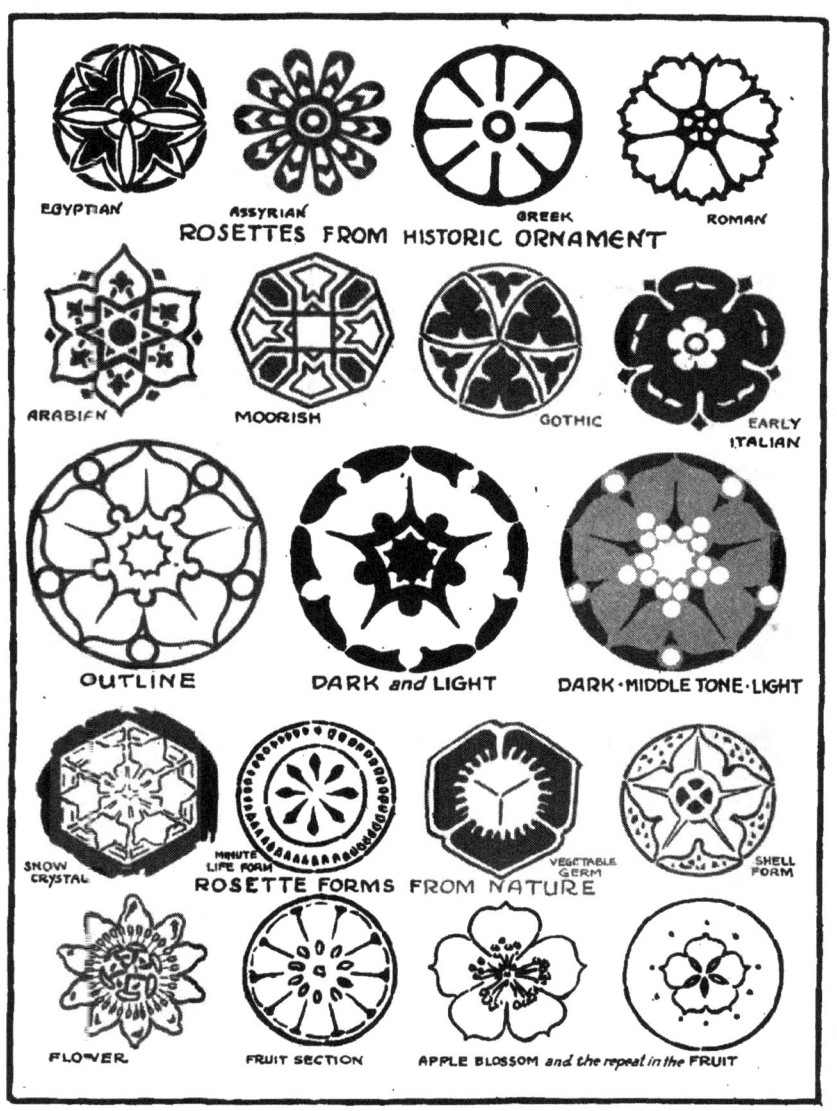

EGYPTIAN   ASSYRIAN   GREEK   ROMAN

ROSETTES FROM HISTORIC ORNAMENT

ARABIEN   MOORISH   GOTHIC   EARLY ITALIAN

OUTLINE   DARK and LIGHT   DARK·MIDDLE TONE·LIGHT

SNOW CRYSTAL   MINUTE LIFE FORM   VEGETABLE GERM   SHELL FORM

ROSETTE FORMS FROM NATURE

FLOWER   FRUIT SECTION   APPLE BLOSSOM and the repeat in the FRUIT

ROSETTE DESIGNS

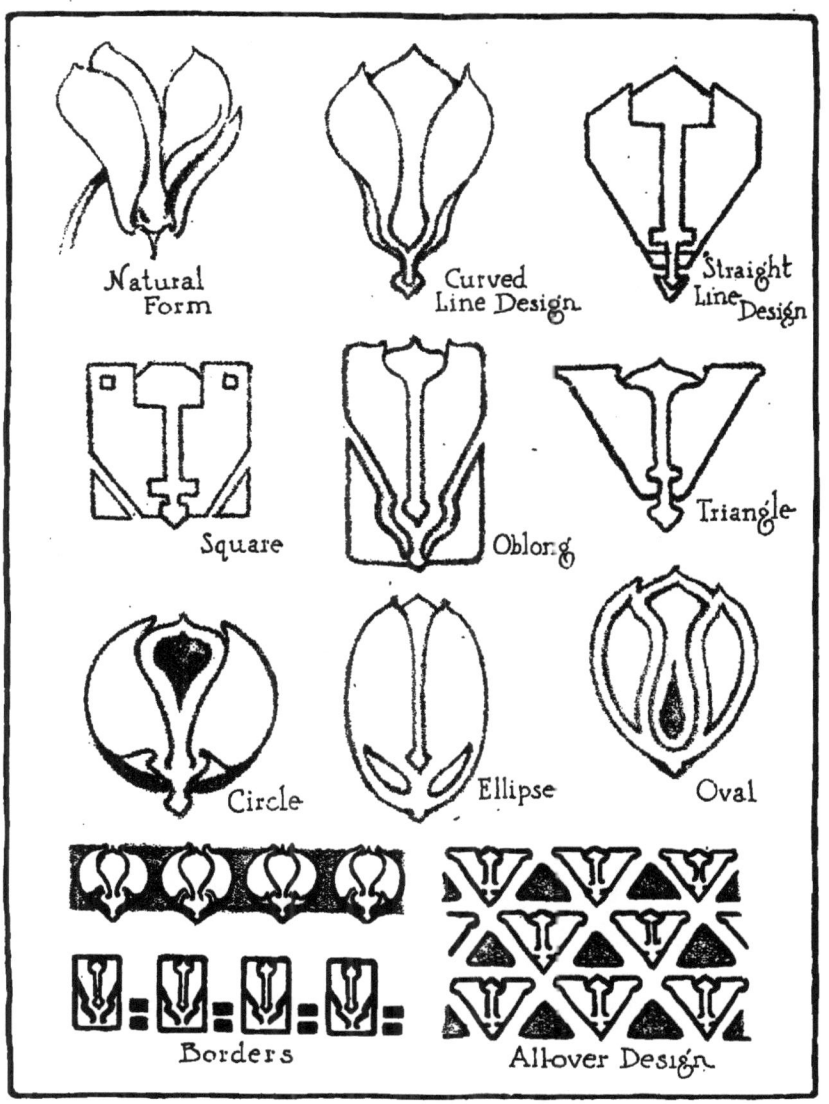

Natural Form

Curved Line Design

Straight Line Design

Square

Oblong

Triangle

Circle

Ellipse

Oval

Borders

Allover Design

HOW TO DESIGN FROM A FLOWER

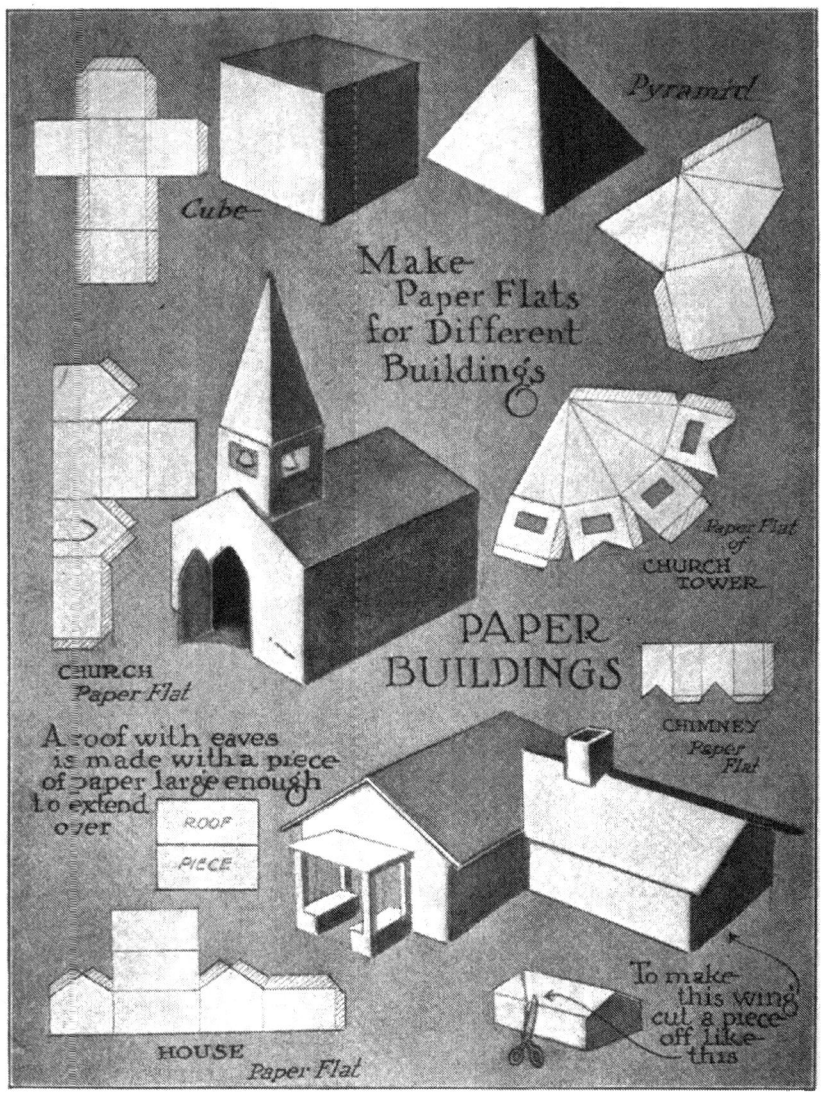

Cube

Pyramid

Make Paper Flats for Different Buildings

Paper Flat of CHURCH TOWER

CHURCH Paper Flat

PAPER BUILDINGS

A roof with eaves is made with a piece of paper large enough to extend over

ROOF PIECE

CHIMNEY Paper Flat

HOUSE Paper Flat

To make this wing cut a piece off like this

PAPER BUILDINGS

TWO-TONE DRAWINGS

11   Applied Art

Free-hand Cut-Out Groups made by cutting Dark and Light papers and mounting on a Gray Background

CUT PAPER STILL LIFE

Black & White Drawings on Toned Background

First decide the tone that will best represent the main part of the object — and paint it.

Then add only the important high lights and shadows over the first tone.

The Lights and Shadows are added

STILL LIFE BRUSH DRAWINGS

STILL LIFE GROUPS. To help the students find good composi-tions or position of the still life groups upon their paper, a cardboard frame with two strings dividing the rectangular opening into four parts will be found helpful. By holding this before the group and moving it, a good composition within the space is located, and the drawing on the paper is made accordingly. The center division strings will guide the student in avoiding central location of objects. The opening in the card should be made in proportion to the pad or paper that is to be used.

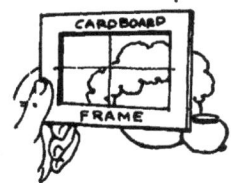

STILL LIFE LIGHTING. To simplify the light and shade on the groups, a back and side partition should be arranged back of the group. A wooden or cardboard box with the front and one side re-moved will make a good stand, as it may be moved without disar-ranging the group whenever it is not to be used for some time. Groups should have one dark side, one light side, and simple shadows.

GROUP PROGRAMS. It will be found that many students have trouble combining material for good groups. For these, the teacher should have a series of cards containing simple outline sketches of interesting and pleasing arrangements that are assembled from time to time. With every still life object in the class collection numbered, corresponding numbers are marked on the diagram. This will make the reassembling of the same arrangement and color an easy matter at any time, and the students will in this way learn correct combina-tions.

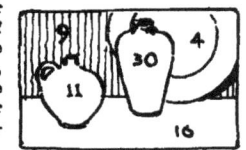

GOOD COLLECTIONS. A great deal of care should be given to the selection of material for still life work. This may be made from inexpensive wares. A good selection of glass and pottery may be made from kitchen ware at any crockery store. Odd bits of cloth, discarded silks and satins, papers, and kitchen ware, which have fulfilled their usefulness at home, may still be good material for the class collection. Boxes and drawers should be used to keep the ob-jects segregated, so that they may be selected without any confusion or lost time.

THE POWER OF SELECTING. Students can learn much about design and color in simply choosing material for a group, and ar-ranging in the best way what they choose. Art is learned not only by hand work, but equally as much by observation work. The power to choose is important. Encourage the student to choose independ-ently of the teacher or others, at the same time being ever willing to discuss the merits of the selection with the teacher or classmates. Do not let the students, in their impatience to commence painting, rush the assembly of the material or their drawing. Two periods spent in selection of material, and as much more in the drawing, will better insure success than a hurried beginning. To say that a draw-ing was sketched in ten minutes adds no merit or value unless it is good. Slow work of course is not to be encouraged, and every stu-dent should be prompted not to waste time. Sensible combinations of objects should be used. Objects should be assembled so as not to occupy the center of spaces; and while contrasts of form and size are desired, these contrasts should not be too great. Mounted prints of good groups drawn and painted by artists should be kept in view of the students, so that they will be influenced in the right direction.

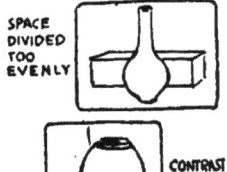

OBJECTS NOT RELATED

SPACE DIVIDED TOO EVENLY

CONTRAST TOO GREAT

Cut Paper on Black Background

Color Harmony *from* Butterfly and Application to Design Work.

Cut Paper and Brush Work

Color Harmony from Flower

NATURE BOOK

Pedro J. Lemos

COLOR HARMONIES FROM NATURE

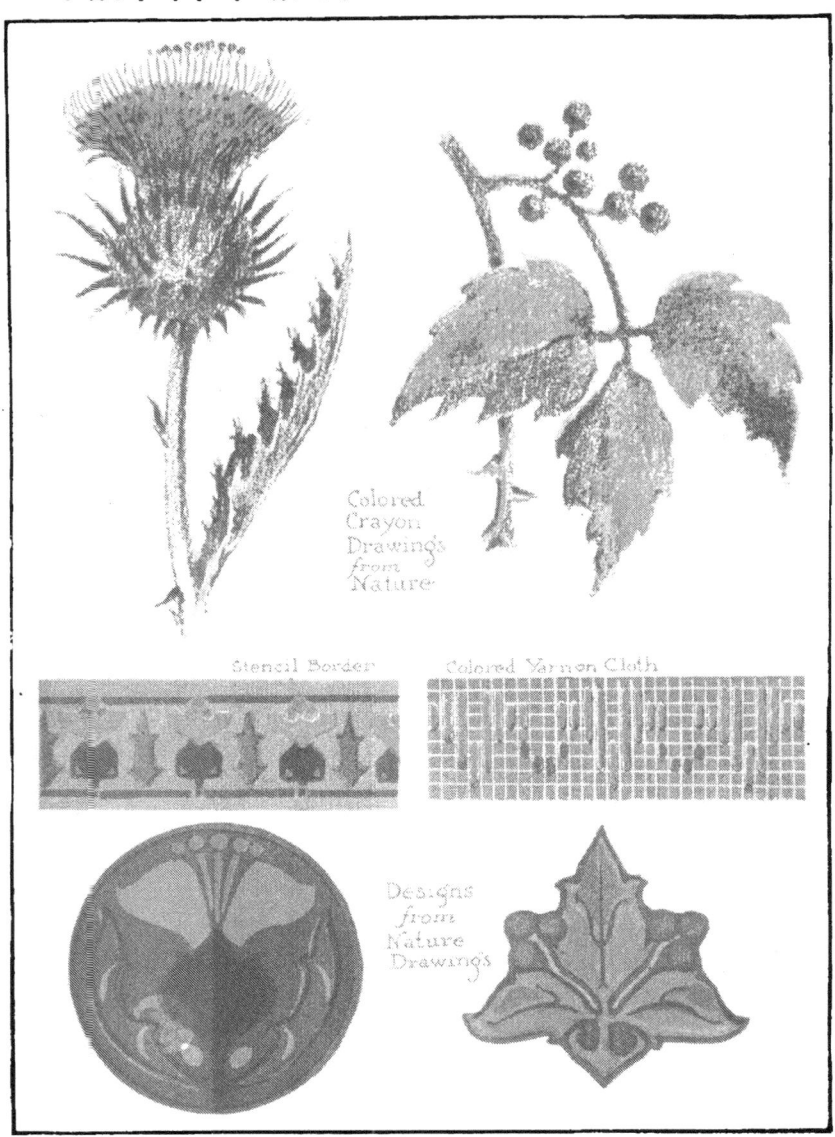

Colored
Crayon
Drawings
from
Nature

Stencil Border   Colored Yarn on Cloth

Designs
from
Nature
Drawings

DESIGNS FROM NATURE FORMS

THE SEVENTH YEAR

DRAWING AND PAINTING

DURING THE SEVENTH YEAR, we should study from leaves, flowers, and plants, making careful drawings of the various parts, so that every possible suggestion may be found for making designs. While we have before used flowers and plants in this way, this year we will give them more attention in many ways.

FIRST WE MUST KNOW THE DETAILS of our subjects, and therefore we will make careful drawings from them before using them in design. We will not use all the details in designing; but where we find it necessary to eliminate any detail, knowing all the parts, we will then know best what parts may be left out.

By making careful drawings, we shall also discover many beautiful parts to plants and flowers, that otherwise we should not see, and learn things about nature that we did not know before.

OUR DRAWINGS MUST BE CLEAR AND DEFINITE, so that we can work from them when the flower or the plant is not in season. The drawing may be larger than the original, if there is need to enlarge parts to make them clear. It must be easy to count the number of petals, and see definitely the way the stems are connected, and see the shape of the leaves.

We should make several views of the flowers, the leaves, and the seed pods, as it will be found that side views, top views, and often back views suggest good patterns.

WHEN STUDYING FROM FLOWERS, if we cut them in half or pull them apart, pleasing design suggestions on the inside will be revealed. Seed pods cut either horizontally or vertically may be used in this way, and buds of various flowers have beautiful patterns in their inner formation.

NATURE IS FULL OF BEAUTIFUL FORMS; and as we found in previous lessons, plants of all kinds give pleasure to the eye by their variation. Different species of flowers may be bell-shaped, round, triangular, and many other forms. The same species of flowers often vary in shape, presenting a change of form in their different growths. Then again flowers on the same plant have numerous shapes, and it may be

(165)

hard to tell which form is the most interesting. Thus we see that Nature uses variation to convey her beauty; and we should not forget that our designs, to be beautiful, must contain variation.

WHEN USING A FLOWER SHAPE, we may find that a certain form fits our space better than the exact form of the flower that we happened to pick. We should not hesitate to change the form so that it will look better, as Nature varies her shapes, and when designing, we must subdue or subordinate our drawings to the purpose of our design.

FLOWER PETALS radiating from a center often vary in their exact shape, or their edges may be a little different. When designing, we have liberty to choose one petal shape that we may prefer, and repeat it in the place of the others. When a flower has two sides different, in a design, both sides may be made alike, or symmetrical. The same arrangement can be made of leaves; and in fact, when we use any part of Nature in design, we may rearrange it to decorate properly the space or material that we are using.

SEVERAL GOOD SHEETS OF DRAWINGS should be made from flowers, and also from leaves, seed pods, and buds, in soft pencil, on paper. These drawings should be carefully planned, so that each sheet will be an orderly arrangement and a permanent record for our further use. From these we can then design almost as well as from the real plant.

A PORTFOLIO to contain our sheets can be made this year; and we should add as many blue prints from leaves, flowers, and branches as we can collect. Also collect pressed flowers and leaves gathered because of their beautiful patterns. If we prepare such a portfolio carefully, and each sheet is thoughtfully arranged, we shall have a small library of material that will be most useful, and one that any artist or designer would prize.

When drawing from a flower or a plant, it will be found easier to work from if it is laid on a white, gray, or black background, whichever gives the best contrast, so as to prevent objects in the room from confusing the actual outline of the plant.

HOLDING STANDS for keeping the plant upright before us on our desks can be easily arranged so as to eliminate the need of always holding the plant in our fingers. Sensitive plants, of course, should be placed in a jar or a bottle with water to prevent their drooping before we have finished drawing from them.

BEFORE COMMENCING THE DRAWING, we should think carefully, and select the branch, cluster, or group of flowers that will best represent our subject. Too, we must be careful to select one that can be depicted in our drawing easily. Therefore one that has a confusion of leaves, or that has too many flowers in one part and too few in others, should be avoided. The simpler branches, or just parts of plants, will be the most satisfactory to commence with. A branch with three to eight leaves and several catkins, seed pods, or blossoms is sufficient for one drawing; for if we need more material, we shall best record it by making a second drawing from another section of the plant.

After making careful drawings in pencil, we should make a number of sheets of brushwork studies, both in black and white and in color.

BRUSHWORK PAINTINGS enable us to study and represent the larger parts of our subject, and prevent us from forgetting about the thing as a whole. The beauty of the entire form of a tree, shrub, branch, or flower is often overlooked, if we give all our attention to the details. In working with the pencil, we have a tool that enables us to seek and record the small parts, while the brush lends itself to the bigger parts. For this reason, artists often work with the two, using the pencil for outlines and small parts, and the brush for working out the larger portions and the backgrounds.

THREE GOOD BRUSH DRILLS are as follows: First, using white or cream paper, outline in pencil the flower or plant arrangement carefully. This outline must be definite and finished enough to prevent any need of guessing how certain parts are to be completed, when worked upon with the brush. Next, all the white or lightest parts of the subject are outlined with a brush line. On all the rest, a dark shade about half value is used, a darker shade being added in the darkest portions. This method is shown on the first drawing on page 182, and is the same method that we have already used with our still life work.

THE SECOND METHOD is to use white and black on gray, and the third method is to use white and gray on black paper. White and black crayon may be used instead of paint, but the drawing will need to be affixed to be preserved. When the black and white paint is used, it should be mixed and first tried on a scrap of paper, to see that it is the right tone, before it is used on the working sheet.

COLOR PAINTINGS should be made over careful outline drawings of the flower or plant, but the pencil lines should not be so heavy that they will be hard to erase after the painting is finished. If we will make our drawing first on another piece of paper (thin paper is best to use), we can erase. as necessary, and trace the outline, when correct, on our working sheet. This will prevent the erasing from spoiling the surface of the paper on which we are to do brush work.

COLOR CRAYON STUDIES also should be made. As has been mentioned before, a rough paper is best for crayon work, and the crayon should not be put on too thick. Several light rubbings should be used where several colors are to be combined.

COLOR NOTES should be made from nature subjects, so that the color harmonies thus secured may be used.in the things we are going to design and construct. We shall find that nature has wonderful color harmonies and color combinations, and that we need only to apply these harmonies to our surroundings to secure pleasing color.

By referring to the color plate in this chapter, we shall see how a record of the colors has been made from the butterfly and the flower, and then used in designs and the decorating of objects. We shall find that there are more of some colors than of others in objects in nature; and the nearer we hold to this proportion, the nearer our harmony will be to that of nature. We find also that some objects in nature have very brilliant and contrasting harmonies, while others have quieter and grayer color arrangements. We should search for these different color harmonies, and make records of them for our portfolio collection.

DESIGN

FLOWER AND PLANT DRAWINGS may be used for the purpose of selecting portions for designs for book covers, booklet pages, titles, wood or metal work, and many such purposes.

TO SELECT GOOD PORTIONS, we will use finders, or cut in a piece of paper an opening the size of the space we wish to fill, and moving this paper over the drawing, select the best section and make a drawing from it. Several such sections selected from one drawing of the manzanita berry, showing where they have been selected, is shown on one of the following pages.

NATURALISTIC DESIGN is the name applied to this kind of design, because a natural arrangement of the plant is retained. Even though the flowers and the leaves may be changed in detail, if the natural lines of growth are retained, it is still a naturalistic design arrangement.

SEVERAL VARIATIONS can be made from one selection once we have decided just the naturalistic arrangement we will use. By using two shades of gray on white paper, or white and black crayon on gray paper, or white and black paint on gray paper, we secure variation by the tone or value arrangements that we use. Several such arrangements are shown on page 182.

SIMPLE DESIGNS should be made of a single leaf or flower after we have spent some time in drawing from nature forms. These can be made with the pencil or with the brush, and various methods are suggested on the following pages.

BORDERS AND BACKGROUNDS can be made by repeating these simple leaf and flower forms one after another so that pleasing arrangements shall be made. If we make our simple designs to conform to certain shapes, like the square, the triangle, the oblong, the circle, the oval, and the ellipse, we shall find that they can be arranged more easily into interesting patterns.

AN EXCELLENT DESIGN DRILL is to cut out a number of such forms from dark paper. Next see how many arrangements, similar to those on page 180, we can make with the form we have cut out. These forms should be about one inch in size, and of thick enough paper to permit us to draw a pencil around the edge and so plan our patterns. We may then finish these with our brush, using black paint or ink only, varying by using outline and black or different shades of black. Afterwards we should try some of the same patterns in color. If these simple forms are pleasing, we can change them into designed flowers or fruits, as on page 181, and our pleasing pattern will be still retained.

DESIGN FOUNDATIONS like this should always be planned, as they will make our work easier and better arranged. Just as we have learned to block in our subjects when drawing, we should also block in when planning our designs.

COMPLICATED DESIGNS are not the best. Designs that have a great deal of "fussy work" and intermingling lines should be avoided. We like the simple melody of music, the simple, clear sentence when reading, and also the simple, restful design.

CUT-OUT DESIGNS will help us to simplify our motifs. By folding several pieces of paper together, we can cut out several motifs at one time. Different shades of paper may be used for cutting, and different backgrounds to paste the cut-out forms upon. Patterns made in color this way may be very beautiful. We should try to make a number of designs in this way, similar to those on page 183.

HANDICRAFT

THE MAKING OF BOOKS should be studied, and we will apply our designs to the construction of booklets and portfolios. The construction of books is important knowledge, and many thousands of people are engaged in this work. At one time, all books were lettered by hand on parchment. This took a great deal of time. Many of these books are still preserved and are beautiful examples of art and skill. When the first type was invented, it permitted more books to reach the people; and in that way, knowledge was increased. There has been no greater influence in spreading civilization than the printed page.

· MANY METHODS are used for gathering and binding the book pages, and these methods should be studied. We can find books, and brief descriptions in the encyclopedia, on the origin of printing and the development of books. The first books printed were beautiful in arrangement, and printers to-day study them as examples.

WILLIAM MORRIS was a famous printer of the nineteenth century. He was a great decorator, designing wall papers, tapestries, furniture, stained glass, and pottery. He is well known as a poet and writer, and is celebrated for the beauty of his printed books. Morris's teaching was summed up in his statement, "Have nothing in your home that you do not know to be useful or believe to be beautiful."

THE PAGES OF THE BOOK should have pleasing margins. Even our composition books, examination papers, and letters should be thus arranged, for no amount of good writing will look well if there are no margins.

MARGINS can be arranged in different ways, a few of which are shown on page 189; and our illustrations, if used, may also be planned in different arrangements. In making up a booklet, it is best to assemble the pages first in their order, and lightly number them. These pages may then be taken apart, as work can be done upon them more easily when they are separate, and they can be put together again when finally completed.

WHEN PLANNING A BOOKLET, we should try to have the cover and the first pages inside (which are called end leaves), as well as each page arrangement, a complete harmony. No part should appear to be so different from the rest, that it is noticeable. Just as we block in our drawings and plan foundation forms for our designs, our handicraft should be first roughly planned. Printers make a rough book first to try different arrangements. This rough book is termed a "dummy." We should make a dummy of our book. Only a few pages need be planned, but such pages should be planned very carefully.

END LEAVES AND BORDERS may be stick printed or stenciled. Borders may be used around the pages, or at the top and bottom only. A color should be used that will harmonize with the lettering or writing, and it should not be stronger than the rest of the page. Writing ink and water color on felt or blotters may be used upon which to press the stick or pencil end.

STENCIL DESIGNS may be cut in stiff paper; and a little library paste added to the water color paint will prevent its running under the edges of the stencils.

COVERS should be made of durable material, as they must protect the rest of the book. We may make them of stiff board covered with paper, or with linen or other artistic cloth. The cover may be made larger than the pages, or trimmed so as to be the same size.

THE COVER DESIGN may then be placed upon this material, either by drawing it in crayon, ink, or water color, or by stenciling or block printing.

TO BLOCK PRINT a design, we should cut the motif out of a piece of linoleum, smooth cardboard, or thick rubber, and mount it on a block of wood. If we place a little oil paint of the proper color, thinned with turpentine, upon a felt pad, we can press the block on this pad, and then on our cover surface.

CORRECT POSITION of each motif is secured by ruling with light lines with pencil or chalk, which will divide the cover up into a number of divisions to guide each impression.

CONSTRUCTION OF BOOKLETS and portfolios is shown on following pages, and other ways will be found by experimenting, and by studying how booklets and books are made that come to our hands. There are so many pleasing folders and booklets made for advertising purposes, that we can collect those which have interesting arrangements, and use them as models from which to work.

COVER LETTERING should be carefully drawn on a separate piece of paper, and then transferred to the cover before being finished. Lettering should never look too large or too small on the cover; and when it is used together with a design, the two should look well together. A good letter to use is shown in this chapter, and is planned by dividing each space into three divisions.

PLANNING LETTERING for a certain space prevents it from being too large or being placed too high or too low. After marking out for the lettering a space that looks well on the cover space, you should then retain the lettering within the space planned. A second way of doing this is to letter the wording out on a thin piece of paper, and then adjust it to the space on the cover, and trace it on for permanent location. Do not crowd the lettering. Keep spaces equal to a letter O between the words, and a good space between the lines. Study the different styles of lettering that you see on book covers.

WE WILL REMEMBER that in drawing, design, and handicraft, the important point is not how much work is placed on our paper or object, but how well that work is done; and we should endeavor to keep our work simple and restful.

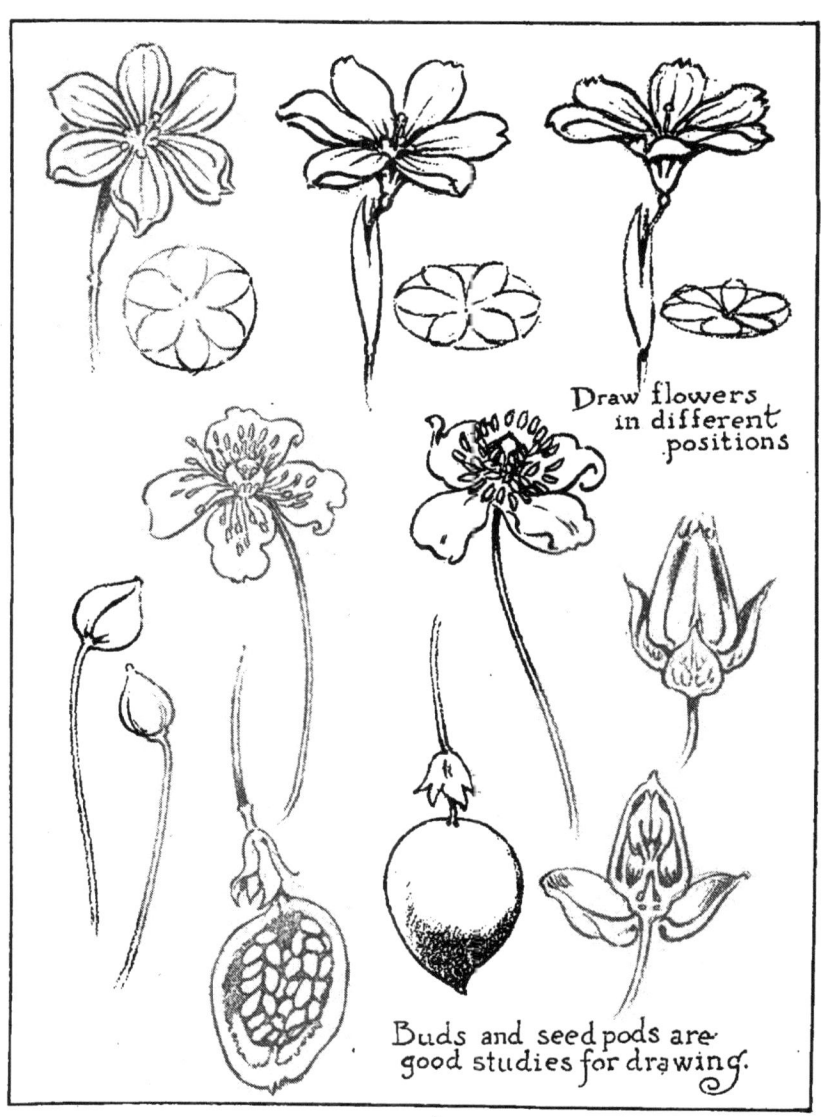

Draw flowers
in different
positions

Buds and seed pods are
good studies for drawing.

FLOWER DRAWING

Study and draw
simple leaves
and twigs

Study
the stem
connections

PLANT GROWTH DRAWINGS

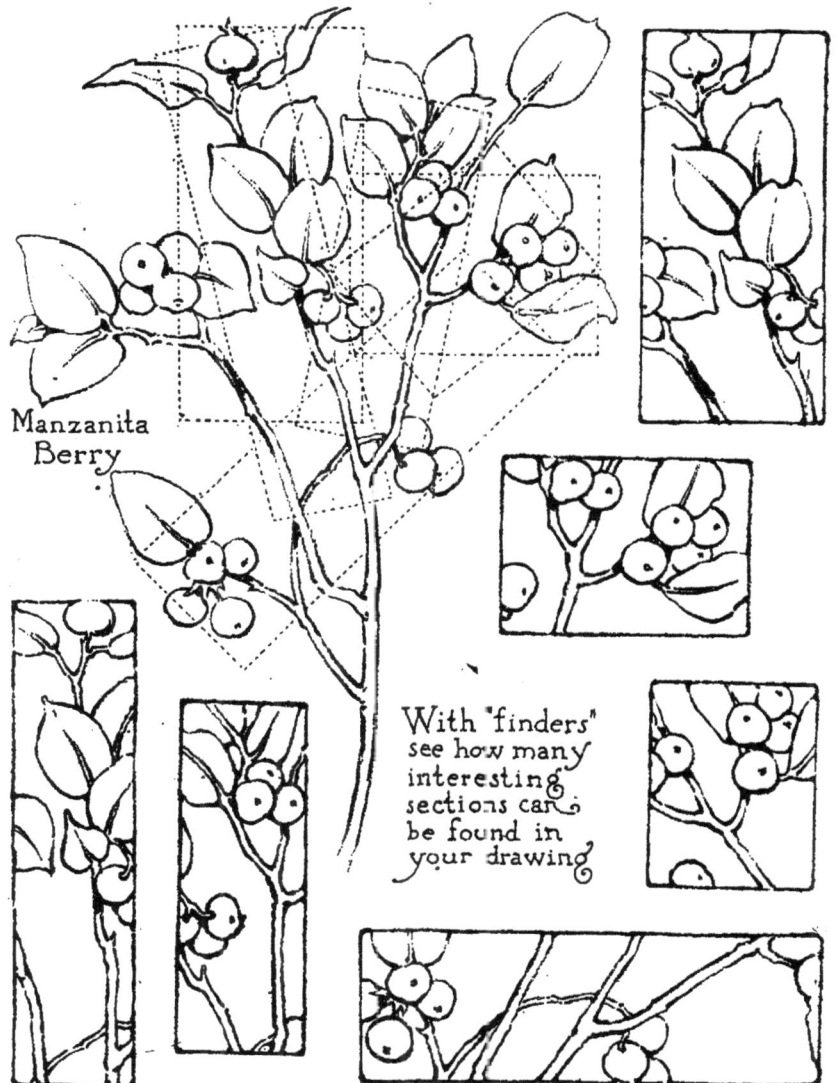

Manzanita
Berry

With "finders"
see how many
interesting
sections can
be found in
your drawing

COMPOSING PLANT DRAWINGS

LIGHT AND DARK PLANT DRAWING

White paint
for the light
parts
A little
black
added to
the white
will make
gray
For light lines
hold the brush upright
With a
full
brush
and
flat strokes
Paint your
subject in
white and
gray on
dark paper

LIGHT AND MIDDLE TONE ON BLACK PLANT DRAWINGS

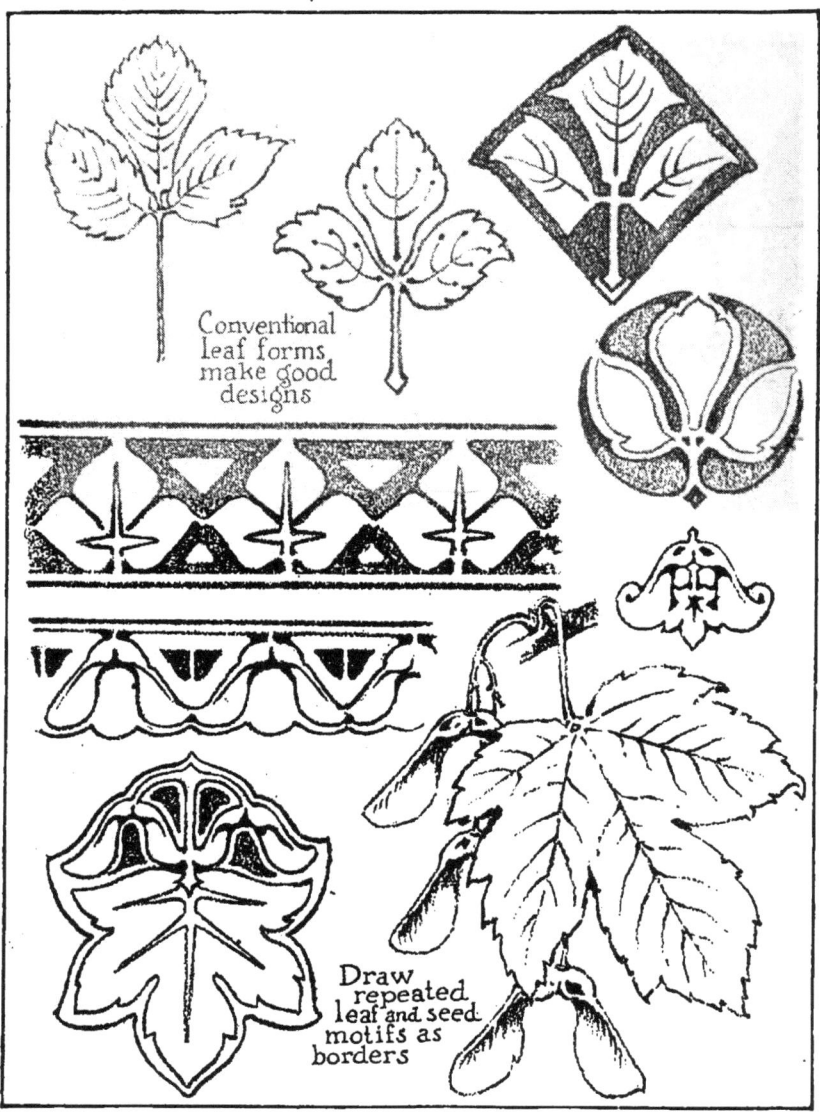

Conventional
leaf forms
make good
designs

Draw
repeated
leaf and seed
motifs as
borders

PLANT DESIGN

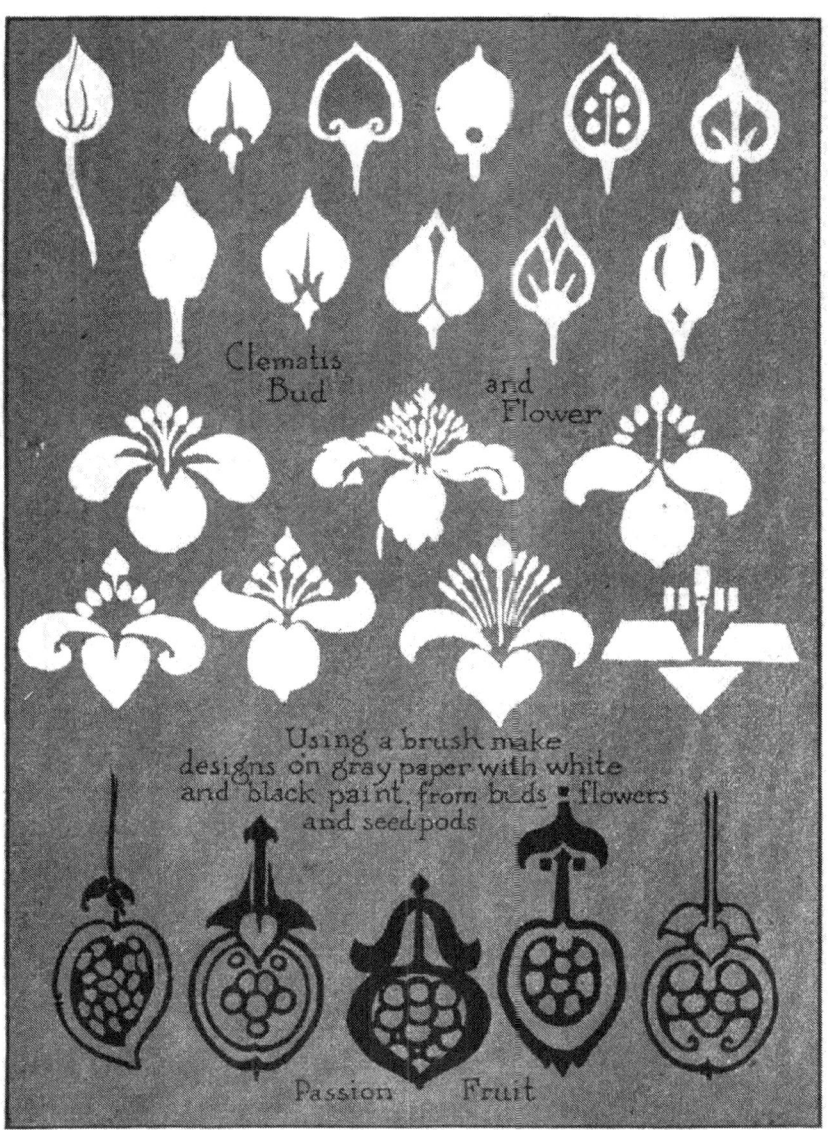

BUD, FLOWER, AND FRUIT MOTIFS

The simplest
geometric forms
repeated
will produce
the best
patterns

Design simple
borders and
all-over patterns
from simple
forms

GEOMETRIC ALL-OVER PATTERNS

By changing
simple geometric
forms into
ornaments
the pleasing
pattern is
still retained

Add but little
detail to the
less simple
motif forms

THE GEOMETRIC PATTERNS DEVELOPED

VARIOUS RENDERINGS OF FLOWER DESIGN

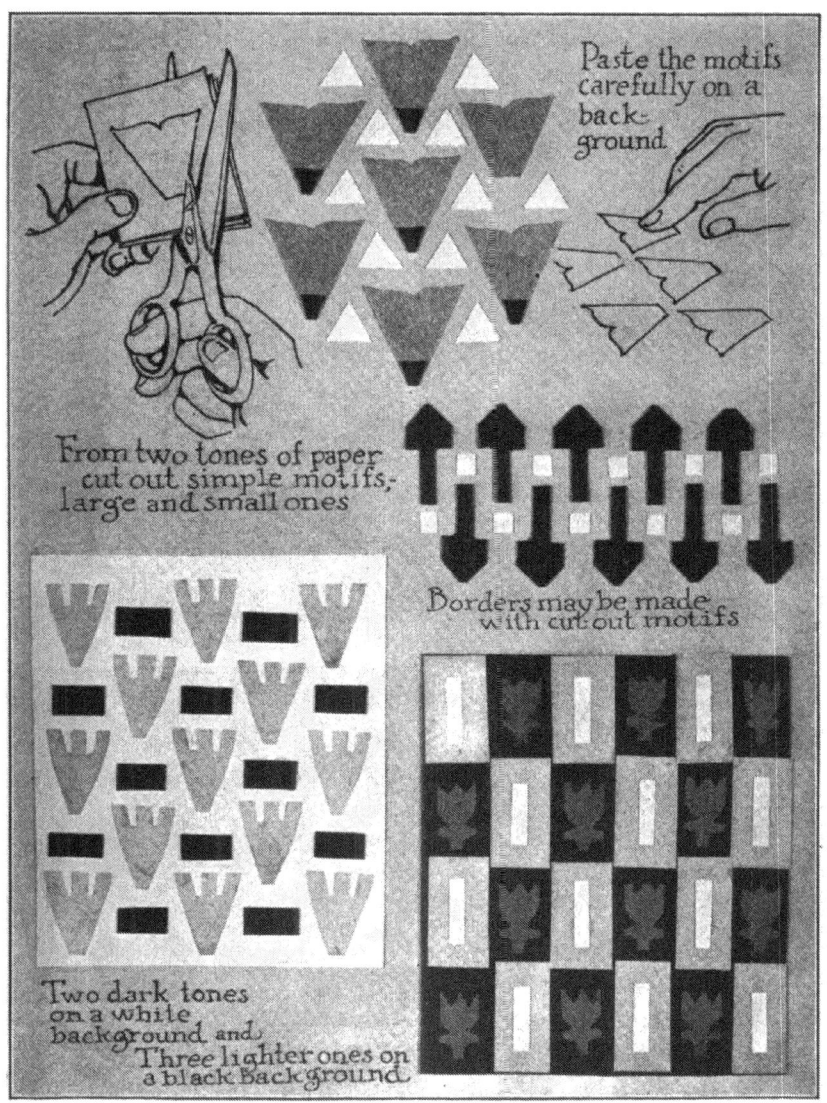

Paste the motifs carefully on a background.

From two tones of paper cut out simple motifs, large and small ones

Borders may be made with cut out motifs

Two dark tones on a white background and Three lighter ones on a black background

CUT PAPER PATTERNS

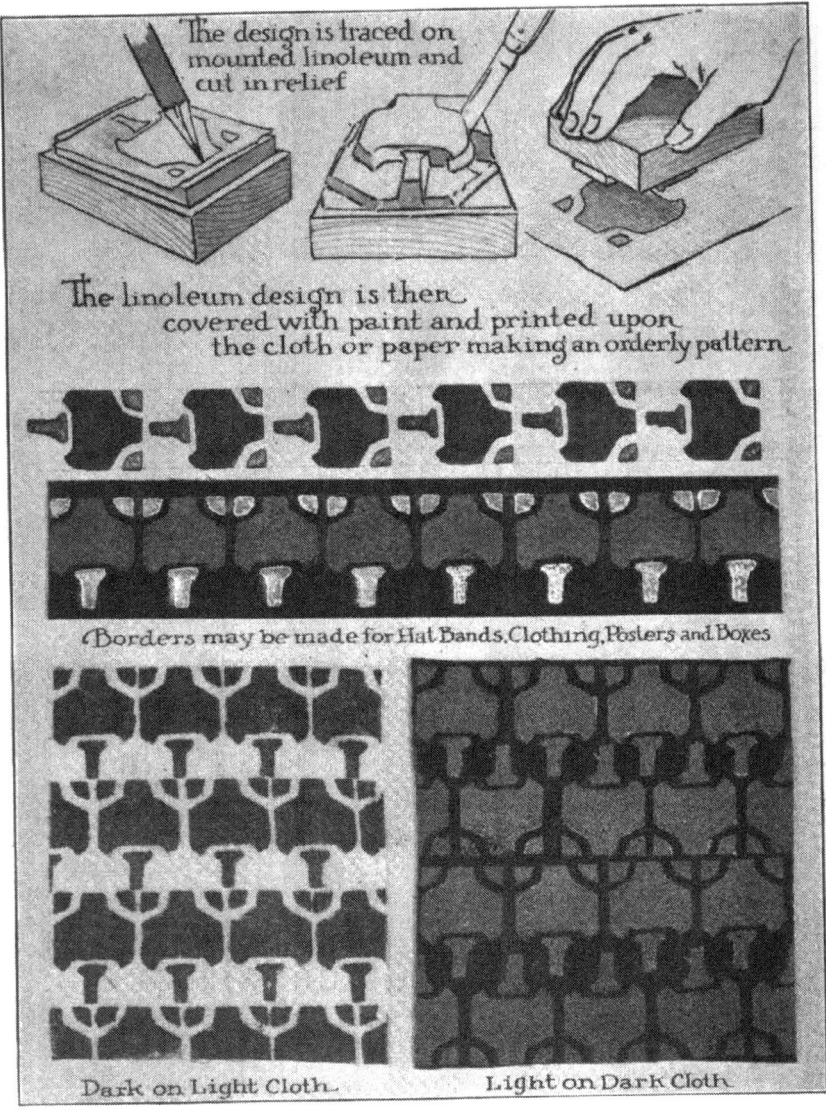

The design is traced on mounted linoleum and cut in relief

The linoleum design is then covered with paint and printed upon the cloth or paper making an orderly pattern

Borders may be made for Hat Bands, Clothing, Posters and Boxes

Dark on Light Cloth   Light on Dark Cloth

HOW TO BLOCK PRINT

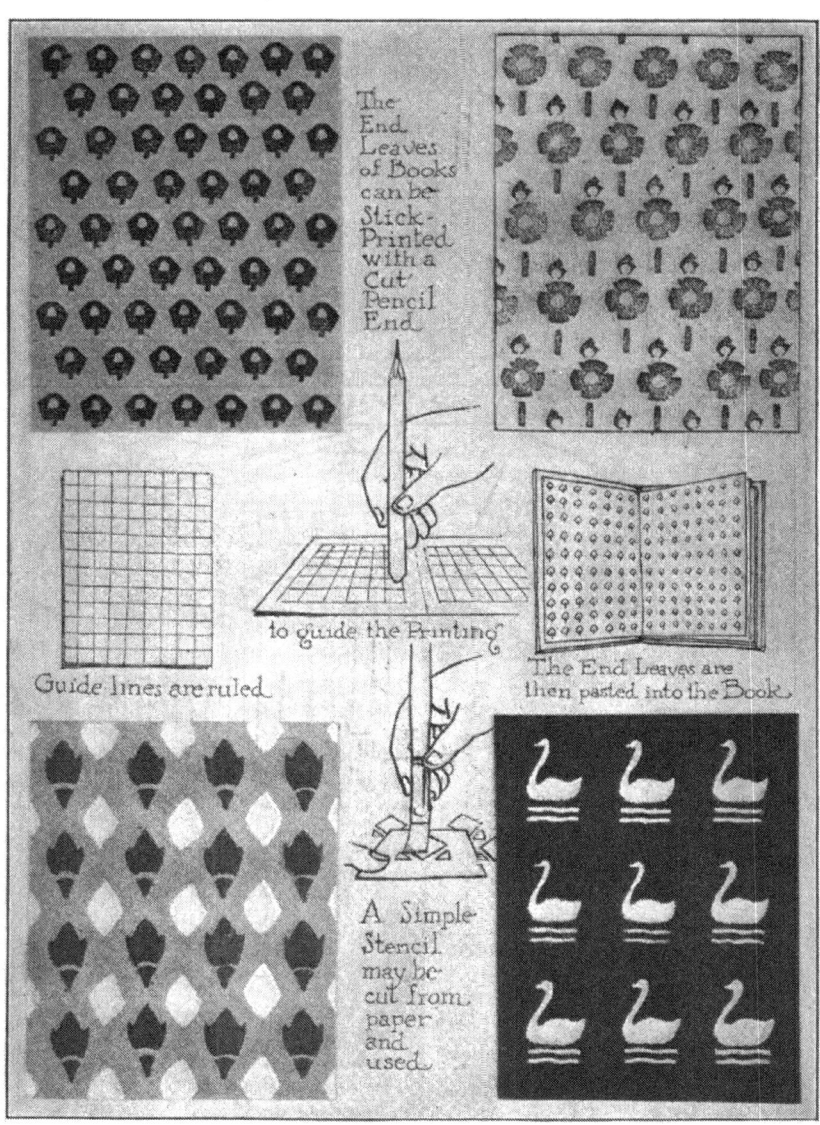

The
End
Leaves
of Books
can be
Stick-
Printed
with a
Cut
Pencil
End

to guide the Printing

Guide lines are ruled

The End Leaves are
then pasted into the Book

A Simple
Stencil
may be
cut from
paper
and
used

STICK-PRINTING END LEAVES

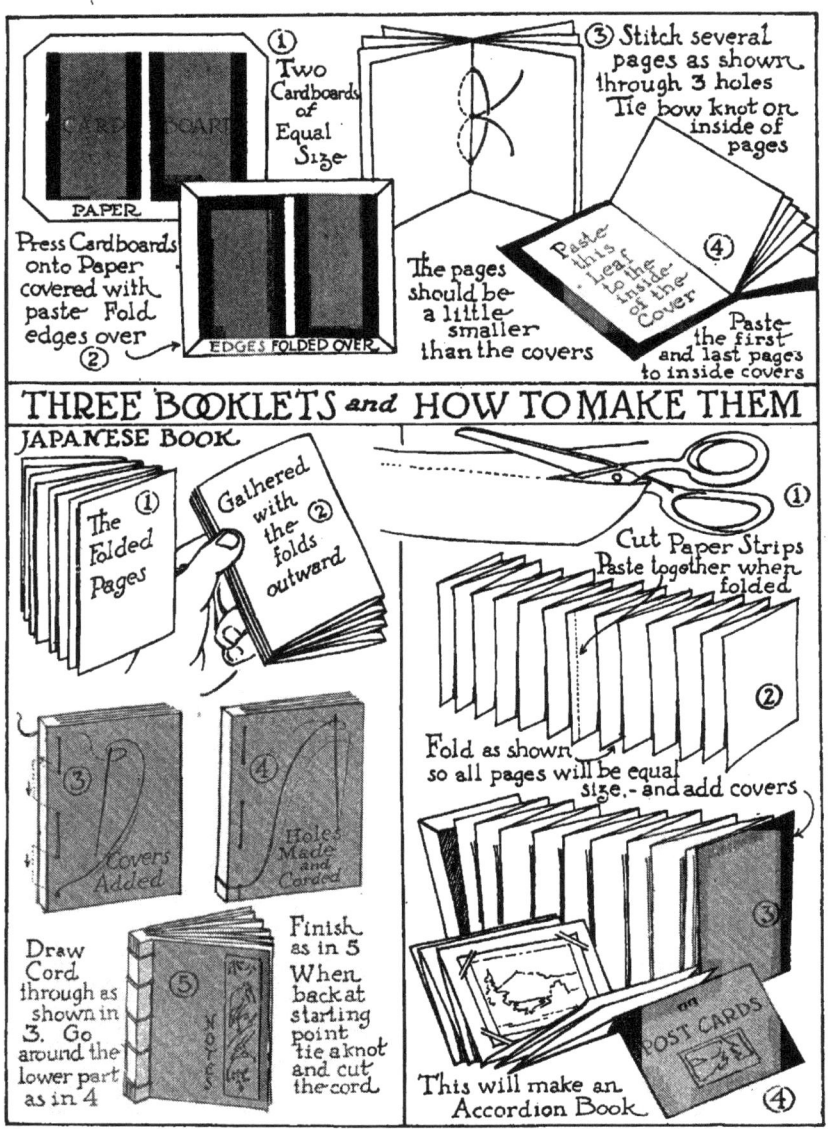

① Two Cardboards of Equal Size

③ Stitch several pages as shown through 3 holes Tie bow knot on inside of pages

CARDBOARD

PAPER

Press Cardboards onto Paper covered with paste Fold edges over ②

EDGES FOLDED OVER

The pages should be a little smaller than the covers

④ Paste this Leaf to the inside of the Cover

Paste the first and last pages to inside covers

THREE BOOKLETS and HOW TO MAKE THEM

JAPANESE BOOK

① The Folded Pages

② Gathered with the folds outward

③ Covers Added

④ Holes Made and Corded

⑤ Draw Cord through as shown in 3. Go around the lower part as in 4

Finish as in 5 When back at starting point tie a knot and cut the cord

① Cut Paper Strips Paste together when folded

② Fold as shown so all pages will be equal size. — and add covers

③

POST CARDS

④ This will make an Accordion Book

BOOKLET CONSTRUCTION

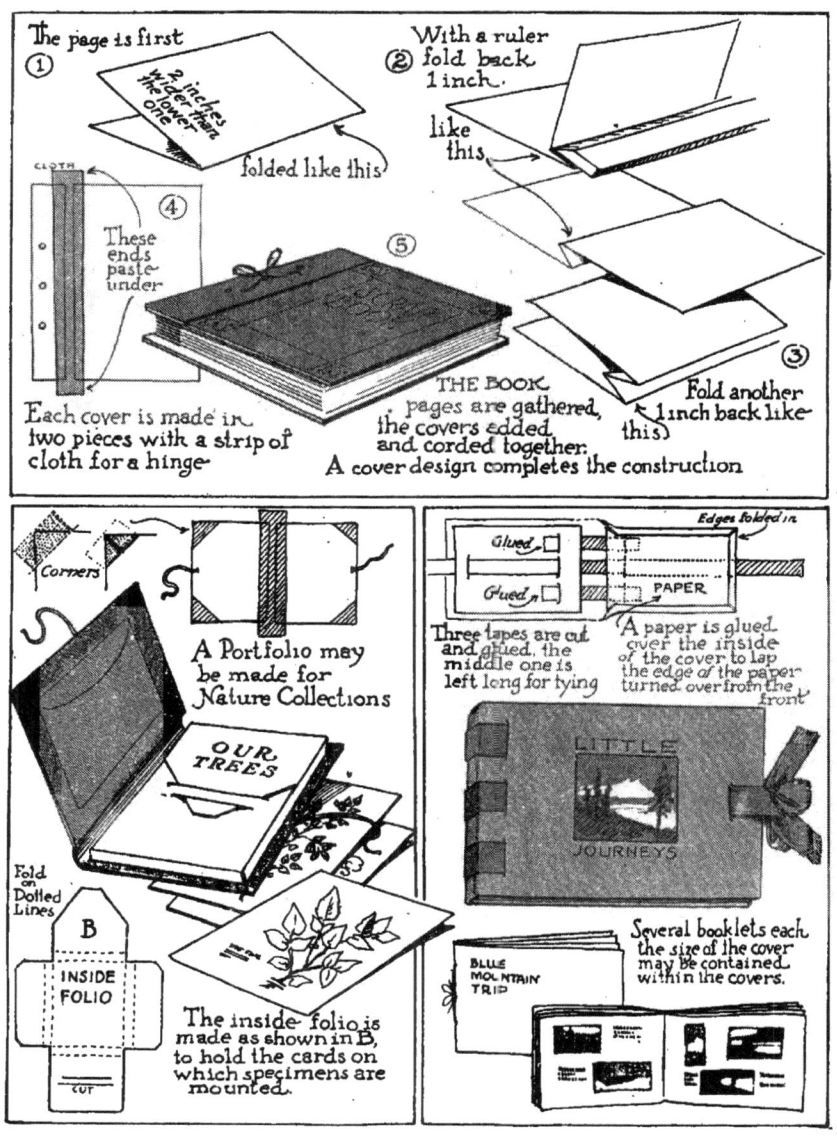

① The page is first folded like this (2 inches wider than the lower one)

② With a ruler fold back 1 inch. like this

③ Fold another 1 inch back like this

④ CLOTH These ends paste under

⑤ THE BOOK pages are gathered, the covers added and corded together. A cover design completes the construction.

Each cover is made in two pieces with a strip of cloth for a hinge.

Corners

A Portfolio may be made for Nature Collections

OUR TREES

Fold on Dotted Lines

B INSIDE FOLIO CUT

The inside folio is made as shown in B, to hold the cards on which specimens are mounted.

Edges folded in

Glued   Glued   PAPER

Three tapes are cut and glued, the middle one is left long for tying

A paper is glued over the inside of the cover to lap the edge of the paper turned over from the front

LITTLE JOURNEYS

BLUE MOUNTAIN TRIP

Several booklets each the size of the cover may be contained within the covers.

THE MAKING OF BOOKS AND PORTFOLIOS

ABCDE
FGHIJK
LMNOP
QRSTU
VWXYZ
1234567890

Points of
V.A.W
should extend
above and

below lines

Triangle
shaped
Letters
should have
a space be-
tween like
this

Top and
Bottom Curve
of Round
Letters should
extend beyond
lines

Plan the
letter S
over
a figure 8

Lettering should always be placed
above the center of the cover

NATURE
NOTES

Plan
Lettering
Carefully

RECIPE
BOOK

Lettering
should
Harmonize
with the
Design

COLOR
NOTES

LETTERING CONSTRUCTION

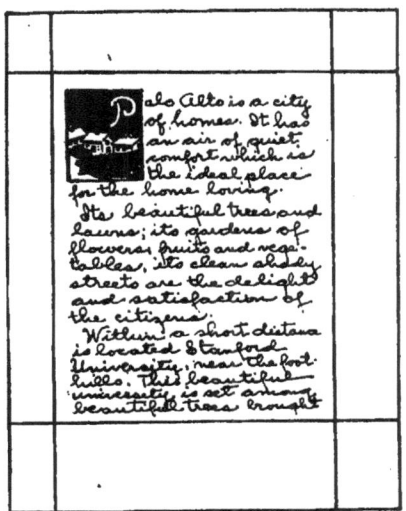

AN INDIAN STORY

...running down the trail as fast as his legs would go to the tepee of White Fox. All the boys and girls who saw little Wah-hee running al so ran after him, so that outside of White Fox's tepee you could see little sisters with papooses on their back and brothers with their bows and arrows and dogs.

While Wah-hee was talking and telling of the strange things he had seen in the Blue Forest, some figures on horseback were seen in the distance.

← This side toward the middle of the book.

Four ways to arrange the pages of your booklet or composition book. Cut pictures from magazines for illustrations.

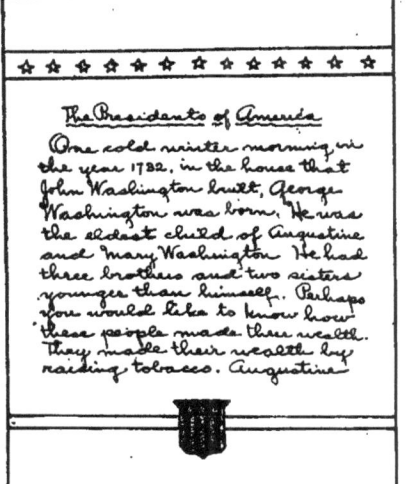

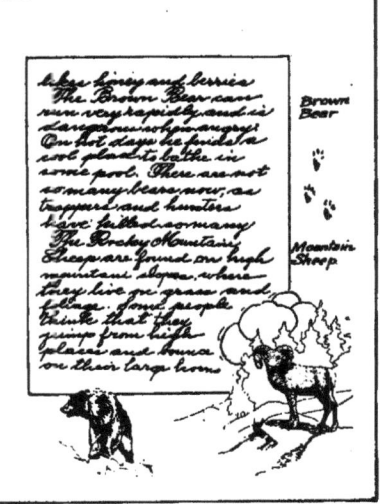

PAGE ARRANGEMENTS

TEACHER'S NOTES FOR THE SEVENTH YEAR

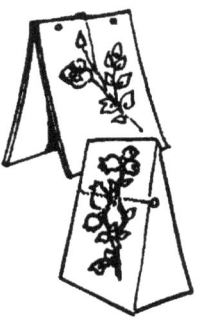

DESK EASELS. These may be made by fastening two pieces of cardboard together at the top or by turning back edges of the cardboard so as to permit them to stand well when placed on the desk. To these, the flower or other subject may be fastened by overhanging string or by an elastic passing across the front. Each student can easily make his own desk easel as part of his handicraft problems. With uniform measurements planned by the teacher, all desk easels will be uniform in proportions, creating more unity in room appearance when the class is at work. Good boards to use are strawboard or tar board, which should be covered with a neutral-colored paper. The neutral-colored paper will serve the double purpose of giving a suitable background and preventing the cardboard from injury by moisture from plants.

THE USE OF PASTE. Most students use too much paste, or too little where it is most needed. A scrap of straight-edged cardboard will be found excellent to distribute the paste over large surfaces. Paste once hardened and then softened is never as satisfactory as fresh paste, for it will have a large amount of hard granules, which will show through the paper pasted. Before any paper is pasted, it should be slightly sponged on one side, and then the paste applied on the opposite side. This prevents curling up of the paper, and faulty drying after it is pasted. A ruler edge, if used to press pasted surfaces down, will help them to stick. Unfastened surfaces are often due to air that has been arrested when the sheet was placed upon the pasted surface. To avoid this, pasted sheets should be placed so that one edge is properly located, and then the rest of the surface should be gradually permitted to roll into place. The sheet should never be dropped onto its location.

SAMPLE LIBRARY. Every printer, designer, and artist retains examples of artistic printed productions that come to his hands. There can be no greater help to the teacher in book construction, lettering, and handicraft than the assembling of such matter for reference. Boxes, portfolios, and scrapbooks may be used for orderly arrangement of all such material, so that the student may readily see how others have executed the problem in which he is interested. Careful mounting on medium gray cards will go far toward increasing the value of such a library.

OTHER HELPS. A visit by the class to a book publishing plant, if possible, will create an interest in the making of books. If such a trip is impossible, a description by the teacher, with examples of progressive book construction, will do much toward creating a greater care and appreciation for books. Printers are generally willing to assist in giving any information for such purposes.

A paper cutter is a great help in cutting paper in the classroom. Different sizes are securable, and insure square corners in cutting.

A safety benzine can for holding gasoline or benzine where such liquids are used in the classroom will prevent accidents and save waste.

LANDSCAPES IN COLORED CRAYON

TREE POSTERS

THE EIGHTH YEAR

DRAWING AND PAINTING

NATURE DRAWING is incomplete without a good knowledge of how to draw trees both in line and in color. We should know how to draw and paint them easily, because the looseness of the foliage and the gracefulness of tree forms require that they be drawn easily, so that they will not appear stiff.

EACH TREE HAS A TYPICAL FORM, which, if identified and first blocked in, will help the finished drawing to have the same character as the tree. We recognize trees at a distance by their shapes; and while there are different species of trees having similar shapes, still in turn the foliages or the way the masses of foliage join the main trunk will be found to be different.

THE CORRECT SHAPE of the tree should be carefully drawn before any of the detail is attempted. After the main mass is drawn, then the larger foliage divisions should be indicated, and the prominent parts of the outline.

TREE OPENINGS, or the spaces of sky or background that appear through the tree, should be carefully outlined. This careful planning of the form, outline, and openings is necessary, in order that once the drawing or the painting is commenced, no hesitation as to where certain parts end and others begin will be evident in the finished drawing.

THE BEST DRAWINGS are those which have the appearance of having been made with confidence and perfect knowledge of the construction of every part. There should be no guessing as to which direction the pencil, crayon, or brush should be carried.

THE BEST FOLIAGE LINES are made in the direction that the foliage grows. Some tree foliages consist of long, drooping leaves, while others consist of large, flat leaves, or of needles, like the pine, which radiate from many points. A little practice on a separate piece of paper, using pencil strokes that indicate the character of the tree foliage, will enable us to secure the right "swing" before doing the real drawing.

A GOOD WAY TO STUDY TREES is to make drawings of them when the leaves have fallen, as the branches make the form of the trees, and the twigs show where the leaves will be. Artists study the skeleton

(191)

of the human figure, in order that they may draw the figure more correctly; and they also draw the tree skeleton, in order that they may know
how to draw the tree better when the leaves are on.

STUDY THE BRANCH CONNECTIONS carefully. Tree limbs
should not be drawn as though stuck on, but as part of the whole tree.
Nature has provided a strong support to limbs as they connect one with
another, and as each large limb connects with the parent trunk. A beginner at drawing trees can always be known by the way the tree limbs
are joined to each other on his drawings.

PENCIL DRAWINGS can be made by holding the pencil flat and
making the strokes so that they follow the right direction. These strokes
should all be of one tone, in order that the tree may appear as a gray silhouette of pencil marks without any darker or lighter parts. Now we
know that the tree we are drawing from has dark sides, and that the
masses of foliage have dark sides, which are always on the opposite side
from where the light strikes.

WHEN IT IS HARD TO RECOGNIZE LIGHT AND SHADE on a
tree, partly close the eyes, and the shades will become simplified, so that
you will know just about how much shade to indicate in your drawing.
The smaller details of shades, or shadows, and the unimportant details
of the outline, should be left off, as they add nothing to the subject, and
would really detract from the strength of our drawing if added.

THE SILHOUETTE IDEA should be used throughout our tree drawings, and can be planned in three steps, whichever of the drawing me-
diums is used, as pencil, crayon, pen and ink, or brush. First, the whole
form should be carefully planned, with the openings and prominent parts
of the outline indicated. Second, the general shade should be placed
within the form outline in a flat value. Third, then the darks are added,
which complete the drawing.

CHARCOAL WORK is a good means of drawing trees. By drawing
our trees large, as is generally done if we use charcoal, we are more
sure to become acquainted with their character, or "anatomy," as it is
called. To do a tree in charcoal, we first put on a flat gray tone to show
the main parts of the tree. Then with a soft eraser or what is called
a "kneaded eraser," we pick out the light spots. Last we add the dark
parts found in the shadows of the foliage and trunk.

INTERESTING TREE DRAWINGS by Japanese artists are shown
on page 199 in this chapter. Notice the direct way in which the little
branches, which grow off to each side of the main trunk, have been put

in. See how the artist has observed the rough, pebbly bark on his tree, and has worked it in. All these drawings have been done with the brush. The more brush work you learn to do, the better artist you will be.

TREES, LIKE PEOPLE, ARE FULL OF CHARACTER. They are not only beautiful and interesting, but they make us think of people. In springtime, the orchard trees, with their beautiful pink and white blossoms, make us think of a bride. And what could resemble an old, crabbed man more than some of the oaks we see growing on the hillside? Battered by wind and weather, they still hold sturdily to their ground, as if to say, "This hill is mine, and I'm going to stick right here." Some pictures of such trees are shown on page 202.

LANDSCAPES made in three tones of cut-out paper are fine practice. They are not only easier to make than those we have just talked about, but in most cases they look better. What could be prettier than the little landscape of the castle up on the hilltop, which you see on page 204? Even if we are drawing in water colors, this is a good style to follow. In making landscapes in cut-out paper, always remember to paste down the parts first that should go underneath. This saves extra work in cutting out and matching pieces.

SOME GOOD LANDSCAPES can also be made by using black and white crayons on gray or brown paper. Crayons are good to use where you wish to make little sketches out of doors and find water colors too inconvenient. Some of our best magazine illustrations are made with a pencil that resembles our crayons in texture.

STAINED GLASS DESIGNS have to be made in the right way or they will not be a success when worked out in the glass. After an artist has made his little color sketch for a stained glass window, the workmen in the factory make a large pattern of it in heavy paper the same size the window is to be. They cut this paper pattern into sections, just as a woman cuts a dress pattern, and use these patterns to cut their glass by. But glass is not as easy to handle as cloth or paper. The colored glass has to be cut with a little glass cutter, which has either a diamond point or a little wheel on it for cutting the glass. When a small groove has been cut, then the glass is broken apart by bending it or tapping it. For this reason, any very long, slim shapes, or shapes that turn corners and come back again, like a horseshoe, will not cut successfully from glass. This is because when the workman tries to cut glass this way, it breaks across the thin parts or at the

13 Applied Art

corners. This is why, in making a sketch for a stained glass design, you should always try to divide it into parts that look as though they would cut easily out of glass. The little thin lines you see in the picture represent the lead strips that are used to hold the glass together.

The last drawing on this page shows the tree used in a pen and ink drawing for a book plate. These book plates are pasted to the inside cover of people's books, so that when the books are lent, people will know to whom they should be returned.

LANDSCAPES give us a fine opportunity to study color. Every time we go outdoors, we can see color all about us. The green grass and the bright flowers, the hillside, the blue ocean, the gorgeous sunset, and the rich moonlight,—all these give us a chance to study color. We soon learn that each color has its own meaning or message for us. No one would think of painting a snow picture in reds and oranges, because these are colors of warmth, and not of coldness.

IN STUDYING TREES, we learn that some are a brighter green than others. Some may be a light yellow-green, and others a deep gray-green quite different from the yellow-green. Some tree trunks are a deep red-brown, others a blue-gray, and still others a tan. The more we study trees, the more color we see in them. You will find that wherever the sunlight hits the leaves, they are colored a golden yellow. Wherever the tree is in shadow, the shadow color has a little purple in it. Many designers get ideas for their color schemes by studying the color combinations found in rocks and trees and flowers.

COLOR DRAWINGS FOR STAINED GLASS are made so as to resemble the effect of the glass. By dripping colors together when they are wet, we obtain the mottled effect found in the stained glass coloring. The next time you go to some place where there is a stained glass window, as a church or a library, take a look at it, and you will see that the blues run into the greens, the yellows run into the reds, and so forth. To obtain this effect, we should first pencil our sketch out carefully. After this is done, we should dampen the drawing all over with plain water on our brush. When the paper is nearly dry, we begin to drip our colors on the drawing. If, for instance, we have dripped on a green tone, we can drip a blue tone right next to it, and let the two colors run together. After the colors have dried, we should outline all the pieces of glass with our brush and black ink or water color. This line will help to hold our drawing together, and represents the lead line found in stained glass. You can make some beautiful little drawings in this manner.

DESIGN

DESIGNING LANDSCAPES is a little different from drawing or painting them. When we make our paintings, we often try to get more or less realistic effects by shading them up with high lights and shadows. In designing landscapes, we keep everything flat and simple, as though it were cut out of paper. That is why paper cut-out landscapes are good training for us. They help us to see our scenes in this flat, simple way.

IN SKETCHING OUT OF DOORS, most young artists become confused. They see around them so much that is good to draw, that they try to do the whole thing on one sheet of paper. The result is naturally very disappointing. They soon give up in despair. The right way to sketch out of doors is to select one thing of interest, like an old oak tree, a little bridge, or some one's cottage.

After you have decided what to sketch, the next thing is to see if you can plan it on paper so that it makes an interesting page, or "composition," as artists call it. On page 206, you will find a series of drawings showing you how to select interesting pictures from scenes around you.

FINE EXAMPLES OF TREES and landscapes done with the brush, and with parts filled in, are shown on page 207. This begins to be like the Japanese style, and will help us to get freedom and confidence in our work. You will notice that the pictures have been planned so that the black spots have been nicely distributed over the design. This "spotting," as designers often call it, helps to hold the picture together and to make it pleasing to the eye. Practice is required to do this correctly and to know just where to put our spots. Notice that the little tree on the left of the picture, and the row of trees in the distance, have been made black to balance off the large black tree on the right-hand side.

VARYING THE THICKNESS of our lines is one way in which we can help give distance in our brush drawings. If you will look again at the drawing, you will see that the trees in the middle of the scene have been made heavier than the mountains away off in the background. This plan of making some of our brush outlines heavier than others, and of keeping them lighter the farther away they get, helps us to make our picture look as though it had distance and atmosphere in it.

TREE BORDERS are a natural step from tree landscapes. They are one means of using the tree sketches we have made in our previous work. On page 208, eight different kinds of tree borders are shown. Every one of these is different, yet each one is beautiful. At the top, we have a row of trees done with a brush in black and white. In making such a border, we should first design our decorative tree, then repeat four or five times by tracing it. In tracing, we should be careful to space our trees just far enough apart to make them interesting, and yet to hold them together. You will notice that the line drawn at the bottom of this border helps to hold it together.

LOOK AT THE TREES on page 209. Here we see two trees from Sicily, a Greek tree, an Assyrian tree, two Persian trees, one Chinese, and one Coptic. The Coptic designs were made by early Egyptians who had turned Christian. Every one of these trees is done in a different way, yet each fits the purpose for which it was intended. We find trees much used in tapestries and rugs, in shawls, tablecloths, scarfs, drapes, and in hundreds of other places. Some of our most beautiful books have covers stamped with tree designs. The ability to draw a decorative tree is worth a great deal to you. Do you think you could make one? Copy some from this tree page, then try one of your own.

HANDICRAFT

THE WASTE BASKETS are made of heavy cardboard laced together with heavy cord or with raffia. The designs may be stenciled on with crayons or opaque water color. Where the parts are not laced together, the corners may be made stronger by putting cloth strips on the inside. Another way to decorate these cardboard objects would be to cut the designs from colored paper and paste them on the cardboard. This way is about the best of any, if done right. In making things like these, be careful to get all the sides alike, and to cut them evenly, so as not to have waste baskets and boxes that are crooked and will not stand up right.

OBJECTS MADE IN WOOD are also shown. A boy or a girl who has a little sloyd saw and can get some thin wood to work with, can learn to make many useful articles, as well as have an enjoyable time. Book ends like those at the top of the page are fine things to make. The designs can be painted on with enamel paints, or with opaque water colors and shellac.

THE FLOWER HOLDER AND THE NECKTIE RACK are two other good objects to make. By putting an ordinary jelly glass inside the little box, we have a very satisfactory flower holder. Care should be taken to make these things neatly and to have the different sides fit together well. Every artist should be a good craftsman too.

HOW TO MAKE A TREE BOOK is shown on page 212. The pictures tell us just how the work is done, step by step. A desirable size for the pages is 6 x 8 inches or 8 x 11 inches. To make the pages, we should take a piece of paper just twice this size and fold it over. This gives us two leaves for our book. Next we put about six or eight of these leaves together and stitch them as shown in step 1 on the drawing. Several of these groups of pages may then be sewed together as in step 2. This makes the inside of our book.

THE BOOK COVERS can be cut from heavy cardboard and pasted to the outside leaves of our book. Then a sheet of heavy paper, any color we like, is folded around the book and glued to the inside of the covers. This is shown in step 4. This makes a practical book and one that is not difficult to put together. Inside you can put sketches of trees, studies of their leaves and buds, and other things of interest about trees. Some neatly written or lettered pages about trees can be put in as shown in the picture. Most of us see and admire trees every day, yet there are not many of us who know much about their names and habits. A book like this would help us to get acquainted with them.

LANTERNS and how they are made is the subject of page 213. We can nearly always buy Japanese lanterns, but it is much more interesting for us to make our own. We can learn to make lanterns which, hung over an electric light globe, will add an artistic touch to our homes. Six different kinds of lanterns are drawn here. They can be made of colored paper, with heavy black paper for the edges. The sides may be made of thin pieces of colored paper pasted over one another, or part of the design may be painted on in transparent water colors.

A PAPER PATTERN should first be made, similar to the one shown at the bottom of the page. The pattern we have here will make the kind of lantern top shown on the left-hand side of the second row. The parts are fastened together with glue, and pressed together well. Try to keep the outside surfaces free from any glue marks, as these would spoil the looks of your lantern. All the lanterns shown were actually made and used, and looked very beautiful when lighted up.

AN ALPHABET that can be made with a brush is the one we shall try this year. This alphabet is very similar in appearance to one used a great deal by architects. It is not only artistic, but is simply constructed and easy to letter. You will notice that the round letters like O and Q are very wide. This is one of the characteristic points of this alphabet.

SOME GOOD DRILLS to try before making your letters are given on page 214. These will make your hand steady, and teach you to make your curved letters more graceful. A picture has been drawn to show you how to hold your brush in making curved letters. This is the way the professional letterers hold their brushes. Holding your brush this way gives you a better control of it and more freedom in turning corners on letters.

TRY THE SMALL LETTERS after you have made the large ones; and last, the numbers. Very few people can make artistic numbers, yet we write numbers almost every day. Do not be discouraged if your hand shakes and does not go where you want it to go, when you hold your brush upright. Little by little, you will find yourself more able to make good strokes with your brush held this way; and the system, once learned, will prove very valuable to you.

OUR MODELING PROBLEM this year will be to plan houses and gardens and to construct them with clay and paper. This is valuable training for us, and will also teach us to observe the homes in which we live, to see how they can be made beautiful and practical. Work of this kind will help us to learn house and garden planning, which is a study that comes very close to everyday life.

DIFFERENT HOUSE PLANS may be sketched on paper before we select the one we are to make. Having decided upon the right one, we can then lay off our garden in the sand table. A little place like the one shown in the picture would be the kind to make. The house can be made of heavy cardboard, painted any colors we like, and the trees and the shrubbery of a little lighter cardboard. The trees and the shrubs will look better if they are torn from paper, rather than cut out, as cutting gives them too stiff an edge.

CLAY can be used for the stones in the path, for the foundation of the house, and for the wall. Little marks scratched into the wall will make it look like stone, or it may be worked up to represent a hedge. Small sticks of wood can be used to make the beams of the pergola. The clay may be made to look more like stone by setting little stones and pebbles into it. When you are through making a place like this, you will not only have had a good time, but will have learned many valuable things.

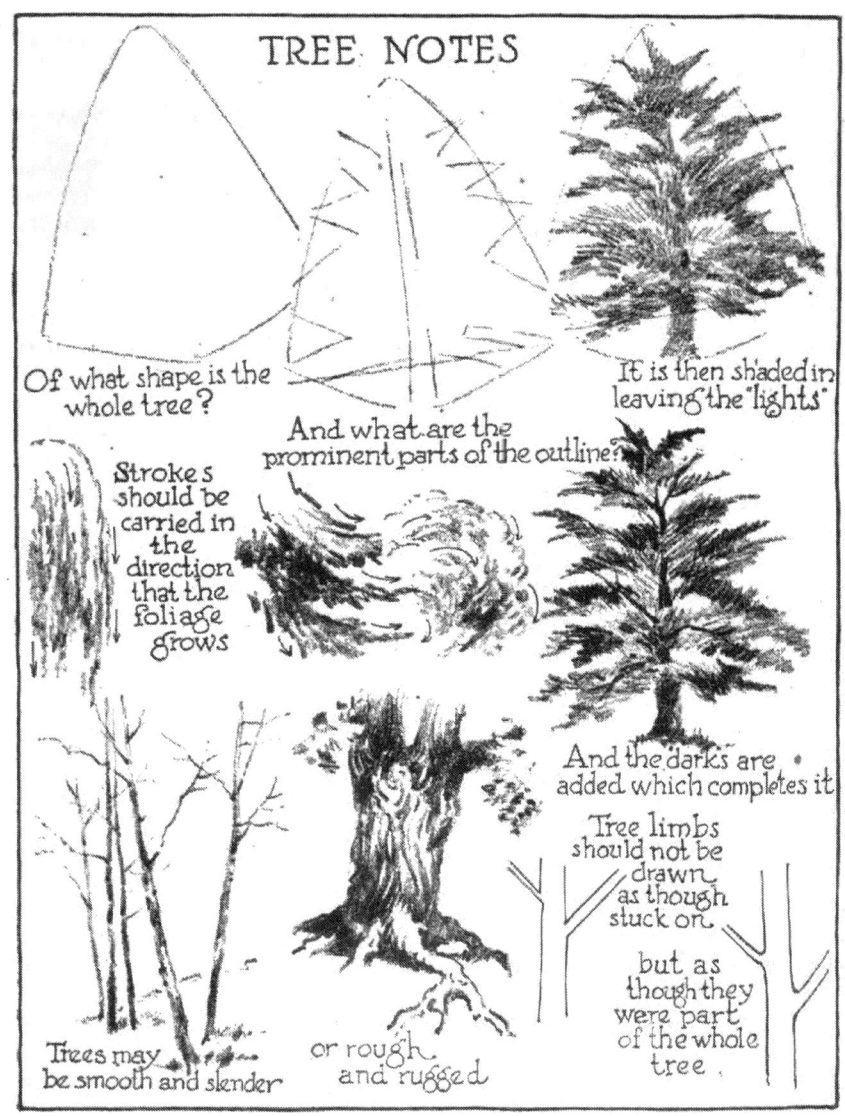

TREE NOTES

Of what shape is the whole tree?

And what are the prominent parts of the outline?

It is then shaded in leaving the "lights"

Strokes should be carried in the direction that the foliage grows

And the darks are added which completes it

Tree limbs should not be drawn as though stuck on

but as though they were part of the whole tree

Trees may be smooth and slender

or rough and rugged

HELPS IN DRAWING TREES

BRUSH WORK
A Silhouette in
Halftone first.
Then the "darks"
are added.

PENCIL WORK
Form is first drawn
in flat tone, leav-
ing the "lights."
Dark tones are
then added.

CHARCOAL WORK
The "lights" are erased
out of the flat tone and the
"darks" are then drawn.

THREE WAYS TO DRAW TREES

JAPANESE BRUSH DRAWINGS

BRUSH DRAWINGS OF TREES

FOUR WAYS TO DRAW LANDSCAPES

CUT PAPER AND CRAYON LANDSCAPES

PENCIL SKETCH

COVER DESIGN

STAINED GLASS

BOOK PLATE

THE APPLICATION OF A TREE DRAWING

PORTIONS OF LANDSCAPE AS PICTURES

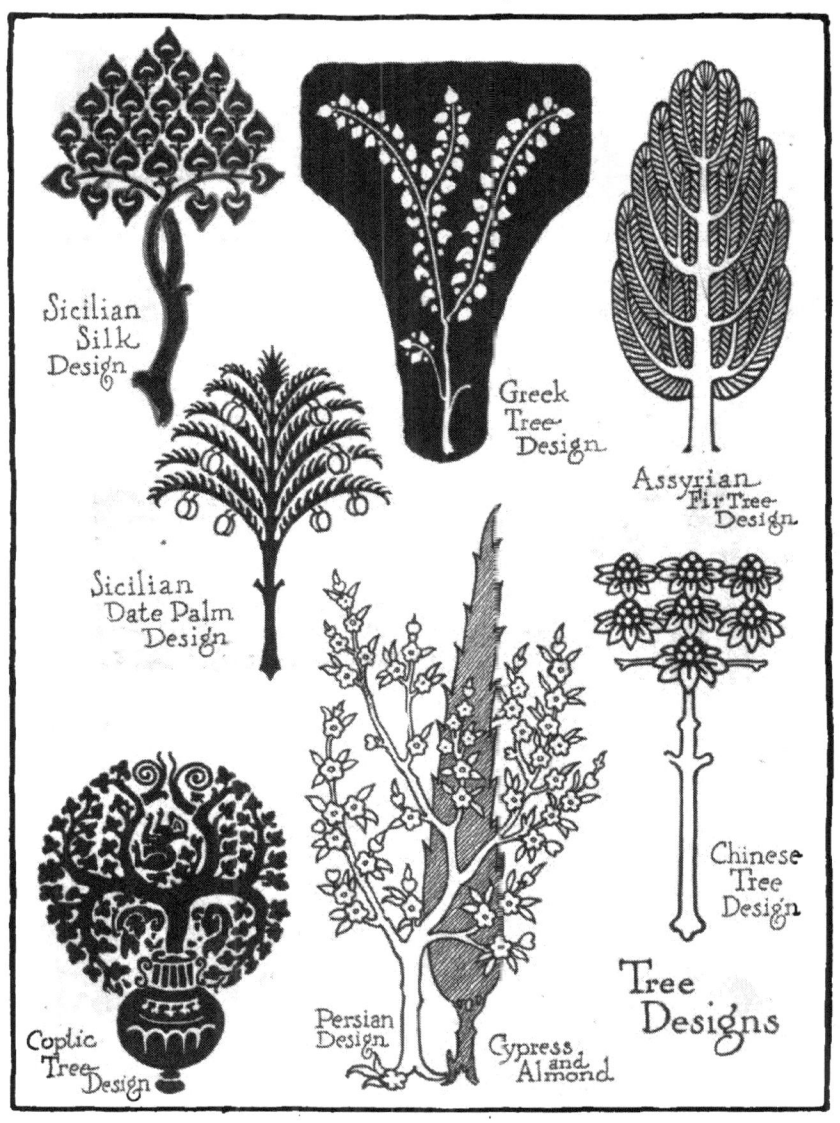

Sicilian Silk Design

Greek Tree Design

Assyrian Fir Tree Design

Sicilian Date Palm Design

Chinese Tree Design

Coptic Tree Design

Persian Design

Cypress and Almond

Tree Designs

HISTORIC TREE DESIGNS

14 Applied Art

Decorate Cardboard Objects with Tree Designs

Waste Baskets

Pencil Holder

Corners may be made stronger with cloth strips

Blank

Calendar and Pad

Desk Tray

Seed Box

CARDBOARD CONSTRUCTION

THIN WOOD
OBJECTS MAY BE
DECORATED WITH
TREE MOTIFS

BOOK SUPPORTS

GLASS

MATCH BOX

PENCIL BOX

FLOWER HOLDER

TIE RACK

PIN CUSHION

THIN WOOD CONSTRUCTION

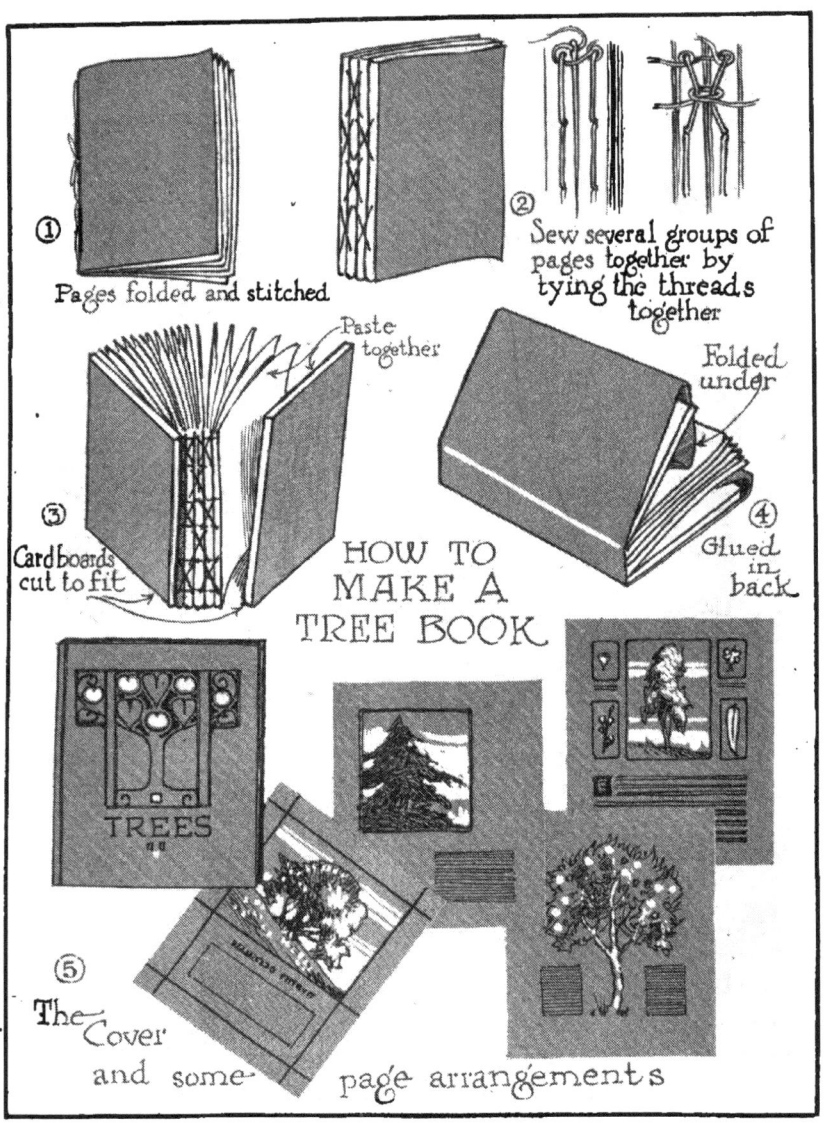

① Pages folded and stitched

② Sew several groups of pages together by tying the threads together

Paste together

③ Cardboards cut to fit

Folded under

④ Glued in back

HOW TO MAKE A TREE BOOK

TREES

⑤ The Cover and some page arrangements

HOW TO MAKE A TREE BOOK

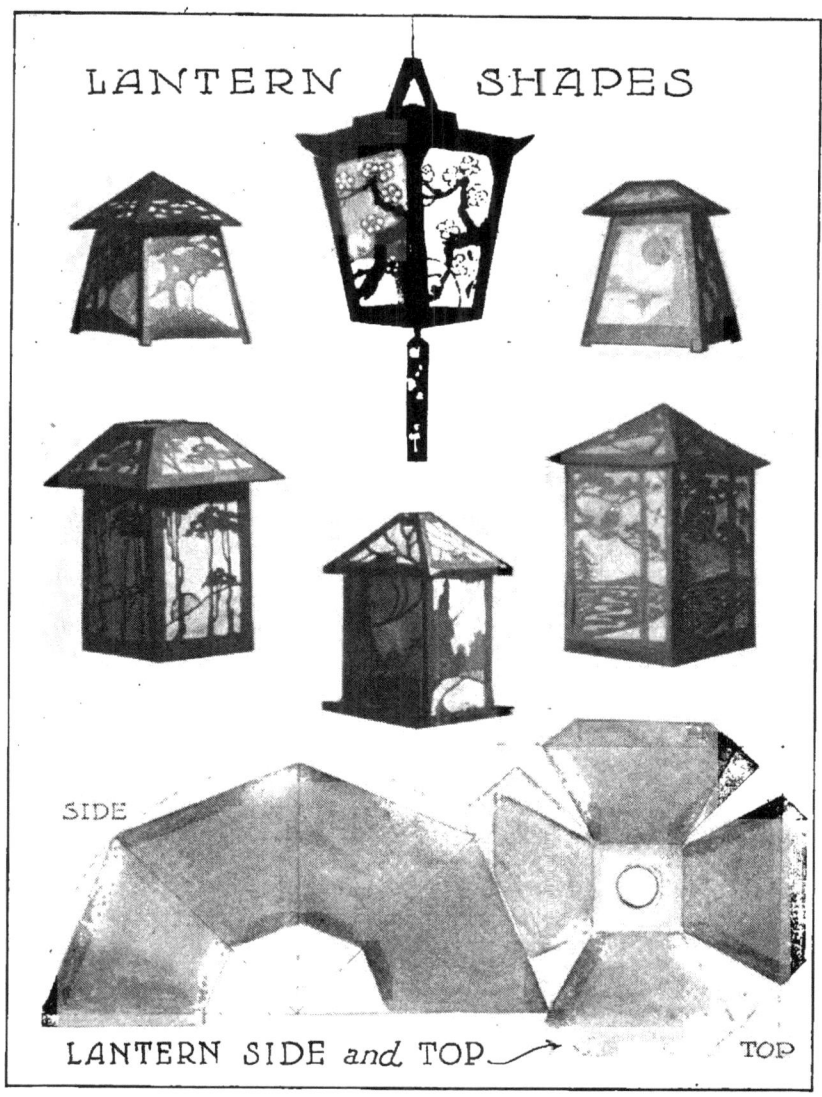

LANTERN SHAPES

SIDE

LANTERN SIDE and TOP

TOP

HOW TO CONSTRUCT PAPER LANTERNS

Good drills

Hold the brush
upright for curves

BRUSH LETTERING

Plan
Houses and
Gardens with
Paper and Clay Forms

HOUSE AND GARDEN PLANNING

TEACHER'S NOTES FOR THE EIGHTH YEAR

TREE SUGGESTIONS. Strong, bold tree pictures either from paintings or from photographs should be collected by the teacher for use in the schoolroom. Good tree pictures are constantly appearing in the various magazines; and if these are mounted on stiff card-board and filed in systematic order, they can be used to good advantage as reference material. A collection of trees applied to industrial purposes, such as stained glass designs, book covers, borders, and decorations, should also be assembled for posting on the reference board. Such a board will go far toward making a class problem successful. Often the students need only the suggestion of how others have worked similar problems, to work out their own successfully. The teacher should post the material in a pleasing way on the reference board. Careless and unbalanced arrangement is sure to create a similar impression upon the students in their own arrangement.

BRUSH DRILLS. Practice with the brush should be continued by the students until they can produce good light and heavy lines in clear, confident strokes. Brush drills showing continuous connecting curved lines in a designed form create rhythmic brush rendering, and other patterns and strokes can be developed to create facility with the brush. The making of a long stem with increasing thickness toward the bottom, and a series of radiating leaves made with single brush strokes, gives the combination drill in the use of the finest line with the heaviest strokes the brush will produce.

USE OF PASTE. If a table or a desk can be arranged for students to do large pasting upon, it will prevent waste of paste and the possibility of students' having paste on their own desks and thus soiling other work. The paste in tubes is the best form for individual use, since just what is needed is used, and the screw top is placed back when the paste is not in use. Have the students learn to use the paste tube correctly. It should be pressed from the bottom, not near the top. As it is emptied at the bottom, the bottom can be rolled up. Where a straight edge of paste surface is needed, if a straight strip of thin paper is laid down along the edge to which the paste is to come, when the paste is brushed, the strip will take the surplus paste. When the strip is removed, the pasted part will remain with a straight edge. Paper that is to be pasted flat in large surfaces should stand for a minute or two before it is laid and pressed upon the surface it is to cover. This prevents the paper from wrinkling, as the paste dampens the paper and causes it to stretch. If pasted down before this stretching is completed, it will not remain smooth.

WOODWORK BENCH. For school work in thin wood, a work-bench simply equipped with a wood vise, a few hammers, a wood miter box, and a saw, will permit the making of more interesting problems. Where a regular woodwork course and equipment are available, the working of wood problems will be an easy matter. To the teacher with limited equipment and space, however, a simple bench and set of tools will give many benefits. And it is encouraging to know that elaborate equipment is not indispensable to good work. Thoughtful use of simple tools has produced some of the world's finest craftsmanship.

A paper over the pasted portion

Rubbed with hand to make paste hold.

A strip to define edge of paste

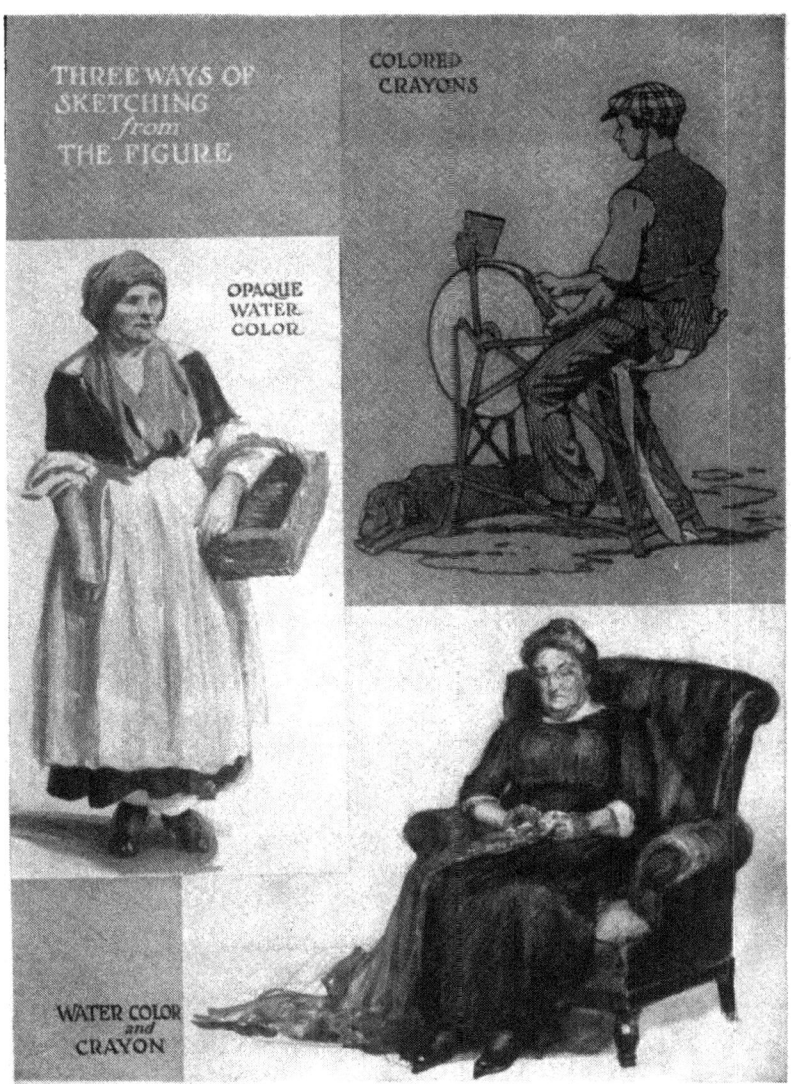

FIGURE SKETCHING

FLAT COLOR FIGURE DRAWINGS

FOUR STAGES IN WATER COLOR PAINTING

WATER COLOR STEPS IN LANDSCAPE PAINTING

CRAYONS ON DARK PAPER

THE ACADEMIC GRADES

DRAWING AND PAINTING

DRAWING is such a pleasing subject and has so many angles to it, that most beginners become confused as to what is the best way to start. A little study soon shows us that some of our simplest forms of drawing are not only the most effective but help us to learn quickly. In the drawing lessons we take up here, we are going to carry our work forward step by step, so that we shall really know how to draw when we are through.

SILHOUETTES are the first kind of drawing we shall make. Silhouettes are those drawings which are filled in solid without any shading. The name "silhouette" came from Etienne de Silhouette, the French minister of finance in 1759. He made the method fashionable by decorating the rooms of his house with these simple, flat drawings.

About one hundred years ago, people made portraits by cutting out a side view of a person's head on black paper. George and Martha Washington had their portraits done in this way. The ancients in Greek and Egypt used the silhouette method of drawing on their temples and vases. It takes skill to do this work well, and it is one of the best kinds of training for an artist.

GOOD ARRANGEMENT and "spotting" of our drawings can be obtained comparatively easily in silhouettes. We have only two things to think of — black and white. Our silhouette may be black against a white background, or it may be white against a black background. Some of these are shown on page 225. Take a look at that page. Every drawing on it is interesting. And each one tells all that need be told. The little boy and girl with the rabbit, the children flying kites, the photographer, the soap bubble party — every one of them tells what the artist wanted it to tell. Even in places where the figures lap over one another, as in the picture of the soap bubble party, or that of the children chasing the turkey, the drawing is easy to understand, and is artistic too.

IN NEWSPAPERS, and other printing where rough paper is used, this kind of work is utilized a great deal. For one reason, it is easier to print. For another, the eye grasps the silhouette quickly. When a man is glancing over his paper in a hurry, he does not care to stop and worry out an elaborate drawing. So it is that advertisements in drawings of this kind have been found to bring good results.

(217)

STUDIES IN LIGHT AND SHADE are the next problems we want to take up after we have studied silhouette work. In silhouettes, we learned to look at our subjects as one flat spot, or "mass." In this way, we learned to get the general shape and character of our objects. In our next step, we want to see if we can learn to draw our subjects by means of simple lights and shades. This kind of drawing is valuable for us, because through it we learn to pick out the high lights and shades of our objects and to put them down on paper. A famous artist once said, "There are only three tones to any drawing — high lights, middle tones, and shadows." So if we learn to pick out the high lights and the shadows, we have mastered the hardest part of drawing.

LIGHT AND SHADE STUDIES are shown on page 226. Some of the drawings are made by using shadows alone. Others have been made by merely using high lights. Two high light drawings are shown at the top of the page. They have been done by using white water color or crayon on gray paper. What could be prettier or more effective than the drawing of the lion in the upper right-hand corner? A few well chosen lines with the white crayon tell the whole story. The drawings done in shadows alone are just as strong. While only the shadow side has been drawn in, the eye makes up the rest of the picture. Look at the drawings of the stewpan and the one of the bowl, at the bottom of the page. Notice that the shadows on the inside of the pan and bowl are on the opposite side from the shadows on the outside. This helps to give the effect of looking into the bowl and the pan.

THE FORM of our objects, and their lights and shadows, have been the steps we have covered so far. Our next step will be to combine these ideas in order to make a completed drawing. On page 227, we have four drawings of a bowl, a spoon, a spool, and an ink bottle, which show how this is done. First we make a silhouette drawing of the object in a medium-toned wash of black water color. If, before we put in our wash, we outline our high lights lightly in pencil, we can paint around them and leave the high lights in the white paper.

THE SECOND STEP in our work is to pick out the shadows of our subject and put them in. This should be done after the gray wash has dried, so the colors will not run together. Half closing your eyes in looking at an object will help you to pick out the high lights and the shadows easily. The last step is to put in some of the necessary details, such as the border on the bowl. By this time, your drawing will be completed. If it is properly done, it will be a good, crisp drawing, and have the effect of modeling your objects in light and shade.

LIGHT AND SHADE studied in this way are a valuable problem. The trouble with most young artists is that they have never had enough of this kind of practice. Doing plenty of this, and doing it well, will go farther toward making you an artist than any other practice you could pick out. Don't be satisfied with three or four drawings. Make three or four pages, and go slowly. Be sure that the high lights and shadows you put in are placed in the very best way. Try to be a reliable artist.

SKETCHING is the next study we are going to take up, after we have perfected our light and shade work. Some people think that the word "sketching" means any quick, hurried drawing scratched on paper. This idea is not bad if in back of these quickly drawn lines there has been some thought and study. An artist who has made a great success of his work said that in making a sketch, if he had only twenty minutes, he would study his model for fifteen minutes, and draw it in the remaining five. This idea of his could not be bettered. Many people draw by taking a paper and starting to put lines on it without stopping to look their subject over and get a general idea of it.

OBSERVATION is a quality that all successful artists try to develop. It is because the Japanese artists have their observation so highly trained and developed, that they are able to make such wonderful drawings from memory. When our power of observation is strong, we see the leading points in our subject that make it what it is. If, for instance, we are sketching a canary bird, we should stop and look for the points that make it different from other birds; such things as, the shape of the bill, the tail feathers, the head, and so forth.

QUICK SKETCHING from models is used a great deal in art schools, because it does not leave the student time to see and put in too much. In this way, he is compelled to put down only the main parts, or "essentials," of his model. Look at the drawing of the milkmaid on the "Quick Sketching" page, 228. When you hold it well off, it tells the story clearly. It shows a Dutch woman with wooden shoes, resting on one foot, with a can of milk in her hands. Yet when we look closely at the shoes, we see that they are made with merely a few well chosen strokes of the pencil.

CHARCOAL is used in art schools because it is an easily handled medium that gives nice shades and tones when used correctly. The paper on which the charcoal is drawn comes in sheets about 20 x 23 inches in size. This paper has a rough, pebbly surface, which catches the charcoal strokes and helps to give an artistic effect. Some beginners try to cover up all the rough dots on their charcoal paper by taking their fingers or a cloth and rubbing the charcoal into the paper. This is just the wrong thing to do, because it gives the drawing a blurred or worn-out appearance. The best drawings in charcoal are those in which a little of the grain of the paper is allowed to show between the charcoal strokes. Drawings of this kind always look more full of life and color. In other words, they give us the same effect that the rays of light give when they strike the surface of the model.

RUBBING with a soft chamois or your finger is all right if done only a little in a few spots to soften lines, but never do it if you can avoid it. The high lights of the drawing are picked out with a soft kneaded eraser. After a student has studied the figure from casts until he can draw the parts well enough, he can then draw the whole figure. He is thus able to make use of the knowledge he has obtained by making his large, detailed drawings of the various parts, such as hands, feet, and so forth.

ARTISTS who are willing to study drawing in this way, become confident of their ability, so that they are capable of producing the highest kind of art work. This is because they are sure of what they are doing, after having made a careful study of the objects they are to draw. Beautiful paintings like those of George Inness, Edwin Blashfield, Maxfield Parrish, John Sargent, and others, have been made by men who spent years in learning the foundation steps in art before they tried the more elaborate things.

PENCIL WORK is closely related to charcoal drawings. Pencil drawings have the advantage that they do not rub out quite so easily as charcoal work. Pencils are good for sketching out of doors, because a pencil and a pad are easily handled in taking trips. On page 231, we have a sketch of a tree done with a blunt-pointed pencil. Below it, we have one done with a small-pointed, soft pencil. Both of these are good drawings. If your work has a tendency to be too soft and delicate, then the top style of drawing is best. Using a blunt-pointed pencil will give your drawing strength and character. If, on the other hand, your work looks a little crude, then try a small point on your pencil.

Artists often make drawings in which they use two and sometimes three kinds of pencils in one drawing. They use their heavy, blunt pencils in the main parts of their drawing, and the finer ones in the details. This has the effect of producing finished looking work, and of keeping

the details softer and more delicate than when only one sort of pencil
is used. The next tree or flower drawing you make in pencil, try
this idea.

STUDYING HEADS is interesting and fascinating. If you try to
draw them, do not become discouraged, but take your pencil and measure
off the relative size of the different parts, and block them in before you
try to finish up your drawing. Watch the shape of the eyes. Be careful
not to make them too much of an almond shape, nor to draw the lower
lid with too hard a line. This gives a stare effect to the eyes. It is
better to make a drawing of a head in an outline with good proportions
than to make one all shaded up and not correctly drawn.

THREE DRAWINGS showing how to sketch a head in pencil, are
shown on page 234. By looking at them, you can get an idea of how
to carry out a drawing like these. It would not be a bad plan to copy
this whole page. Then, when you come to make a sketch of your own,
you will already be familiar with the method. Notice that the general
character and proportions of the finished drawing are the same as those
of the first two drawings, except that it is more complete in detail and
shading.

PERSPECTIVE is a subject many students do not care to take
up, because they are not able to understand it readily. On pages 236 to
241, most of the points we ought to know, are brought out very clearly.
If we look them over and follow them step by step, we shall have no
trouble to understand what is meant by perspective. It is the art of
drawing, upon a flat surface, objects as they appear to the eye, regard-
less of their actual size or distance. If we do not make our drawings
with reference to perspective, the objects in them will seem to be out
of proportion.

A RAILROAD TRACK is a fine example of perspective. In looking
down the track, we find that the farther away the ties are, the smaller
and closer together they appear to be. The two tracks seem to run together, and the telegraph poles along the side seem to get shorter and
closer together as they disappear into the distance. To draw such a
picture, we should understand the laws of perspective. At the bottom
of page 236, you will see a picture of the Doge's Palace in Venice.
Notice how everything in the picture seems to come to a point. Some
white ink lines have been drawn on the photograph to help you see this
easily. Everything we look at has this same appearance in a greater or
a less degree.

THE HOUSE AND THE ROAD right above the palace picture are other examples of this "receding" of lines, as it is called. See how the road seems to come to a point, and the telegraph poles seem to grow smaller. In the picture on the right, we are standing in the middle of the road. In the one on the left, we are to one side of it. Take a good look at the picture at the top of this page. Here we have a sketch of a winding road with some trees to one side of it. Suppose you were to stand where the man is in the first picture on the page. Your eyes would be on a level with the horizontal line you see in the picture, or the horizon line. If you were to go away up on a hill and look down at the same road, then the horizon line would seem higher in the air, because your eyes would be higher up. The second picture on the page helps to show this idea.

WHEN YOU STOOD down low, as in the first picture, people on the road would look like those you see in the third picture of that row. If you went up on the hillside and looked down, you would see the tops of people's heads, as in the last picture. This shows us that the horizon line will appear higher or lower according to where we stand, and that the objects we see will look different when we look at them from different directions.

THE POINT where all the lines seem to come together is called the vanishing point, and is always on a level with our eyes. If we go up higher, the vanishing point is higher; if we are low, then our vanishing point seems low. Look at the second page of perspective drawings. Here we have a picture of a book held up above our eyes and one held below our eyes. Notice in each drawing how the receding lines go to the vanishing point, which is always on a level with our eyes.

AN INTERIOR OF A ROOM is difficult for those to draw who do not understand perspective. But when we know that lines all seem to converge, or run together to one point, we can figure our drawing out easily. A simple way to do a room interior is shown on this second page. If we decide about where the level of our eyes comes, and put a pencil dot there, we can thumb-tack one end of a strip of cardboard to that point. Then all we have to do is to swing our cardboard strip back and forth and rule pencil lines along it to give us our receding lines. This will make the drawing of the room quite simple.

GEOMETRIC SHAPES, such as squares, etc., always look smaller on the side that is farthest away from our eyes. Look at the middle drawing of page 237. Notice how the square seems to get smaller as it goes away from you. Look at the square wooden frame. See how much shorter the farthest side seems to be. After learning to draw simple objects so that they recede correctly, we can then begin to use our knowledge of perspective in more elaborate forms. At the bottom of this second perspective page, 237, we have a picture showing how we can first block out an oblong form lightly in pencil and get it so that it recedes properly. When this is done, we can cut up this oblong into steps, houses, or whatever will fit into the space. This way of working makes it easier to do objects that are more or less cut up.

THERE ARE TWO KINDS OF PERSPECTIVE. The one where the front of our object is parallel with us is called "parallel perspective." The one where the object is turned at an angle is "angular perspective." In drawing objects in angular perspective, we find that we must have two vanishing points. In parallel perspective, we need only one vanishing point. In either case, the vanishing points are always on a level with the eye.

ROADS that slant downward always converge at a point below the horizon. Those which slant up, converge at a point above the horizon. A flat road converges at the vanishing point on a level with our eyes. The same rule works with the slanting roofs of houses. Notice that in one of the perspective diagrams on page 238, the proper way to draw roofs of houses is shown.

"OBLIQUE PERSPECTIVE" is the name given to lines that slant up or down and recede to points of their own. It is only when lines or faces of objects are absolutely level, or the upright sides of objects rest on a level, that they converge to points on the horizon. On this same page, we have a diagram showing how a road would be drawn if part of it were flat and part slanting, downhill and uphill. You will see that the downhill part converges below the level of the eye, the uphill part above the eye level, and the flat part on the level of the eye, or the horizon line.

ROADS THAT ZIGZAG like those shown at the bottom of the page, have several vanishing points, all of which are on the horizon line. The light pencil lines show how this road should be planned out. Roads that zigzag and also slant should be drawn like the sketch on the right-hand side of the one just mentioned. While these ideas may seem a little confusing, they will be found easy to understand if you will look at the drawings carefully. We learn more easily by studying drawings than by reading written descriptions.

ARCHITECTS make a great deal of use of perspective. Often what is known as a plan of a building is given to them, and they are asked to make a perspective picture of it. Plan drawings show the buildings as though you were looking down at the top of them from an airplane. On page 240 is explained how side views of buildings can be made from plan drawings. First we draw the plan on our paper. Above it, we rule a horizontal line, which is to be our horizon line. Then we rule a vertical line right through the point of the building which is nearest us, and up through the horizon line. This gives us our two vanishing points. All that is left is to find out how high our building is to be, and to make the vertical line of our side view drawing in proportion. Then we draw lines from the ends of this vertical line to our two vanishing points, and this gives us our building.

FIGURES of people are drawn by perspective also. As we can see by the working page, 240, they appear smaller when farther away. If they are all in one row, then they can be drawn by the use of lines like those in the drawing on the lower right-hand corner, which has a farmer in it. If the people are scattered, like those in the lower left-hand drawing, then horizontal lines are drawn out from lines that recede to the vanishing point, and the people are sketched within them.

CURVED OBJECTS may be drawn in perspective, too. An easy way to draw a circle in perspective is to sketch a square in perspective and then put your circle inside of it. This idea will be a big help. Look at the diagram in the lower right-hand corner of the sheet of curved objects on page 241, and you can see how much easier it is to draw an oblong first and then put the two curves inside of that. The farther above or below your eyes a curved line is, the more it seems to curve. This idea is shown in the upper right-hand corner. You will notice that the curves at the top of the row, which are closer to the level of the eye, are quite shallow, but those lower down become more and more deep and circular. Perspective is an interesting subject, once you begin to get hold of it; and it is worth your trouble to learn how to use it. Try the simple objects first, and then go on to the more difficult subjects.

SILHOUETTE ILLUSTRATIONS

15 Applied Art

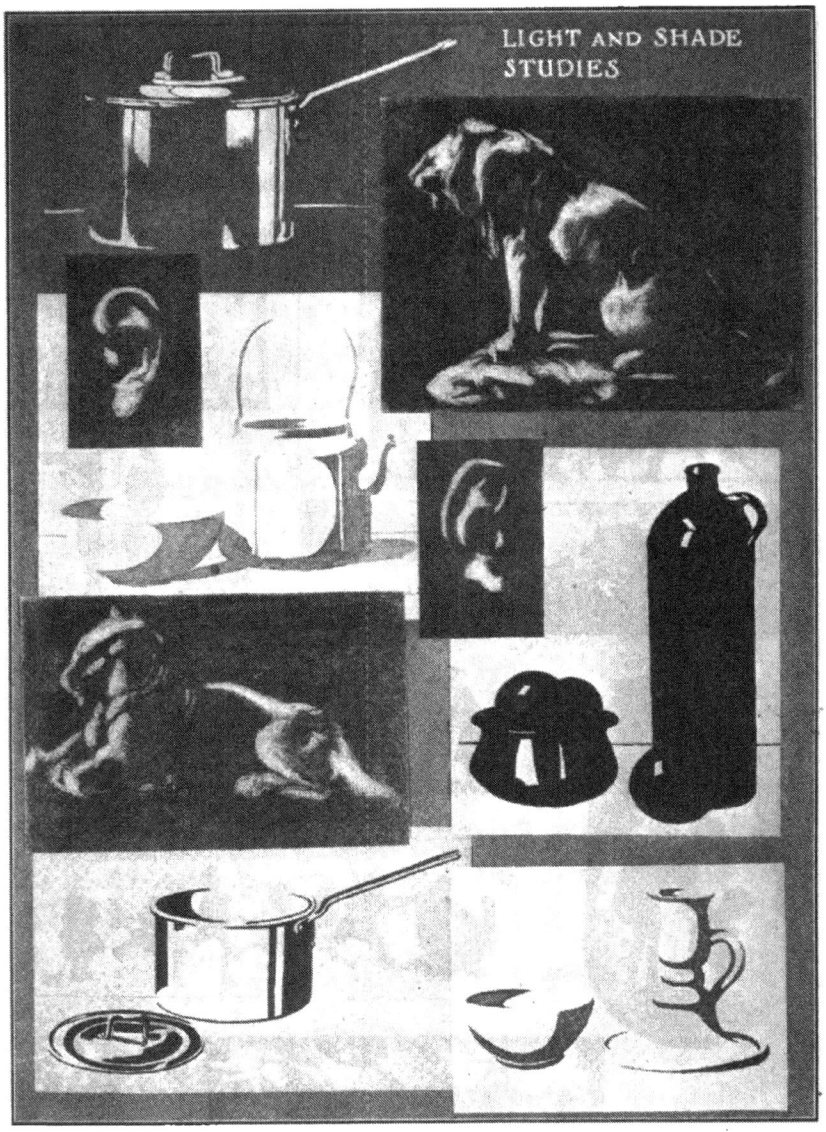

LIGHT AND SHADE STUDIES

FOUR STEPS IN LIGHT AND SHADE

FIGURE SKETCHING

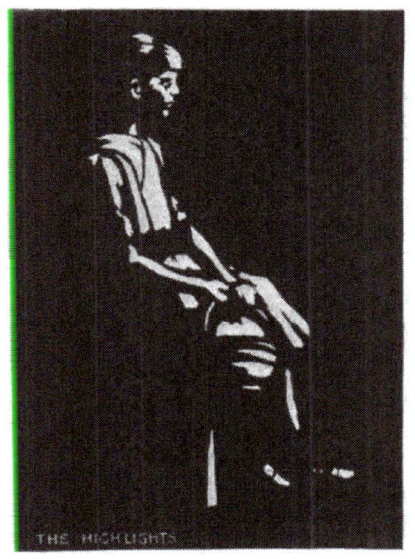

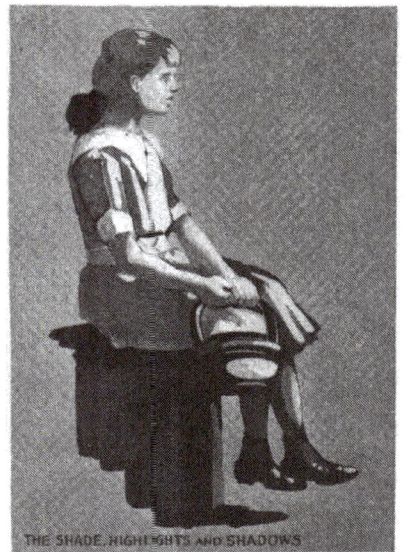

THE HIGHLIGHTS

THE SHADOWS

THE SHADES

THE SHADE, HIGHLIGHTS AND SHADOWS

FOUR WAYS TO SKETCH A FIGURE

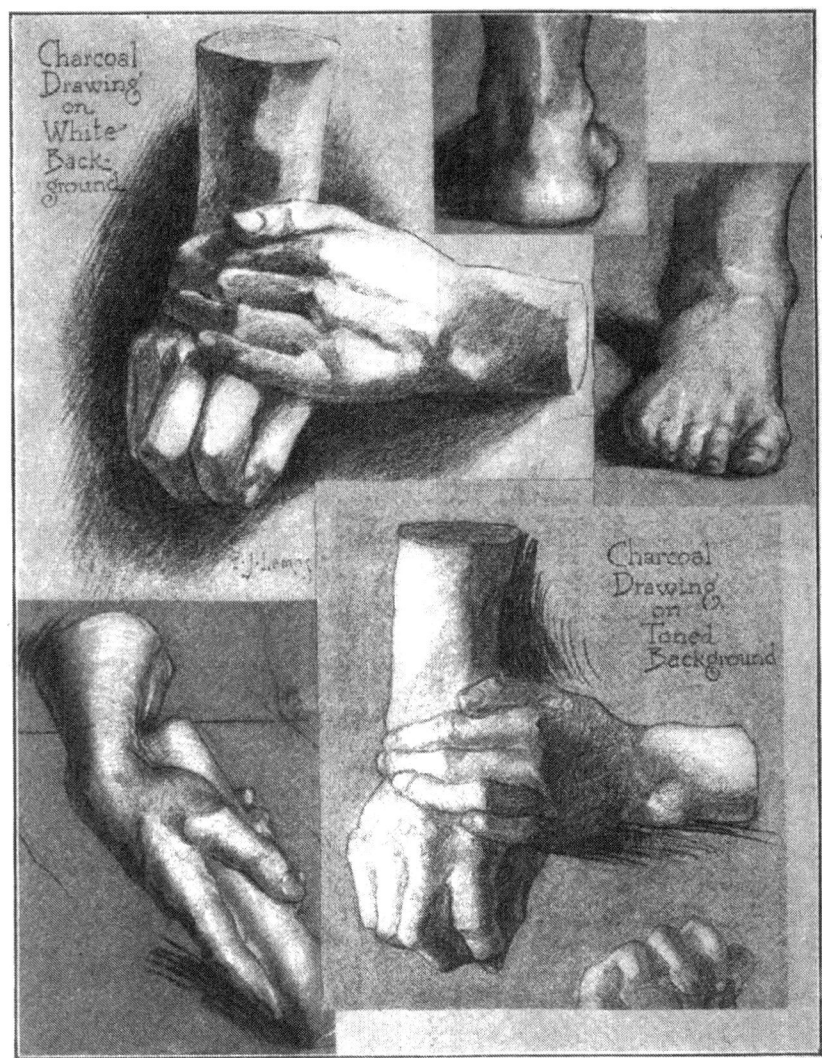

Charcoal
Drawing
on
White
Back-
ground

Charcoal
Drawing
on
Toned
Background

CHARCOAL DRAWINGS FROM CASTS

Drawn with a soft blunt pointed pencil

Drawn with a small pointed soft pencil

PENCIL DRAWINGS FROM TREES

OUTDOOR SKETCHING IN PENCIL

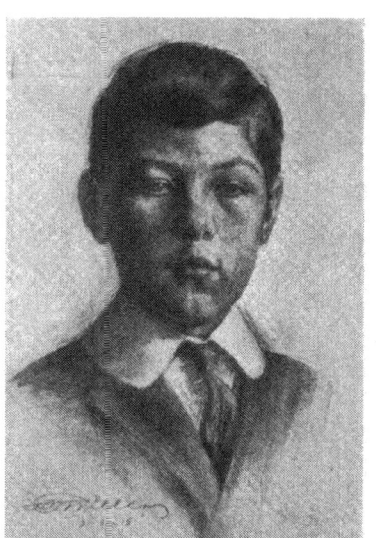

FOUR WAYS TO DRAW A PORTRAIT

APPLIED ART

PERSPECTIVE IN NATURE

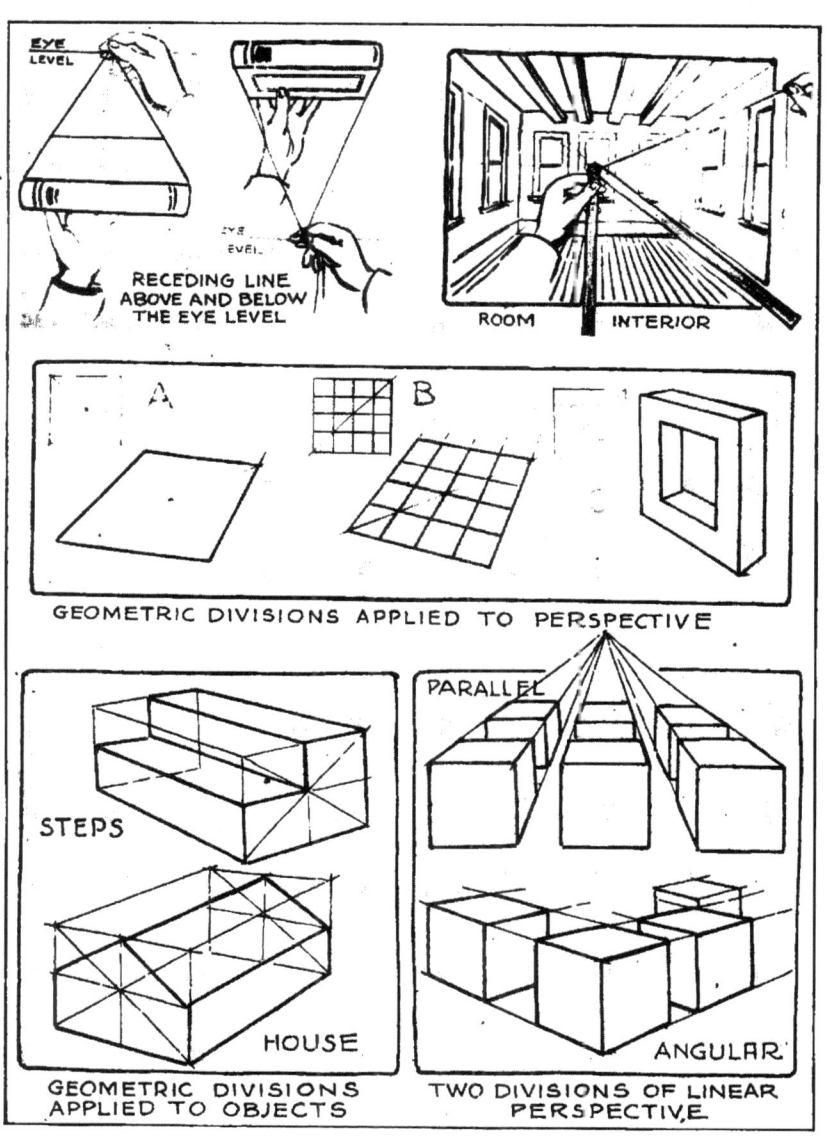

EYE LEVEL

RECEDING LINE ABOVE AND BELOW THE EYE LEVEL

ROOM INTERIOR

A

B

GEOMETRIC DIVISIONS APPLIED TO PERSPECTIVE

STEPS

HOUSE

GEOMETRIC DIVISIONS APPLIED TO OBJECTS

PARALLEL

ANGULAR

TWO DIVISIONS OF LINEAR PERSPECTIVE

PARALLEL AND ANGULAR PERSPECTIVE

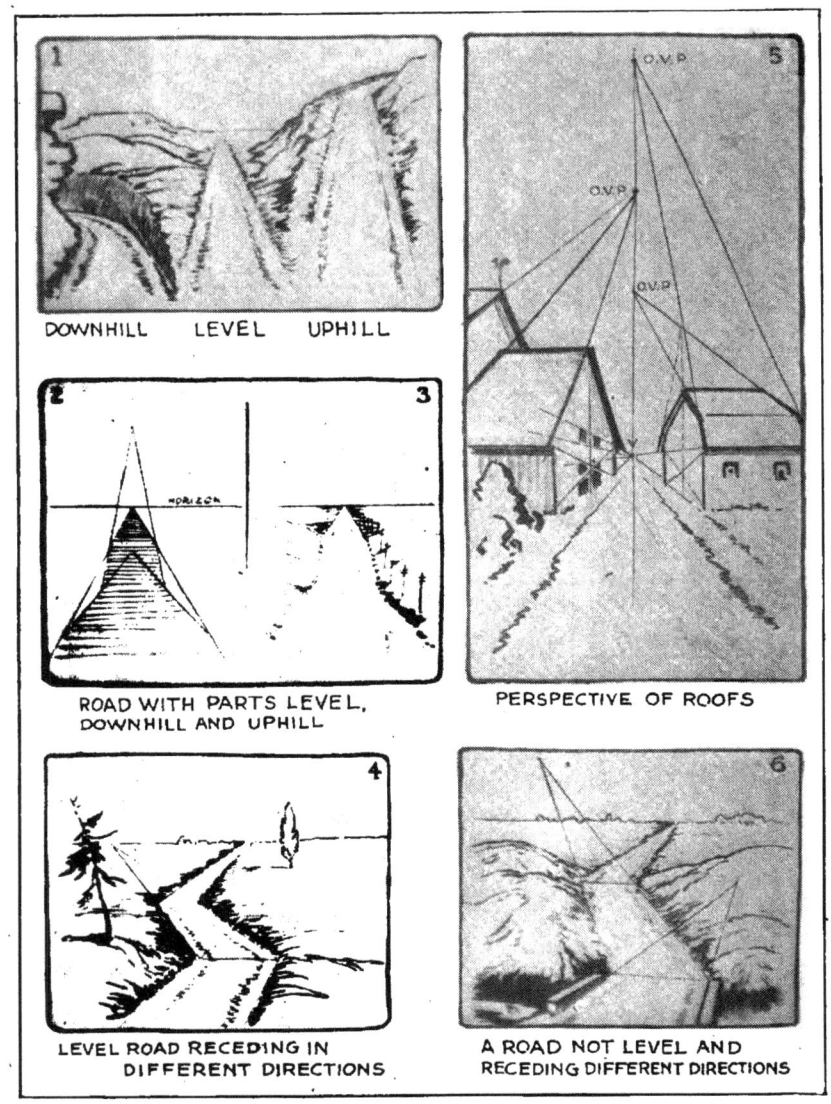

1   DOWNHILL   LEVEL   UPHILL

ROAD WITH PARTS LEVEL,
DOWNHILL AND UPHILL

PERSPECTIVE OF ROOFS

LEVEL ROAD RECEDING IN
DIFFERENT DIRECTIONS

A ROAD NOT LEVEL AND
RECEDING DIFFERENT DIRECTIONS

OBLIQUE PERSPECTIVE

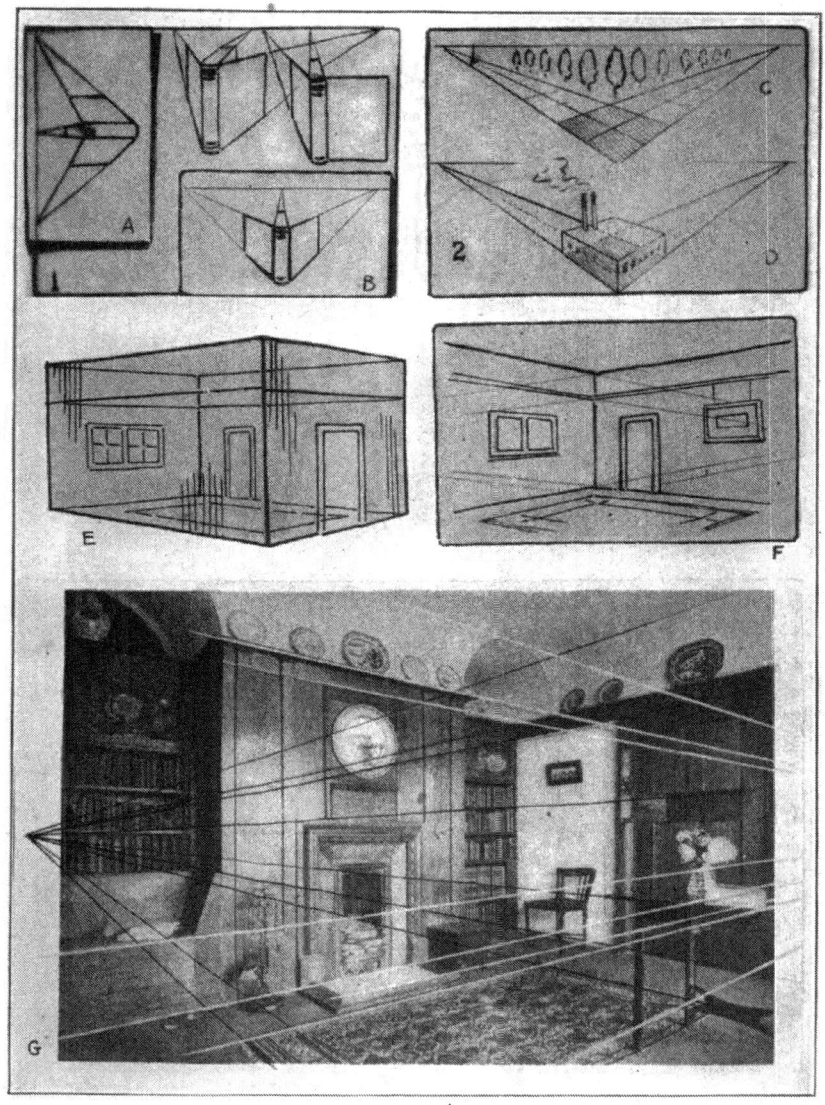

TWO-POINT PERSPECTIVE

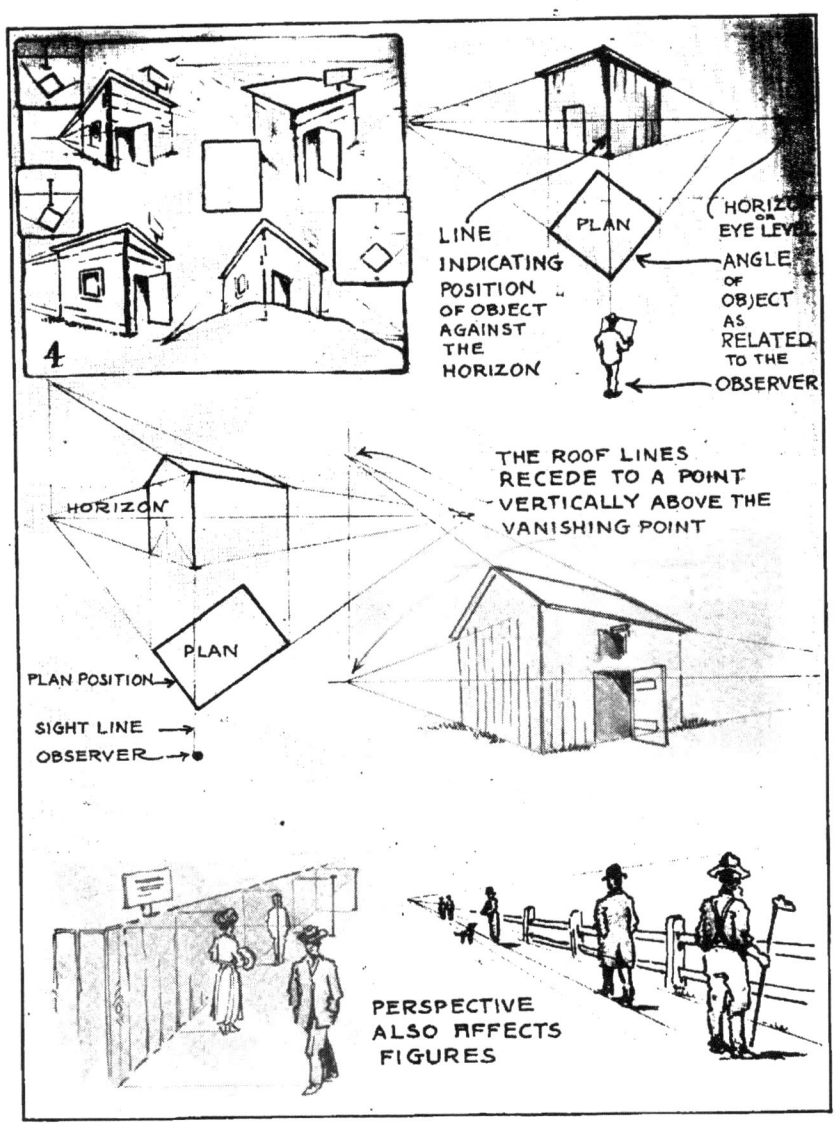

4

LINE INDICATING POSITION OF OBJECT AGAINST THE HORIZON

PLAN

HORIZON OR EYE LEVEL

ANGLE OF OBJECT AS RELATED TO THE OBSERVER

THE ROOF LINES RECEDE TO A POINT VERTICALLY ABOVE THE VANISHING POINT

HORIZON

PLAN

PLAN POSITION

SIGHT LINE

OBSERVER

PERSPECTIVE ALSO AFFECTS FIGURES

PERSPECTIVE FROM PLAN SKETCH

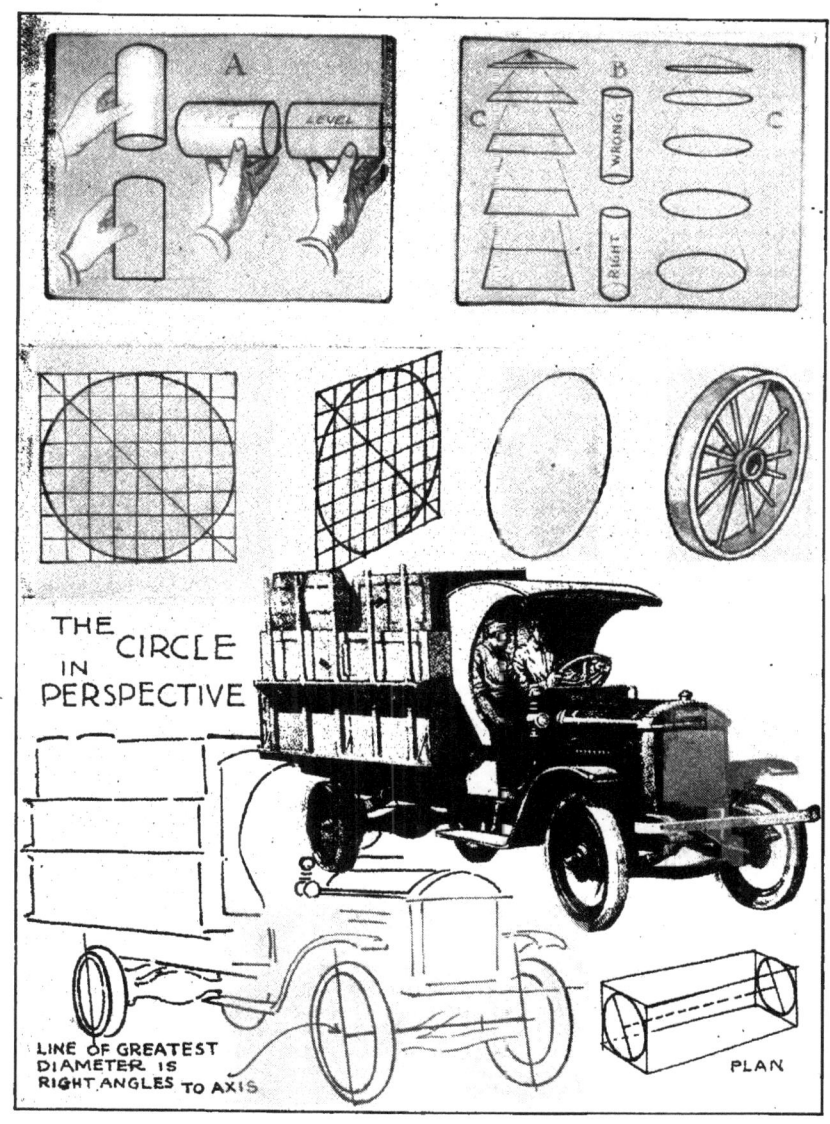

THE CIRCLE IN PERSPECTIVE

16 Applied Art

TEACHER'S NOTES ON DRAWING

OUTDOOR SKETCH EQUIPMENT. For outdoor work, as simple and light an equipment as possible should be planned. For pencil or crayons, a pad with sheets gummed at one edge only will serve the purpose. For water colors, it is best to have a pad that has the four edges gummed firmly, with the exception of one little place to permit the insertion of a knife point. This allows each sheet to be taken off as it is completed, leaving the next sheet clean and in condition for the next sketch. If a second cardboard is fastened with a cloth or strong paper hinge pasted on the bottom board of the pad, it will serve as a pocket into which completed work can be slipped, along with reference sketches.

For a simple, light board, either building boards made of paper or real wood can be arranged as shown, with two legs, so that these legs can rest on the ground and form an outdoor desk when the lower edge of the board is resting on the worker's lap.

For water color sketching, where water is not available from a near-by point, a small fruit jar or wide-mouthed bottle can be easily carried if a string is tied around it so as to form a handle.

SKETCH CLASS BACKGROUNDS. A few large drapes or frames with stretched sign painter's cloth that is covered with wall tints serve admirably for figure backgrounds. A few different colored backgrounds will be valuable in working from figures, as contrast of color is given, which permits the working class to see the subject. To place the model against a wall with much pattern, or against a space that is broken up with tables and blackboards and shelves, is to bring into the subject a number of detracting elements. Three backgrounds that will be valuable are one of a neutral gray, one of a warm tone, and one of a cool tone. These three backgrounds will cover the needs of almost any sketch class. If the figure posing can stand on a platform about one and a half feet to two feet above the class, this will permit the students to see the model more easily. For a person beginning to pose, ten minutes should be the maximum length of each period. Later he may pose for fifteen or twenty minutes. Chalk marks around the feet of the model will generally aid in retaining the same pose with reference to the sketches of different students. The exact head position can be secured from the drawing of the previous pose.

Sketch Class

After the students have sketched continuously from the figure for several periods, then let them have a limited period for quick sketching, allowing one, two, three, five, ten, or fifteen minutes for a sketch. Such rapid sketching will give time only for the general characteristic lines — a factor that is important but generally overlooked where much time is devoted to the one subject.

MATERIAL FOR STILL LIFE WORK. For still life work, the teacher should have a group of things that lend themselves to high light sketching, such as glass objects and those with shiny surfaces. There should also be a group of things that cast interesting shadows for the shadow drawings. A collection of such material and other good objects can be made gradually and assisted by the students. As previously suggested in grade outlines, if such articles are listed and numbered, the teacher can then readily locate them as needed.

COLORED CRAYON

WATER COLOR

INK AND WATER COLOR

DECORATIVE LANDSCAPES

GIFT CARD DESIGNS

DECORATIVE FLOWER PANELS

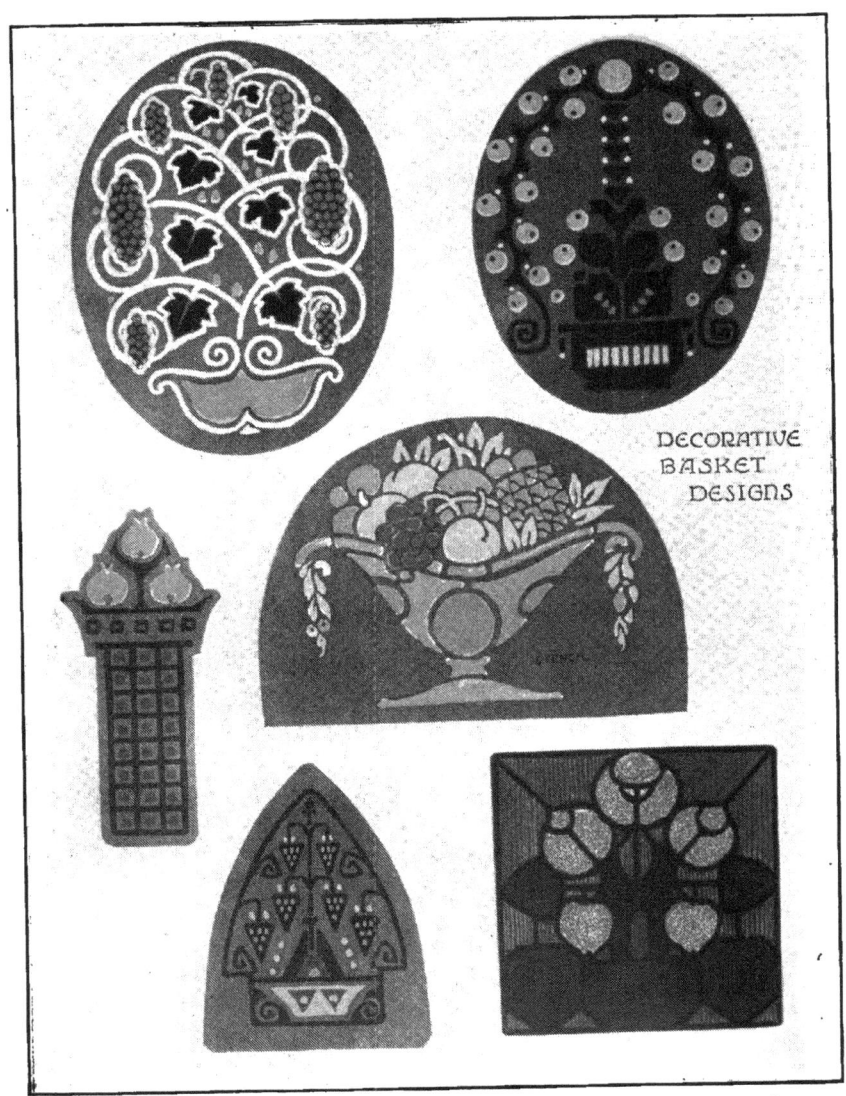

DECORATIVE
BASKET
DESIGNS

BASKET DESIGNS

THE ACADEMIC GRADES

DESIGN

DESIGN is coming to be more and more important in art work. People have begun to realize that design enters into practically every form of art. Artists who understand design always do better work as a result. In the European art schools, it was found that beginners did much better in design if they were restricted to a few simple lines and dots at first. In this way, they were led to think of a pleasing arrangement of these spots on the paper. As a result, students learned to draw and paint designs that were beautiful because they had agreeable proportions and arrangement of lights and darks.

OUR FIRST PROBLEM in design is to take only dashes and dots and make borders with them. We shall first make two borders with vertical lines and dots alone. Then we shall make two by using vertical and oblique lines in the same border; and last, we shall make one with oblique lines only. The secret of making artistic borders in this way is to watch the design made by the white space between the lines, as well as the black design made by the lines themselves. Sometimes the prettiest part of your design will be made by the white background spots.

A GOOD RULE is, never to have the space between the lines the same width as the lines themselves. This prevents your design from being monotonous and confusing. Notice that on page 251, the space between the lines is less than the width of the lines themselves. The best medium to use in making these designs is black paint and a square-pointed brush. The kind of brush used by show card artists is just right for this work. Or a strip of cardboard dipped in ink will do.

DESIGN DEVELOPMENT is our next problem. Many artists say that they can draw, but that they have trouble thinking up designs. This second problem helps us to cultivate the ability to develop or create designs. First on page 252 are given four spots exactly alike. We are to take these and vary them in size, location, etc. Notice how much more interesting the spots become when they are varied. After making three or four designs like this, we change them still more by working our spots up into more elaborate shapes. You can see that all the designs on this page have the same general formation. By varying the shape of the spots, it is possible to originate dozens of different designs.

(243)

VARIOUS PATTERNS made by repeating spots in borders and all-over designs are shown on page 253. Almost any spot will make a good border when it is repeated in a pattern. If you will look at this page closely, you will notice that the same spot has been used to make a border, an all-over pattern, and two circular patterns. One of the circular patterns is in black and white, and the other is in three tones. Designs like these are very satisfactory if worked up in attractive colors.

FLOWERS AND PLANTS are among the best sources of design. Nature is full of suggestions for beautiful designs and patterns. Look at designs made from the columbine, on page 254. Even the leaves and the seed pods have been used as suggestions for designs. Any one of these single designs, or "motifs," as they are called, would work into a splendid design for a border or all-over pattern. All the designs on page 254, except one, are bi-symmetric. In other words, both sides of the design are alike. The motif at the extreme right toward the bottom of the page is what is known as an "occult" design, because the two sides balance each other although they are not alike.

DESIGNERS who make a success of their work are well acquainted with what are known as the basic rules of design. When we come right down to it, there are not a great number, and they are easy to remember. One of these rules is that of repetition, or rhythm. Any simple motif repeated gives us this rhythm. It is like the beating of time in music. Nature decorates many of her forms by means of this rule. Look at the designs on page 256. See how the repetition of spots in the leopard, the peacock, and the seed pod have made them decorative. Sometimes this repetition is in lines, like a border; and often it is a series of spots radiating from a center, like the petals of a flower. Chains, jewelry, wall-paper, and borders on vases or buildings, are all examples of designs made beautiful by repetition.

RADIATION is another feature of good design. Radiation is seen everywhere in nature, from the wings of the birds to the fingers of our hands. It is especially seen in the leaves and the flowers. By radiation, we mean the graceful growth of the various parts of a design from some central spot or axis. On page 257, we have a row of diagrams showing how the design may radiate from a center like a flower; from a point like a palm leaf; from an axis or a base, as many plants do; or from a curve, like some vines. When we draw a jumble of spots like those in the lower left-hand corner, we have a poor design. The minute we make these same spots radiate from a common point, the design begins to have character.

MANY FAMOUS PAINTINGS owe much of their beauty to radiation. Some of the famous Greek statues and paintings are full of radiation lines. The painting, Pot of Basil, by Alexander, a sketch of which is shown here, has fine radiation in it. Radiation is found in architecture, too, and there are few good designs that do not have it in some form.

MEASURE is a third essential in design. When we speak of measure, we refer to the relative proportions of the various parts of a design to each other. In the chart showing measure suggestions, on page 258, look at the picture of the three stands and vases in a row. Notice how much better the second drawing, where the vase is larger than the stand, looks than the one in which the stand and the vase are the same height. Drawings like the first have the effect of both parts fighting for your attention. The same thing is true of the black panel that is divided exactly in half. The one that has a small rectangle at the top and a large one underneath is by far the better.

THE GREEKS recognized the effect of good proportion in design, and originated what is known as the "golden oblong." This space, which is considered to be the most ideal we can use, has a short side about three fifths of the long side. The Greeks also discovered that an area was most pleasing divided somewhere between one half and two thirds the length of the whole area. Nature has many examples of what is called graded measure. This occurs in places like a butterfly's wing or a sea shell, where the spots are practically the same 'shape, but get smaller and smaller.

BALANCE is an important element. If we see a book or a plate projecting over the edge of a table, we are not satisfied until we put it where it will not fall off. In the same way, designs that are not well balanced affect our eyes. There are two kinds of balance, bi-symmetric and occult. The human figure is a fine example of bi-symmetric balance, because both sides are alike. In occult balance, the various parts appear to balance each other, although they are not alike. A kangaroo or a leaning oak tree is a fine example of occult balance. On page 259, notice how the heavy tail on one end of the kangaroo balances, or makes up for, the head and the front legs hanging over on the other side. In the oak tree, see how nature has grown a bunch of leaves and branches back to one side to make up for the leaning tree trunk.

IN MAKING DESIGNS, we may cut up our spaces in various ways, as shown in the designs of birds on page 259. In the first one, we have a bi-symmetric or like-sided design. In the second, we have an alternate design, or one in which the design is divided in half, but where one half has the bird at the top and the other has it at the bottom. In the third one, the axis, or line that divides the two birds, runs diagonally from one corner to the other of the rectangle. This last style of diagonal balance is used a great deal in posters and paintings.

ALL-OVER PATTERNS also are a fine design study. All-over designs are used in rugs, linoleums, wall paper, tapestries, and hundreds of other places. You cannot look very far without seeing something in which an all-over pattern has been used. To draw these so they will come out right, we must first lay out a pattern over which to trace our motifs. There are several styles of patterns. Six of the most important are shown on page 261. The square pattern is simple, the lines in it being ruled at right angles and the motifs put in the squares. The slip pattern is something like the square, only the rows of motifs are slipped up and down so as to alternate. This gives a pattern somewhat like a brick wall with the bricks on end. The circle pattern is easy to understand. The easiest way to block it out is to rule lines representing the centers of your circles, and make your circles with a compass.

THE OBLIQUE PATTERN is like the square one, except that the squares are turned obliquely. With a T square and a triangle, this is easy to make. The scale pattern is found in many tapestries. It consists of rows of half circles alternating. Series of horizontal and perpendicular lines drawn across your paper are an aid in putting in your compass lines. The hexagon pattern is the hardest to do. If you will take a triangle that has angles of thirty and sixty degrees on it, this will help you to put in the diagonal lines. These diagonals should be exactly the same distance apart. With these in, the rest will be simple. The way to make your all-over pattern is to make just one motif on thin paper, and trace it off by putting a piece of graphite paper under it. Of course, your design should fit the space in which it is to go.

VALUES are the next step in our design. By values, we mean the gradation of tones or colors from light to dark. A splendid drill in values is the making of what is known as a "value scale." For this, we should get some good water color paper, and block off small rectangles, say about 1¼ x 3 inches in size. Next take your black water color and fill in one of these rectangles with a jet-black tone. Then add a little water, and make one slightly lighter, and keep doing this until you have a scale of five or six tones running from black to white. This is the best kind of training for your eye. A value scale is given on page 262.

FOR DESIGNS, a value scale of only three or five values would be sufficient, as designs having simple tones are the best. In the tiger lily drawing, we have six different designs made by using different kinds of value combinations. The way to make your tones dry flat is to put a light wash of plain water over the paper first, then flow the color over it.

THE FOUR DIVISIONS OF DESIGN are shown on page 263. These are naturalistic, conventional, geometric, and abstract designs. Naturalistic designs show the subject in its realistic form, but plans it so as to make a pleasing arrangement with a given space. No modeling is attempted, but the tones are kept flat. This is the idea on which most of the Japanese art is based. Conventional designs are made by taking the most typical lines and curves found in the subject and putting them in a design of conventional form. All parts, even the details, are drawn in this conventional manner. Most conventional designs are bi-symmetric, or like-sided; yet an occult arrangement may be used. Book covers, jewelry, borders, etc., have many conventional designs.

GEOMETRIC DESIGNS are the ones based on cross-ruled paper. This cross-ruled paper has light lines ruled up and down and at right angles, to form hundreds of little squares. The design is made over these squares, and should contain in it no lines that do not run either at right angles or at an angle of 45 degrees. Geometric designs are made mostly for rugs and other textiles that must be woven on looms. The mechanical working of the threads as the cloth is woven, makes necessary the drawing of the designs in this way.

ABSTRACT DESIGNS are much used lately. They are somewhat similar to conventional designs, except that they are so far removed in appearance from the original subject, that there is little or no resemblance. For instance, in looking at the abstract design in the lower right-hand corner of page 263, we know that it is based on a flower, but it might be any one of several species. Abstract designs retain only the suggestion of the subject, rather than its natural appearance. Designs of this kind require a pretty good knowledge of design; but when you once learn to make them, you have acquired something that will be a great aid to you.

BLUE PRINTING is a good way to become started in designing from flowers. This is taken up in the chapter on handicrafts, and is a big help in keeping definite records of flowers and plants. A sheet of designs made in charcoal, from flowers, is shown on page 264. Notice how carefully the artist has planned his flowers on the paper so as to make a pleasing arrangement. Also see how the spots of white and black have been so placed as to balance each other. Every one of these designs is interesting. One way to make charcoal drawings of flowers is to thumb-tack a piece of charcoal paper on a smooth drawing board. Then, with a knife, scrape some charcoal dust from a piece of charcoal. Rub this dust over the paper with a soft cloth or chamois until it makes an even tone all over. With this as a background, you can then sketch in your flower drawing by using charcoal for your dark parts and picking out the whites with a kneaded eraser.

AN EASY WAY to get your design on the paper without mussing up the charcoal background, is to draw your flower outline on the paper with a hard pencil before rubbing the charcoal dust on the page. Then, when you rub the gray background on, you will be able to see the outlines of your flower drawing, as the dust will not stick to the graphite.

INSECTS, as well as flowers, are prolific sources of design. Look at page 265, and see the wonderful designs worked out from insects. The butterfly is one of the best insects we can find for design suggestions. Its natural markings almost make the design for us without any further trouble. Designs like those on that page are suitable especially for handicraft metal work. See how the butterfly at the bottom of the page has been worked into a paper knife. Get from the library pictures of butterflies, and see if you can work out some good borders.

BIRDS are still another source for design. Parrots, peacocks, blue jays, robins — all kinds of birds — have been used in design motifs. The peacock is especially adapted to this purpose, because its markings are so decorative. The Japanese and the Chinese use the peacock a great deal. The best plan in making bird designs is to make them very conventional. Do not try to make a picture of a bird, but try to make a pleasing conventional arrangement of spots and lines, based upon the bird form.

ANIMALS also may be used in design, although they are much harder to draw than are most birds and insects. Animals used by the designers of different nations are shown on page 267. Notice the queer border of little animals that look like decorative deer, in the Peruvian border. The Chinese and the Japanese are very fond of designs resembling dragons. In medieval days, designers produced queer looking designs called "gargoyles." These gargoyles were used on the tops of buildings, and were a combination of various animals all worked into one. Take some paper and see if you can work out a design for a square, using rabbits like those in the Spanish design for a start.

ALL THESE DESIGNS we have been talking about can be used in many ways. We may stencil them on sofa cushions, or tool them in leather for a table mat or for book ends. They might be carved in wood, or worked out in stained glass or in pottery. Designs based on flowers, insects, birds, and animals are found in every country. The Indians weave them in their baskets, the Africans paint them on their shields, the Northern Indians carve them on their totem poles. Man has always taken from nature most of his suggestions for ornament. We should plan our designs so that without exception, they can be properly worked out in the kind of material we intend to use.

LANDSCAPES done in different tones are a step forward in decorative design work. Page 269 shows a fishing village worked out in tones. Six different styles are shown. This kind of work is valuable for us, because it soon teaches us what parts of our drawing to make dark and what parts light in order to produce a good design. The same value scale you used in flower designs will work out well in these decorative landscapes. Always keep your tones flat. Do not try to model them. The flat decorative style of drawings is the one that is desirable.

ONE OF THE BEST PAGES in this chapter is 271. In this page, we see the many ways in which designers and craftsmen put their design ideas to use. Years ago most people had never heard the word "design." All they thought of as connected with art was painting. An artist sometimes spent years in making what he called his "masterpiece," in hopes that it would sell for a large sum and that he would become famous. Many young artists in those days nearly starved while they were trying to produce pictures that people would like. To-day many artists receive good salaries for work that they enjoy doing.

IN THE LAST PAGE considered, we have first a sketch of an oak tree as we would make it on one of our sketching trips. You will notice that this particular tree is very well drawn and is nicely balanced. Next to this sketch is a design of this same tree worked out to fill a circle. Look at the edges of the circle, and you will see how the artist has curved the lines of his tree so that they run gracefully into the circle itself. A design like this one would be well adapted to cutting out in metal, as copper or brass, because it holds together.

THE OAK TREE DESIGN arranged so as to be adapted for an ornamental iron gate is shown next. Observe how the character of the oak tree has been kept even though the design has been made in the twisted scrolls necessary to this kind of iron work. Iron grill work was very popular in the early days, and there are fine examples of old French and Spanish iron work on some of the buildings of New Orleans and other cities.

A STAINED GLASS DESIGN of the oak is shown next. You can see the design has been planned so it will cut up into glass parts as is necessary in stained glass work. To give the picture a complete effect, some figures have been put in the foreground and a ship in the background. At the bottom of the page is a little sketch showing how this stained glass window would look over a bookcase or a buffet. Next to our stained glass design, we have one worked out in geometric lines for a curtain. Notice how the square lines of the design fit in with the square space in which it is set. This design could be worked in cross-stitch, or other medium, on the curtain. A little sketch next to it, shows how the curtain would look with this design upon it.

THE SAME TREE is shown worked on a piece of furniture, such as a chair; worked in hammered brass on a fireplace hood; and on a cover for a guest book. This guest book cover could be in tooled leather, and the chair design could be either carved or stenciled on the wood. A good looking little hope chest is also shown with the tree design carved on the ends. The bands of this chest could be made of copper. A pair of book ends with the tree worked in leather or carved in wood are shown too. So we get here a pretty fair idea of some of the uses to which we can put the design we have learned to make.

AS A LAST WORD, let us put down some don'ts. One of them is, Don't start to color your design before you are sure you have spaced it well in pencil. Another is, Don't put too much into your design. Keep it simple. If your design doesn't look right, try taking out parts instead of adding some. Don't rub too much with your eraser the paper on which you intend to put color. If you do, the surface will be spoiled for taking color well. Make your sketch on a piece of thin scratch paper and trace it off.

IN PLANNING YOUR DESIGNS, keep in mind the following rules:
1. Avoid too many crisscross lines or angles.
2. Do not make all parts alike in size, but vary them.
3. Do not use too many different forms.
4. Avoid making motifs too large or too small for their space.
5. Relate your design to the space or object to be ornamented.
6. Keep all the parts of your design related.

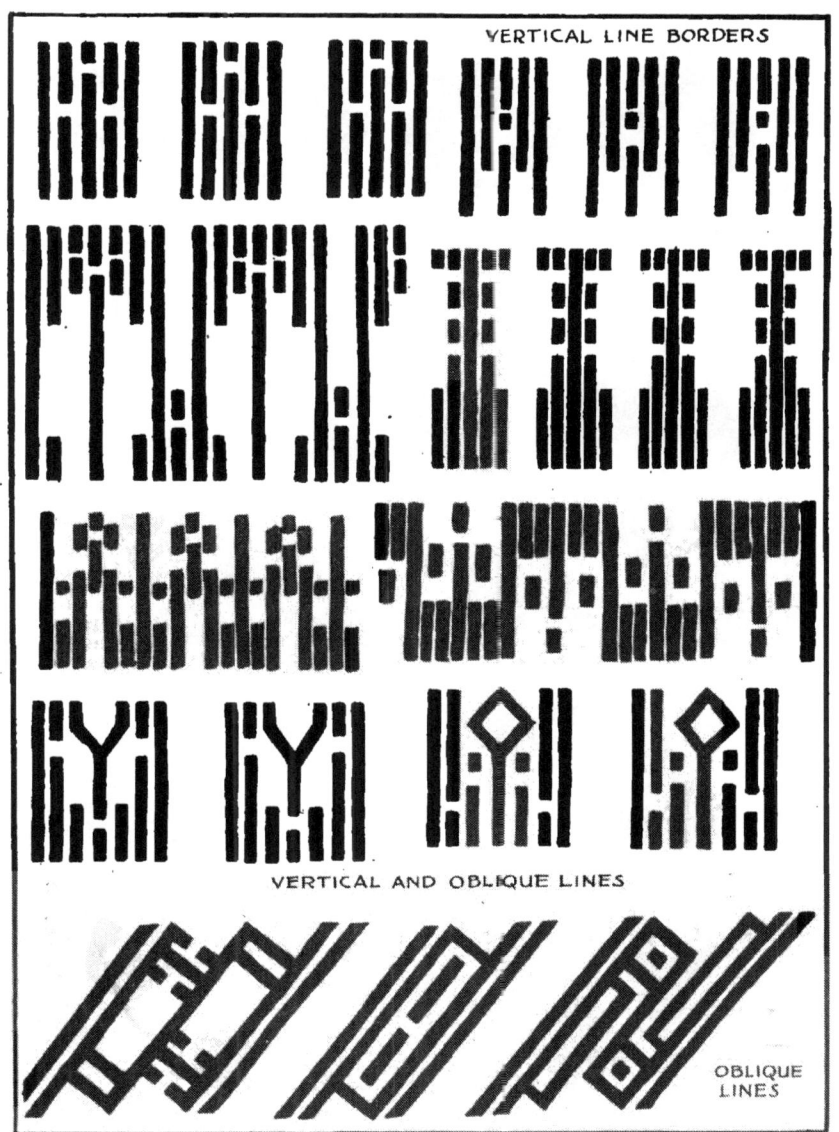

LINE BORDER DESIGNS

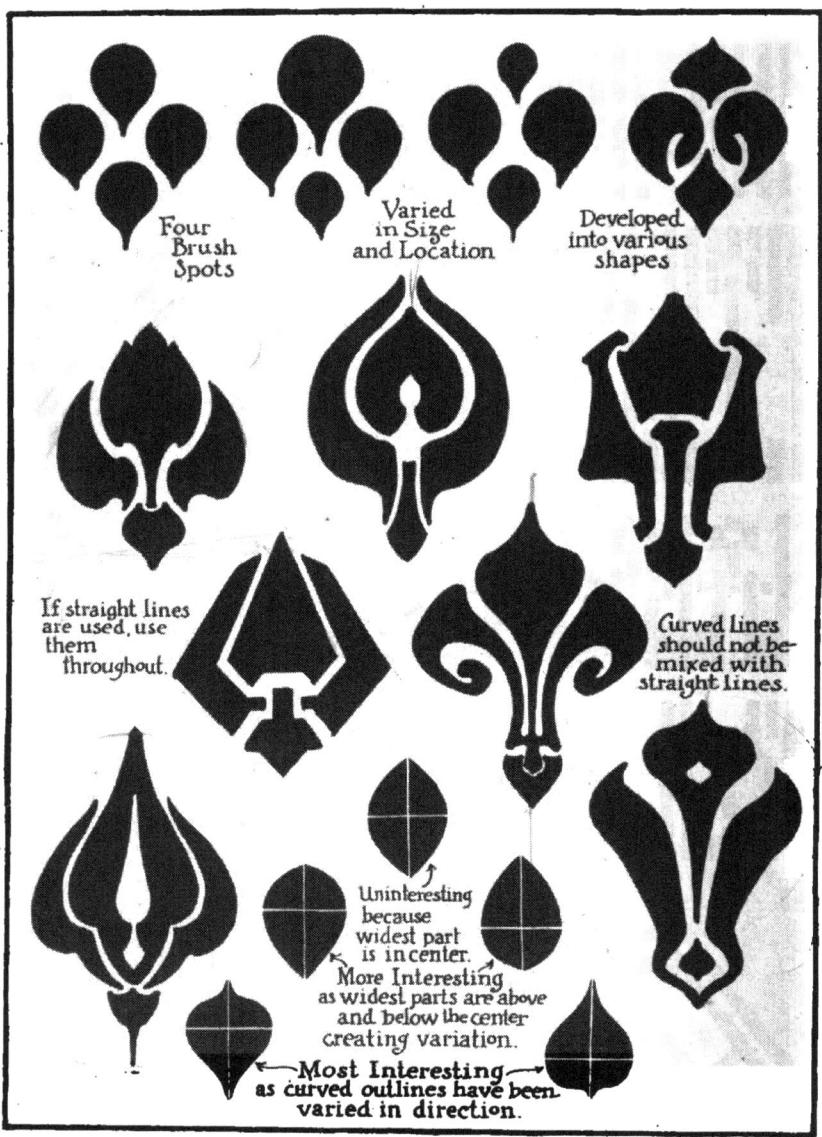

Four
Brush
Spots

Varied
in Size
and Location

Developed
into various
shapes

If straight lines
are used, use
them
throughout.

Curved lines
should not be
mixed with
straight lines.

Uninteresting
because
widest part
is in center.
More Interesting
as widest parts are above
and below the center
creating variation.
Most Interesting
as curved outlines have been
varied in direction.

DESIGN MOTIFS FROM SPOTS

REARRANGEMENT OF THE SAME MOTIF

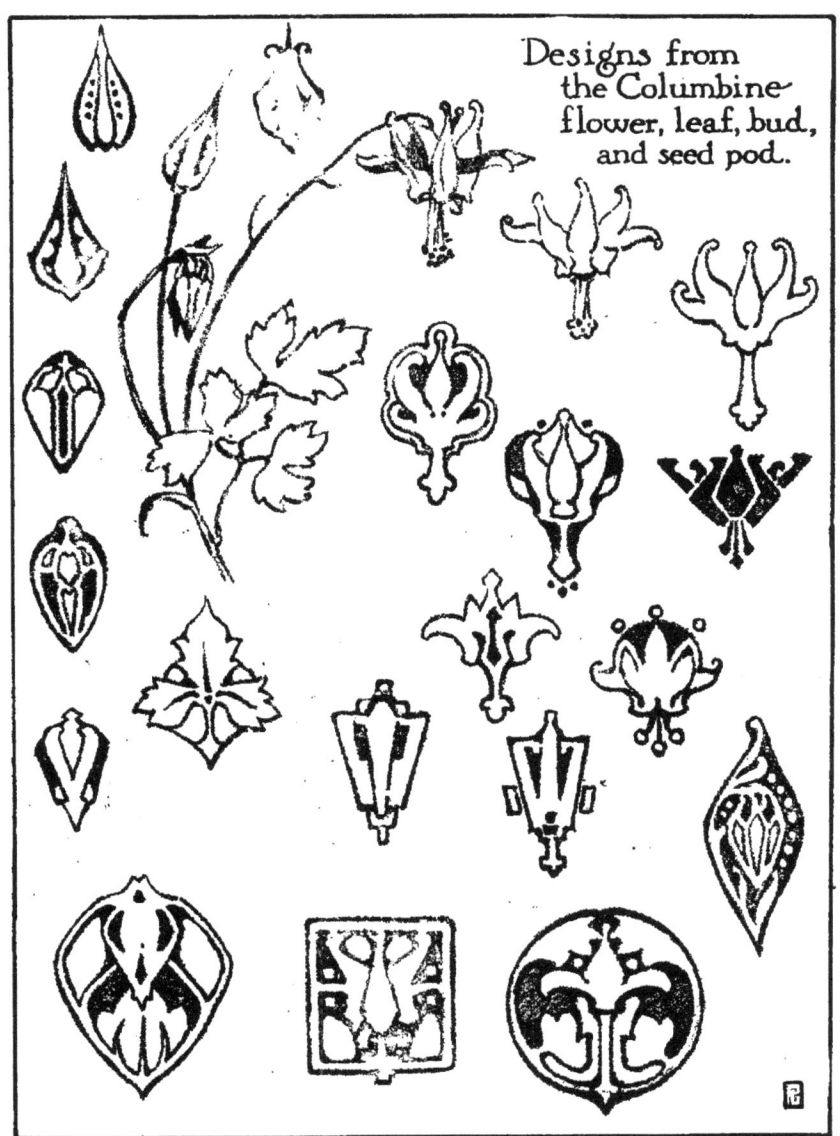

Designs from the Columbine flower, leaf, bud, and seed pod.

DESIGNS FROM FLOWERS

FLOWER MOTIFS

Rhythmic Repetition in Nature.

Radial

Design is Simplified by working patterns over geometric forms.

Any simple motif repeated produces rhythm.

Disorder

Order

Variation may be produced by contrast of size, opposition dark & light and by color

Variation by Opposition

Variation by Contrast

All-Over Patterns

Radial Repetition

Cross St. Ambroïs Paris

Moorish

Greek

Egyptian

Greek

Italian Majolica

St. Peter's Chair-Rome

Early China

REPETITION IN HISTORICAL ORNAMENT

REPETITION IN DESIGN

RADIATION IN DESIGN

17   Applied Art

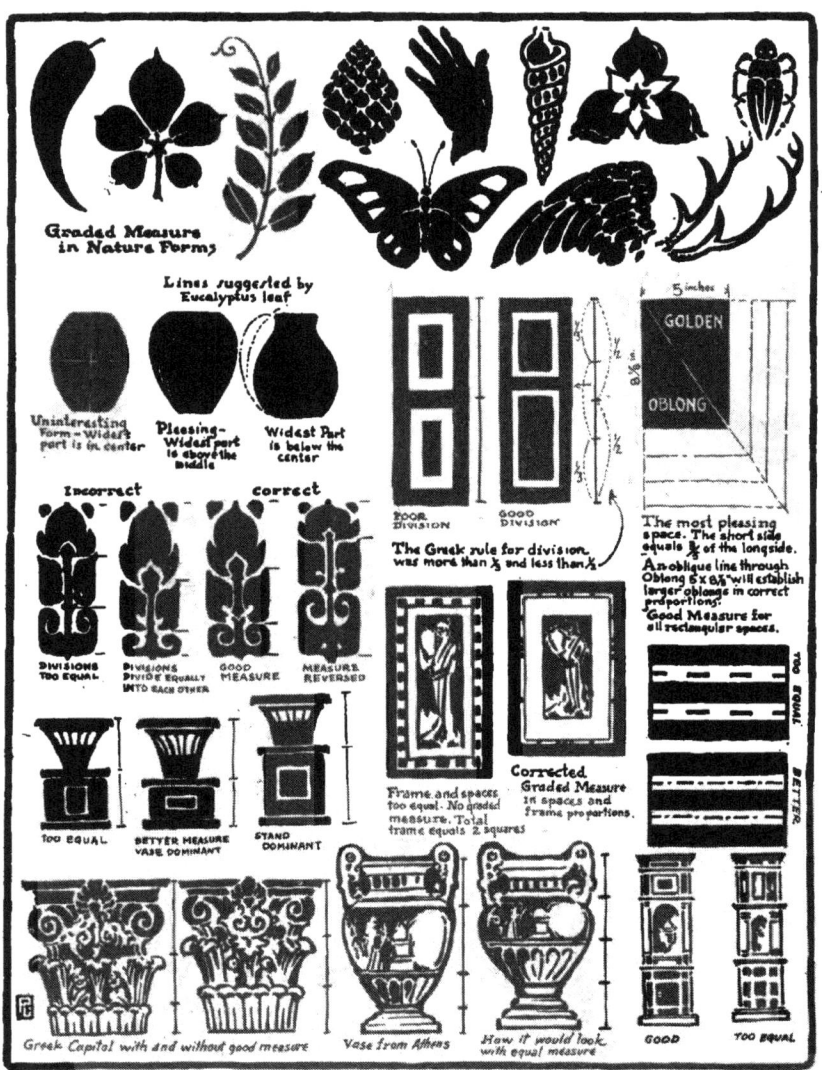

Graded Measure in Nature Forms

Lines suggested by Eucalyptus leaf

Uninteresting Form - Widest part is in center

Pleasing - Widest part is above the middle

Widest Part is below the center

Incorrect

Correct

DIVISIONS TOO EQUAL

DIVISIONS DIVIDE EQUALLY INTO EACH OTHER

GOOD MEASURE

MEASURE REVERSED

POOR DIVISION

GOOD DIVISION

The Greek rule for division was more than ⅓ and less than ½

GOLDEN OBLONG

5 inches

8⅛ in.

The most pleasing space. The short side equals ⅝ of the long side.

An oblique line through Oblong 5 x 8⅛ will establish larger oblongs in correct proportions.

Good Measure for all rectangular spaces.

TOO EQUAL

BETTER MEASURE VASE DOMINANT

STAND DOMINANT

Frame and spaces too equal. No graded measure. Total frame equals 2 squares

Corrected Graded Measure in spaces and frame proportions.

TOO EQUAL

BETTER

Greek Capital with and without good measure

Vase from Athens

How it would look with equal measure

GOOD

TOO EQUAL

MEASURE IN DESIGN

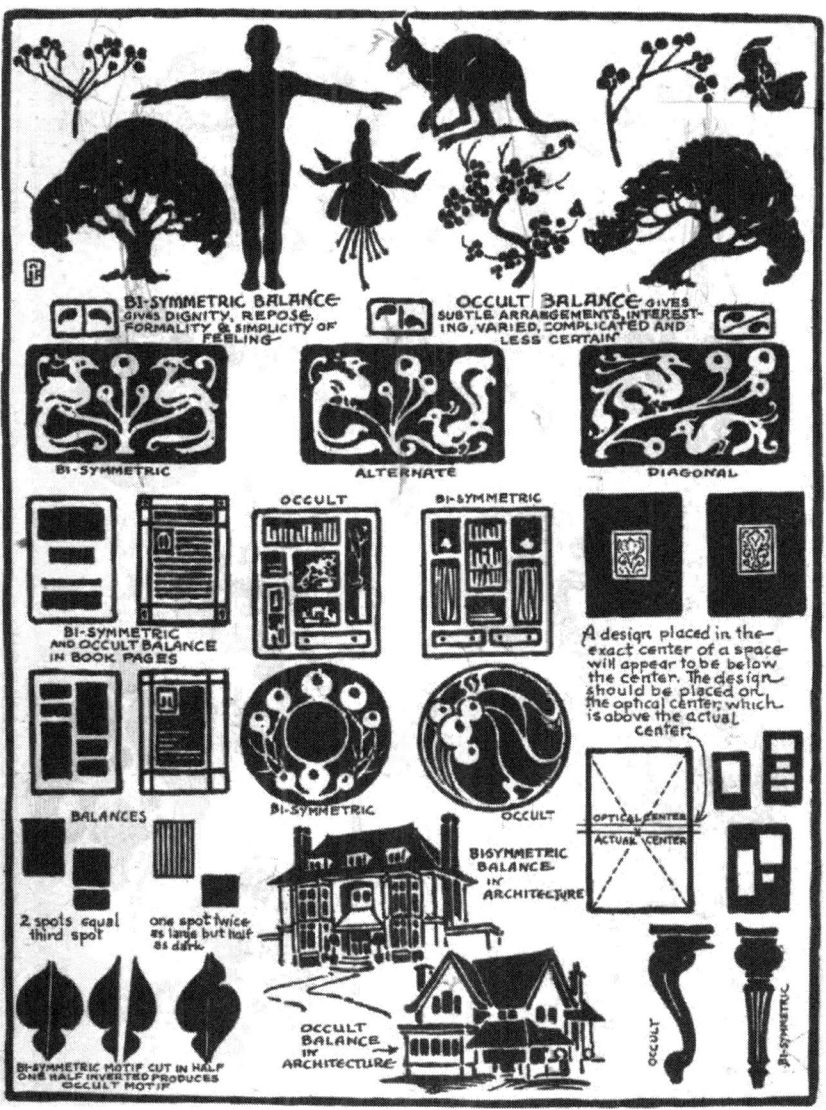

BALANCE IN DESIGN

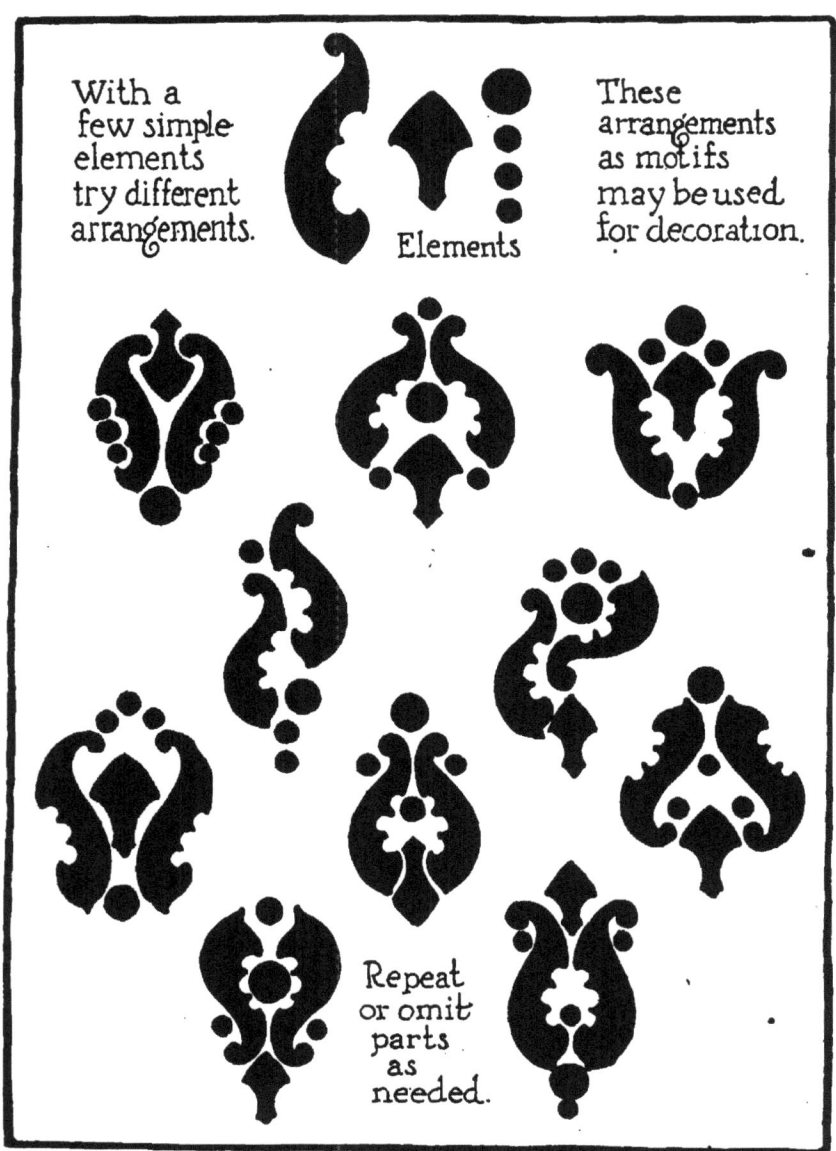

With a few simple elements try different arrangements.

Elements

These arrangements as motifs may be used for decoration.

Repeat or omit parts as needed.

VARIED MOTIFS FROM THE SAME ELEMENTS

SQUARE

CIRCLE

SCALE

SLIP PATTERN

OBLIQUE

HEXAGON

ALL-OVER PATTERNS

DIFFERENT ALL-OVER PATTERNS

VALUE SCALE
Made by taking
intense black and
pure white and
making tone steps
between these two
values. Three
values will do
for designs, as the
tones should be
simple.

DIFFERENT VALUE ARRANGEMENT WITH THE SAME SUBJECT

THE FOUR DIVISIONS OF DESIGN

RUBBED CHARCOAL FLOWER DESIGNS

INSECTS IN DESIGN

HISTORIC BIRD MOTIFS

Oriental

Haida
Indian

Spanish

Byzantine

Japanese

Italian

Coptic

Aztec

Peruvian

Hopi
Indian

The Animal in Design

HISTORIC ANIMAL MOTIFS

LIGHT AND DARK LANDSCAPE DESIGNS.

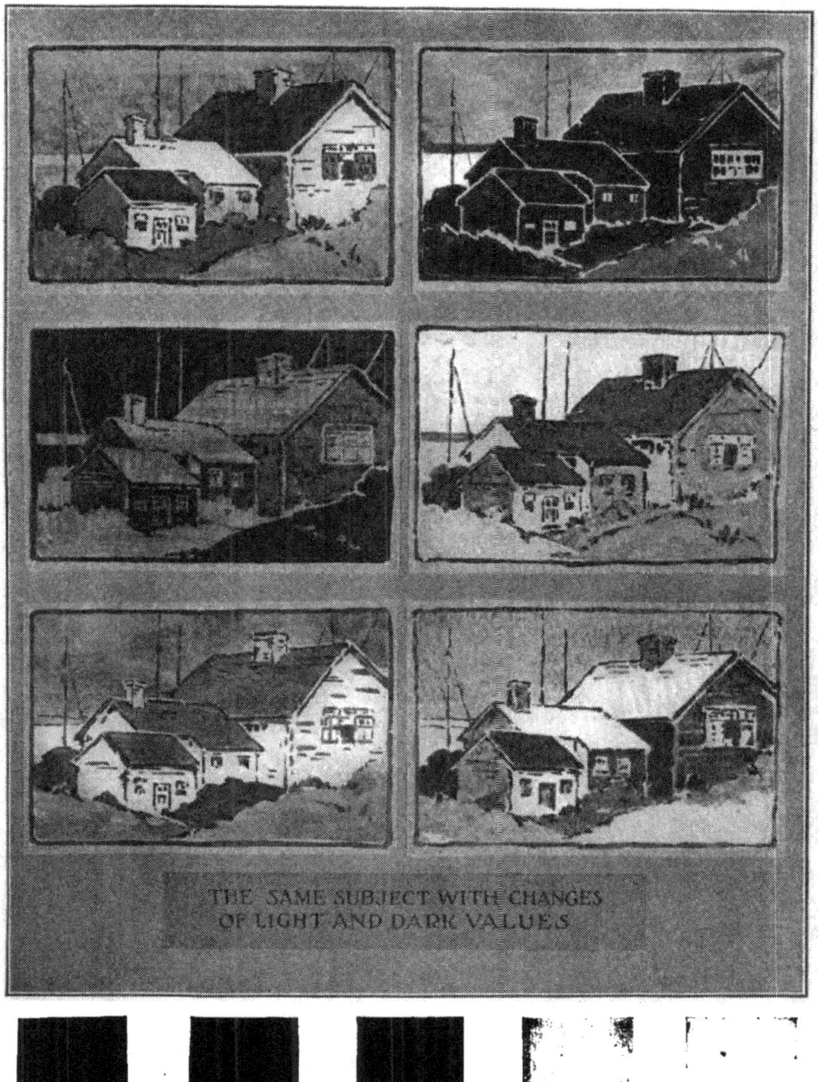

THE SAME SUBJECT WITH CHANGES
OF LIGHT AND DARK VALUES

VALUE STEPS IN LANDSCAPE WORK

DECORATIVE LANDSCAPES

TREES IN APPLIED ART

TEACHER'S NOTES ON DESIGN

NATURE DESIGN OBJECTS. Nature supplies many excellent subjects that demonstrate design principle. While many of these objects are perishable, others can be preserved easily, and should be gathered and exhibited in the classroom. Flower forms and animal and marine growths should be drawn so as to accent the design principle for which they have been selected, and the drawing should be carefully arranged and assembled with the nature design collection. Students are certain to become keener and more appreciative admirers of nature if they recognize that nature is ready to assist them in their handiwork by suggestions toward beauty. The teacher should take the class occasionally on a "nature design journey," during which the students should make notations and collections of everything that tends toward illustrating the design principle.

BUTTERFLIES, BIRDS, AND ANIMALS. The use of butterflies, birds, and animals by designers as sources for design suggestions is very general. Color harmonies, patterns for surfaces, and motifs for design use are repeatedly to be found in such forms. The women of Persia gather butterflies into cages, that they may look at them while they weave the beautiful textiles for which their country is famous. One of the best inspirations toward good design in a classroom is to secure a number of mounted butterflies or birds and animals and use them for subjects in design either in their entire forms or merely as color suggestions; or parts of the subject can be used as suggestions for a border or an all-over pattern. It will be surprising to the teacher who thinks that every conceivable suggestion toward design has been secured from a given butterfly or bird, to find some student later who will make an entirely new adaptation. Some students have a greater range of originality and adaptation than the average. These students should be employed by the teacher to help in developing similar vision in other students.

FABRICS AND WALL PAPER. The study of useful application of all design should follow or be interwoven with every design problem. In the use of all-over patterns or borders made from repeated forms, many good examples will be found to occur in printed, woven, and dyed textiles. Splendid repeated designs will also be found in wall paper. Small sections of fabrics and wall papers can be secured inexpensively. These can be mounted on cards, and kept to display whenever a problem will be helped by their use. There are magazines also that picture buildings and rugs and patterns from many parts of the world. These should be collected and mounted, and added to the reference files of design patterns. The use of a design pattern or single motif used in different ways, for an all-over design, should be one of the prominent problems of the design class, and can be stimulated if the teacher has some such problem that has been successfully accomplished, on display where the students can easily see it.

WALL PAPERS AND TEXTILES

THE USE OF DESIGNS THAT ARE NOT GOOD. If students hear of and see only artistic designs, yet inadvertently they may develop, in their search for originality, trends that are not desirable, and they may not be aware of their faults. The teacher will have no trouble in finding plenty of carpet designs showing flowers in huge, realistic form; and rug designs with cats and dogs in pictorial arrangements; frames with many ornate, unrelated ornaments; wall papers with effects of much interweaving, and perspective garden effects; poorly designed book covers; furniture and houses with impossible ambitions. Seeing these, or their pictures, will prove one of the most positive ways of impressing upon the students what not to do. Examples of pleasing, quiet, and unobtrusive articles that are fitted to their purpose, and that design which enriches without defeating utility, should be put alongside the poor examples. Such an exhibit and its lessons will never be forgotten by the student.

INCORRECT DESIGN APPLICATIONS

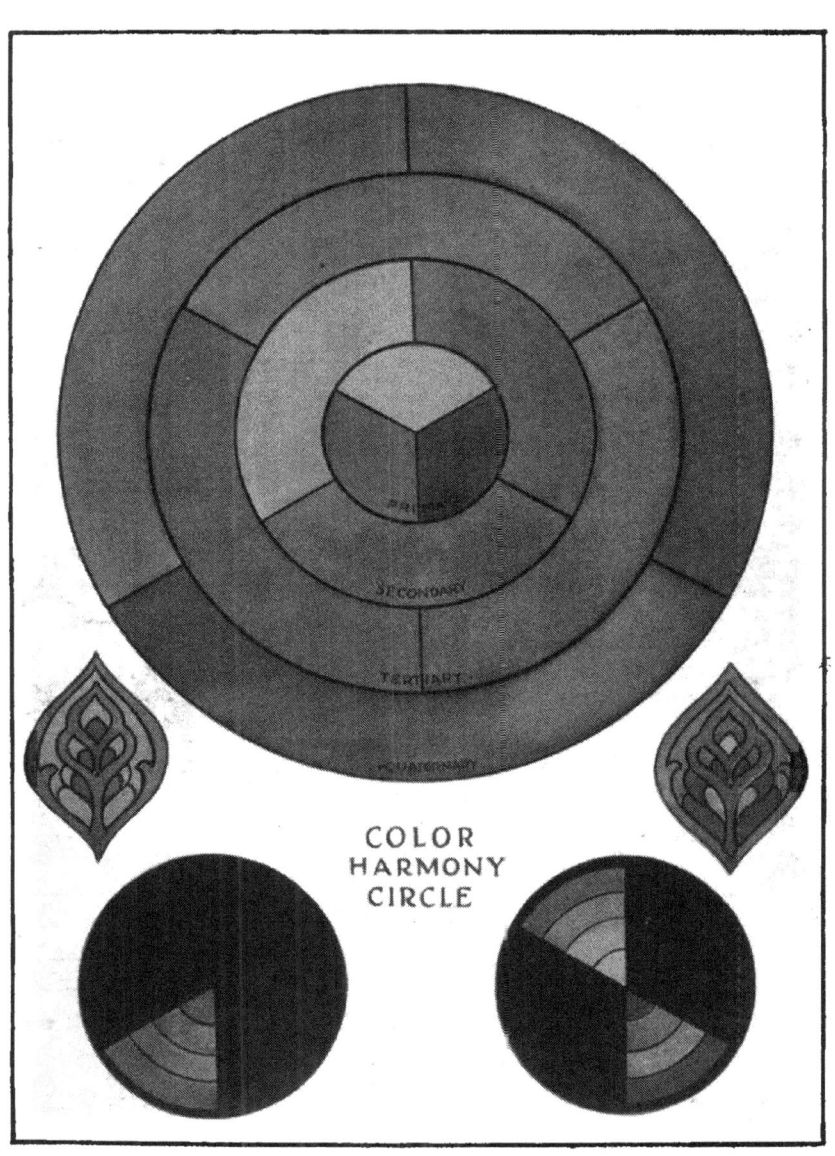

COLOR
HARMONY
CIRCLE

COMPLEMENTARY COLOR WHEEL — COLOR CHART NO. 1

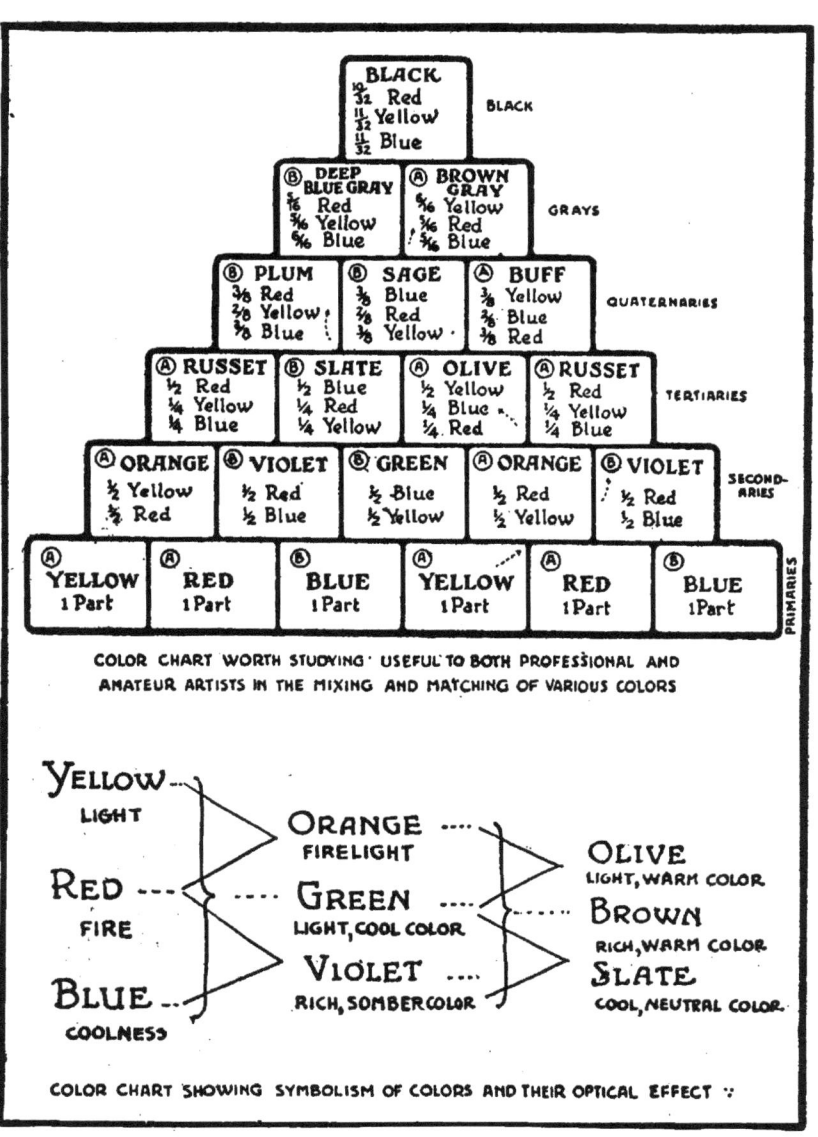

BLACK
10/32 Red
11/32 Yellow
11/32 Blue

BLACK

ⓑ DEEP BLUE GRAY
5/16 Red
5/16 Yellow
6/16 Blue

Ⓐ BROWN GRAY
6/16 Yellow
5/16 Red
5/16 Blue

GRAYS

ⓑ PLUM
3/8 Red
2/8 Yellow
3/8 Blue

ⓑ SAGE
3/8 Blue
3/8 Red
2/8 Yellow

Ⓐ BUFF
3/8 Yellow
2/8 Blue
3/8 Red

QUATERNARIES

Ⓐ RUSSET
1/2 Red
1/4 Yellow
1/4 Blue

ⓑ SLATE
1/2 Blue
1/4 Red
1/4 Yellow

Ⓐ OLIVE
1/2 Yellow
1/4 Blue
1/4 Red

Ⓐ RUSSET
1/2 Red
1/4 Yellow
1/4 Blue

TERTIARIES

Ⓐ ORANGE
1/2 Yellow
1/2 Red

ⓥ VIOLET
1/2 Red
1/2 Blue

Ⓖ GREEN
1/2 Blue
1/2 Yellow

Ⓐ ORANGE
1/2 Red
1/2 Yellow

ⓑ VIOLET
1/2 Red
1/2 Blue

SECONDARIES

Ⓐ YELLOW 1 Part

Ⓐ RED 1 Part

ⓑ BLUE 1 Part

Ⓐ YELLOW 1 Part

Ⓐ RED 1 Part

ⓑ BLUE 1 Part

PRIMARIES

COLOR CHART WORTH STUDYING · USEFUL TO BOTH PROFESSIONAL AND AMATEUR ARTISTS IN THE MIXING AND MATCHING OF VARIOUS COLORS

YELLOW
LIGHT

RED
FIRE

BLUE
COOLNESS

ORANGE
FIRELIGHT

GREEN
LIGHT, COOL COLOR

VIOLET
RICH, SOMBER COLOR

OLIVE
LIGHT, WARM COLOR

BROWN
RICH, WARM COLOR

SLATE
COOL, NEUTRAL COLOR

COLOR CHART SHOWING SYMBOLISM OF COLORS AND THEIR OPTICAL EFFECT ⁖

COLOR CHART A

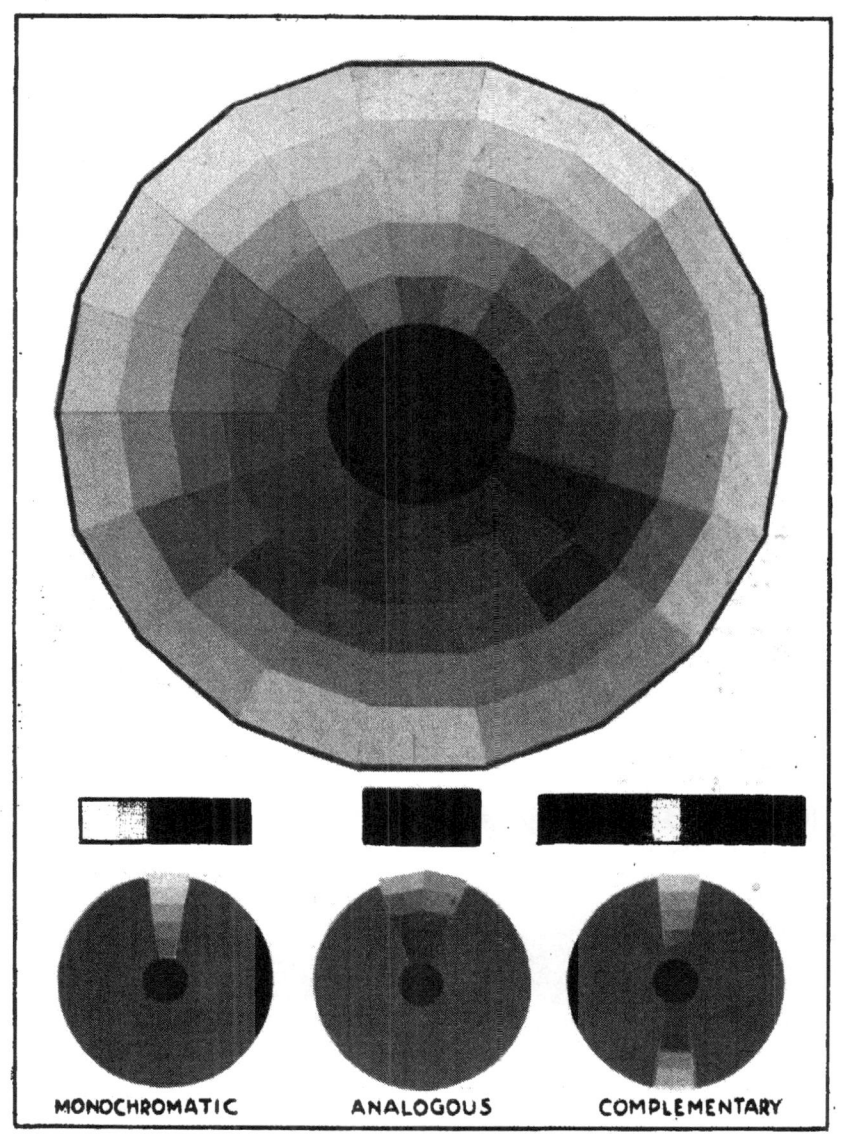

MONOCHROMATIC   ANALOGOUS   COMPLEMENTARY

COLOR HARMONY WHEEL — COLOR CHART NO. 2

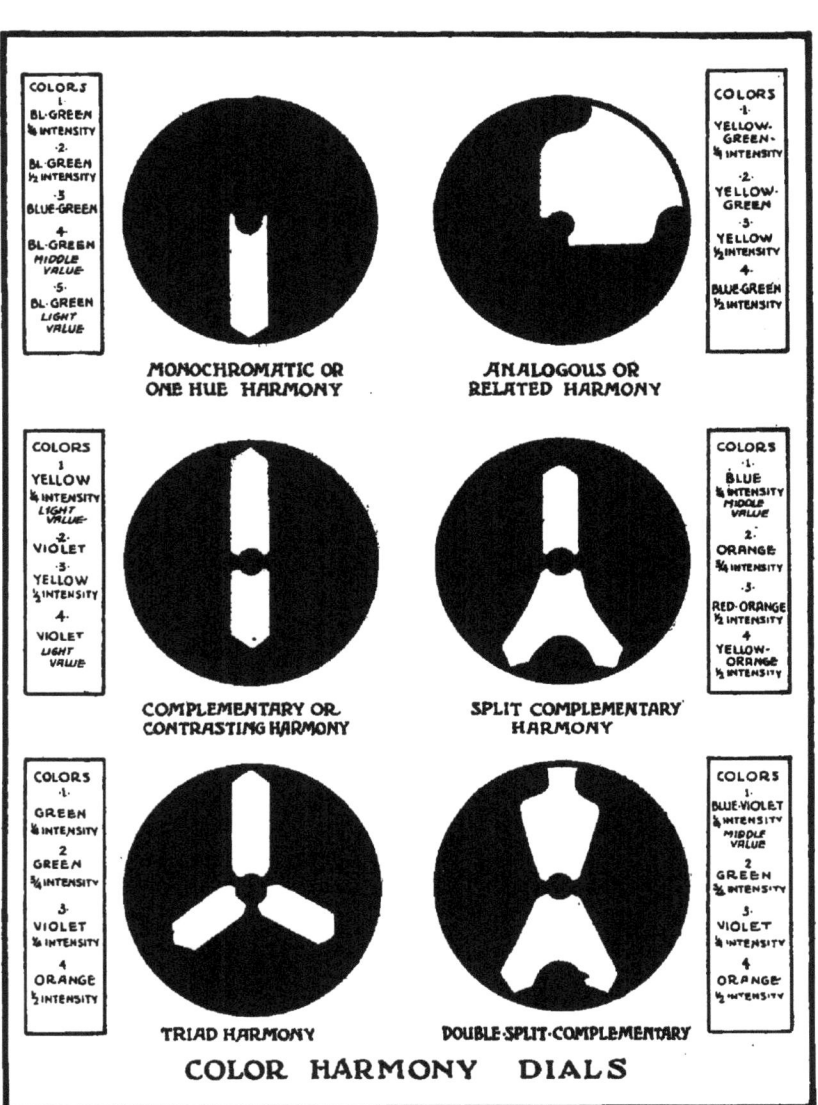

COLORS
1.
BL·GREEN
⅞ INTENSITY
·2·
BL·GREEN
½ INTENSITY
·3·
BLUE·GREEN
4·
BL·GREEN
MIDDLE
VALUE·
·5·
BL·GREEN
LIGHT
VALUE

MONOCHROMATIC OR
ONE HUE HARMONY

COLORS
·1·
YELLOW·
GREEN·
⅞ INTENSITY
·2·
YELLOW·
GREEN
·3·
YELLOW
½ INTENSITY
4·
BLUE·GREEN
½ INTENSITY

ANALOGOUS OR
RELATED HARMONY

COLORS
1
YELLOW
⅞ INTENSITY
LIGHT
VALUE·
·2·
VIOLET
·3·
YELLOW
½ INTENSITY
4·
VIOLET
LIGHT
VALUE

COMPLEMENTARY OR
CONTRASTING HARMONY

COLORS
·1·
BLUE
⅞ INTENSITY
MIDDLE
VALUE
2·
ORANGE
¾ INTENSITY
·3·
RED·ORANGE
½ INTENSITY
4
YELLOW·
ORANGE
½ INTENSITY

SPLIT COMPLEMENTARY
HARMONY

COLORS
·1·
GREEN
⅞ INTENSITY
2
GREEN
¾ INTENSITY
·3·
VIOLET
⅛ INTENSITY
4
ORANGE
½ INTENSITY

TRIAD HARMONY

COLORS
1
BLUE·VIOLET
⅞ INTENSITY
MIDDLE
VALUE
2
GREEN
¾ INTENSITY
3·
VIOLET
⅛ INTENSITY
4
ORANGE
½ INTENSITY

DOUBLE·SPLIT·COMPLEMENTARY

COLOR HARMONY DIALS

COLOR CHART B

Application of
Nature Colors
to Design Harmonies

COLOR HARMONIES FROM NATURE

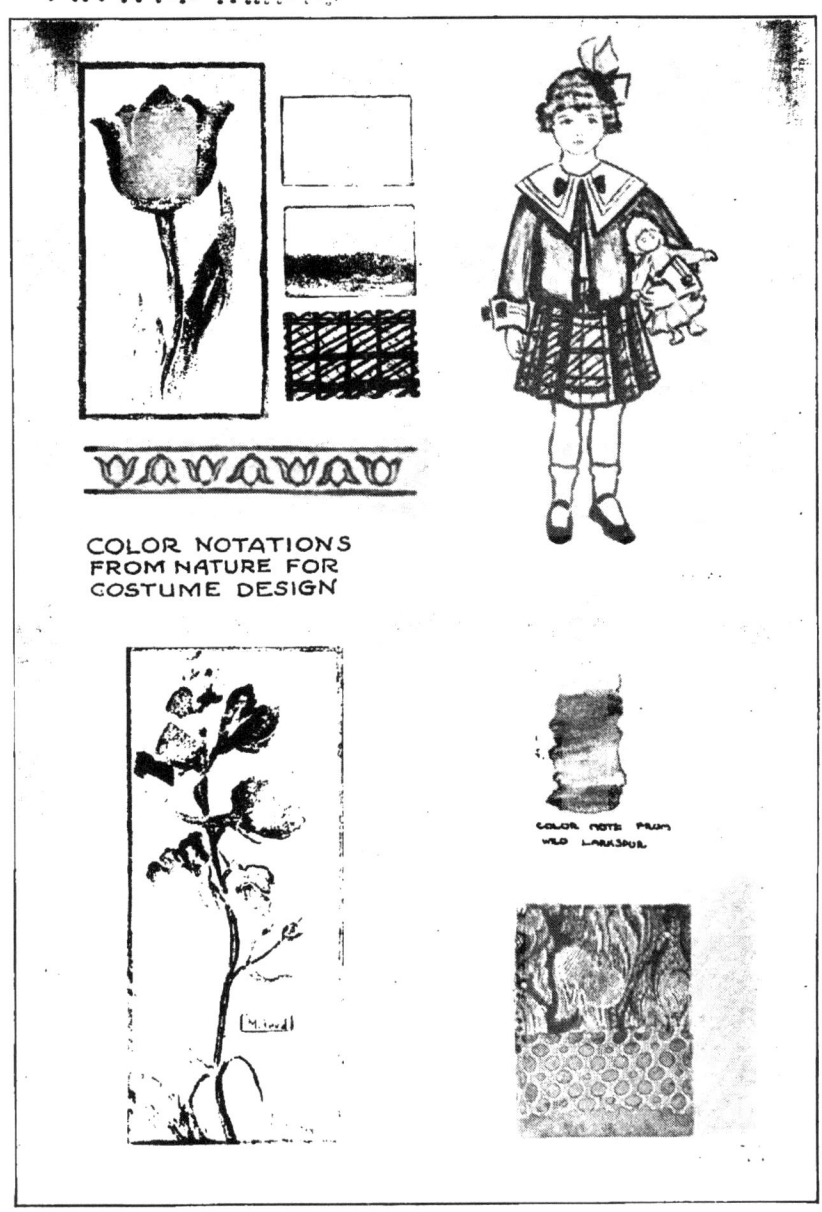

COLOR NOTATIONS
FROM NATURE FOR
COSTUME DESIGN

COLOR NOTE FROM
WILD LARKSPUR

THE USE OF NATURE COLORS FOR COSTUMES

COPTIC
WEAVING
300 A.D.

COLOR NOTATIONS FROM TEXTILES

JAPANESE
BROCADE
1800 A.D.

COLOR HARMONIES FROM TEXTILES

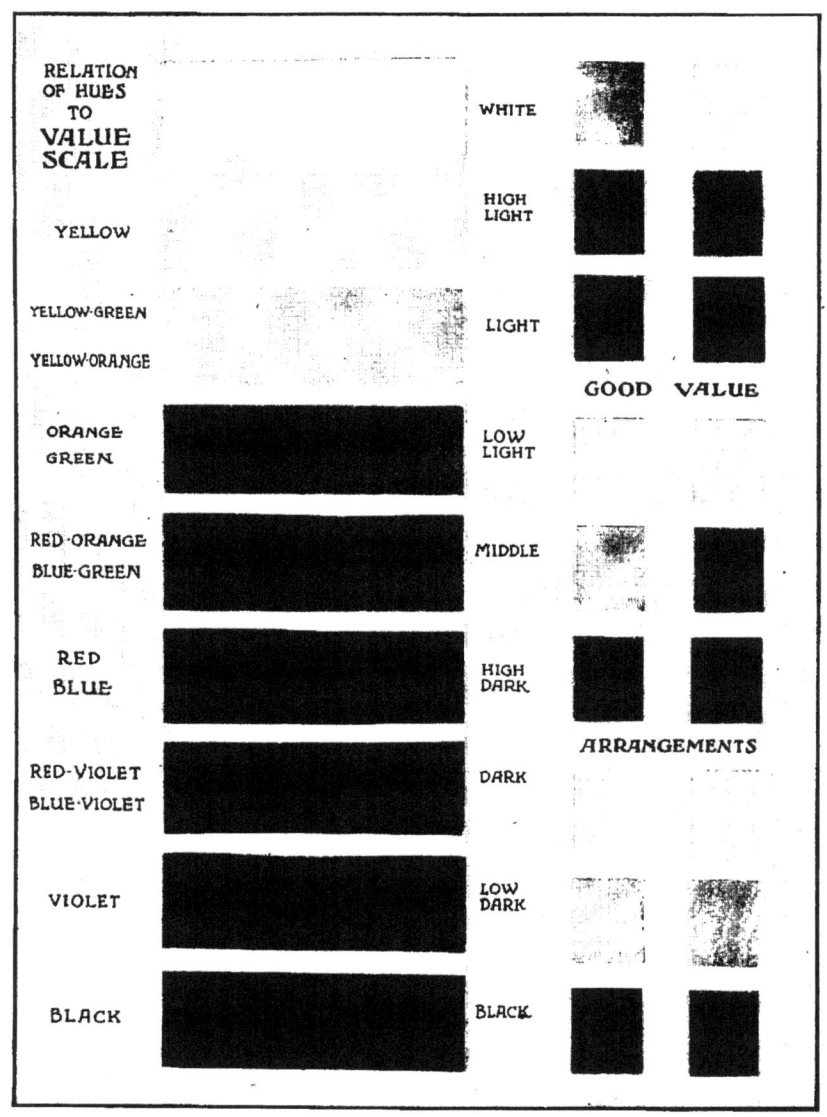

RELATION
OF HUES
TO
**VALUE
SCALE**

YELLOW

YELLOW-GREEN

YELLOW-ORANGE

ORANGE
GREEN

RED-ORANGE
BLUE-GREEN

RED
BLUE

RED-VIOLET
BLUE-VIOLET

VIOLET

BLACK

WHITE

HIGH
LIGHT

LIGHT

LOW
LIGHT

MIDDLE

HIGH
DARK

DARK

LOW
DARK

BLACK

GOOD VALUE

ARRANGEMENTS

THE NEUTRAL SCALE

Leather

Carved
Wood

Printed Fabric

Silver Pendant

Stencil

Weaving

Etched
Metal

Painted
Box Cover

COLOR DESIGNS FROM PLANT FORM

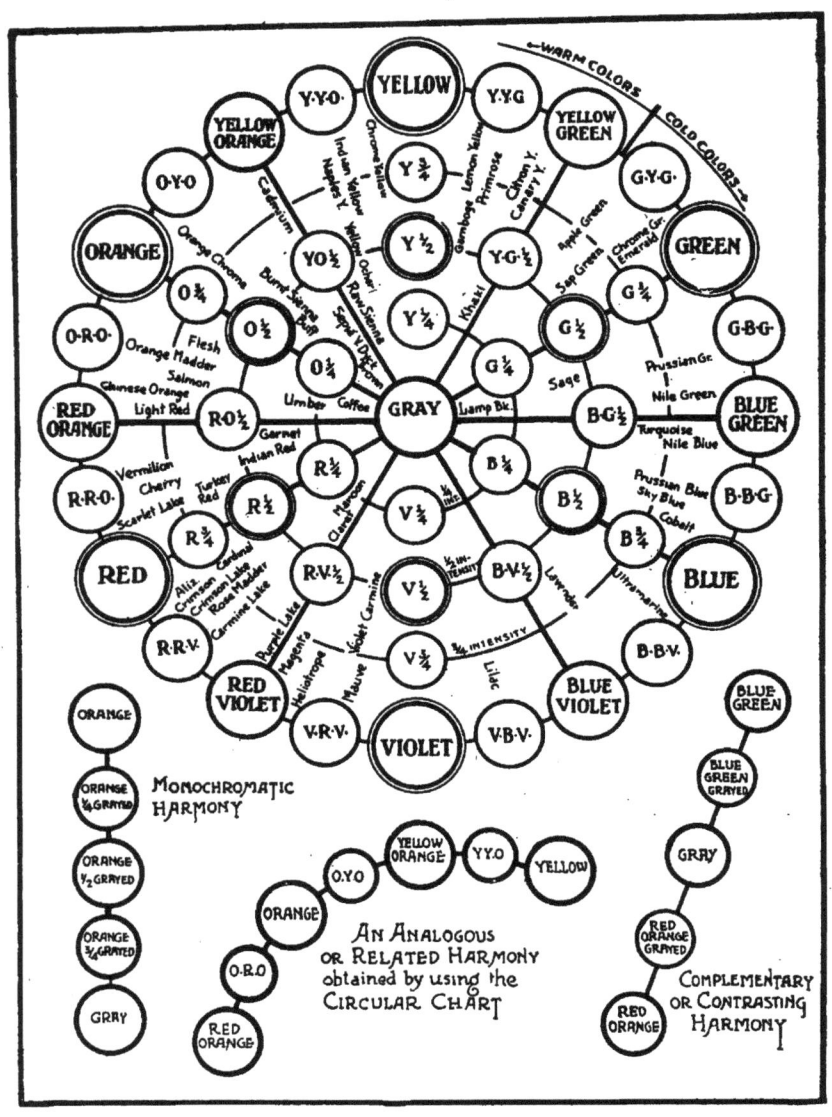

THE RELATION OF PIGMENTS TO THE COLOR WHEEL

THE ACADEMIC GRADES

COLOR

, COLOR is the next subject we shall take up. It is a fascinating subject to study. To some people, color is a difficult subject. This is generally because they try to do wonderful things with color before they have learned the basic principles.

NEW COLOR THEORIES are constantly being discovered and suggested by educators. Some teachers of color adopt every new theory that comes along, and the result is generally a bewildered class, and oftentimes a bewildered teacher. Color is not confusing if we are willing to start right. One of the main troubles in studying color lies in the fact that people fail to realize that a theory which can be successfully illustrated with a prism and light rays, may not work out at all with oil or water color pigments.

ALL PAINTS CONTAIN SOME SEDIMENT, because of the ingredients from which they are made. It is this sediment which makes the use of color from a practical standpoint quite different from the study of the theorist experimenting with light rays.

PRIMARY COLORS are called by that name because from them it is possible to obtain all the other colors. Various colors have been named by artists as being the correct primary colors. But the color theory which names yellow, red, and blue as the three primary colors, has been proved the most successful from a practical standpoint. All the other colors can be worked out by combinations of these primaries.

ENGRAVERS base their work on this theory. By using a series of color filters, our modern photo-engravers are able to make plates which, in three printings, of yellow, red, and blue, give us all the colors found in nature. Sometimes a fourth plate of black is added to give the picture the gray tones. If you will take a good magnifying glass and look at the color prints in this book, you will find the little dots of yellow, red, and blue running all through them.

INTERIOR DECORATORS also base their color work on this theory. If you will look at the color chart with yellow, red, and blue in the center, entitled "Color Chart No. 1," you will see a color wheel, which is used largely by decorators. Every one who uses it finds it successful. This chart starts with an inner circle of the three primaries, yellow and red and blue.

(273)

THE SECONDARY COLORS, as they are called, are found in the second circle. These colors are made by combinations of the primaries. From this circle, we find that yellow and red make orange; yellow and blue make green; and red and blue make violet. In the third circle, we find the third or tertiary colors, which are made by mixing the secondary colors together; as, violet and orange to make russet, orange and green to make citrine. The fourth circle has the quaternary colors. The location of the colors on the chart not only shows how the colors are made, but also helps the artist to figure out color schemes. This latter point is the leading feature of this particular chart.

GOOD COLOR SCHEMES can always be worked out by the use together of the colors found in any of the wedge-shaped sections shown on this same chart. In this case, the artist finds he is using what are known as related or analogous colors. These colors have to a greater or less extent some common color running through them all. Contrasting colors have the tendency to enrich or emphasize each other when used together, as in the case of the pie-shaped sections that lie directly opposite each other. These contrasting colors are suitable to use in such places as posters, billboards, car cards, and other places where brilliance and emphasis are desired. On the other hand, related or analogous color schemes are preferable when the softer harmonies are needed, as in room decorations, fabrics, and costumes.

THIS COLOR WHEEL is a great aid to students in devising color schemes for themselves, instead of relying upon the teacher, as is generally done. In addition to helping the students to decide the *kind* of colors to be used, it also helps to determine the *amount* of each color. For instance, in looking at the color wheel, we find that in the triangle selected, the area of plum color is seven or eight times as large as that of red. In planning a design or poster, the pupil should use plum in the larger areas, and red in the smaller ones.

COLORS ON THE OUTER RIM of the color wheel are much less brilliant than those in the inner circle, so they can be used in a greater proportion than the brilliant colors. Thus we find that the chart automatically works out a rule much used by designers, which says: "The smaller the area, the brighter the color; the larger the area, the grayer or softer the color."

ANOTHER COLOR CHART, and an unusually useful one, is found on the reverse side of the Chart 1. This chart may look a little complex at first glance, but in reality it is not. It shows the mixing and development of colors from the primaries clear on to the grays and to black. It starts at the bottom with the primary colors, and keeps building up until it finishes off with the deep grays and black. From this, the student can see the transposition from the brighter colors to the softer and grayer colors.

THE CORRECT PROPORTION of primary colors needed to make any of the other colors is also shown in this chart. By looking at the diagram, we see immediately that buff can be made of $\frac{3}{8}$ yellow, $\frac{3}{8}$ red, and $\frac{1}{4}$ blue. In other words, if the student took one part yellow, one part red, and a little less than one part of blue, he would come pretty close to a good buff. Of course, some allowance will have to be made for the variation of colors in the different boxes of students, but the chart gives the right start.

GOOD COLOR SCHEMES are easily worked out from this chart. You will notice that in the upper left-hand corner, a little circle has been drawn with an A and a B lettered in it. All the colors lettered A are related or analogous to one another. All those marked B are related to each other. In this way, we find that blue, green, slate, sage, and blue gray are related. If the artist wishes to obtain a combination of colors that have contrast, all he needs to do is to combine a color that is marked A with one marked B. The farther up on the pyramid these colors are, the more certain the artist is of obtaining a pleasing combination of contrasting colors. If you use adjoining colors on rows next to each other, following a course similar to that shown by the light dotted line, you are sure to obtain the most perfect contrasts.

ANOTHER COLOR WHEEL is Color Chart No. 2 in this same chapter. Color wheels similar to this have been in use for some time past. In this wheel, the various colors are placed around the circumference of the circle. Between the three primary colors are the secondary colors and the mixed hues. The colors in their standard form are shown in the third circle. The grayed colors are given in the two inner circles, and the lighter values or tints of the colors in the two outer circles.

GRAYED AND BRILLIANT COLORS are in this way shown as well as the various hues and values. A fine way to use this color wheel is to make three little dials of cardboard that will fit the color wheel. One of these dials will be merely a straight strip of cardboard. With this particular dial, ordinary complementary color schemes are worked out very quickly. For instance, if we swing one point to green, we find the other point resting on its complementary color, red.

WHEN SELECTING COLORS in this way, avoid using two colors from the same circle. If, for instance, you select a brilliant red for one of your colors, then you should select a grayed green to go with it, or a tint of the green. A little black used as a third color for the darkest note will give a perfect color combination.

SPLIT COMPLEMENTARY HARMONIES are easily understood after you refer to this last color wheel. Instead of a dial with one straight line, as before, we make a cardboard open dial like the one in the diagram on the reverse page, Chart No. 2, which has a double-forked opening at one end. If we turn the single point of the opening to green, the double forked point will register red-orange and red-violet, both of which can be used with green without any danger of clashing. Split complementary harmonies are better than the straight complementary color schemes, from the fact that they give more refinement and variety of color.

THE DOUBLE SPLIT COMPLEMENTARY HARMONY is obtained by making a cardboard open dial that has the opening ends split into narrow forks as shown on the same page. If we turn one end of the dial so that the forks point to red-orange and red-violet, then the other pointed forks rest on yellow-green and blue-green. If we analyze these colors, we discover the interesting fact that the green in one set offsets the red in the other set. We also see that the yellow offsets the violet, and the blue offsets the orange. For this reason, double split complementaries are always fine harmonies to select in working out color schemes, as they contain a combination of both related and contrasting colors.

TRIAD HARMONIES are obtained by making a cardboard dial as on Color Chart B, the openings of which include colors that are one third of a circle apart. The points will rest on such colors as orange, green, and violet, or yellow-orange, blue-green, and red-violet. This gives a color scheme which has variation and yet does not clash. It is a useful color scheme, because many professional orders, such as magazine and book covers, call for schemes on three colors. In the selection of colors for a triad harmony, one of the colors should be used in its full intensity or brilliancy, and the others in more grayed or neutral tones.

A COLOR SENSE, or instinctive ability to select colors that may well be used together, is the natural gift of some people. To them, certain colors must not be used together, because they do not "look right." These people are fortunate in a way; but the study and use of such charts as are here shown and described will help them to decide on their colors more readily and to be surer of their ground. For the color students who are not so fortunate as to be naturally gifted with a "color eye," the value of these charts is almost beyond estimation.

NATURE is crowded to overflowing with color in its many phases. The more we study color and look for it, the more we see of it in our surroundings. A student who begins to try painting from nature out of doors begins to see and put down color that he never before realized was there. He sees purple in his shadows where he thought there was only brown or black. He sees cream and blue in his high lights where once he thought he saw only white. In the same way, the nature student discovers color when sketching birds or leaves, rocks or shells. The little flower that at a quick glance he believed to be two-colored, may prove to be made up of seven or eight varying colors, shades, and tints.

PROFESSIONAL ARTISTS depend upon Mother Nature for their color inspirations. Many exquisitely wonderful rugs and fabrics have been based on color schemes that some clever and thoughtful artist has obtained from a leaf or a flower. Study the page showing color harmonies from a leaf. Here we see how the colors obtained from it have been used in various ways, such as a room interior, landscape, etc. How many beginners would have thought that such a pleasing interior decoration could be developed from such a simple source?

SEA SHELLS, BIRDS, ROCKS, the bark of trees, butterflies, insects, and dozens of other sources in nature are all good places to get a start in developing color schemes. Sometimes an ordinary little rock picked up on the hillside or on the seashore will reveal an interesting and unique color scheme that can be used in many ways. If the colors are used in the same proportions found in nature, the results are bound to be better than if the colors are used in any other proportions. You will be surprised to see how gray and soft most of the colors really are that we find in nature.

ORIENTAL FABRICS and prints are also good sources of color. How many of us are there who have not stopped and admired the beautiful, soft colors of some well made Oriental rug? Or, in other instances, it may be a piece of ancient dress goods of historic interest which contains the exquisite coloring. On one of the color pages, we see how color notations have been made from fabrics that have come down from past generations. If there is a museum in your locality, keep your eyes open the next time you visit it, and you will see in the vases, the old furniture, the tapestries and fabrics, many splendid color notes that it would pay you to jot down for future use.

A VERY SUCCESSFUL ARTIST made it a habit to carry with him a little notebook in which he put down various things that would help him in his art work. Among the items he never failed to enter were unique color schemes he came across through the day. When he was working on some order, such as a book cover, a poster, or a bit of pottery, he would often find in his notebook a suitable scheme. Thus the little book paid him for his trouble many times over.

MATCHING COLOR is really more difficult than most people think. Those of us whose eyes are not fully developed to a true color sense, may think that we have matched a color when in reality we have not. To some people, all green looks practically the same; but to the real color artist, there are many greens, and they are all individual. In the European countries, people have been trained to see color more correctly than here in America. Not long ago an American firm turned out some fabrics that were not quite satisfactory. For some reason, the colors looked harsh and glaring. This was in spite of the fact that, as the superintendent claimed, they had followed the same color scheme as that used on a much admired piece of European goods.

THE COLOR ARTIST was called into the conference, and he soon proved to the manufacturers that the colors used on their fabric were much more brilliant than those found in the European cloth. He did this by cutting a little circle out of a piece of cardboard, and placing the cardboard on the cloth in such a way as to show each color in turn. When he did this, the European colors were found to be in reality quite gray, but they looked more brilliant because of being placed next to one another — a fact observed in all complementary colors.

"HUE" is the name given to the various *kinds* of colors. For example, hues that most of us can easily think of are yellow, red, and blue, orange, green, and violet. There are many other, hues besides these. "Hue" means the *kind*, or *type*, of color in question.

"VALUE" is the term applied to the amount of light or dark in a color. We might have a drawing all made up of one color, but using different *values* of that color. The picture might show a light green sky, and a medium green lake, and a deep green tree, and yet have all painted from the same tube of paint. Values in colors are obtained in different ways. If we wish to obtain a light tint of any water color we are using, we generally add water to it. This allows more of the white paper to show and gives our tone a lighter value. If we wish to make our tone darker, we add black to it. In using oil paints, we add white to our color to lighten its value.

INTENSITY is the quality of color that is the most difficult for students to understand. When we speak of the intensity of a color, we refer to the brilliancy of the color, or the speed with which its light waves travel to the eye. A very pure, crisp color is generally an intense one. Some of our colors have more intensity than others. Yellow, for instance, travels toward the eye twelve times faster than violet, and is therefore a considerably more intense color.

THIS INTENSITY, or brilliancy, of a color may be grayed or subdued by the addition of some of its complementary to it. For example, if we have a green that looks far too brilliant, we add a little of its complement, which is red, and this subdues the color without killing any of its richness; or if we have a design with blue and orange in it, and we find the colors too brilliant, we can easily remedy this by mixing a little blue into the orange and a little of the orange into the blue. In this way, we reduce the intensity of the color, though we may not change its value or hue.

COMPLEMENTARY COLORS are very easily found if we use any of the charts shown and described in this chapter. However, to make clear the meaning of the term "complementary," it may be well to explain that two complementary colors used together have the quality of completely satisfying the optic nerves of the eye. This can easily be proved if you will cut from a piece of bright red paper a little circle. Next take a pen and make a little dot of ink about $1/16$ of an inch in size on a piece of white paper. Take these two pieces of paper out into the sunlight. Look hard at the red disk for a few minutes, then switch your eye to the black spot on the white paper. To your surprise, you see a faint, hazy circle there of gray *green*, which is the complementary color of red. In other words, the optic nerves of your eyes have been supplying the missing complement.

COMPLEMENTARY COLOR SCHEMES, for this reason, are always pleasing, because they satisfy the eye. Now, in order to be able to determine what these complementary colors are, it is only necessary to remember that a complementary color scheme contains the three primary colors in it. We know that the three primary colors are yellow, red, and blue. If we have yellow, we mix together the two *remaining* colors, red and blue, to find its complement. These two colors give violet, which is yellow's complement. In the same manner, we find that red's complementary is made by mixing the remaining primaries, which are yellow and blue. Blue's complementary, orange, is made by mixing the remaining primaries, which are yellow and red. So we find that red's complementary is green; yellow's, violet; and blue's, orange.

COLORS MAY BE WARM OR COLD. That is, the optical effect of color on the eye gives us a sensation of warmth or coldness. Yellow, orange, red, and brown are always regarded as warm colors. Blue, blue-green, and blue-gray are known as cold colors. In such work as interior decoration, it is well to realize and use this quality of color. Thus in a room all done in soft greens and grays, a little touch of golden buff, vermilion, or orange will give the whole room a cheerful appearance. This bit of color may only be a vase on the mantel or a rug on the couch, but it has its effect. A little dark hall may be made to look lighter and more hospitable by tinting it in warm buff color, as this color reflects light and has a warm glow to it.

THE SYMBOLICAL SIDE OF COLOR is a feature that interests all artists. As well as being interesting, it is also useful. All colors have their optical effects on the eye, and the stimulus carried along the optic nerves to the brain gives us certain sensations.

For instance, we all know of the excitement displayed by a bull when a red cloth is waved under his nose; and even a turkey gobbler generally becomes excited when red is displayed in his vicinity. This is because red has an almost irritating effect upon the mind. It causes quick vibrations of the optic nerves, which thus transmit to the brain a nervous sensation of high intensity. For this reason, red wall paper would never do for any one's study or library, particularly for a nervous person's.

A COLOR SYMBOL CHART is shown, giving some of the symbolism of colors. We find that yellow is a great reflector of light, and hence has a light-giving quality. Blue is a cool, retreating color, and indicates restraint. It is a desirable color to use in its grayed form for such things as backgrounds. So in turn we find green to be a cool, restful color, as any one can verify by going out into the hills on a spring day. Violet is a somber, rich hue; while orange is warm and brilliant, combining the warmth of red with the light of yellow. The farther we go from the primary colors, the softer and more neutral the hues become, until at last we find ourselves in the warm and cool grays, and finally reach black.

ALL OUR COLORS have a history or a symbolical association that has come down to us through the centuries. White and black have always been typical of light and darkness. Most nations consider black as a sign of sorrow, darkness, or mourning.

THE SOFTER GRAYS AND BROWNS are always associated with retirement or sorrow. Their very neutrality of color unconsciously registers a feeling of quietness or somberness upon our dispositions.

YELLOW is the color of the sun and of gold; and with many of the ancient nations, it was symbolical of wisdom. Yellow is significant of gayety and cheer, and is the color that reflects light the most. It is the closest to white light in its brilliancy.

ORANGE is a flame color. Its brilliancy appeals to children and savages. But it is typical of knowledge, as it represents the lamp, the torch, and the flame,— all symbols of knowledge. When the wisdom of God came to Moses in the wilderness, it came as a burning bush. Then the Spirit, which was to lead into all truth, came to the disciples at Pentecost as a flame of fire.

RED is symbolical of love and of fire. It is a vigorous color, and in its more sinister forms, is typical of war, passion, and anarchy.

GREEN is our springtime color, and is typical of fertility and abundance. The Bible likens a righteous man to a green tree whose leaves do not wither. In the early Christian art, the cross was often represented as green, because of its potency.

BLUE is typical of constancy, because, like the sky, it endures forever. Nothing permanently changes our blue sky; and Paul said, "We can do nothing against the truth." Blue was the favorite color of the Scotch Covenanters. "True blue" is a term we often hear.

VIOLET, made of blue and red, represents truth touched with passion and love. Violet is also the color of shadows, and is the mourning color of China. In Christian art, the penitent Magdalene wears violet.

THE ABOVE NOTES help to give us a slight idea of the symbolical meaning of colors. If we get so that we can use our colors understandingly, we not only produce better effects, but we know that we are working in the right direction. The colors we use should be adapted to the place and to the subject to which they are to be applied. If we are planning a poster for a spring scene, then we should use the colors typical of spring, and not browns and reds, the colors of autumn. If we wish to have a rich, dignified design, we should be careful not to put in it light, delicate colors, nor strong, violent colors, which would not be associated with our subject.

TEACHER'S OUTLINE ON COLOR

NATURE COLOR SOURCES. Color notations can be best secured from nature; and the teacher can collect stones, bark, leaves, and many other nonperishable sources of good color harmonies. The students also should gather such material to study and to copy the colors from. These color harmonies should then be applied to the different handicraft problems as suggested in the preceding chapter. A small case or library shelves could be arranged to hold such a permanent collection. A collection that is related to color is one made up of material gathered from nature showing how birds, plants, and animal life are protected by colors that conceal them in their environment. Stuffed birds or animals with interesting color or pattern should be secured as part of the collection.

COLOR TEXTILES. There are many textiles made each year, that have good patterns and color arrangements. If small sections of these are secured and kept by the teacher for reference or as examples, they will be found to be helpful. If students see things similar to their own problems, but are being made and used, they have an incentive in their work. Textile samples should be big enough to include a full unit of the design motif, and should be mounted on cards, the warm-colored textiles being grouped on one sheet, and the cool-colored textiles on another. Or the printed cottons could be in one set, and the woolens and the silks in other sets. A collection of this kind will be of immense value in the study of design and color, and will prove of educational interest in several other studies.

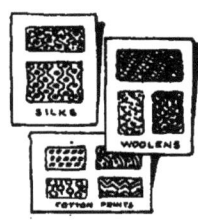

COLOR ILLUSTRATIONS. Many color illustrations have fine color harmonies. Prints that appear in magazines, reproducing paintings by Maxfield Parrish, Jules Guerin, Edmund Dulac, and others, give excellent examples of pictures formed on analogous and complementary color harmonies. These prints help students to understand that a pleasing color harmony is an important part of picture building. A good problem is to have other designs and applications take their color from some one of these pictures or part of a picture. Interior decorators often secure their entire scheme of color decoration from some picture that is to hang in the room.

COLOR SCHEMES FROM COLOR PRINTS

COLOR ANALYSIS. The study of color scientifically will be an interesting aid to one who is studying color artistically. A number of color tests can be used to demonstrate color divisions and optical effects. The following are a few optical illusions that illustrate how certain colors appear to necessitate their complement before the human eye is satisfied. Taking a small disk of strong prismatic color and putting a small black spot the size of a pinhead in the center, gaze steadily for a minute or two at this central spot. Then pass a white card over one half of this disk, and you will see the spectral complement fill the uncolored half of the circle. Again cover one half of the circle, gazing at the exposed half. Remove the card, and the exposed half will appear purer in color, as the spectral complement has been added to the portion formerly colored, making it grayer.

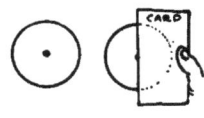

Take two color disks of complementary colors with a space and a dot between them. Let the eye pass back and forth from one to the other slowly, then stop suddenly over the dot midway between, and there will be seen a white light disk surrounded with a grayer tone. This is because the complementary colors have united in a white light for a total unity. Cover either disk, and after gazing at the remaining one awhile, look at the spot where the other one was, and its specter will appear.

RED

Repeat this operation with two disks that are not complementary, and the color specter between the two will not be a white light, but a specter of the combined complements of the two disks. If, for instance, the disks are green and violet, the two complements of these colors are red and yellow, therefore the specter will be a light orange disk.

GREEN

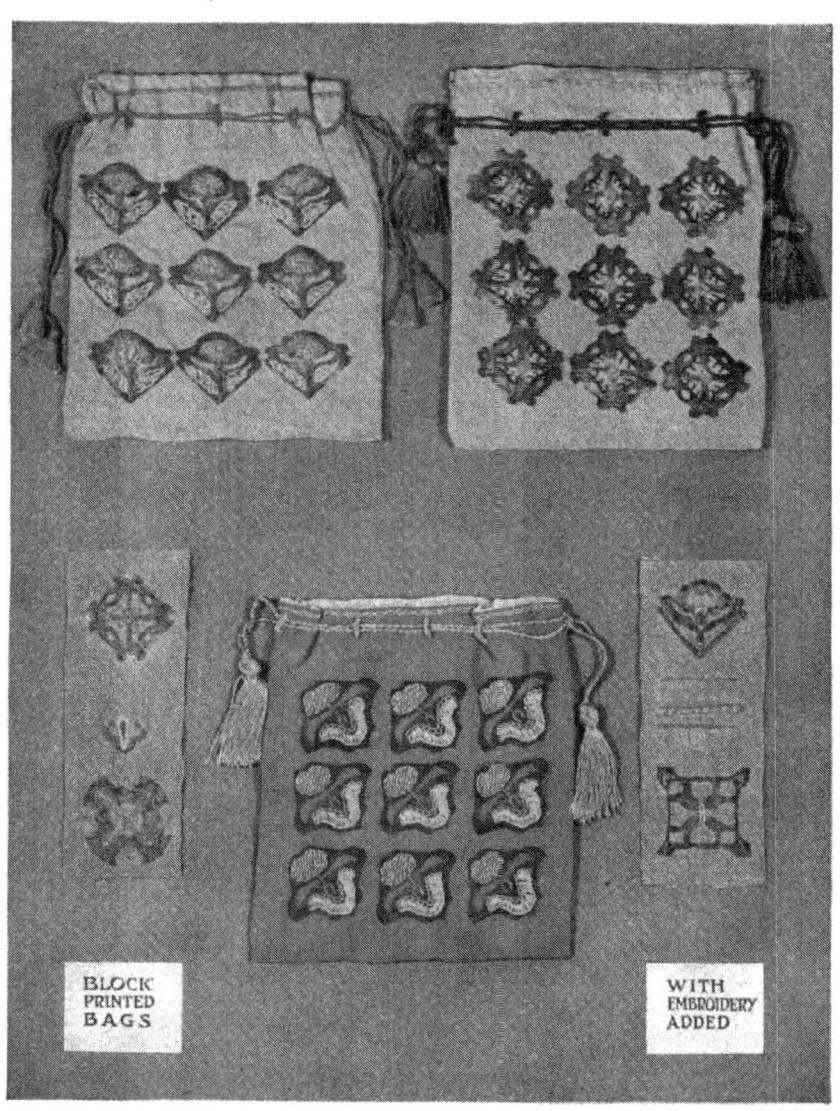

BLOCK
PRINTED
BAGS

WITH
EMBROIDERY
ADDED

BLOCK-PRINTED AND EMBROIDERED BAG

TEXTILE DECORATION METHODS

THE ACADEMIC GRADES

HANDICRAFT

IN OUR DESIGN, we studied how to work out motifs from the various sources in nature. We learned that flowers, birds, insects, and animals all are full of splendid suggestions for designs if we but know how to look for them. See on page 291 how the artist has worked out the interesting motifs in the lower half of the page, from the redwood tree. With these little motifs to start with, a designer could work out dozens of beautiful things, ranging all the way from a book cover to a border for your living room.

WHEN FLOWERS are scarce and the flower season is gone, we often wish we had some way of keeping a permanent record of those we do not have an opportunity to draw. One way of doing such a thing is to make what are called blue prints. To do this, we first buy a roll of rapid blue print paper at an art store. Next we buy, or borrow from the mechanical drawing department, a printing frame such as photographers use. One about 8 x 10 inches in size is large enough. We then pick some flowers we would like to get prints of, and take them, with the printing frame and paper, to a dark room. Any ordinary room with the blinds closed will do. We cut off a piece of the blue print paper large enough to fit inside the frame. If the frame is pretty large, then just cut a piece big enough to cover the plant. We open the frame and place the plant next to the glass, and the paper on top of it. Then we put the back of the frame on and turn the frame over.

THE NEXT THING to do is to expose the picture. By letting the sunlight hit directly on the plant through the glass for three or four minutes, we make our print. After we have done this, we take our print back into the dark room and release it. By holding our paper face up under running water, we develop our print and produce a picture of our plant in a white silhouette against dark blue background.

STENCILING

STENCILS, after they are designed, are made in the following way: First purchase some stencil paper at an art store. This paper has been oiled or paraffined so as to be waterproof and easier to cut. After you have made your design on thin paper, trace it on the stencil paper by slipping a piece of graphite paper under your design. When the design is traced, take a sharp knife and cut your stencil out against a

(283)

piece of hard wood or cardboard. Be careful to cut into the corners as well as you can, so as not to rip your paper when lifting out the parts. If you have made any mistakes in the construction of your stencil, you will soon discover them when you cut it out. By holding your finished stencil against a piece of white paper or up to the light, you can get a fair idea of how it will look when color is stenciled through it.

TO STENCIL, we may use various ideas. The first way to try stenciling is to do it with opaque water color. We suggest this because water color is easier to handle than oil paint, and will do to practice with. On page 294, we have some stencil decorations. These have been done either on fabrics or on wall paper, with opaque colors or with oil paints. In stenciling, we take the material we wish to stencil, and thumb-tack it over a piece of blotter or several layers of newspaper. Then we take a brush that has short, stiff bristles, like those used for oil paintings, and mix our color. It is best not to get too much paint on the brush, or the paint will go on too heavy.

WITH THE STENCIL pinned over the place we wish to stencil, we then stipple our color on the paper. This stippling method is the only good one for stenciling, as the paint is allowed to go through the openings and is less likely to leave too much in the corners. When our stencil paper gathers too much paint, we can unpin it and wipe off the surplus from around the edges.

IN USING OIL PAINTS, the secret is to use the colors with but little turpentine mixed into them. In painting pictures, artists use turpentine or linseed oil to mix their paints. In stenciling, the less used the better. Put in only enough to make your paints work well from your brush. If too much is used, your design will run and look blurred on the edges. On cloth, oil paints are always used, as water color would not last. In using oil paints, we must be careful not to smear colors already put on.

SOFA CUSHIONS, table runners, window drapes, scarfs, and dozens of similar useful things, can be decorated by stencil work. For materials that are going to be washed or subjected to considerable wear, the artists use a mixing fluid in place of the turpentine. This mixture is made of the following:

                    3 ounces of turpentine
                    10 to 12 drops of vinegar
                    4 to 6 drops of lemon extract

BLOCK PRINTING

BLOCK PRINTING may be termed the twin brother of stenciling. Block prints, too, are used to transfer designs to cloth, but in a little different way. Take a good look at page 296, which explains perfectly how block printing is done. First you take a piece of ordinary linoleum or cardboard and glue it on a block of wood. Next you draw or trace your design on this surface and cut it out with a sharp knife. This leaves your design in relief as is shown in the illustration. The linoleum or the cardboard is much easier to cut than wood.

OIL PAINT is next brushed on the block with a flat bristle brush. The block is then ready to stamp on the cloth. Under the linen or muslin or other cloth we may be using, there should always be several layers of newspaper. This helps the block to sink into the cloth and allow the paint to get a firm hold. The design is thus transferred to the fabric. The block should be held flat and pressed firmly onto the cloth in printing.

BATIK WORK

BATIK WORK is another form of handicraft used to decorate fabrics. Although some people have the idea that batik work is a new method, this handicraft has been practiced for many years by the natives of Java. These natives have brought this work to a high state of perfection, and they produce it with but two colors.

THE WORD "BATIK" means "to design," and batik work certainly allows us to exercise our designing ability. To start right, we should plan our design in light masses against a dark background, so that the pattern is composed of bold lines and parts. Trace the outline of this pattern on the cloth, cotton or silk, and outline firmly with a soft pencil.

WAXING is done by stretching the cloth over a frame or a picture stretcher. Melt up a wax made of one half beeswax and one half paraffin. Put it on the design with a brush while the wax is melted, so that it will flow easily. The wax should be melted over a hot flame or stove. The wax should go through the cloth; so any part visible from the under side should be touched up with wax. The pencil lines will keep the wax from spreading. The cloth is then removed from the frame.

DYEING is done by using diamond or other easy dyes. When the dye is cold or nearly so, you can crumple up your cloth with its wax pattern and dip it into the dye. After it has been well immersed, it is taken out and dried. When dry, it is placed on newspapers and the wax is pressed out with a hot iron. Any wax remaining can be washed or brushed off with gasoline.

THIS KIND OF BATIK, of course, is not permanent if washed very often. Those who wish to secure a permanent color should use sulphur dyes. These are made as follows:

Part One

¼ lb. of dyestuff (sulphur dye)
¼ lb. sulphide of soda (concentrated)

Dissolve this, using only enough water to allow the solution to become clear. Bring it to boiling.

Part Two

Sal soda (½ the weight of the dyestuff, or ⅛ lb.)
Salt (3 times the weight of the dyestuff, or ¾ lb.)

PARTS ONE AND TWO are combined, and boiled until dissolved. The dye is used when cold. Use enamel, wooden, or ironware cooking utensils. After dipping, hang the cloth in the air to dry. This darkens the color and makes it fast. These dyes may be secured from Metz and Company, of New York City, and come in yellow, blue, brown, and green. Both stencil and batik work are beautiful arts in the hands of a true craftsman.

TIED AND DYE WORK is made by tying or stitching the cloth at regular distances. Sometimes pebbles are tied in several places. The cloth is then dipped into a dye. The dye does not affect the parts tied, or the parts gathered where stitched. When the cloth is untied, the tied parts appear as a design, as shown on the bottom of page 298.

TOOLED LEATHER

TOOLED LEATHER is an interesting kind of work for craftsmen. A kind of leather known as tooling calf has the best reputation for this kind of work. As a substitute, many craftsmen have been using what is known as tooling sheep. This leather is not so thick as calfskin, but it has a fine surface for tooling.

TOOLS especially made for leather work can be bought at leather supply shops or at art stores. How to use one is shown on page 300. The design is made on thin paper. When satisfactory, it is traced on the leather. This is done by simply dampening the leather all over with a soft cloth or sponge and then tracing on your design. No graphite paper is necessary, as the leather, when damp, yields to the pencil.

When the design is traced, it is then modeled as shown here. Always keep your tool between yourself and the design you are tooling. This helps you to keep your design in relief.

LEATHER can be left its natural color or stained with leather dyes. After the dyes are dry, a gasoline wash of any desired color may be put over the whole. This wash is made of about two parts of white oil paint to one part of any oil color desired. The oil paint is thinned down with plenty of benzine or gasoline so as to make it fairly weak. This wash is brushed over all the leather and allowed to dry. The surplus is then rubbed off with a soft cloth. To bring out the color and give a finish, a final polish may be put on with a little ordinary tan shoe polish and cloth. Leather articles are both practical and beautiful.

GESSO WORK

GLASS, METAL, AND WOOD may all be decorated with gesso. To make it, we use the following formula:

Part One

10 tablespoons of whiting mixed with water to a thick cream
6 tablespoons of liquid glue

Part Two

1 tablespoon of varnish
4 tablespoons of linseed oil

Stir part two into part one and boil for ten minutes in a double boiler. It is sometimes better to stir the linseed oil in after the gesso has nearly finished boiling. Pour the gesso, when cooled slightly, into an open-mouthed bottle and cork well. This keeps it in good condition.

THE WAY to use gesso is shown on page 302. It should be stippled on the designs, as it goes on quicker that way. The gesso can be built up to any height, although a good craftsman never makes things in too high a relief. When the gesso is dry, any mistakes may be colored with oil paints or water colors. If water colors are used, a coat of shellac or clean varnish should be given them to hold down the color.

METAL WORK

PAPER KNIVES, trays, book ends, bowls, table lamps, and many other useful things may be made in copper. After your design has been made, it is scratched on copper with a metal point, or traced with indelible tracing paper. The design may be finished up in several ways. It may be cut right out of the metal, or etched in. Another way is to cut out the design on a separate piece and rivet it on the main piece. Copper rivets can be hammered into place by flattening out the blunt end with a hammer.

THE WAY to make a paper knife of copper is shown on page 304. The copper is hammered, or planished, as it is called, to give it a mottled pattern. Next the design for the outline is traced off and cut out. A design may be etched on the handle in the following way: First, paint all your paper knife over with asphaltum varnish. This may be purchased at a paint shop, and is diluted with benzine to make it flow easily off the brush. In painting the paper knife, leave exposed only the part you wish the acid to etch. When the asphaltum is dry, then dip the knife in a solution of nitric acid.

THE NITRIC ACID SOLUTION should be composed of one part of nitric acid to five parts of water. Perchloride of iron may be used in place of nitric acid. It works more evenly, and may be purchased at any engraver's supply house. After the knife has been etched until the desired depth is obtained, it is taken out, washed under running water, and the asphaltum is removed with benzine or gasoline. The design will be found to be in relief. The copper is then rubbed down with emery cloth and finished off with beeswax and a soft cloth.

VARIOUS WAYS of producing copper work are shown on page 305. A is a photograph of a book end with stained glass set in back of the design. B shows one with leather back of the copper. C shows a book end in which the design was etched, and the center spot made of a little piece of stained glass set into a copper rim. D is a book end with a triptych design in leather set into the openings. E is a tray with the design cut out of the corners, while F shows a tray and a paper knife with a butterfly design cut out and riveted on the main piece. G is a tray with the corners etched in. H shows a row of watch fobs. I is a paper knife with a design etched and "repoussed," or hammered up from the back. J is one with the design cut out. K is one with a riveted design on it, and L shows one cut out and riveted on the main piece. The center spot is a mother-of-pearl blister or some inexpensive stone.

BOWLS are more difficult to construct; but if you are careful, good results can be obtained. A flat circular piece is used, and is hammered as shown. It is hammered over a block in which a hollow has been chiseled out. This allows the copper to bend under the hammer strokes. When the copper becomes too stiff and brittle from hammering, it is "annealed." The annealing is done by heating the copper over a gas flame and plunging it into a tub or basin of cold water. This method softens the copper so that it can be hammered more. Never try to hammer the copper when it is too hard, as it has a tendency to crack if not annealed often enough.

THE FLAT PIECE of copper may in this way be gradually rounded out and finished as shown. A border design may be etched into the bowl in the same way explained for the paper knife. This same method, as shown on page 306, may be used for bowls and trays of various shapes.

CEMENT POTTERY

CEMENT POTTERY and the way to make it are shown on pages 307 and 308. By this method, tiles, vases, bowls, and other useful articles may be made. On page 307, the way to make tiles is shown. First get two sizes of small sable brushes, a putty knife, several small dishes, a spoon, a fine mesh sieve, and a piece of glass. This will be your equipment.

TO MAKE MOLDS, follow the ideas shown in the diagrams. Clay or modeling wax should be used for the first mold. When this mold is finished, the plaster is poured over it to make the plaster mold. After an hour, the plaster may be removed and allowed to dry well. When dry, the plaster mold is oiled, and in turn used for a mold over which to pour the concrete.

THE CONCRETE used for these tiles is composed of a mixture of one part of fine sand and one part cement. When the cement has set for two days, it may be removed and finished as shown in the first column. If cement colors are to be used, then mix the concrete colors.

TO MIX COLORS, proceed as follows: Place a little of the desired color on the glass and add dry cement to it, reducing the color to the correct tone. Ordinary Portland cement may be used, or white cement, if light tints are desired. Next add a little water to make a thin paste. Any tile to be colored should be left one day out of the mold, then soaked three hours in water before the color is applied. Put on a spoonful of the color, shake the tile slightly on an even surface, and pour off any surplus. Bubbles may be dissolved by pricking with a pin immediately after the surface has been coated.

WHEN THE TILE has been colored, place it carefully in a tray, and add enough water to reach a little more than half way up the side of the tile. Let the tile remain in this water four or five days, adding

19 Applied Art

more water to replace that which may evaporate or be absorbed by the tile.

ANOTHER WAY OF MAKING A TILE is shown in the second column; while a third, called majolica, is shown in the third column. Plasticine and plaster of Paris are used for all the molds.

FOUR OPERATIONS are needed in making bowls and vases:
1. Making the original model.
2. Making the molding case from the model.
3. Pouring the concrete into the molding case.
4. Releasing the mold and completing the cast.

The first step is to build the vase or bowl form desired, from modeling wax or clay. Make the form solid, not hollow. Keep the contour alike on all sides. Any vase or bowl can be duplicated in cement by making a plaster mold from it. The inside of the bowl should be filled with sand or wadded paper, and a false neck built over the mouth with clay or modeling wax. Oil the surface of the vase.

THE SECOND STEP is to place your first model upon a piece of oiled glass or tin. Marking off about one third of its diameter, build a narrow strip of clay or wax on two sides from top to bottom. This ridge should extend far enough out to meet the molding case or metal strip, and you should look over both the walls and the outside case, to be sure there are no loopholes for the plaster to leak out. The sections of the mold are then made in three parts, as shown in the last row of page 308. Notice the two little holes that have been cut into the first plaster section before the second one is poured. These are to form keys, so that you can lock your parts together in putting your plaster mold in place. When the three parts are finished, they are oiled on the inside and tied together. They are next turned upside down and oiled, and a mold is made for the bottom. The plaster mold is then ready to use.

TO COMPLETE the vase, pour in the cement mixture clear up to the top. After one half hour, the mold may be "rotated." This is done by revolving the mold, at the same time pouring out a little of the concrete. Experimentation will soon show you how often to rotate. Every half hour is a good average. About three rotations will make the shell of the vase thick enough. The mold may be removed after drying for several days.

DESIGNS FROM A NATURE DRAWING

BLUE PRINTS MADE DIRECT FROM THE PLANT BY SUNLIGHT · ·

BLUE PRINTS FROM FLOWERS

JAPANESE STENCILS

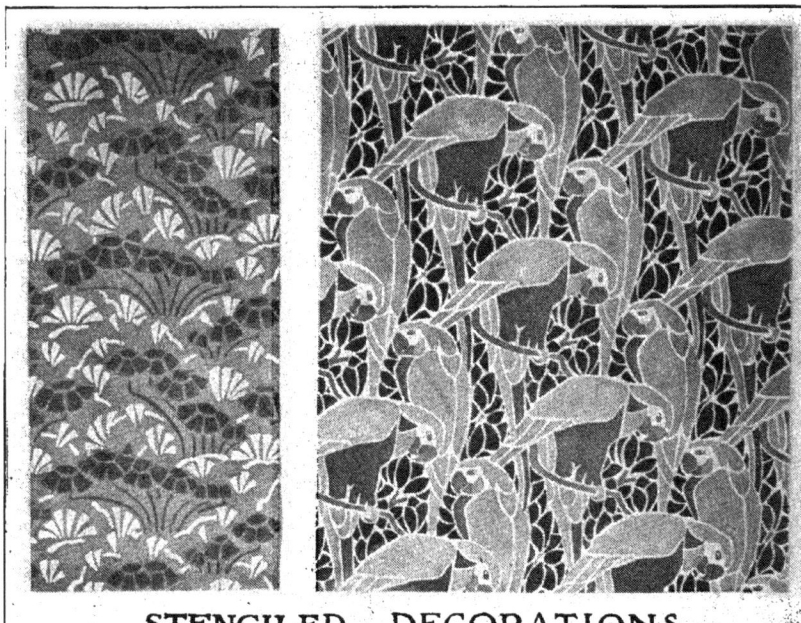

STENCILED DECORATIONS

GOOD STENCILED DESIGNS

ABCDE
FGHIJK
LMNOP
QRSTUV
WXYZ

STENCIL ALPHABET

The Stencil

The Flower Sketch

STENCIL DESIGNING

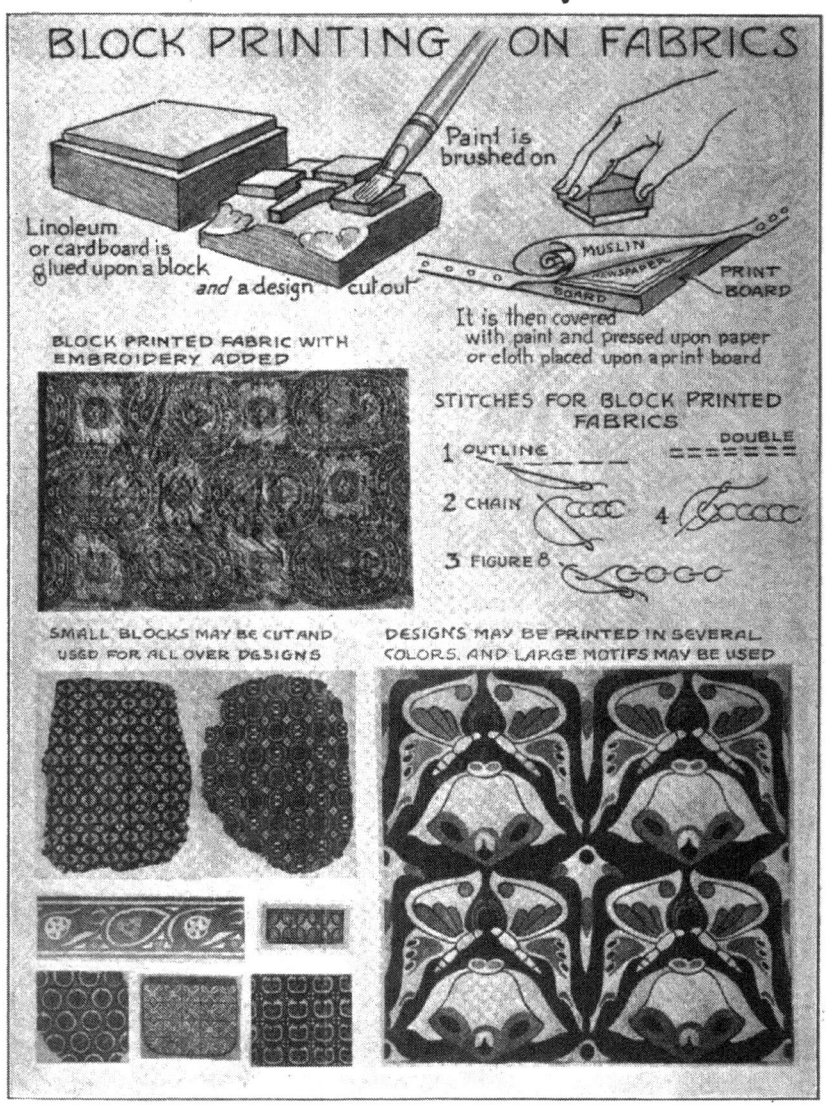

BLOCK PRINTING ON FABRICS

Linoleum or cardboard is glued upon a block *and* a design cut out

Paint is brushed on

It is then covered with paint and pressed upon paper or cloth placed upon a print board

MUSLIN
NEWSPAPER
BOARD
PRINT BOARD

BLOCK PRINTED FABRIC WITH EMBROIDERY ADDED

STITCHES FOR BLOCK PRINTED FABRICS

1 OUTLINE   DOUBLE
2 CHAIN   4
3 FIGURE 8

SMALL BLOCKS MAY BE CUT AND USED FOR ALL OVER DESIGNS

DESIGNS MAY BE PRINTED IN SEVERAL COLORS, AND LARGE MOTIFS MAY BE USED

HOW TO BLOCK PRINT

BLOCK PRINT PATTERNS FROM THE SAME MOTIFS

EXAMPLES OF BATIK AND TIED AND DYED WORK

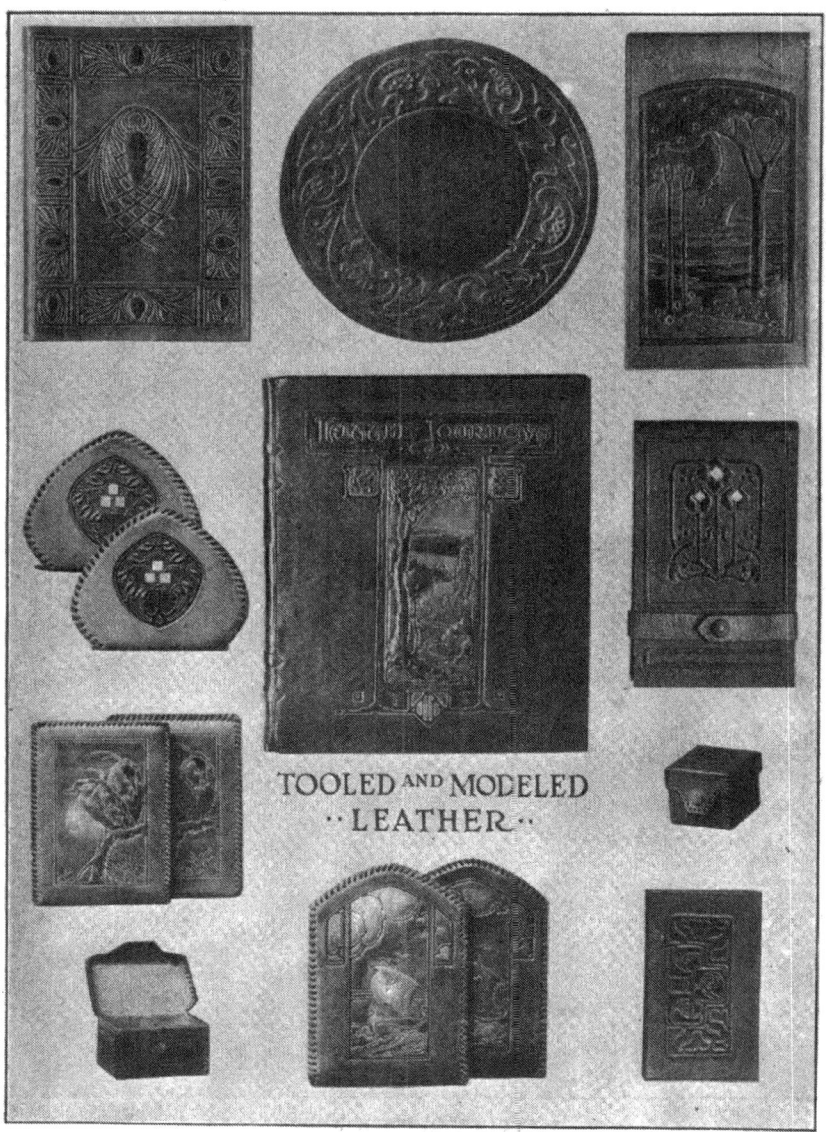

TOOLED AND MODELED
·· LEATHER ··

EXAMPLES OF LEATHER CRAFT

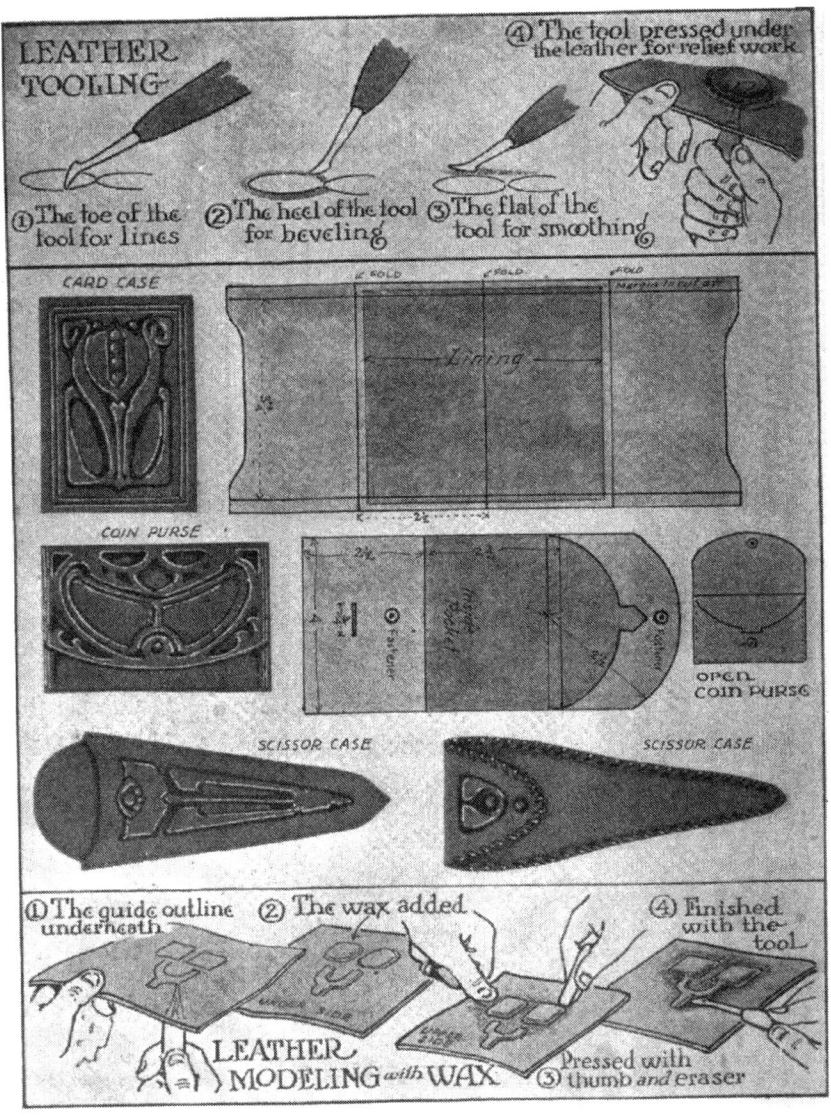

TOOLED LEATHER WORK

LEATHER LACING AND COLORING

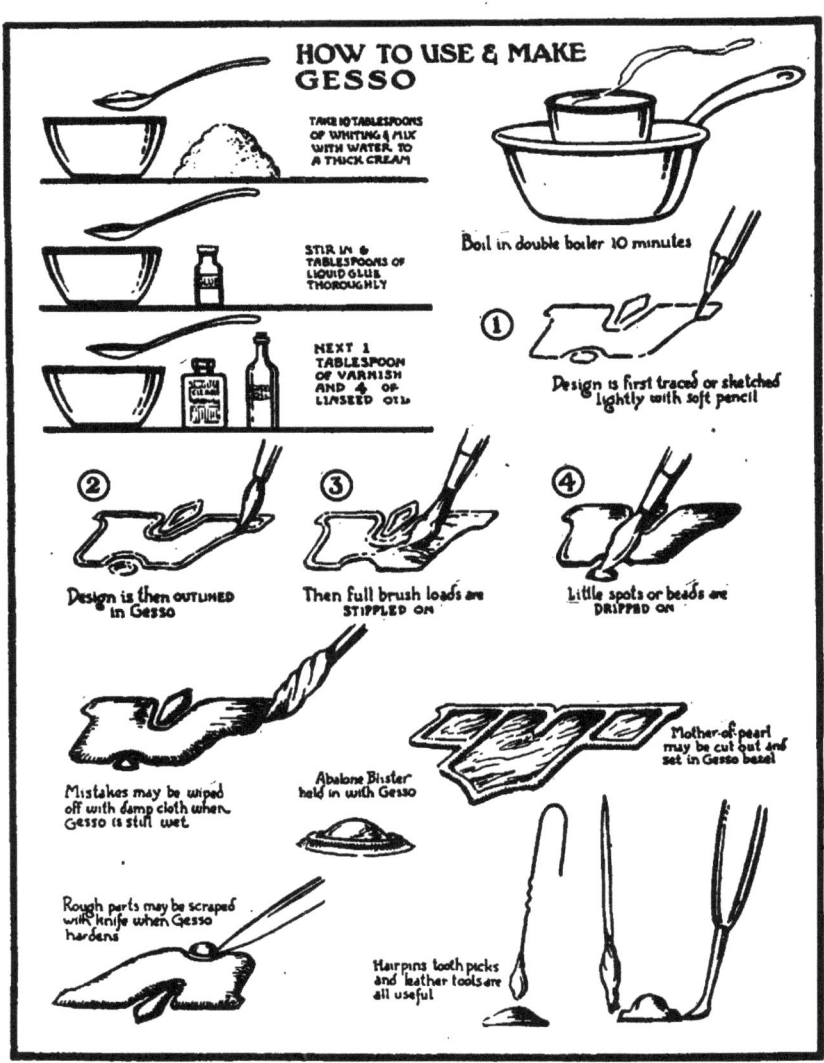

HOW TO DO GESSO WORK

GESSO
DECORATED
ARTICLES

EXAMPLES OF GESSO WORK

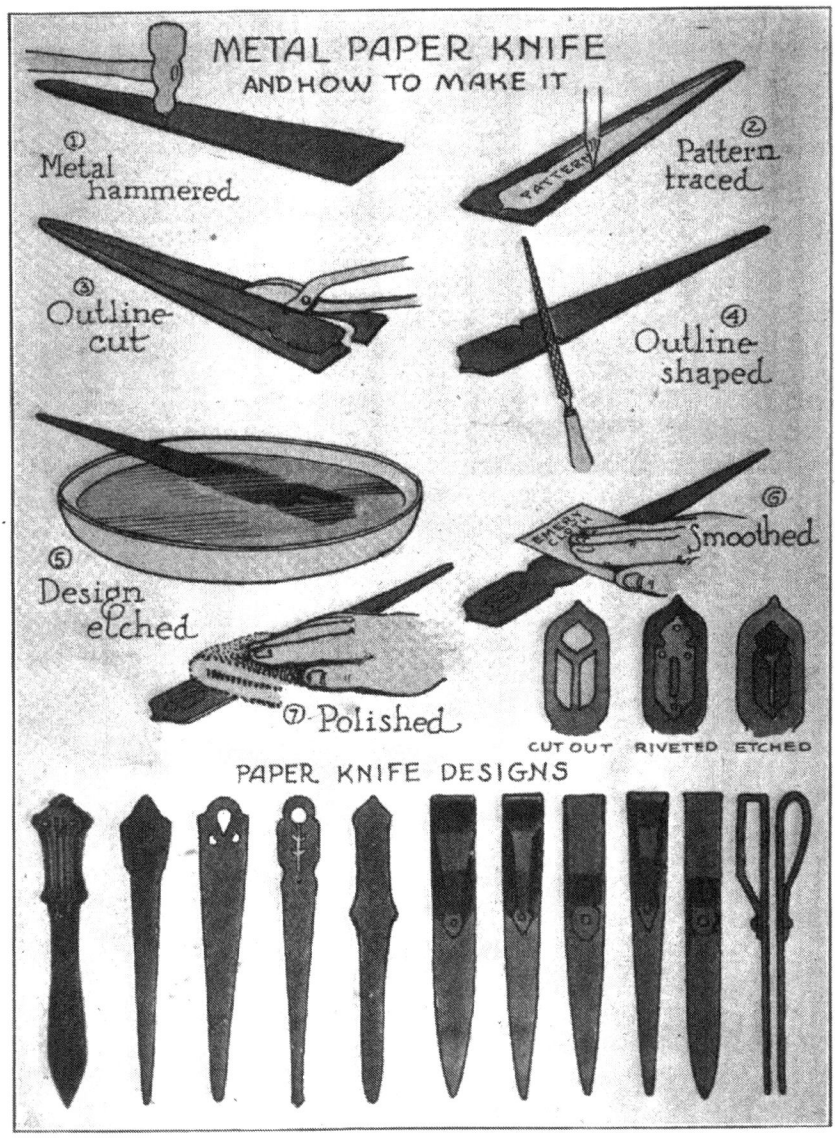

HAMMERED METAL WORK

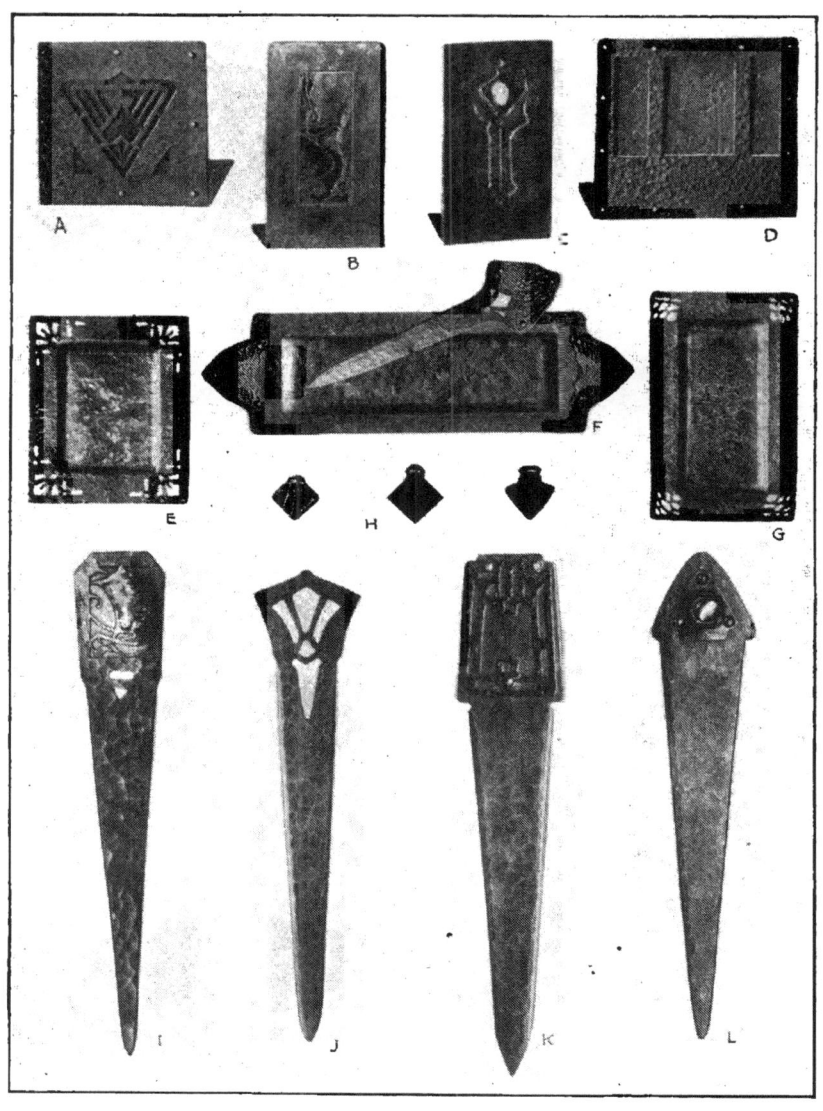

HAMMERED METAL OBJECTS

20 Applied Art

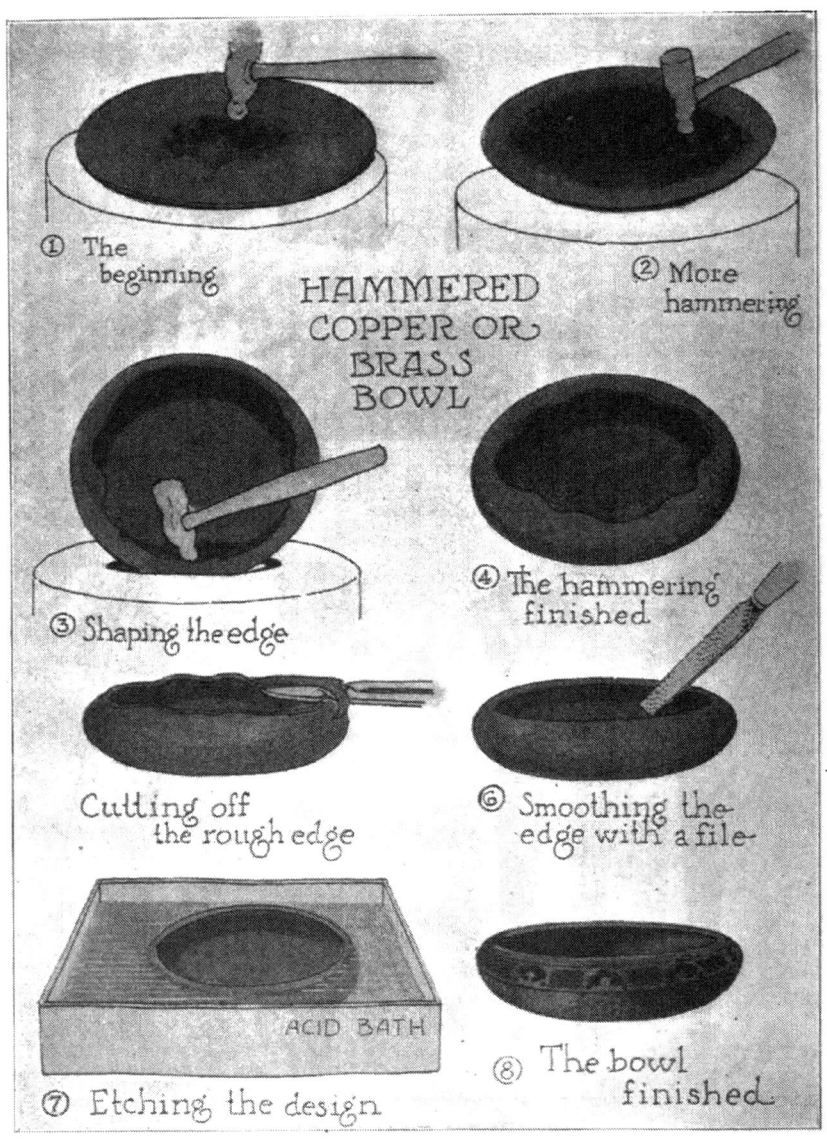

① The beginning

HAMMERED
COPPER OR
BRASS
BOWL

② More hammering

③ Shaping the edge

④ The hammering finished

⑤ Cutting off the rough edge

⑥ Smoothing the edge with a file

ACID BATH

⑦ Etching the design

⑧ The bowl finished

HAMMERED COPPER WORK

Incising a design on a plaster tile

It is dampened oiled bars placed around it and plaster poured into it

This result is used for producing

a cement tile which may have a second color brushed into the incisions and finished with a wax rub

A clay layer may be cut through and placed on glass or oiled paper and cement poured into the mold.

A second color is poured into the openings and then leveled

Retaining Bars may be adjusted in this way to fit any size tile

Square Cardboards placed and pressed into the tile backs

Mix the proper colors and drip into place after oiling the surface

Over the colors pour cement

After it is hard pry it apart

and thus obtain an incised tile in several colors

MOLD
TILE

CEMENT TILE WORK

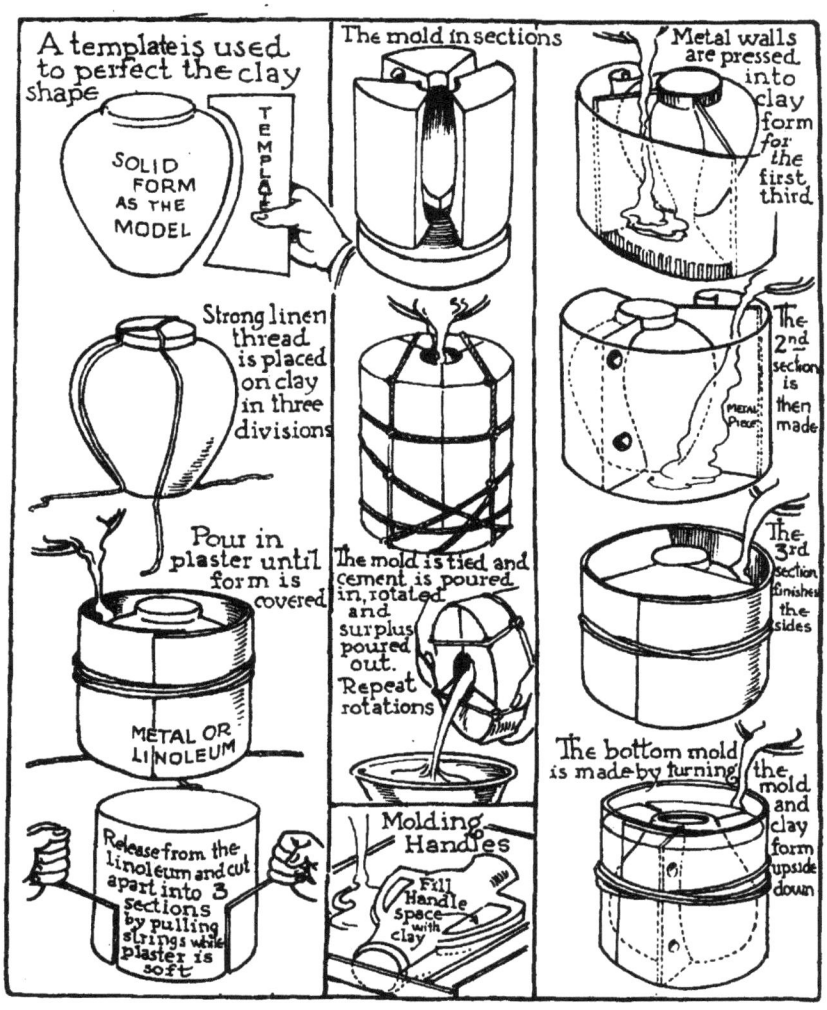

HOW TO MAKE CEMENT POTTERY

CEMENT TILES AND POTTERY

TEACHER'S NOTES ON HANDICRAFT

HANDICRAFT TABLE. It will be repeatedly found that a general working table for various handicrafts will be essential in the classroom. On such a table, stencil paints, bottles of leather dyes, poster paint, and other such materials can be placed; or shelves near can hold the material, and the table can be used by the students to mix such of the materials as they may individually need. An oilcloth or linoleum cover on the table will enable the monitor or the students to keep the top clean. If the rule is established and followed that each student put material in its proper place after using it, and that covers be kept on the several containers, the materials will be kept in good condition, and better results will be obtained in the problems.

STENCIL WORK. The difficulty with most students' stencil work is that the students make one of two mistakes. They either use too much paint on their brushes, or they mix the paint too thick. The paint should be thinned with turpentine or gasoline until it will color the fabric without leaving the paint in streaks or in piles against the stencil edges. If the brush contains too much paint, it should be wiped on the edge of the paint dish until there is but little left. A few strokes on a folded newspaper will absorb surplus paint. The brush should then be tried on waste pieces of the material before the actual stencil is used. Paint mixed in a white dish will appear different in color when brushed upon a colored fabric. A good way is to place a glass over the fabric and mix the color on the glass to harmonize with the fabric color underneath.

MIXING STENCIL PAINT ON GLASS

OVER THE TEXTILE TO BE COLORED

LEATHER DYEING. Better results will be achieved in coloring leather if the student does not attempt to secure the full color at one time. Diamond dyes, or the paper strips used to secure color for photographs, are good to use for coloring leather. The color is applied with a brush just as water color is used. Where colors are to be mixed, they should not be mixed before they are put on the leather, but a thin wash of each should be placed on the leather portion that is to have such color. If the colors are mixed together before being applied to the leather, they often coagulate and lose their hues. Large surfaces should be covered by the use of a sponge or a large brush. The leather should be thoroughly dampened before large washes of color are applied, to eliminate the possibility of hard edges.

A SPONGE IS USED TO COLOR LARGE LEATHER SECTIONS

HAMMERING METAL. In forming bowls or deep depressions in copper or brass, a short section of tree stump or heavy timber set on end will be serviceable. Different shaped hollows can be hammered or cut into the surface of the upright stump. The metal is held over the hollow and hammered. This results in the metal's taking the shape of the hollow, and the metal shape is guided by the moving of the metal at each successive blow of the hammer. The metal should be softened occasionally by annealing. This is done by placing it in a flame until it is red, then plunging it into cold water.

TO ANNEAL METAL

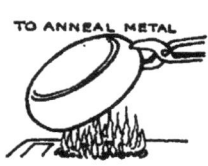

ETCHING TRAY. A good etching tray can be made of roofing paper. The paper can be folded at the corners without cutting, so that it will not leak. If this is placed within a box or tied about with a strong cord, it forms an acid tray that will last a long while. Small metal problems can be etched in a deep porcelain dish or in the glass trays used by photographers in developing their work.

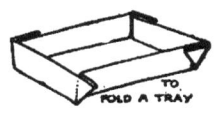

TO FOLD A TRAY

THE ACADEMIC GRADES

LETTERING

LETTERING is a subject that students once thought did not have much to do with art. This was because they were mostly familiar with the form of letters we see printed in magazines and newspapers on a press. Naturally, when we are familiar with letters that are made in lead type and printed by machinery, we are likely to connect lettering itself with something mechanical. But what is known as free-hand lettering has always been, and is now, one of the most artistic forms of work.

THE ORIGIN OF OUR ALPHABET is a good subject to study, because it is not only interesting, but it gives us a better idea of what these letters originally represented and how they were developed to their present state. A good many years ago, the Egyptians used a form of writing that was made up of "story symbols." In other words, when the kings and the nobles wished to record the result of some great war or other important event, they had the story chiseled out in rock or stone. To put down these records, the scribes used picture forms to represent the ideas they wished to express. We find in the Egyptian inscriptions, pictures representing water, fish, some of their sacred birds, and other such symbols. These figures in time became an established thing, and they were taken up and used by the Egyptian priests, who in those days held power next to royalty itself.

THE PRIESTS, in using these story symbols, simplified them so as to make the inscribing of the records easier. As a result, they gradually produced what is known as the hieratic form of Egyptian writing. This hieratic form was much easier to make than the original pictures, as you can see by looking at the chart on page 319. If you will observe the little map on that page, you will see an arrow line starting from Egypt and going from there to Phœnicia, then to Greece, and last to Rome. This line shows how the Egyptians' story symbols traveled.

THE PHŒNICIANS were an energetic people living on the border of the Mediterranean Sea. They were great traders and merchantmen. In their dealings with the Egyptians, they were quick to see the possibilities of such symbols as a means of recording their business transactions; and they took the Egyptian story symbols and adapted them to their needs. Being practical, they simplified the symbols still more, and

(311)

put them more into the form of a regular alphabet. The Phœnicians traded with the Greeks also, and soon their alphabet began to be noticed by the Greek nation.

THE GREEKS not only adopted the Phœnicians' alphabet, but they changed its forms so as to make them more beautiful. This is natural, when we remember how much the Greek nation loved and developed art. Besides making the alphabet simpler and more beautiful, the Greeks changed the direction of reading and writing these forms. The Phœnician writing always ran from right to left, but the Greeks changed it so as to read from left to right, as our writing does to this day. In time, the Romans began to learn of this alphabet used by the Greeks, and it was not long before they too were using the alphabet. To the Romans belongs the credit of developing our alphabet to its highest state, as the alphabet they perfected is known as about the most beautiful in the world, the classic Roman.

THIS CLASSIC ROMAN ALPHABET is much used at the present time, and we can hardly go down the street without passing some library or other public building that has its name or some other inscription in this kind of letter. Thus far, no alphabet has been designed that is superior to the classic Roman. It is a letter that goes well almost any place, and its letters are so graceful and yet dignified that it is well adapted to inscriptions, plaques, medals, coins, and other similar work. Because practically all our modern alphabets are based on the classic Roman, we are going to study it and learn how to make it.

THE VARIOUS NAMES given to the different parts of the letters are indicated on our first lettering page. The upright lines in the letters are known as *stems*. The little finishing ends on the letters are known as *stubs* or *serifs*. The round curve on letters like R and P is called a *lobe*, while the swinging lines like those on R and K are known as *swash lines*. These names are given so that in referring to them we shall know what part of the letter we are talking about.

THE THIN AND THE THICK STROKES in the Roman alphabet are the most difficult for beginners to remember. Just what parts are thin and what are thick is a question that always comes up. To make this easy, it is only necessary to remember the following rules:

1. The vertical strokes are thick except those in the letter N and the first line on the M.

2. Horizontal strokes are thin, as well as all the strokes that run up from left to right.

3. The round letters should always be made taller than the straight ones, because, having no corners, they *appear* smaller than the straight letters do.

4. For the same reason, the points on the letters A, V, M, and W should be made to extend past the guide lines a little, so as to make them look large enough.

GUIDE LINES are the light pencil lines that the artist rules to help in his lettering. In this way, the lines are kept straight, and the size of the letters is kept uniform. You will find, in looking at them, that the round letters in the classic Roman are wider than the straight ones, and that the letters M and W are about $1\frac{1}{4}$ times as wide as the straight letters. The letter I, being so narrow, always has less room on the line. You will note that the straight lines are all finished off with the little strokes called serifs. These serifs should always be the same shape in letters of the same alphabet.

THE SMALL LETTERS of the alphabet, as those on page 320 are called, were gradually developed by the artists and the scribes, from the large, or capital letters. They were the result of people's trying to make the capital letters rapidly. This attempt to do rapid lettering resulted in the artists' making letters that were more round and swinging. In a few centuries, we find that most of the writing was done in these small letters. In looking at them, you will see that they differ from the large letters in several ways.

SMALL LETTERS have lines projecting above and below the body of the letters. These are called ascending and descending strokes. These strokes are found in letters like b, d, f, h, and k. The small letters also are made within guide lines. Some artists find that by building their letters over a letter O, they get more uniform shapes. The ascending strokes are about three fourths the height of the body of the letter. The descending strokes extend about the same distance below the line. You will notice that these small letters have also stubs, or serifs. On the second lettering page, we have a diagram that gives the names of the different parts of the small letters.

AN EASY WAY to learn to letter is to get some cross-ruled paper that has little squares on it, and work your letters over that. Make a good copy of both the small letters and the large letters to use for reference. Then see how many of the letters you can make from memory. It is only when you can draw these letters from memory that you begin to accomplish something.

A FAMOUS ARTIST once said, "When in doubt, use Roman." By this, he meant that the Roman alphabet is one that can be used anywhere successfully. Yet there are places where another kind of letter would be more appropriate for the subject. One of these kinds is known as the text letter. This letter is found in almost every country. The English, the French, and the Germans all have text letters. The text, or Gothic letters, as they are sometimes called, are pleasing to look at. For instance, look at the top alphabet on page 322. The alphabet shown here is one of the clearest of all the text alphabets.

THE SMALL LETTERS of these alphabets are on page 323. You can see that the small letters have the same general character as the large letters of the same alphabet. A good way to learn how to do the top set of letters, the English text, is to study the letter O. This letter is really the basis for most of the other letters of the set. After you have learned to draw an O, you can easily construct such letters as the b, d, g, and e over it. In this text letter, the vertical strokes are thick, and so are the oblique ones that run downward from left to right. The thin strokes are those which go upward from left to right. You will notice in the small uncial letters, that while there is a similarity to those of the text alphabet, they contain more curves. These small uncial letters are easy to make, easy to read, and very artistic. In fact, the large and the small uncial letters are a fine alphabet to learn.

LEARNING HOW TO SPACE LETTERS is the next important thing we shall study after we learn how to construct letters. Page 321 shows how our letters may be condensed or expanded to fit certain spaces. One look at the page will quickly show how the letters may be varied. There are oftentimes places that allow little room up and down but plenty horizontally; in such a case, short, wide letters, called extended letters, are used. In other instances, the space is crowded horizontally, but has plenty of room vertically. At times like this, the artists use what is called a condensed letter, one that is very tall and narrow.

THIS METHOD of condensing or extending letters helps us to give our letters the desired prominence, yet it allows us to put them into arbitrary space. Extending and condensing letters is only one way of changing them. In the bottom half of the page are shown some other ways of varying letters. One way is to make the width of the letter lines different, as in the word "Vary" on the left-hand side.

In this way, we can make the face of our letters look heavy or light. A light letter is used where only a delicate style of letter is needed. A heavy, bold letter is used in places like billboards, advertisements, or posters, which are to be read quickly. Another way to vary letters is by changing their serifs. These serifs may be made round or square or pointed, like those shown on the right-hand side of the page. About ten different styles of letters are made here by changing their serifs. The thing we should be careful of is to keep the serifs the same in all the letters on the line.

LETTERS HAVE CHARACTER, just as people have. For this reason, we should always try to use the kind of letter that will go with the rest of the picture in which the wording is used. In other words, letters should be adapted to their environment. For instance, it would not be good taste to use light, delicate, lacy letters on a poster advertising machinery. It would be just as bad to use heavy, massive letters in a cover advertising delicate laces. If we keep this idea in mind, it will help us to use our letters in the right way.

LETTER CHARACTERS are shown on page 324. At the top, we have a light and graceful letter; and at the bottom, a heavy one. In between the two are three other styles of letters, all with different characters. Each style of letter has its own place, where it is best fitted to be used. A strong letter like the fourth row would be suitable on a book cover design or a street car advertisement. The plain, dignified style in the third row would be good used in article headings, or book frontispieces. Advertisements that appeal to feminine buyers, or such things as candy box covers, would look well if done in either of the two fanciful styles shown at the top. The quicker we learn to think of our letters as having character, the sooner we shall be able to use them in the correct way. A row of little designs, using letters ranging from the light to the massive style, are shown on the page we have been talking about.

ARTISTS who do a large amount of lettering, like poster or show-card men, make use of what are called lettering pens. These pens are a modern adaptation of the reed pens used by the scribes and monks in olden times. They enable us to make good letters with little effort. There are various kinds of pens. About the easiest one to use at the beginning is the one known as the ball-pointed. These ball-pointed pens are satisfactory because they are made in such a way that we may write with them in any direction without fear of their sticking into the paper. The pen is dipped into the ink and held so that the flat tip of the pen is flat on the paper. We then proceed to letter just as though we were using a pencil. A little motto lettered with one of these pens is shown at the top of page 325.

ANOTHER PEN, and one a little more difficult to learn to use, is shown next on the page. This pen has a square end, and makes a square, angular letter. It is harder to use, because its square end makes us twist the pen around to get our different strokes; but with a little practice and patience, you can soon master this pen. Still a third pen, one that makes both a narrow and a heavy stroke, is shown in the lower left-hand corner. By holding the pen as shown in the picture, you are able to make letters that have both heavy and light strokes, like those of the motto. Text and uncial letters are easily made with this sort of pen. The horizontal and up strokes are made with the thin part of the pen. The vertical and down strokes are made with the thick part.

THE LAST PEN shown on the page is the one used most by letterers. It has a stub-shaped point, which is cut at a slight angle, as seen in the picture. These pens come in about twelve different sizes, so that an artist may make either wide or narrow lines. By holding the pen at the same angle as we letter, we produce the thin and the thick strokes of our letters automatically. In other words, the pen does the work. While this may sound easy, a little time is required to be able to get steady strokes and execute the letters gracefully. In letters like those in the motto, the decorative scroll lines at the ends of the letters are put in with a smaller pen.

INK FOUNTAINS are furnished with these pens, and may be slipped on the pen points. These fountains enable you to letter several lines without redipping the pen. They also give your pen a crisper and more clean-cut line. Some of these pens come with fountains already attached to them. Others have one fountain to a set of pens, necessitating changing the fountain for each different size of pen used. All these pens may be purchased at any art store. They should be kept clean when you are using them, or else your strokes will not look sharp.

GOOD EXAMPLES of hand lettering are shown on page 327. Here we have a fair idea of the demand for hand lettering. We find it used everywhere, both in illustration work and in advertising. On that page, there are several examples of the use of classic Roman. The word "graphica" and the letters under it are all exact copies of the classic Roman letters. Notice how artistic that whole block of letters is. It is not only a graceful style of letter, but one that is easy to read. In the little motto in the upper right-hand corner, we have a modern adaptation of the Roman. The letters used in this motto are heavier and a little stiffer than the regular classic Roman. "Old Hampshire Bond" and the words "Bush Terminal" are two good examples of the text letter used in a business imprint. In cases where only a few words are used, these text letters are distinctive and agreeable to look at; but they would not be practical if it were necessary to use a large number of words. Another letter shown here in several places is called an Italic script letter. "Italics" is the name given to any letters that slant, and "script" implies a letter that resembles writing. "The Kewpies and the Glorious Fourth" is a good example of these letters.

INITIAL LETTERS are another way of using our alphabets in art. These decorated letters are used at the beginning of articles, to give them a little artistic touch. The use of these letters dates back to the early days when the scribes decorated their pages of illuminations with a large colored initial at the top. A group of good initials is shown on page 328, and also some of the kind that we should not make. In every one of the good initials, you will notice that the design is consistent and holds together. Even in the letter A in the upper right-hand corner, the decoration is so designed that it holds together inside its border.

MONOGRAMS form a splendid field for the study of lettering. Monograms are used everywhere, from business stationery to motor cars. Good monograms are used by some people all their lives, if they have found one they really like. Most monograms consist of an artistic arrangement of the initials of the owner's name. Sometimes these are designed so as to be easily read. At other times, they are difficult to make out. The kind of monogram we draw depends upon whom we are making it for, and also upon what that person likes best. Some of the monograms we have on page 329 have been designed for business firms, like the Tiffany Studios. Others, like those in the fourth row, have been made for private stationery. In some cases, you will notice that the letters are made by the white background instead of the black ink. Monograms like this are always attractive.

CALLIGRAMS are similar to monograms, with the exception that they contain the whole word instead of the initials alone. Calligrams were very popular among kings and nobles in medieval days. The letters in them were so planned as to make a pleasing design unit rather than to be easy to read. In the calligrams we have here, I am sure you would have no difficulty in making out the words. The secret of making good monogram or calligram designs is to imagine that your letters are like putty, which you may mold. Then if you will sketch in pencil the general outline of the shape you wish your monogram to be, you can, by twisting them around, make them fit this space.

ANOTHER WAY that helps in monogram work is to put down lightly in pencil the two or three letters you wish to monogram. With them down before you on the paper, you can look at their general formation and see what part of each letter may be twisted or swirled to balance off the others. There is no combination of letters that cannot be worked out into a good monogram, in spite of the fact that people often say the contrary. Study the monograms shown, then try to make one with your own initials. Try putting it in different shaped spaces, like a circle, a triangle, and a square.

IMPRINTS often have lettering in them. By imprints we mean a design used by people, generally in business, as a sort of sign or seal. These imprints, or trade-marks, as most of them are called, are used by firms as a sign by which the public can recognize their goods. Some firms value their trade-marks at millions of dollars. This is because they have advertised these trade-marks to such an extent that people get to ask for goods with those marks on them. Of course, a trade-mark is not worth much if it is not backed up by good products; but the firms that advertise their trade-marks take good care that their products satisfy people.

BOOKPLATES are closely related to trade-marks. They have been used for hundreds of years. People like George Washington and Paul Revere used bookplates in their days. In fact, Paul Revere not only used them, but he designed and carved them in wood for other people. The original idea of a bookplate was to mark a book so that, should it be lent or lost, it would be returned to its owner. For this reason, many old bookplates were found with verses such as this one:

> "By him who bought me for his own,
> 　I'm lent for reading, leaf by leaf.
> If honest, you'll return the loan;
> 　If you retain me, you're a thief."

IN DESIGNING bookplates, we may work them out with several ideas in mind. One would be like a coat of arms, wherein shields, crests, monograms, etc., would be used. This kind of bookplate is very dignified, and is termed "heraldic." Another idea is to incorporate into the design some of the hobbies or the occupation of the one for whom the plate is made. For instance, if a girl likes flowers, the design may have a picture like the second one in the bottom row on the bookplate page, 331. If a boy likes to be out of doors tramping and fishing, then these ideas are worked in. A man may be an author or a poet; and when he wants a bookplate, the artist generally works in these ideas for him.

The Kewpies
and the
Glorious Fourth
by
Rose O'Neill

"A BLESSED COM~
PANION IS A
BOOK; A BOOK THAT
FITLY CHOSEN IS A
LIFE-LONG FRIEND."
DOUGLAS JERROLD.

Old·Hampshire·Bond

GRAPHICA
A MAGAZINE FULL
OF BUSINESS-GETTING IDEAS FOR
CANADIAN BUSINESS MEN

Phipps
Hats

OAK LEAF
OVERLAY
PAPER

Bush Terminal
International Exhibit
Building New York

HOME COMPANION

Buying from
a Poorly
Printed Catalog

The
PROMISED
LAND

GOOD EXAMPLES OF HAND LETTERING

EXAMPLES OF HAND LETTERING

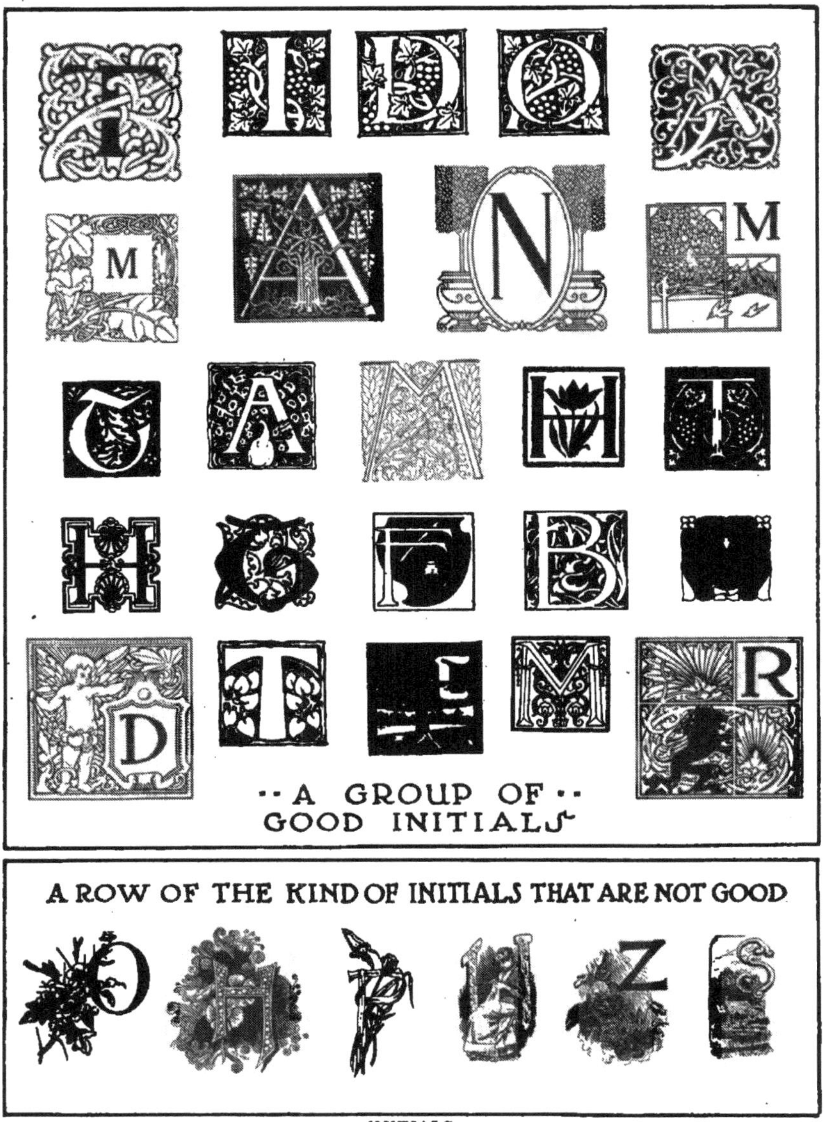

.. A GROUP OF ..
GOOD INITIALS

A ROW OF THE KIND OF INITIALS THAT ARE NOT GOOD

INITIALS

BOOKPLATE DESIGNS

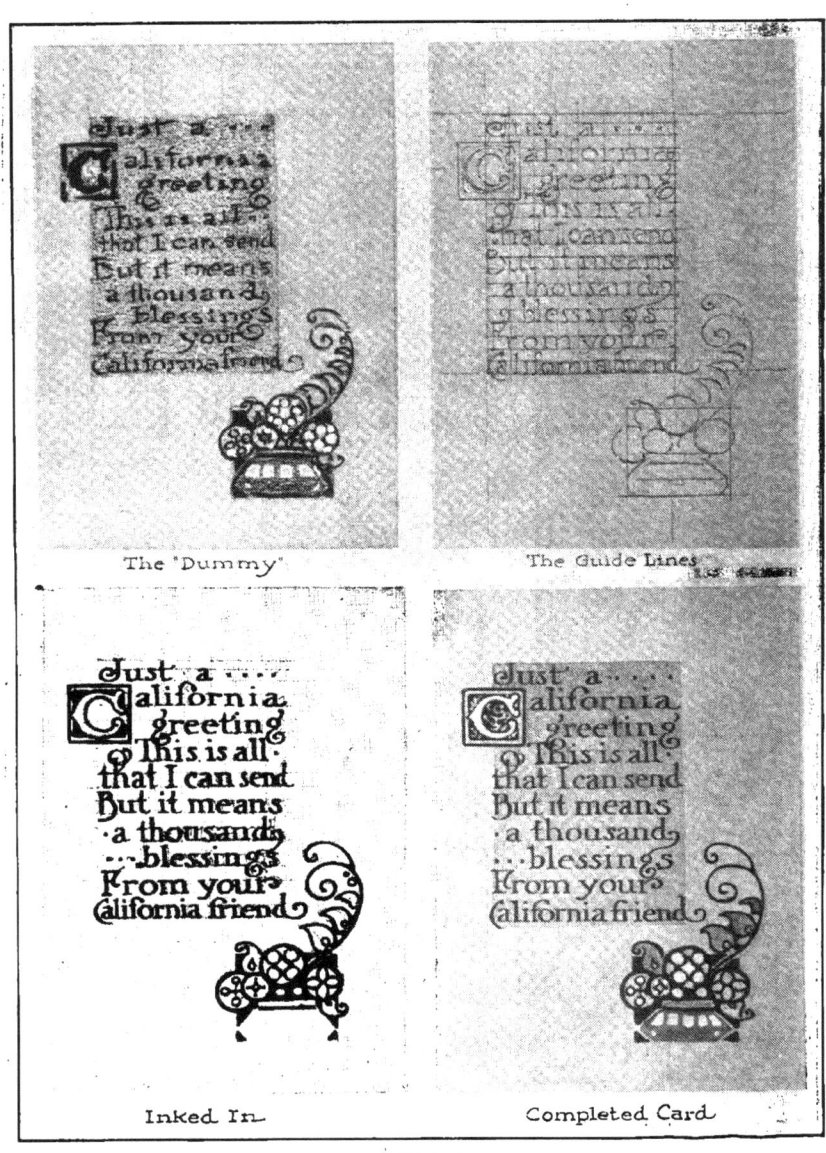

FOUR STEPS IN LETTERING A CARD

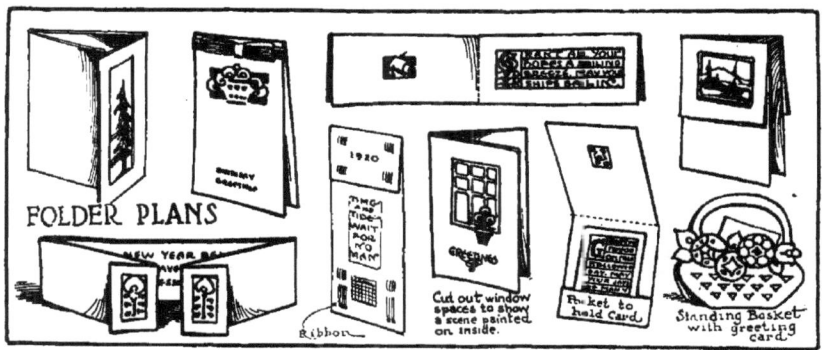

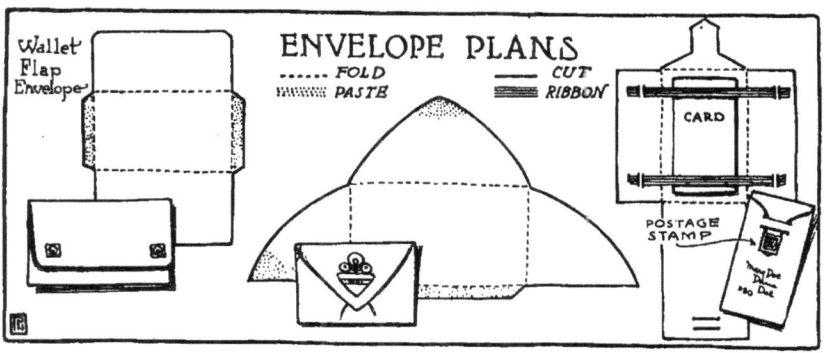

CARD AND ENVELOPE CONSTRUCTION

TEACHER'S NOTES FOR LETTERING

GOOD LETTERING appears everywhere in magazine advertising. Poor lettering also appears; and the teacher should assemble both kinds on mount boards, to illustrate clearly to the student the preferred letter forms. Large forms of well drawn letters should be made on large sheets of paper, so that the students can have posted an influence toward perfect lettering. Have the students always on watch for examples of correct lettering and also incorrect forms. There is no better way to develop a good knowledge than by observation combined with practice.

HOUSE
INCORRECT

HOUSE
CORRECT

LETTERING STROKES can be well executed in a large, free way by the use of a wide, flat brush. To demonstrate how and where the thin and the wide strokes should occur, use a wide brush dipped in ink. If the brush is always held in the same position, it will produce the narrow parts of a letter with every up stroke, and the wide parts with every down stroke. Let the students letter with a brush in this way, or else with the flat side of a piece of chalk on the blackboard, until they know just where every thin and every wide part of each letter should come. A cardboard strip about one half inch wide will work very well on paper if it is dipped into writing ink. The use of lettering pens will also demonstrate the good formation of letters when these are made so large that they need to be outlined.

ENVELOPE AND CARD EXAMPLES. With the problems of lettering will always come the application of lettering. Folders, cards, booklets, and envelope forms should be gathered as examples of simple and pleasing forms of printing arrangements. These should be filed in separate boxes, and additions should be made to the collection as regularly as possible. Various ways of making simple bindings should also be assembled, so that when lettering is applied to booklets and folders, the work will be done on material that is practical and durable. A mount containing well lettered pages and booklets, to which students can constantly refer, will prove a fine influence toward good forms. Let the students know that the proportions, spacing, and coloring selected for lettered pages play as important a part as the actual letter form; that the parts must be combined well if the whole is to be successful.

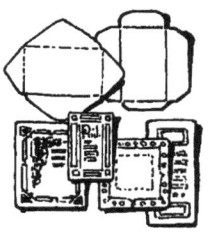

LETTER CHARACTER. The fault of much of the lettering produced in classes is that it has little relation in type or character to the purpose to which it is applied. Lettering used for a flower advertisement should surely be different from that used for the book cover of a school report. The different forms of lettering developed through the ages are related to the characteristics and types of those times. The classic, dignified lines of the Roman letter are identified with the classic architecture of that time, just as the Gothic form of lettering is an echo of Gothic architecture. The harmony of a letter form with its purpose and time is a problem which all students should keep in mind.

FLAT COLORS

HEAVY OUTLINE and SHADOWS

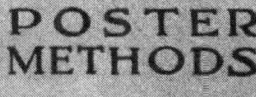
POSTER
METHODS

STENCIL

LIGHT OUTLINE and TINTS

CUT-OUT PAPERS

POSTER DESIGNS

The
Book Plate
in color

TWO-COLOR ADVERTISING DESIGNS

COLORED BOOK PLATES — COVER DESIGNS

THE ACADEMIC GRADES

ILLUSTRATION

BY ILLUSTRATION, we mean the kind of drawing that is found in magazines, newspapers, and books, to illustrate stories and articles. Almost every beginner in art wants to do this kind of work, because it looks attractive. Before trying to make illustrations, it is necessary for us to learn how to draw. It is for this reason that we have spent so many lessons in giving you a good foundation training. With this training, we can now go ahead and use our ideas combined with our drawing ability to make good illustrations.

"TECHNIQUE" is a word given by artists to the various styles or methods of doing work. The first technique we are going to study is that done either with pen and ink or with brush and ink. In other words, the next few pages of drawings have been done in black ink on white paper. A page of silhouettes is shown first,— 343. These silhouettes will always be one of the best ways of making illustrations. Look at these, and see how strong and effective they are, and yet how artistic. The very simplicity of such drawings makes them good. In work of this kind, we should always try for a pleasing arrangement or design of the black spots, one in which they balance well. The big areas may be put in with a brush, and the thin lines with a pen. Try copying one of the sea pictures.

THE NEXT TECHNIQUE we want to study is known as cross-hatch pen lining. In this technique, we secure our shades and tones by crossing the pen lines over one another at an angle. Before trying to draw a picture in this style, we should practice making shades by drawing a little technique chart like that in the lower right-hand corner of page 344. You will notice that the lines do not cross each other at right angles, but at a slant. This keeps our technique from being too hard and stiff. In drawing our lines, we should wave them a little, like those you see in the chart. This also makes the drawings more artistic.

IN THE LIGHT TONES, the lines run only one way. In the deepest tones, they may cross four or five times. In making these darker tones, we should be careful not to cross lines over lines that are still wet. If we do this, it makes our lines heavy and blotted looking where they run together. So as not to become confused, it is a good idea to block out lightly in pencil the place where the different tones stop. This will help you to see just where to stop when stroking over your lines.

INCREASED pen lines offer another way of doing pen and ink work. This is a more difficult style to execute than the crosshatch. As you can see on page 345, the lines all run in the same direction. The darker tones are made by drawing the lines closer together and by pressing down more on the pen. We should first practice several series of lines like those in the chart at the bottom of the page, before trying a drawing in this technique. To make a drawing in this style, we must be sure of our strokes, and work slowly. Hurried strokes will result in the lines running together and making "muddy" looking drawings.

STIPPLE WORK with the pen is always interesting to do. It is a fairly easy medium for beginners to learn, although, to be done well, it must be done slowly. Stipple work is done by making little dots with the point of the pen. By increasing the size of these dots, or making them closer together, we are able to make graded shades and tones in our drawings. There are several ways of making stipple drawings. One is called close stipple. This kind of stipple is made by keeping the dots separate but making them very close together. In order to do this correctly, we must follow a definite direction in making our dots, so as not to run them together. A good way to do this is to start by making several circles on various parts of our drawing surface, then stippling dots around the outside of these circles until the various series of circles run into one another. This gives us a definite direction to follow, and at the same time keeps the technique from looking too stiff. See page 346.

FREE STIPPLE is a technique in which the artist does not try to keep his dots separate, but runs them together in such a way that it has the appearance of a charcoal drawing. In doing free stipple, we have to be careful not to go over the same dots too many times, as this will make a black spot that will stand out prominently. Repeat stipple is very similar to free stipple. The difference between the two is that in the repeat stipple, the dots are kept separate for the lighter tones. Then to make the darker tones, a second layer of dots is put between the first dots after they are dry. This kind of stipple is a fine one for beginners to try, as it allows us to go over places that we did not get just right at first. Other ways are shown on page 346.

SPATTER WORK is very much like stipple, but more easily done. If you will look at spatter drawings on page 347, you will see that they are made up of dots something like stipple, only more irregular. Spatter work can be engraved and printed just like any other pen and ink work, if done right. The way to do good spatter work is as follows:

First purchase at any drug store some powdered gum arabic. Dilute this in water until you have it about the consistency of mucilage. Then mix a little blue water color with it. Mix just enough to give it a slight tinge of blue. The next step is to have your drawing ready. To do this, we draw on Bristol board, in pencil outlines, the subject we want to make. The lines should be fairly heavy, so that we can see them easily when we start to spatter. In some cases, it is a good plan to outline your drawing with a thin ink outline instead of pencil, as this is easier to see through the spatter.

Next we paint the gum arabic over the parts we do not wish the spatter work to touch. When the gum is thoroughly dry, we then put on the spatter work in the following manner: First take a toothbrush and a piece of wire screening. Take the stopper of your waterproof drawing ink bottle and rub ink with it into the bristles of the brush. Next hold the wire screening about an inch or two above the surface of your drawing, and rub the inked bristles of the brush back and forth across the wire screen. This will cause dozens of little ink dots to spatter down upon the paper; and these spattered dots give spatter work its name.

By painting gum arabic over the parts you do not wish to have any darker, and spattering the rest, you can obtain a drawing with several degrees of shade, all done in spatter work.

WHEN THIS SPATTER is dry and your drawing is done, you can then hold it under running water. The gum arabic will wash away, leaving a completed drawing. Sometimes, if the gum arabic has a little tendency to stick, you can loosen it by dabbing it lightly with a piece of cotton. The ink you use for this work must be waterproof, or it will wash off when the gum arabic is washed away. When the drawing has been washed out, it should be placed on a piece of blotter to dry. A soft, simple drawing can be obtained in this way, similar to those in the picture.

SCRATCH BOARD is another medium used by many artists. This kind of board comes in many designs and patterns, all planned with the one idea of enabling the artist to produce good work in a short time. There are various kinds of boards that are a success. Two of these are shown on page 348. The stipple surfaced board has a mechanical dot stamped upon it, one which resembles that made with pen and ink on paper. We make these dots appear by simply rubbing over the board with a soft, black pencil — the blacker, the better. The heavier we press on the pencil, the blacker the dots will be, and the darker the tones. In this way, we can produce soft and delicate tones, like those in a pencil drawing. These tones done on stipple scratch board will reproduce and print well, if done properly. We should be careful not to smudge up our lines on the scratch board, as then the engraver cannot photograph them.

LINE SURFACED BOARD is similar to the stipple board. It has black lines printed on it, which are used for the middle tones of the drawing. If we wish to make a lighter tone, we scratch the surface of our board, and it produces dots similar to those you see in the baby's hair in the picture. If we want a pure white, we scratch still deeper into our board, and we get down to the white paper itself. This scratching should be done with a sharp knife blade.

TONES DARKER than our gray background are produced by rubbing across our printed lines with a soft, black pencil. This gives us crisscross lines like those in the sailboat. We can get a jet black by using drawing ink. In this way, in a short time, we can have five distinct values, or tones, in our drawing, without much effort. It takes some practice to handle this board right, but a little experimentation with a small piece of the board will soon show you how it works. A good way to keep the surface of the board clean is to sketch your drawing first on a piece of thin paper. When this has been done to suit you, trace it off on the scratch board with a piece of graphite paper. ·

STILL LIFE drawings made in pen and ink are valuable practice. To do these properly, we must block out our drawing first in pencil, indicating the places where the shades are to go. If we are not quite certain as to the directions the lines should take, we should put them in with pencil before trying them in ink. It is a wise plan to copy a still life drawing, like one of these on page 349, before trying to make one yourself direct from objects. This practice will help you to see how the lines should go on various surfaces. On page 349, we have two kinds of technique shown. The top picture has its tones done in crosshatch. In the bottom one, a style more like the increased line is used. Both are valuable techniques to learn.

THE FLOWERS shown on page 350 are done in several styles or techniques. We have a flower done in a decorative outline, such as one would use for a flower analysis drawing. Just below it is one done in what is called a bold outline, more filled in with black masses. At the top, we have a nasturtium done in short strokes by increased lines, and next to it is a fuchsia executed in crosshatch work. In the center is a flower done in the long, sweeping strokes much used by newspaper artists. At the bottom, we have a row of pansies done in a combination of two techniques — the increased and the crosshatch together. The idea used in the flower drawing on the left, where the pen strokes make a gray background with a white flower on it, is a good one to remember. See if you can make a drawing of a flower, like this one. It would not hurt to copy this whole page, before trying to make an original flower drawing.

BUILDINGS are more difficult than other drawings, because there are so many details to care for. While a flower or landscape drawing may permit of many deviations from the original, we have to be careful in drawing buildings, else they will look crude or lopsided. One of the most beautiful drawings in this book is the one of Reims Cathedral, in the upper right-hand corner of page 351. Here this famous building is shown in all its delicate architecture. The lights and shades on it have been so handled as to give the effect of a building sparkling in the sunlight. This drawing is done in short, broken lines.

IN DRAWING BUILDINGS, be sure to pick out a simple subject first, like an old shed or a log cabin. Make it in the style that comes easiest to you, then try other techniques. If your work is too weak and delicate, try the heavy strokes. If your work looks crude, make some drawings in a technique like the one used in the cathedral drawing.

RENDERING pen and ink drawings from photographs is shown on page 352. At the top, we have a photograph of pine trees. Below it, we have the same composition worked out in four different ways. The first is simplest, and is done like a decorative outline. A drawing of this kind helps you to get good compositions, and keeps you from thinking too much of shades and high lights.

THE SECOND DRAWING is done in shadows only, similar to some of the drawings we made in still life work. This problem is a good one to try next, because it helps us to decide just where the shadows come. A drawing like this can be done with a brush. The third drawing is made in what is known as decorative rendering. This decorative rendering differs from the other kinds in that the various parts are made more definite and mechanical. For instance, notice how the leaves have been done in the trees. See how the lines have been put in on the grove of trees in the background. This style is used a great deal in magazine illustrations.

TWO DRAWINGS made by professional artists, from the same photograph, are shown on page 353. Each artist was asked to make the drawing in his own technique, and here we have the results. Each is a fine piece of work, and each has its distinct style. The top one has more detail worked into it, and is executed in what artists call a "full tone." By this, they mean that all the gradations from black to white are shown. Notice the confident way in which all the lines have been put in. In the lower drawing, the artist has used a bolder stroke and more of a decorative style, yet the general character of the two drawings is practically the same. In the second drawing, observe how the shades of the tree on the left have been done in almost one simple black shade. A drawing like this would print well on almost any kind of paper.

DIFFERENT GRADES of pen and ink drawing must be used on different kinds of paper. Because of the coarse fiber of some papers, it is impossible to print a finely drawn picture upon them. On the other hand, some magazines are printed on paper that will take any picture, no matter how closely drawn it may be. An artist always finds out the kind of paper on which his illustration is to go before he starts to make it. If it is to go on a rough surface, such as newspaper, then he uses a style similar to the silhouette or the outline drawing of Washington on page 354.

AN OUTLINE DRAWING will print on practically any kind of paper, because it has no fine lines to catch the ink and print a blurred line. Many posters are worked in this style. The drawing in the lower left-hand corner is called a "half shade," because it has in it about half the number of tones found in the portrait above it. In this case, we have a drawing that will print especially well on a medium grade of paper, which is the kind of paper used by most magazines. You will see here that all the important shadows have been put in, such as the shade on the side of the face and the black in the coat.

THE FULL SHADE DRAWING in the last picture is the best looking of them all. It contains practically all the tones found in the photograph, and naturally takes more time. In this one, even the background has been indicated in vertical decorative strokes. All the minor shades on the face have been shown also. Because of all these little lines, it is necessary for the engraver to exercise more care in making the engraving, and the printer more care in printing it. The surface of papers on which these fine line drawings are printed is smoother and more glossed than that used for the other drawings. See if you can copy the half shade portrait of Washington.

PORTRAITS done in many ways by professional artists are shown next, on page 355. They vary all the way from the simple shadow drawings of Lincoln to the highly decorative drawing of Robert Burns. Some are in crosshatch, some in stipple, and some in simple outline, like the one of Rockefeller. In the lower left-hand corner, we have a little pen and ink sketch of a lady's head, by Harrison Fisher, magazine illustrator. A fine portrait of a pilot, done in stipple, is shown in the center. Notice that no matter what technique the artist has used, he has kept it consistent. Any one of these here shown is worth copying. Try the easiest ones first, like those of Lincoln and Rockefeller.

EIGHT DIFFERENT WAYS of making the same drawing are shown on page 356. This page will bear considerable study. Every drawing is good and adapted to various places. At the top, we have one in simple outline. Next to it is a strong decorative drawing. The first one in the second row is done in stipple dots. The second one in that row has been done in crayon pencil on rough paper. The fifth drawing is done with a fine brush for coarse paper; while the sixth is a drawing on line scratch board. The first one in the bottom row is done in a strong style of black wash, and is the kind used for magazine work. The last one is also a wash drawing worked out on gray paper with white and dark paint.

A PAGE OF DECORATIVE DRAWINGS is next shown. You will notice that these pen drawings are done in a flat, poster style. There are no weak or delicate lines in them anywhere. They have been executed with the idea of keeping a good arrangement of light and dark spots. See how strong the two landscapes in the center look. Yet they balance well. In these decorative drawings, you will observe also that such things as leaves and water are treated in a very conventional manner. See how the leaves have been made of series of little ovals put close together. In this decorative style of drawing, do not try too much for high lights and shadows, but work more for flat tones.

WASH DRAWING is another means that artists use in illustrating. On page 359 are shown several good ways to make this kind of drawing. The picture of the ship shows us the way we should first put in our flat washes, or undertones. Over these we can then work our details and darker tones. All this should be done in transparent water color, so as to build up the tones one on top of the other. Wash drawings that are to be engraved and printed should always be drawn with more contrast than we need in the finished effect, because wash drawings lose some of their contrasts in being reproduced.

A COMBINATION of crayon and wash is often used by professional illustrators. In this kind of drawing, the artist first sketches his drawing lightly with his crayon pencil. Next he puts in his flat washes as those in the boat drawing are done. When these are dry, he finishes his drawing by putting in his deep tones and details with the crayon pencil. Drawings done in this way have a crisp, clean-cut style, and can be completed fairly rapidly. Some artists make their drawing with the crayon pencil, then fill in the necessary tones with washes of transparent water color.

PEN LINES AND WASH are often used together. The little Belgian girl is drawn this way. In these drawings, the artist outlines his picture in waterproof drawing ink. Then he fills in his tones with washes of black. This is a very rapid way of working, and also gives a good drawing. The sharp black pen lines help to offset the tendency of the engraving and printing to soften the drawing. By the use of waterproof ink, the lines are prevented from running when the wash is put on. All these wash drawings must be done in black and white. No color should be used, as it will not photograph properly. Drawings done in color can only be reproduced by the use of color filters and color plates. This necessitates making what is called the "three-color half-tone," which is very expensive. Two-color and three-color half-tones are used on the covers of many magazines. The color engravings in this book have been made in this way.

OPAQUE WASH is sometimes used in illustration. The opaque wash drawings on page 360 help you to see how they are done. In the center, we have a pastoral scene done in opaque wash. At the sides and the bottom are little sketches showing how to go about making such a drawing. The wash being opaque, it enables us to put a light tone over a dark tone. This is something we cannot do in transparent wash. In using opaque wash, we should always keep our color well stirred up as we use it, to avoid mottled effects. Opaque wash is made by mixing white water color with black water color, in different proportions, according to the tone, or shade, wanted.

FLAT TONES are first put on. Then our lighter and darker values follow, as is shown in the little sketches. By putting in our backgrounds first, and building our drawing up over them, we can finally round it out to the finished effect we see in the big picture. The way to handle details like the sheep is a good problem to study.

GRAY BACKGROUNDS are often used in wash illustrations, especially in making decorative drawings, like that of the leopard on page 361. The artist puts on first his foundation shades, then his deep blacks and pure whites. This method has two desirable features. It is not only a rapid way of working, but the gray background helps you to know just how much contrast your drawing needs, and at the same time helps to hold your whole picture together.

PEN AND BRUSH DRAWINGS

COMBINING PEN AND BRUSH WORK

CROSS-
HATCH
PEN
LINES

EXAMPLES OF CROSSHATCH PEN LINES

EXAMPLES OF INCREASED PEN LINES

White Ink Stipple over the black parts

Close Stipple

Free Stipple

Free Stipple

Repeat Stipple

Close Stipple

Set Stipple

Pen and Ink Stipple Methods

STIPPLED PEN WORK

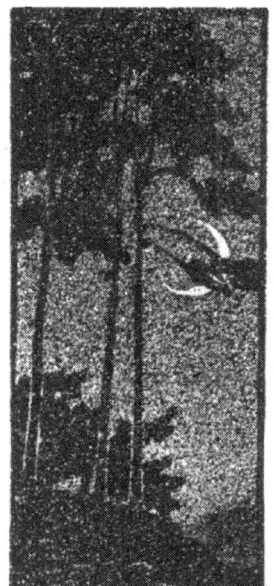

SPATTER WORK DRAWINGS

SPATTER DRAWINGS

Stipple Surfaced
Scratch Board

Line Surfaced
Scratch
Board

SCRATCH BOARD DRAWINGS

PEN AND INK STILL LIFE DRAWINGS

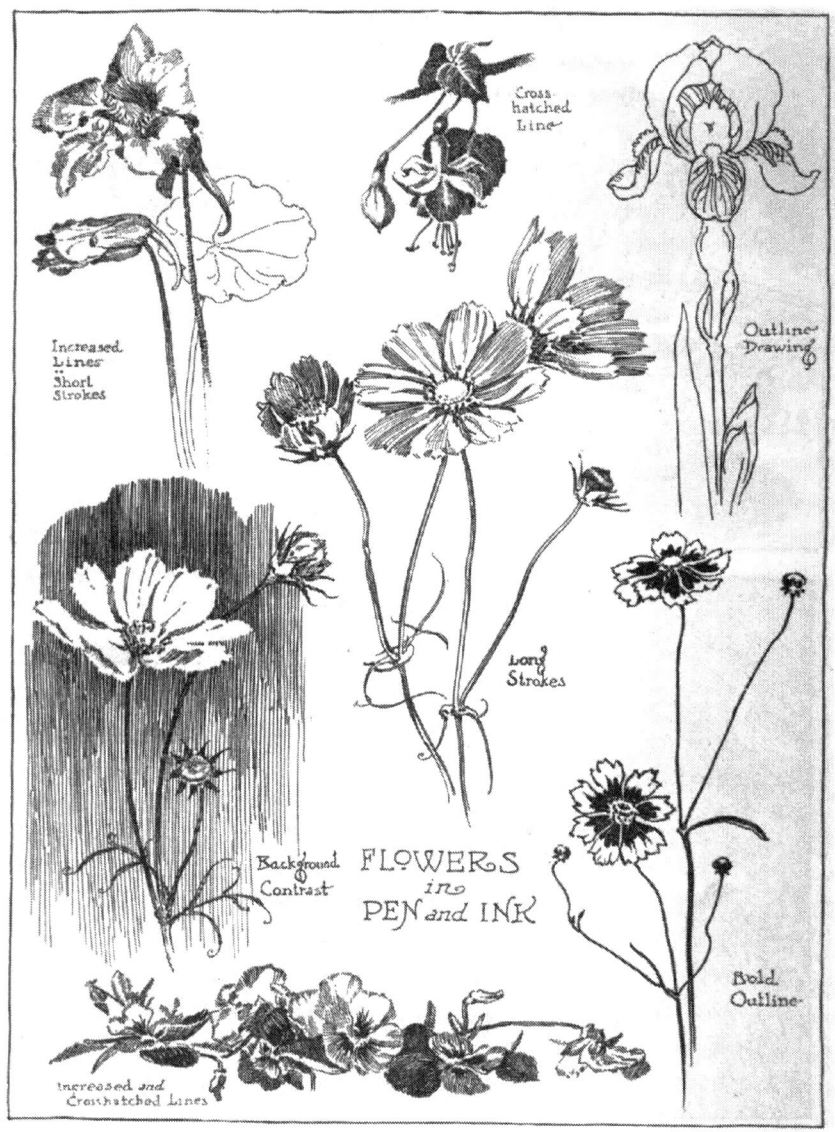

Cross hatched Line

Outline Drawing

Increased Lines Short Strokes

Long Strokes

Background Contrast

FLOWERS in PEN and INK

Bold Outline

Increased and Crosshatched Lines

PEN DRAWINGS FROM FLOWERS

LINE
and STIPPLE

SHORT
BROKEN LINE

OLD BRIDGE
KIRKMICHAEL
PERTHSHIRE N.B.

QUICK LINE
LINES ACCENTED ON
CENTER OF INTEREST

BOLD, COARSE
LINES

OUTDOOR PEN AND INK SKETCHES

THE SCENE, AND FOUR STYLES OF PEN RENDERING

TWO RENDERINGS FROM THE SAME SUBJECT

THE SUBJECT

OUTLINE PORTRAIT for NEWSPAPER and ROUGH PAPER

HALF SHADE PORTRAIT for MEDIUM GRADE PAPER

FULL SHADE PORTRAIT for FINE GRADE PAPER

THREE WAYS OF DRAWING A PORTRAIT IN PEN AND INK

PEN PORTRAITS

EIGHT WAYS OF DRAWING THE SAME SUBJECT

WASH DRAWINGS METHODS

EIGHT WAYS OF DRAWING THE SAME SUBJECT

THE ACADEMIC GRADES

WASH DRAWINGS METHODS

OPAQUE WASH DRAWINGS

LIGHT AND DARK WASH ON GRAY BACKGROUND

TEACHER'S NOTES FOR ILLUSTRATION

PEN AND INK SUBJECTS. Photographs and prints of well defined subjects, and those with good patterns of objects or trees against a background, make the best subjects for pen and ink drawings. Those which the teacher decides are simple enough for students' use, may be collected from magazines and photographs. To prevent these prints or photographs from becoming injured while being used, they can be protected by a sheet of celluloid on the front, and backed by a firm cardboard. They are fastened with a clip or pasted on the edges. The celluloid can be used for protecting other prints whenever subjects are changed. A uniform size of mount board will allow easier filing, and reuse of celluloid and backing material.

THE SUBJECT

FRAGMENT COPIED FOR STUDY

CARE OF EQUIPMENT. Drawing ink should be kept well corked, to prevent evaporation and thickening. White paint also should be kept covered, to prevent drying out. When water colors or paint dry hard, they can be softened by the addition of a little glycerin and water. Drawing papers and mount boards should be kept in flat drawers or flat portfolios. Having decided on the part to be used, the student should restore the balance to the portfolio. Such a practice prevents waste of paper. Brushes should not be permitted to dry with paint or ink on them, since that ruins their elasticity and points. Brushes should not be left for long periods in water cups, as this destroys their shapes. Insist on the care of equipment.

DRAWING INK BOTTLE GLUED TO FLAT BOARD

KEEP COVER ON

PREVENTS SPILLING INK

THE USE OF REPRODUCTIONS is good if they are used understandingly. The students should be well informed that a pen drawing which has been engraved and printed, is usually reduced in size, and the lines are therefore very much smaller and closer together than they appeared in the original. Therefore, in copying, about the same number of lines should be made to appear for the given space, and the copy should be drawn about twice as high as the print. A student may form an undesirable habit of always copying and never doing subjects of his own. Copying should be done only where a certain influence on technique or rendering is desired. It can be accomplished in no better way than by copying some particularly well done section of the subject containing the admired rendering.

CELLULOID HELD ON WITH CLIPS TO PROTECT THE PRINT

A COVERING PAPER WILL PROTECT THE SUBJECT

FIGURING PROPORTIONS. When drawing in pen and ink or wash for illustration, it is generally best to make the drawings large. To increase a rectangular space to a larger proportion, the simplest and most satisfactory method is shown in the diagram opposite. To find the dimensions of a drawing that is to be reduced to a smaller measure, a diagonal line is made from corner to corner of the drawing (usually on the back), and, either the width or the height measurement having been set off on the border line, a right angle from this point will give the point of the other corner where this right angle intersects the diagonal line. A little experimenting will prove this a very simple method of checking up proportions.

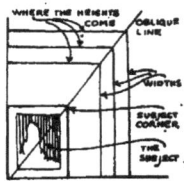

WHERE THE HEIGHTS COME

OBLIQUE LINE

WIDTHS

SUBJECT CORNER

THE SUBJECT

LESSON OUTLINES FOR THE GRAMMAR GRADES

A teacher cannot expect to teach drawing successfully without a good knowledge of drawing and painting, and he should surround himself with every available help. Connect all study of art as closely and naturally as possible with other lines of work. Cultivate observation, and encourage sketching from natural objects. Train the senses, the mind, and the hand to work together.

Make an effort to have good pictures on the walls, and lead the children to study and discuss them. Ruskin says, "A room without pictures is like a house without windows." Help the children to observe beautiful and appropriate forms in everyday objects. Let them learn to be interested in furniture, household belongings, etc., and in how such things are made, and to appreciate whatever is especially well designed in form and color.

Example is the most effective means of teaching drawing. The teacher must lead, not push; must draw, not talk. Showing how is best accomplished by doing, not explaining. The teacher is to accompany the following outline with the chapter illustrations of the book.

FIRST YEAR. First Semester.

1. Observation of surroundings and of objects in nature and their shapes.
2. Relation of the circle, the ellipse, and the oval to nature objects. Compare shapes of things gathered to these geometric shapes.
3. Teach placing of material on desks; and teach directions, such as left, right, top, bottom, under and over, left to right, front to back, etc.
4. Draw leaves and grasses with colored crayons.
5. Make borders with dots and dashes.
6. Make designs with cut-out, circular papers. Change the cut-outs to flowers by cutting the edges.
7. Teach simple, straight line alphabet. Letter pupil's name and school's name.
8. Make paper bookmark with design or colored crayon flower.
9. Make simple basket and simple box.
10. Letter name and decorate with round cut paper flower.

FIRST YEAR. Second Semester.

1. Conversational lesson regarding the seasons.
2. Teach drawing simple trees with crayon. Show pictures. Speak of the horizon.
3. Draw landscape on board, children to use their gray paper and black

(363) .

and white crayon in reproducing this. Fill in both sky and foreground, using trees in space below horizon.

4. Draw flowers and leaves with white and black crayons, on gray paper. Repeat them with light and dark colored crayons on dark paper.

5. Cut out simple forms and animals from light and dark paper. Mount the problem on a background.

6. Cut out flat paper baskets and mount, pasting paper flat flowers with basket.

7. Weave paper mats. Decorate with crayon marks.

8. Cut paper mats and borders from folded paper. Use as decorations to other things.

9. Teach simple lettering, using it for paper protective cover of school books. Use name of pupil and school. Use simple cut-out design from paper to decorate center of cover.

10. Model with clay or modeling wax, making round objects and flat objects. Make birds and animals to place on tree twigs for sand table.

SECOND YEAR. First Semester.

1. Conversational lesson about action. Games and action poses illustrated. Teacher to make action lines on board. Straight line means inaction; oblique line means action; vertical line means repose.

2. Teach making of action figures with simple lines. Make action figure of "Bobby and Fido."

3. Draw action figures in colored crayon lines. Illustrate running, jumping, throwing, etc.

4. Draw toys in outline with crayon on white paper. Use toys with shapes that can be drawn in the flat. Study sizes of parts.

5. Draw with crayon in silhouette forms, using simple objects. Draw also using color but making forms in a silhouette manner.

6. Make an A B C booklet.

7. Illustrate A B C booklet with simple object drawings.

8. Letter an alphabet of small letters. Letter three words.

9. Make simple borders with squares and parts of squares added to crayon lines.

10. Cut out travel pictures and mount.

SECOND YEAR. Second Semester.

1. Simple story to be read by teacher. Children to illustrate it with action figures.

2. Draw objects and toys with white and black crayon on gray paper. Draw the same in colors on white paper.

3. Draw straight line trees on geometric paper.
4. Letter a short verse in small letters with capitals.
5. Cut out from patterns paper animals that will stand up.
6. Color paper animals with crayons.
7. Make flat paper bowls and flowers. Use colored paper.
8. Make paper baskets and boxes and decorate in colors.
9. Make stencil and cut-out designs for booklet covers.
10. Model objects and animals from clay balls.

THIRD YEAR. First Semester.

1. Show good pictures, and let children tell of beautiful things and places they saw during vacation.
2. Let children tear from paper, using as subjects some of the things that are to be found in the schoolroom. The teacher may post large bird and animal subjects as guides.
3. Cut a bird and an animal from white paper and mount on black paper. Do the same with black paper and mount on white.
4. Draw simple subjects within six geometric forms.
5. Make designs from cut-out paper shapes.
6. Cut out an alphabet from folded squares, each pupil to cut out two letters.
7. Cut out name in alphabet and mount.
8. Make simple objects in colored crayon, with some shading.
9. Make colored crayon drawings from flowers.
10. Cut snowflakes from folded paper.

THIRD YEAR. Second Semester.

1. Make a paper model for an action figure, teacher to supply hectograph outline.
2. Have children put paper models of action figures in different positions and trace.
3. Children to make action figure drawings and illustrate geography lesson.
4. Conversational lesson on trees and their shapes. Show relation of trees to six geometric shapes.
5. Pupils to draw trees within simple shapes.
6. Cut paper trees.
7. Cut vase forms from black paper.
8. Cut vase forms from colored paper. Decorate with crayons and mount with cut-out colored paper flowers.
9. Make Noah's ark and animals.
10. Model objects from square forms.

FOURTH YEAR. First Semester.

1. Conversational lesson on brush work, paints, and use of colors.
2. Drill in use of brushes and paints.
3. Drill on mixing of colors.
4. Silhouettes of simple objects with brush.
5. Silhouettes of trees.
6. Simple water color landscapes.
7. Dividing of squares into designs.
8. Brush lines on square designs.
9. Coloring of square designs.
10. Painting of flowers in water colors.

FOURTH YEAR. Second Semester.

1. Conversational lesson on Japanese brush drawings. Show examples if possible.
2. Brush drills from leaves and plant forms in silhouette.
3. Brush drills in three values,— light, dark, and middle tones.
4. Brush drills in use of white paint with dark on gray board.
5. Brush drill of simple brush lettering.
6. Still life objects in water colors.
7. Illustrated poems.
8. Window curtain problem.
9. Wax stencil work.
10. Stick-printed designs.

FIFTH YEAR. First Semester.

1. Talk and lesson on birds. Their colors and forms.
2. Lesson on drawing birds. Characteristic lines.
3. Lesson on brush drawing of birds, based on the oval.
4. Make bird booklet.
5. Make bird border.
6. Make bird design in colors within a circle.
7. Make geometric bird.
8. Cut paper animals.
9. Cut simple alphabet letters from paper.
10. Cut bird poster and cut lettering for it.

FIFTH YEAR. Second Semester.

1. Line sketches with brush from animal pictures.
2. Abbreviated line drawings of birds and animals. Refer to Japanese brush pictures.
3. Sketches in dark and light crayons from birds and animals.
4. Cut bird and animal shapes from paper.

5. Make borders and all-over patterns by pasting down these cut-outs, and add brush marks between figures to fill in.
6. Dark and light bird and animal designs on gray paper.
7. Make simple paper and wood animal toys.
8. Make an animal poster with lettering. Cross-stitch birds and animals on cloth.
9. Stencil birds or animals on cloth.
10. Model from live bird or animal.

SIXTH YEAR. First Semester.
1. Lesson on different drawn lines. Illustrate accented lines.
2. Pupils to draw from grasses and plants in pencil.
3. Pupils to draw from still life objects in accented lines. Give memory work.
4. Design simple motifs from flowers.
5. Design motifs to fill six geometric shapes from one flower.
6. Make rosettes in black and white.
7. Cut still life groups from paper. Mount.
8. Make several sheets of line lettering.
9. Make sheet of flower motifs in color with black outline.
10. Make rosettes in colors. Apply with stencils.

SIXTH YEAR. Second Semester.
1. Drill in memory drawing from objects.
2. Draw objects in different positions.
3. Draw curved surfaces of objects at different heights.
4. Draw square objects at different angles.
5. Make still life drawings, and use finders to select good picture arrangements.
6. Make selected arrangements in flat tones.
7. Compass drills of circles and arcs.
8. Make compass designs.
9. Make light and dark drawings of objects on dark paper. Call attention to shapes and locations of high lights.
10. Make a bowl from clay coils.

SEVENTH YEAR. First Semester.
1. Talk and review on importance of design. Show good design examples and applications. Accent importance of nature as design source.
2. Make drawings of flowers or seed pods for design use.
3. Make drawings of leaves and berries for design use.
4. Make composition from drawings, with finders.
5. Make single design motifs from leaves.

6 Make repeated leaf and seed motifs for borders. Make in colors.

7. Make geometric forms and use as all-over patterns.

8. Repeat problem, changing geometric forms to flower or leaf motifs.

9. Make designs in black on colored paper, cutting motifs with scissors.

10. Use designs in block printing paper and cloth with linoleum blocks.

SEVENTH YEAR. Second Semester.

1. Brush drawings in black and white paint on gray paper from flower or leaves.

2. Designs in white and black paint on gray paper from previous flower drawings.

3. Drawings in different tone values from flower study. Use finders for composition.

4. Use designs for block printing and stenciling cloth problems.

5. Talk and plan for booklet design and construction.

6. Make dummy and plan page arrangement.

7. Write or letter pages of booklet.

8. Make cover for booklet.

9. Design cover and assemble.

10. Study and draw lettering alphabet and add title to book cover. Complete.

EIGHTH YEAR. First Semester.

1. Picture study from prints or photographs of good tree paintings.

2. Sketches in pencil or water colors from good examples of tree pictures.

3. Sketching from tree branch.

4. Sketching from trees if possible.

5. Brush drawings from trees in black and in color.

6. Tree designs. One, two, and three trees.

7. Design tree borders.

8. Plan a tree book or folder.

9. Construct the tree book or folder.

10. Study of season's coloring. Make tree picture in colors showing season's coloring.

EIGHTH YEAR. Second Semester.

1. Landscape study continued; study different arrangements of landscape pictures.

2. Make brush outline drawing of landscape and find several smaller compositions from it with finders.

3. Make dark and light arrangements from one of the previous problems.

4. Arrange one of the landscape scenes to fit different proportional rectangles.

5. Plan and cut out landscapes from black, gray, and white paper. Do the same with black silhouettes over water color skies with sunset effect.

6. Use tree on book plate, cover design, or other application.

7. Apply tree in cardboard work.

8. Make lantern with tree design.

9. Apply tree to thin woodwork.

10. Letter tree poem, and decorate with decorative tree drawing.

Note.— All problems are to be varied as teacher's work requires. Other problems in chapters may be substituted for those given in the above outline.

LESSON OUTLINES FOR THE ACADEMIC GRADES
DRAWING AND PAINTING

1. Problem in General Form.

Arrange a simple group, and have students draw it in silhouette only. Next allow them to sketch a simple landscape or sky line in the same manner. Use 8 x 10 inch paper.

2. Problem in Light and Shade.

Arrange still life groups, and have students sketch them first in shadows only, then in high lights only (using gray paper for high light drawing), and last, make a complete drawing, using light and shade in the same study. 8 x 10 inch paper.

3. Problem in Antique Cast Drawing.

Students should make at least ten sketches of the important casts in charcoal. A good order to follow is ear, nose, mouth, eye, hands, feet, toes, etc., up to the more difficult casts. Work for simplicity of tones and planes. Make all drawings large, on regular full sheets of charcoal paper.

4. Problem in Figure Sketching.

Have a member of the class pose for sketching. Allow only a simple "blocked in" sketch for the first three or four times. Later allow longer poses and more detail worked out. 8 x 10 or 10 x 12 inch paper.

Let students make pencil or charcoal sketches of heads from well defined photographs or prints. Have them keep the planes broad and simple. Next they may try a portrait sketch from a posed model.

5. Problem in Landscape Work — Houses.

If possible, allow students to make sketches out of doors from old houses, cabins, or barns. Some good sketches may be seen through schoolroom

24 Applied Art

windows. House sketches may be made also from photographs or prints. 8 x 10 inch paper.

6. Problem in Landscapes — Trees.

Have each student make at least two good sketches of trees. These sketches should be done fairly large, say about 5 x 7 inches, with lead pencil. If no outdoor sketches are available, then photographs or prints may be used. Etching prints make good material for any copy work that may be done.

7. Problem in Perspective Rules.

Students should copy and learn the basic rules of perspective. Arrange groups of boxes above, below, and on the level of the eye, and have students make perspective drawings in pencil. Students should also make at least ten drawings of objects, using perspective lines. 8 x 10 inch paper.

·8. Landscapes in Perspective.

Have students make outdoor sketches or sketches from photographs using perspective lines. They should make at least one sketch showing subjects below the level of the eye, and one above eye level. 8 x 10 inch paper.

9. Two-Point Perspective.

Let students take from a magazine a print of a room interior, and locate the perspective lines, ruling in these lines with a hard pencil or red ink. Next have them make a sketch showing a factory building drawn in two-point perspective.

10. Projection and Circles in Perspective.

Arrange groups of cylinders and cones for perspective sketching. Show students how to block out a circle made from a square to obtain correct perspective.

Have the class draw a wheel in various perspective angles as shown on the working chart. At least four drawings of circles in perspective should be made. All these perspective drawings should be made on good 8 x 10 inch architect's detail paper.

DESIGN

1. Problem in Unity.

Take dot and dash motifs and work out four designs about 2 x 4 inches in size. Next work out a border, using one of the best of these designs.

2. Problem in Mass.

Given four brush spots by teacher, students reconstruct five designs from them, as shown on page 252. Have students keep the space between parts narrow, so the design will hold together. Make in black and white about 3 x 5 inches each.

3. Problem in Surface Pattern.

Teacher to give each student a geometric shape, as on page 253. Student to arrange these forms into a border. Next an all-over pattern, about 8 x 10 inches. Last, a circle including a radial pattern, as shown on page 253. Circle to be 6 inches in diameter.

4. Problems in Flower Analysis.

Students to take any simple flower and make a flat, simple sketch from it; also to develop about four or five designs from the flower, all to be grouped well on a sheet of either white or gray paper, 12 x 18 inches. Use flat colors.

5. Study of Repetition.

Students to study the chart on page 256, and plan a border in colors which contains pleasing repetition. Size about 2½ inches by 8 inches.

6. Study of Radiation.

Study the radiation examples on page 257. Plan a simple design in black and white about 4 x 6 inches in size, using radiating lines as its basis. Next work out the same design motif in flat colors.

7. Study of Measure and Balance.

Work out a design to fit a panel 11 x 15 inches in size. Then work out a border around the panel, using a good division of spaces.

Develop two designs to fit circles about 6 or 8 inches in diameter, one design to be bi-symmetric, and the other to be an occult one. Designs may be in black and white or in colors, as decided by teacher.

8. Study of Four Divisions of Design.

From flowers or flower prints, make up (1) a flower sketch, (2) naturalistic, (3) conventional, (4) geometric, (5) abstract designs. All these can be made approximately 3 x 5 inches in size on one sheet of gray paper. Use flat colors.

9. Bird and Insect Design.

Allow each student to choose either an insect, a bird, or an animal as subject, and work out in flat colors on gray or light brown paper a decorative design from this subject. Difference must be made clear by teacher between ordinary copying of a subject and decorative rendering of it. Size about 5 x 7 inches. Next have the student work out this design in some crafts motif, as a tile, stencil, or a stained glass window.

10. Landscapes in Design.

Have students make a decorative landscape not smaller than 6 x 8 inches, in black and white, on gray paper. Next have them work out this same subject, using variations of light and dark values as on page 269. Last, ask students to adapt their landscape to some form of industrial art, such as a design for a fireplace, a book end, or a chest. This last design may be in grayed colors.

HANDICRAFT

✓1. PROBLEM IN BLUE PRINTING.

Have students each make two or three blue prints from flowers, if possible. Ask them to try for nice arrangement of parts. If flowers and printing frame are not available, allow students to make a sketch in charcoal from some flower catalogue or post card. Size, about 6 x 9 or 8 x 11 inches.

✓ 2. PROBLEM IN STENCIL WORK.

From flower design of Problem 1, or from another design, have students make a design for stencil work. Make plain the fact that the parts must be planned so as not to fall apart when cut.

When the design has been well drawn, then students should trace it to stencil paper and cut it out with a sharp knife. Next allow them to try out the stencil with opaque water colors on toned paper, such as gray or tan.

Students desiring to do so, can be allowed to work out the same design on cloth, such as linen for a sofa cushion, a school bag, or a table runner.

3. PROBLEM IN BLOCK PRINTING.

Follow the same procedure as in stencil work. First have a block print design made. Next trace it on linoleum blocks, and cut it out with a sharp knife. Then try the linoleum blocks out with opaque water colors on toned paper.

Finally the students can produce their crafts design in oil paints on various articles, as a school bag or a book cover.

4. PROBLEM IN BATIK OR RESIST WORK.

Allow students to work out a strong, simple design in charcoal on gray paper. When it is satisfactory, trace it with graphite paper on cloth and paint in with wax. When dry, the whole fabric can be immersed in *cold* dye. When it is again dry, iron out the wax with a hot iron. Batik designs for cushions, waists, curtain drapes, etc., may be made in this way.

5. PROBLEMS IN LEATHER.

Ask students to decide on a simple object to be made in leather, as a coin purse, or a table mat. Have them work out a good design on light brown paper. When the pencil outline is correct, they can tint the parts of the design as desired, with soft or grayed tones of water color.

This design is then traced on leather by dampening the surface of the leather and tracing off the design with a hard pencil. No graphite is needed, the pencil point leaving an indentation in the soft leather. ·

The design can then be tooled and stained, and the article assembled. Patterns should be made of heavy paper and tried out before the leather is cut.

6. ADVANCED PROBLEMS IN LEATHER.

Students qualifying should be allowed to work out more advanced problems in leather, making such things as book ends, magazine covers, wallets, etc. Always have students make heavy paper patterns and assemble them to make sure that the right construction is used.

Buttons and clasps will be put on at any fair-sized glove or dry goods house, at a nominal price.

7. PROBLEMS IN METAL WORK.

If permissible, have students work out a few problems in copper — simple problems, such as paper knives, book ends, and simple trays, which do not require much equipment. A few saws, hammers, and drills will almost do the work. Besides sawing, etching acid may be used to produce designs on the copper. A paper knife is a good subject to try first.

8. ADVANCED PROBLEMS IN METAL WORK.

For more advanced work, such objects as trays, bowls, and vases may be worked out. It is advisable to restrict the efforts to small objects, as the results are sure to be more satisfactory. A small flower bowl or a card tray is a good subject for students who wish to continue in copper work.

9. PROBLEM IN CEMENT WORK.

Have the students work out on paper and in flat colors a design for a simple tea tile. This design can then be in turn worked out in modeling wax. From this wax design, the plaster of Paris mold and the cement tile may be cast. This forms a very interesting and practical craft when properly done. A light finish with floor wax may be given to the tiles when they are completely dry.

10. ADVANCED PROBLEM IN CEMENT WORK.

Students wishing to continue in cement work may work out on paper a design for a vase or a flower box. This design should be actual size, and the colors should be worked out in grayed tones on the paper sketch. The work may then be carried out according to instructions in the chapter on handicrafts.

In the case of the flower box, the four sides are cast separately, then cemented together and to the bottom.

COLOR

1.-STUDY OF COLOR — COLOR CHARTS.

Have students make up a color wheel similar to Color Chart A. The correct colors can be obtained from colored paper booklets such as are sold by school supply houses. By cutting out the desired colors and pasting them in place over a pencil outline, the color wheel can be readily made. Care should be taken to paste the color values in the correct place. The Milton Bradley color booklets have the colors printed on each sheet, and are practical from this standpoint. With this color wheel, the cardboard dials also should be made. Size of wheel, 12 inches in diameter.

2. COLOR DIAGRAMS.

With the color wheel as a basis, ask students to work out four sets of color schemes: (1) complementary, (2) split complementary, (3) triad, (4) analogous or related. These color schemes should be drawn on water color paper in panels about 1½ inches wide. The schemes should show the colors in the correct proportion to each other. In other words, the gray or softer colors should cover larger areas than the brighter colors.

3. INTERIOR DECORATORS' COLOR WHEEL.

Have students make a copy of Color Chart B. It should be done in water colors instead of cut papers. This will allow students to practice in the matching and mixing of colors.

The chart will look best if the colors when dry are outlined with a compass and black drawing ink. Size about 8 inches in diameter.

4. STUDY IN ROOM HARMONIES.

With the color wheel just made, students should work out a color scheme for a room. This can be done in a panel 4 x 7 inches. It should show the ceiling, the frieze, the side wall, the woodwork, and the floor colors, in strips. The side wall color should occupy most of the panel, the ceiling next, and the woodwork the least.

One color scheme may be made in related colors, and one in complementary colors. Advise students against having the colors too brilliant.

5. COLOR FROM NATURE.

Ask students to bring to school a leaf, a stone, a shell, a bit of bark, or some other object from nature, having a pleasing color scheme. From this object, they should make a color panel, showing the colors in the relative proportions in which they are found in the original. The panel should be about 1½ x 4 inches. Next they should work up a design for a tile or a border, using these same colors in the same proportions. Design and panel should both be on one sheet. This sheet may be 10 x 12 inches.

6. FLOWERS IN COLOR — COLOR STUDY.

Students are to make on gray paper, in opaque colors, a copy of a flower and two designs from it. These designs may contain gold or silver in small amounts, or may be outlines in black or some deep color. Size 10 x 12 inches.

7. HARMONIES FROM FLOWERS.

With a flower as a basis, work out a sheet of designs for textiles. This page should not contain more than three or four designs, and the colors should not be too rich. The brighter colors may be put in with embroidery. Size of sheet, 10 x 12 inches.

8. TEXTILES AS A COLOR BASIS.

From some good textile, such as is obtainable in high grade interior decorators' shops or at any museum, have students make a color scale. With this color scale as a basis, ask them to plan a design for a table runner or scarf. The design may have no similarity to the original textile, or it may be a variation of it. The colors should be in practically the same proportion as the original. This design may be later worked out on cloth if desired. Size of design optional.

9. COLOR IN POSTERS.

Have students work out a good color scheme in complementary harmonies from their color wheel. Next plan a poster about 12 x 18 inches in size, for some article, as a breakfast food or a flower shop.
The flower shop will lend best possibilities.
Pencil out a design, being careful not to use too much lettering. Fill in with opaque colors, keeping the color in large masses.

10. COLOR IN ILLUSTRATION AND DESIGN.

Let students work out a design in three colors for a book cover. This design should be 8 x 11 inches in size, on toned paper. The original sketch should be made on thin paper, and traced off when satisfactory.

The design should include the backbone of the book, and should contain lettering, as name of book, name of author, etc., and be made strong in style. Emphasis, care, and finish in this problem make the book covers a fairly difficult piece of art work.

LETTERING

1. STUDY OF ALPHABETS.

Explain to class the origination and development of our alphabet. Have them draw a chart showing the development from the Egyptian hieroglyphics to the Roman letter, as shown at the bottom of page 319. Size 3 x 5 inches.

2. STUDY OF CLASSIC ROMAN LETTERS.

Have students make a careful copy of classic Roman letters in pencil on an 8 x 10 inch sheet of pen and ink paper. When corrections have been made, students may ink the letters. Have them learn the various parts of the letters, as stem, spur, etc.

3. PROBLEM OF SPACING.

Ask students to draw with single strokes and in pencil only, an alphabet in condensed letters and one in extended letters, as on page 321. This problem is mainly for training the eye, and need not be carried beyond the pencil stage, unless the term's work allows time for inking. Size of condensed alphabet, 3½ x 5 inches; extended alphabet, 4 x 6 inches. Next have students take some simple word, as "artist" or "lettering," and letter it in a condensed letter and also in an extended letter. Depth of letters, not less than ¾ of an inch.

4. STUDY OF LETTER VARIATIONS.

With page 324 as a guide, letter any short word in three different strengths of letters; as, light face, medium, and bold. Keep all the words comparatively the same depth and length, but vary their strength.

5. STUDY OF LETTERING PENS.

After sketching lightly in pencil a motto of not more than two lines, try inking it with a *ball-pointed pen*. This pen is the easiest for beginners. Do not have too much ink on your pen, and have a board on which your drawing may rest at a slight angle. Try several mottoes, improving each time.

Next try one of the same mottoes, then a new one, with the regular lettering pen, shown at the bottom of page 325. If the work is not satisfactory, practice a series of strokes and scrolls with the pen until familiar with the way it works. Be sure to use the little brass fountain on the pen, as this gives a crisper stroke. Size of mottoes, about 2½ x 3½ inches.

6. STUDY OF TEXT LETTERS.

Students should copy the English text letter at the top of page 323. This alphabet will be found useful for such things as Christmas cards, church programs, etc. Capital letters to go with these are given on page 322. Students should be allowed their choice between English text and the flourished black letters, but should be required to execute one well. Size 1½ x 3½ inches.

7. STUDY OF PEN LETTERS.

Make a copy of the alphabets on page 326, and ink it. These alphabets are easy to learn and pleasing to look at. With these as a basis, have students design a simple window card, using *letters only*. Size of card, 8 x 10 inches. Wording optional, as, "Spring Hats," "Church Program," etc. Two colors may be used.

8. MONOGRAMS.

Have students look up some good monograms. These may be found on stationery, in magazines, etc. Be sure that modern monograms are selected, not the old-fashioned, interlaced letters. Have one monogram designed to fit a circle and one for a rectangle. Size of circle, 2½ inches in diameter; rectangle, 2½ x 4 inches. Two or three colors may be used. Do not use too many bright colors in the one monogram. See page 329.

9. GIFT CARDS.

Ask students to bring gift cards to school for such celebrations as Christmas, birthday, Thanksgiving, etc. Study the designs on page 333, and sketch on the board some of the most interesting patterns. Next have the students either write or select some suitable verse or motto and letter it with a lettering pen. Have them block everything lightly in pencil for correction before inking.

Cards may be done in black drawing ink, tinted with colors, similar to old style illuminations. Tinted papers may be used, as cream, tan, light gray, etc. Students may also make envelopes to hold cards or booklets.

10. BOOK PLATES.

Study the history of book plates. Have students plan one for themselves or for a friend. It should be appropriate for the person whose name is used. Avoid overelaborate plates. A simple one well done will be much more admired than a weak attempt at a subject too difficult for the student.

Book plates should be done in black ink on white paper. If the student desires to have them engraved and printed, the drawing should be made twice the size of the book plate when finished. The printer can then print from the engraved plate on any tint of paper desired.

ILLUSTRATION

1. Study of Pen and Brush Drawings.

Students should select a strong, simple drawing similar to a silhouette and copy it. Use a medium-sized brush for large areas, and put in fine strokes with a pen. See page 343. It is better if students take a strong photograph or print and render it in this manner, rather than make an exact copy of a picture.

Size — not smaller than 4 x 6 inches.

2. Study of Techniques.

First make a chart on an 8 x 10 inch page, showing the various techniques in small rectangles about 1½ x 3 inches. Techniques should include crosshatch, increased line, accented line, and stipple work.

After these have been done satisfactorily, the student should select a simple subject and render this subject in at least two of these techniques. Crosshatch and stipple are easiest for beginners. Next he should draw another subject in the two remaining techniques. Avoid drawings that are too small. None should be smaller than 4 x 6 inches. Also do not allow the students to try heads when they are not capable of doing so.

3. Spatter Work.

Look up some magazine illustrations in flat tones. These illustrations may be wash drawings or photographs, but they should contain distinct flat tones. After these have been penciled heavily, the drawing should be finished in spatter work with waterproof ink and a toothbrush.

See text for instructions in spatter work. Size about 5 x 7 inches.

4. Problem in Nature Drawings.

With flowers or flower prints as models, have students make careful pencil sketches, about six inches high, of a flower. The various tones should be blocked in and some of the technique lines tried out in pencil before the inking is begun. A safe way to ink is to put in the blackest tones first and work up to the high lights. See page 350. Do not attempt too much detail.

5. Still Life in Pen and Ink.

Arrange a fairly simple group. Have students complete it in light pencil lines. When this has been done satisfactorily, let them go over these lines in ink. Do not permit students to block out a sketch and ink it in roughly without any definite idea as to the direction of their pen lines. This may be done later, but not until students are more confident and familiar with techniques. The group should be on 8 x 10 inch pen and ink paper.

6. Decorative Rendering.

Students should be allowed to copy a good piece of decorative pen and ink work. Next let them take a piece that has been done in the naturalistic style and execute it in decorative rendering. In this work, the lines should be bolder and more formal than in the naturalistic. See pages 357, 358. A ball-pointed pen is desirable for this. Size 4 x 6 inches or larger.

7. Ross Board.

Procure a sheet of No. 37 or No. 12 Ross board. Have the students make a little landscape or marine sketch on thin paper, then trace on Ross board, and finish with soft pencil, ink, and scratch knife. About 3 x 5 inches will be a good size. This shows students' working of Ross board without too much waste of material.

8. Transposition from Photographs.

From some good photograph, work out a pen and ink drawing. Allow students to use any technique they have most confidence in. Various values should be carefully blocked before they are inked. Make about 5 x 8 inches. Portraits may be worked in the same manner by students of exceptional ability.

9. Wash Drawings — Transparent.

With a good print as a study, make a light pencil copy of it. Next finish in transparent wash as shown on page 359. Let the first tints dry well before putting in finishing detail. Drawings may also be outlined in waterproof ink and filled in with wash tones. Size 6 x 8 inches or over.

10. Opaque Wash Drawings.

On light gray-white or tan paper, try making a water color drawing, using opaque colors. See page 360. In this medium, the whites may be put over the darker tones, as in oil paintings. For this reason, the medium tones may be put down first. After a drawing has been done in this manner, permit students to try a poster illustration in about three or four colors. This poster should be about 8 x 11 or 10 x 15 inches in size. It may contain lettering if desired.

"The best teaching is that which results in fitting the student to study
intelligently without a teacher."